BUSINESS ETHICS

BUSINESS ETHICS

Ethical Decision Making and Cases THIRD EDITION

O. C. Ferrell
University of Tampa
University of Memphis

John Fraedrich
Southern Illinois University at Carbondale

HOUGHTON MIFFLIN COMPANY   Boston   New York

Sponsoring Editor: Jennifer B. Speer
Senior Associate Editor: Susan M. Kahn
Assistant Editor: Yuka Sugiura
Managing Editor: Nancy Doherty-Schmitt
Senior Production/Design Coordinator: Sarah Ambrose
Associate Project Editor: Gabrielle Stone
Editorial Assistant: Christian Zabriskie
Senior Manufacturing Coordinator: Priscilla Bailey
Marketing Manager: Michael B. Mercier

Cover Designer: Peter Blaiwas

Printed in the U.S.A.

Library of Congress Catalog Card Number: 96-76899

Student Book ISBN: 0-395-79084-0

Examination Copy ISBN: 0-395-79085-9

3456789-CS-00 99 98

Contents

PART TWO   CASES   **219**

Preface

*T*he headlines in your local newspapers, *USA Today*, *The Wall Street Journal*, or *Business Week* tell you that business ethics is becoming one of the most important concerns in business. A scandalous government investigation or a lawsuit by investors, employees, or customers is reported daily. Many of these events stem from ethical misconduct, resulting from the failure of a company to incorporate ethical compliance into its organizational policies. Many of these ethical concerns evolve into legal problems for the company and destroy its organizational trust with the public and other stakeholders.

The business of helping organizations improve their ethics is growing rapidly. The catalyst has been the implementation of the Federal Sentencing Guidelines for Organizations by the United States Sentencing Commission. The guidelines, approved by Congress in November 1991, broke new ground by providing incentives for organizations that develop ethical compliance programs to prevent misconduct. The goal of the guidelines is to encourage organizations to take action to prevent business misconduct and to be "good citizen corporations." The business of helping implement business ethics programs is a billion dollar industry, with firms such as KPMG Peat Marwick, Arthur Andersen and Co., and many small consulting firms developing organizational ethics programs for companies. Large corporations are hiring ethics officers who report directly to the president and who provide oversight for ethics policies and training.

GOALS OF THIS TEXT

Personal ethics is important but may not be sufficient to handle ethical decision making in a business organization. Personal values that an individual learns through socialization may not provide specific guidelines for complex business decisions. Just deciding what constitutes an ethical issue is often difficult. What is deceptive advertising? What actions could be defined as price fixing by competitors or by the Department of Justice? When should an accountant report inaccuracies discovered in an audit? The purpose of this book is to help you improve your ability to make ethical decisions in business by providing you with a framework that you can use to identify, analyze, and control ethical issues in business decision making. Your own values and ethics are important in this process.

For our purposes, and in simple terms, we define business ethics as comprising moral principles that guide behavior in the world of business. We recognize that many people use the terms "business ethics" and "social responsibility" interchangeably, although each can be viewed from a different perspective. We view social responsibility as an attempt to maximize positive effects and minimize negative effects on society. By studying business ethics and social responsibility you begin to understand how to cope with conflicts between your own personal values and those of the organization in which you work.

Many ethical decisions in business are close calls. It often takes years of experience in a particular industry to know what is acceptable. We do not, in this book, provide ethical answers but instead attempt to prepare you to make informed ethical decisions. First, we do not moralize by telling you what to do in a specific situation. Second, although we provide an overview of moral philosophies and decision-making processes, we do not prescribe any one philosophy or process as best or most ethical. Third, by itself, this book will not make you more ethical nor will it tell you how to judge the ethical behavior of others. Rather, its goal is to help you understand and use your current values and convictions in making business decisions and to encourage you to think about the effects of your decision on business and society.

Many people believe that business ethics cannot be taught. Although we do not claim to teach ethics, we suggest that by studying business ethics a person can improve ethical decision making by identifying ethical issues and recognizing the approaches available to resolve them.

It is important to recognize the relationship between personal morals and ethical business decisions. Whereas abstract virtues linked to the high moral ground of truthfulness, honesty, fairness, and openness are often assumed to be self-evident and easy to apply, business decisions involve complex managerial and social considerations. Some business ethics perspectives assume that ethics training is for people who have unacceptable personal moral development, but that is not necessarily the case. Since organizations are culturally diverse and personal values must be respected, a collective agreement on organizational ethics (that is, codes reasonably capable of preventing misconduct) is as vital as other managerial decisions.

ORGANIZATION OF THE TEXT

In writing *Business Ethics, third edition,* we have strived to be as informative, complete, accessible, and up-to-date as possible. Instead of focusing on one area of ethics such as moral philosophy or codes of ethics, we provide balanced coverage of all areas relevant to the current development and practice of ethical decision making. In short, we have tried to keep pace with new developments and current thinking in teaching and practices.

Part One, "Understanding Ethical Decision Making," consists of 10 chapters. The purpose of these chapters is to provide you with a framework to identify, analyze, and understand how business people make ethical decisions and deal with ethical issues. Several enhancements have been made to chapter content for this edition. Some of the most important are listed here. Chapter 1 has been revised to introduce important changes in the institutionalization of business ethics in society. The "Development of Business Ethics" section includes important changes that provide incentives for ethical compliance programs. Chapter 3, "Applying Moral Philosophies to Business Ethics," has expanded coverage of the relativist perspective and of virtue ethics. "The Legal Dimension" section of Chapter 4, "Social Responsibility," now contains a detailed overview of the Federal Sentencing Guidelines for Organizations. Chapter 5, "An Ethical Decision-Making Framework," has been completely revised to reflect the most recent findings regarding ethical decision making in organizations. A new section on ethical issue intensity is included in the revised decision-making model. Expanded material on interpersonal relationships in the organization is included in Chapter 7, "The Influence of Significant Others in the Organization." Chapter 9, "Development of an Effective Ethics Program," has been completely revised and contains a framework for developing an effective ethical compliance program that is compatible with the recommendations of the Federal Sentencing Guidelines for Organizations. Chapter 10, "International Business Ethics," has been completely rewritten to reflect the increasing dynamics of the area. New topics include cultural relativism, the possibility of universal international ethics, and new business issues in international business ethics.

Part Two consists of 15 cases that bring reality into the learning process. All of the cases have been written or revised specifically for this text. The companies or situations are real, names or facts have not been disguised, and all cases include developments up to June 1996. By reading and analyzing these cases, you can gain insight into ethical issues and decision making.

Three appendixes provide further real-world examples and practice in identifying and weighing ethical issues. These appendixes include association, industry, and company codes of ethics. They also include an ethics game, developed by Lockheed Martin Corporation, that more than 100 companies use to train their employees.

EFFECTIVE TOOLS FOR TEACHING AND LEARNING

Many tools are available in this text to help both students and instructors in the quest to improve students' ability to make ethical business decisions.

Each chapter opens with an outline. Immediately following the outline is an "Ethical Dilemma" section that gets students thinking about ethical issues related to the chapter. The short vignette describes a hypothetical incident involving an ethical conflict. Questions at the end of the "Ethical Dilemma" section focus discussion on how the dilemma could be resolved. At the end of each chapter there is a chapter summary and an important terms list, both of which are handy tools for review. Also included at the end of each chapter is a "Real-Life Situation" section. The vignette describes a realistic drama that helps students experience the process of ethical decision making. The "Real-Life Situation" minicases presented in this text are hypothetical; any resemblance to real people, companies, or situations is coincidental. Keep in mind that there are no right or wrong solutions to the minicases. The dilemmas and real-life situations provide an opportunity for the student to use concepts in the chapter to resolve ethical issues. Following each real-world case in Part Two are questions to guide students in recognizing and resolving ethical issues. For some cases, students could conduct additional research to determine recent developments, since many ethical issues in companies take years to resolve. Students can study the codes of ethics in appendixes A and B to determine ethical issues that companies attempt to control. Finally, appendix C, "Gray Matters," which is new to this edition, describes nine business situations. Working independently or in groups, students can practice making ethical decisions—an exercise that is sure to lead to lively discussions.

The *Instructor's Resource Manual with Test Bank* contains a wealth of information. Teaching notes for every chapter include a brief chapter summary, detailed lecture outline, and notes for using the "Ethical Dilemma" and "Real-Life Situation." Detailed case notes point out the key issues involved and offer suggested answers to the questions. A separate section provides guidelines for using case analysis in teaching business ethics, and it provides three additional cases that can be discussed in class or used for outside assignment or examination purposes. Detailed notes are provided to guide the instructor in analyzing or grading the cases. Teaching notes with suggested scoring guidelines for the "Gray Matters" exercises in appendix C are also provided. A test bank provides multiple-choice and essay questions for every chapter in the text. Finally, a video guide provides detailed information and teaching suggestions to assist instructors in smoothly integrating the use of the videos in their course. The videocassette contains four video segments on business ethics: "A Living Legacy" by the Hershey Foods Corporation (21:12 min.); "The History of Dayton's" by the Dayton Hudson Corporation (35:43 min.); "Tobacco Advertising" by the American Heart Association (9:17 min.); and "Ethics: Good People Finish First" by the Martin Marietta Corporation (15:22 min).

ACKNOWLEDGMENTS

A number of individuals provided reviews and suggestions that helped to improve this text. We sincerely appreciate their time and effort.

Greg Buntz
University of the Pacific

Peggy Cunningham
Queen's University

Joseph M. Foster
Indiana Vocational Technical
College—Evansville

Terry Gable
University of Memphis

Robert Giacalone
University of Richmond

Suresh Gopalan
West Texas A&M University

Charles E. Harris Jr.
Texas A&M University

Kenneth A. Heischmidt
Southeast Missouri State University

Walter Hill
Green River Community College

Jack Hires
Valparaiso University

David Jacobs
American University

Nick Lockard
Texas Lutheran College

Terry Loe
University of Memphis

Nick Maddox
Stetson University

Phylis Mansfield
University of Memphis

Randy McLeod
Harding University

Carol Nielsen
Bemidji State University

Cynthia A. M. Simerly
Lakeland Community College

Debbie Thorne
University of Tampa

Wanda V. Turner
Ferris State College

Jim Weber
Marquette University

Ed Weiss
National-Louis University

The authors wish to acknowledge the many people who assisted us in writing this book. We are deeply grateful to Barbara Gilmer for helping us organize and manage the production process. Debbie Thorne, University of Tampa, provided advice and guidance on the text and cases. Margaret "Peggy" Cunningham, Queen's University, provided helpful advice and support. We offer special thanks to Gwyneth M. Vaughn, who assisted in developing case content and who played a major role in editing and developing the chapter content. Phylis Mansfield and Terry Gable, University of Memphis, contributed cases to this edition. In addition, Dawn Yoshizumi and Tanuja Srivastava provided assistance in the preparation of the cases. Finally, we express appreciation to the administration and to our colleagues at the University of Tampa, the University of Memphis, and Southern Illinois University at Carbondale for their support.

We invite your comments, questions, or criticisms. We want to do our best to provide teaching materials that enhance the study of business ethics. Your suggestions will be sincerely appreciated.

O.C.F.
J.F.

This book is dedicated to:
Linda

O.C.F.

Debbie and my children
Anna, Jacob, Joshua and Lael.

J.F.

BUSINESS ETHICS

PART ONE

Understanding Ethical Decision Making

CHAPTER ONE

An Overview of Business Ethics

AN ETHICAL DILEMMA*

KIM BROWN STOPPED by Carie's office after they had come back from their marathon sales trip through Carie's new territory. Carie had just been hired as a new sales rep and was learning her territory from Kim, who was being promoted to regional sales manager. Carie asked Kim to help her with her expense-account sheet. Kim explained to Carie how the forms were to be filled out and then described how to get reimbursed for items that are "expenses" but that were not on the forms. For example, Kim said, "You can't include tips, so one way you can be reimbursed is by increasing the amount on your cab fares. As you can see, most cab drivers stamp the receipt and let you fill in the amount."

As Carie hesitated, Kim defended this practice by telling her that the company assumes that a little padding occurs for such added expenses. "Besides," Kim added, "I've been with the company for five years and am a regional rep. I should know what's okay to do."

As Carie was filling out the expense sheets, she knew that if she did not pad, her totals would conflict with Kim's.

Questions

1. Who is affected?
2. What is the ethical situation?
3. What should Carie do?

---

*This case is strictly hypothetical; any resemblance to real persons, companies, or situations is coincidental.

Business ethics is one of the most important, yet perhaps most misunderstood, concerns in the world of business today. The field of business ethics deals with questions about whether specific business practices are acceptable. For example, should a salesperson omit facts about a product's poor safety record in a sales presentation to a client? Should an accountant report inaccuracies discovered in an audit of a client, knowing that the company will probably be fired by the client for doing so? Should an automobile producer adopt a costly new safety device that could save thousands of lives but would make the cars too expensive for many consumers to afford? Regardless of their legality, the actions taken in such situations will surely be judged by others as right or wrong. By its very nature, the field of business ethics is controversial, and there is no universally accepted approach for resolving its questions. On the other hand, government is encouraging organizational accountability for ethical and legal conduct. Organizations are being asked to prevent and control misconduct by implementing ethics programs.

Before we get started, it is important to state what this book is and what it is not. First, it does not moralize by telling you what is right or wrong in a specific situation. Second, while it provides an overview of group and individual decision-making processes, it does not prescribe any one philosophy or process as best or most ethical. Third, by itself, this book will not make you more ethical, nor will it tell you how to judge the ethical behavior of others. Rather, its goal is to help you understand and use your current values and convictions in making business decisions and to encourage you to think about the effects of your decisions on business and society. To this end, we aim to help you learn to recognize and resolve ethical issues within business organizations. The framework developed in this book therefore focuses on how organizational ethical decisions are made and on ways the organization can improve ethical conduct.

In this chapter, we first develop a definition of business ethics and distinguish it from the concept of social responsibility. Next we examine the evolution of business ethics in North America. Finally, we provide an overview of our framework for examining business ethics in this text.

BUSINESS ETHICS DEFINED

The term *ethics* has many nuances. Ethics has been defined as "inquiry into the nature and grounds of morality where the term morality is taken to mean moral judgments, standards and rules of conduct."[1] It has also been called the study and philosophy of human conduct, with an emphasis on the determination of right and wrong. *The American Heritage Dictionary* offers these definitions of ethics: "The study of the general nature of morals and of specific moral choices; moral philosophy; and the rules or standards governing the conduct of the members of a profession."[2] One difference between an ordinary decision and an ethical one lies in "the point where the accepted rules no longer serve, and the decision maker is faced with the responsibility for weighing values and reaching a judgment in a situation which is not quite the same as any he or she has faced before."[3] The other difference relates to the amount of emphasis placed on the person's values when the decision is being made. Consequently, values and judgments play a critical role in the making of ethical decisions.

Building on these definitions, we can begin to develop a concept of business ethics. Most people would agree that high ethical standards require both businesses and individuals to conform to sound moral principles. However, some special aspects must be considered when applying ethics to business. First, to survive, businesses must make a profit. Second, businesses must balance their desires for profits against the needs and desires of society. Maintaining this balance often requires compromises or tradeoffs. To address these unique aspects of the business world, society has developed rules — both legal and implicit — to guide businesses in their efforts to earn profits in ways that do not harm individuals or society as a whole.

Most definitions of business ethics relate to rules, standards, and moral principles as to what is right or wrong in specific situations. For our purposes and in simple terms, **business ethics** *comprises moral principles and standards that guide behavior in the world of business.* Whether a specific required behavior is right or wrong, ethical or unethical, is often determined by the public as embodied in the mass media, interest groups, and the legal system, as well as through individuals' personal morals and values. Although these groups are not necessarily "right," their judgments influence society's acceptance or rejection of a business and its activities.

SOCIAL RESPONSIBILITY AND BUSINESS ETHICS

The concepts ethics and social responsibility are often used interchangeably although each has a distinct meaning. **Social responsibility** is the obligation a business assumes toward society. To be socially responsible is to maximize positive effects and minimize negative effects on society. Social responsibility includes economic, legal, ethical, and voluntary responsibilities.[4] The **economic responsibilities** of a business are to produce goods and services that society needs and wants at a price that can perpetuate the business and satisfy its obligations to investors. The **legal responsibilities** of businesses are the laws that they must obey. At a minimum, companies are expected to be responsible for their employees obeying local, state, and federal laws. **Ethical responsibilities** are defined as behaviors or activities that are expected of business by society but are not codified in law. Many businesspeople refer to this set of responsibilities as the spirit of the law. Debates over ethical issues are often resolved through civil legal actions. For example, Denny's restaurant chain paid $45.7 million to black customers who complained that they were ignored or treated rudely by Denny's employees.[5] Finally, **voluntary responsibilities** are those behaviors and activities that society desires and business values dictate. For instance, giving to charitable organizations and supporting community projects are forms of volunteerism for a company.

The idea of social responsibility became prominent during the 1960s in response to changing social values. Many businesses have tried to determine what relationships, obligations, and duties are appropriate between the business organization and society. For example, the Internet involves many ethical issues related to individual rights of privacy and property, as well as questions of community standards. Some companies are obtaining e-mail addresses and sending unwanted junk mail, usually product advertisements. The Federal Trade Commission is studying ways to protect privacy and respect First Amendment rights of free speech.[6] Prodigy, a major on-line Internet service, has operators at its headquarters who monitor for obscene language, attempts by adults to enter children's chat rooms or impersonate someone else, or other suspected devious acts.[7] Internet communication is almost completely unregulated, but by the time you read this, some regulation will probably exist. On-line service companies such as Prodigy and America Online will have to continue establishing ethical standards for their networks. Social responsibility, then, can be viewed as a contract with society, whereas business ethics has to do with carefully thought-out rules of business organizational conduct that guide decision making. Business ethics relates to rules and principles that guide individual and work group decisions; social responsibility concerns the effect of organizational decisions on society.

THE DEVELOPMENT OF BUSINESS ETHICS

The study of business ethics in North America has evolved through five distinct stages: (1) before 1960, (2) the 1960s, (3) the 1970s, (4) the 1980s, and (5) the 1990s.[8] As we move toward the twenty-first century, business ethics is rapidly changing. Most companies see the advantages of improved ethical conduct in business.

Before 1960: Ethics in Business

Before 1960 the United States had gone through several agonizing phases of questioning the concept of capitalism. In the 1920s the nation experienced what was called the Progressive Movement, which attempted to provide citizens with a "living wage," defined as income sufficient for education, recreation, health, and retirement. Businesses were asked to check unwarranted price increases and any other practices that would hurt a family's "living wage." In the 1930s came the New Deal, which specifically blamed business for the country's troubles. Business was asked to work more closely with the government to raise family income. By the 1950s the New Deal was repackaged into the Fair Deal by President Harry S. Truman; this program defined such matters as civil rights and environmental responsibility as ethical issues for businesses to address.

Until 1960 ethical issues related to business were often discussed theologically. Religious leaders raised questions about fair wages, labor practices, and the morality of capitalism. Catholic social ethics, expressed in a series of papal encyclicals, included concern for morality in business, workers' rights, and living wages; for humanistic values rather than materialistic ones; and for improving the conditions of the poor. Some Catholic colleges and universities began to offer courses in social ethics. Protestants also developed ethics courses in their seminaries and schools of theology, and addressed issues concerning morality and ethics in business. The Protestant work ethic encouraged individuals to be frugal, work hard, and attain success in the capitalistic system. Such religious traditions provided a foundation for the future field of business ethics. Each religion applied its moral concepts not only to business, but also to government, politics, family, personal life, and all other aspects of life.

The 1960s: The Rise of Social Issues in Business

During the 1960s American society turned to causes. An antibusiness attitude developed as many critics attacked the vested interests that controlled the economic and political sides of society — the so-called military-industrial establishment. The 1960s saw the decay of inner cities and the growth of ecological problems, such as pollution and the disposal of toxic and nuclear wastes. This period also witnessed the rise of consumerism — activities undertaken by independent individuals, groups, and organizations to protect their rights as consumers. In 1962 President John F. Kennedy delivered a "Special Message on Protecting the Consumer Interest," in which he spelled out four basic consumer rights: the right to safety, the right to be informed, the right to choose, and the right to be heard. These came to be known as the **Consumers' Bill of Rights.**

The modern consumer movement is generally considered to have begun in 1965 with the publication of Ralph Nader's *Unsafe at Any Speed,* which criticized the auto industry as a whole, and General Motors Corp. in particular, for putting profit and style ahead of lives and safety. GM's Corvair was the main target of Nader's criticism. His consumer protection organization, popularly known as Nader's Raiders, fought successfully for legislation that required automobile makers to equip their cars with safety belts, padded dashboards, stronger door latches, head restraints, shatterproof windshields, and collapsible steering columns. Consumer activists also helped secure passage of several consumer protection laws, such as the Wholesome Meat Act of 1967, the Radiation Control for Health and Safety Act of 1968, the Clean Water Act of 1972, and the Toxic Substance Act of 1976.[9]

After Kennedy came President Lyndon B. Johnson and the Great Society, which extended national capitalism and told the business community that the U.S. government's responsibility was to provide the citizen with some degree of economic stability. Activities that could destabilize the economy began to be viewed as unethical and unlawful.

The 1970s: Business Ethics as an Emerging Field

Business ethics began to develop as a field of study in the 1970s. Theologians and religious thinkers had laid the groundwork by suggesting that certain religious principles could be applied to business activities. Using this groundwork, business professors began to teach and write about corporate social responsibility. Philosophers entered the arena, applying ethical theory and philosophical analysis to structure the discipline of business ethics. Businesses became more concerned with their public images, and, as social demands grew, many businesses realized that they had to address ethical issues more directly. Conferences were held to discuss the social responsibilities and moral and ethical issues in business. Centers dealing with issues of business ethics were established. Interdisciplinary meetings brought business professors, theologians, philosophers, and businesspeople together.

By the end of the 1970s, a number of major ethical issues had emerged, such as bribery, deceptive advertising, price collusion, product safety, and the environment. *Business ethics* became a common expression and was no longer considered an oxymoron. Academic researchers sought to identify ethical issues and describe how businesspeople might choose to act in particular situations. However, only limited efforts were made to describe how the ethical decision-making process worked and to identify the many variables that influence the decision-making process.

The 1980s: Consolidation

In the 1980s business academics and practitioners acknowledged business ethics as a field of study. A growing and varied group of institutions with diverse interests promoted the study of business ethics. Business ethics organizations grew to include thousands of members. Five hundred courses in business ethics were offered at colleges across the country, with more than forty thousand students enrolled. Centers of business ethics provided publications, courses, conferences, and seminars. Business ethics was also a prominent concern within leading companies, such as General Electric Co., The Chase Manhattan Corporation, General Motors, Atlantic Richfield Co., Caterpillar Inc., and S. C. Johnson & Son, Inc. Many of these firms established ethics committees and social policy committees to address ethical issues.

In the 1980s, the **Defense Industry Initiative on Business Ethics and Conduct** (DII) was developed to guide corporate support for ethical conduct. In 1986 eighteen defense contractors drafted principles for guiding business ethics and conduct.[10] By 1996 there were fifty-five members representing over 50 percent of the prime contracts with the Department of Defense. This effort established a method for discussing best practices and working tactics to link organizational practice and policy to successful ethical compliance. First, the DII supported codes of conduct and their widespread distribution. The codes of conduct had to be understandable with details provided on more substantive areas. Second, member companies were expected to provide ethics training and to develop communication tools to support the periods between training. Third, defense contractors were to create an open atmosphere where employees felt comfortable reporting violations without fear of retribution. Fourth, companies needed to perform extensive internal audits and develop effective internal reporting and voluntary disclosure plans. Fifth, the DII insisted that member companies preserve the integrity of the defense industry. Sixth, member companies had to take on a philosophy of public accountability. These six principles became the foundation for the United States Sentencing Commission's sentencing guidelines for organizations (discussed in the next section).[11]

The 1980s ushered in the Reagan/Bush eras, with the accompanying belief that self-regulation, rather than regulation by government, was in the public's interest. Many tariffs and trade barriers were lifted, and businesses merged and divested within an increasingly global atmosphere. Thus, while business schools were offering courses in business ethics, the rules of business were changing at a phenomenal rate because of less regulation. Corporations that once were nationally based began operating internationally and found themselves mired in value structures where accepted rules of business behavior no longer applied. While corporations had more freedom to make decisions, the government was developing new mandatory federal sentencing guidelines to control firms that were involved in misconduct.

The 1990s: Institutionalization of Business Ethics

The Clinton administration has continued to support self-regulation and free trade. However, it has also taken unprecedented government action to deal with health-related issues, such as teenage smoking. Its proposals have included restricting cigarette advertising, banning vending machine sales, and ending the use of cigarette logos in connection with sports events.[12] The Clinton administration has supported the concept of organizational accountability for misconduct and damages.

The **Federal Sentencing Guidelines for Organizations,** approved by Congress in November 1991, have set the tone for organizational ethical compliance programs in the 1990s. The guidelines broke new ground by codifying into law incentives for organizations to take action, such as developing effective internal ethical compliance programs to prevent misconduct.[13] Provisions in the guidelines mitigate penalties for businesses that strive to root out misconduct and establish high ethical and legal standards.[14] The guidelines focus on firms taking action to prevent and detect business misconduct in cooperation with government regulation.

The federal government created the United States Sentencing Commission to institutionalize ethical compliance programs and thus help prevent legal misconduct. Organizations are being held responsible for the misconduct of their employees. If a company lacks an effective ethical compliance program and its employees violate the law, it can incur severe penalties. At the heart of the Federal Sentencing Guidelines for Organizations is the carrot-and-stick approach: by taking preventive action against misconduct, a company may avoid onerous penalties should a violation occur. A mechanical approach using legalistic logic will not suffice to avert serious penalties.

The company must develop corporate values, enforce its own code of ethics, and strive to prevent misconduct (a "good citizen" corporation).[15]

The United States Sentencing Commission evaluates the effectiveness of an organization's ethical compliance program according to these seven criteria: (1) development of standards and procedures capable of detecting and preventing misconduct (a code of conduct), (2) appointment of high-level personnel responsible for the ethical compliance program, (3) care in delegation of substantial discretionary authority to individuals with a propensity for misconduct, (4) effective communication of standards and procedures via training programs and publications (ethics training), (5) establishment of systems to monitor, audit, and report misconduct, (6) consistent enforcement of standards and punishments in the organization, and (7) reasonable steps taken in response to an offense as well as continuous improvement of the ethical compliance program.

Business ethics today is an evolving field of study, concentrating on ethical issues in business activities. Business ethical issues can be approached from the perspective of law, philosophy, theology, or social sciences; or they can be dealt with in a pragmatic spirit, seeking solutions for specific managerial problems. The study of business ethics does not mean simply moralizing about what should or should not be done in a particular situation. Rather, it systematically links the concepts of ethical responsibility and decision making within the organization. Business managers, academics, and the government are attempting to develop systematic guidelines that can help individuals and organizations make ethical decisions.

WHY STUDY BUSINESS ETHICS?

The Problem

Concerns about ethical wrongdoing are almost epidemic today. The mass media report unethical activities in government, business, sports, religion, science, and medicine on a daily basis. An Ethics Resource Center survey of four thousand employees indicates that workers witness many instances of ethical misconduct in their organizations. The specific percentages are noted in Table 1–1. Note that workers report multiple observations of ethical misconduct; therefore, each category is an independent question of observed misconduct.

When asked about acceptable practices and whether they would bend the law in doing business with certain organizations or entities, approximately one-quarter of the businesspeople polled in another survey said that they would write bad checks, invade the privacy of job interviewees, pirate software, steal clients, and inflate their sales (see Figure 1–1). Some of the groups against which these businesspeople would bend or break the spirit of the law

TABLE 1–1 The Unethical Worker

Percentage of Workers Who Say These Ethical Infractions Are Committed by Coworkers	
Lying to supervisors	56%
Falsifying records	41%
Office theft	35%
Sexual harassment	35%
Alcohol and drug abuse	31%
Conflict of interest	31%

Source: Ethics Resource Center survey, as reported in *USA Today,* October 18, 1995, p. B1. Permission provided courtesy of the Ethics Resource Center, 1120 6th Street, NW, Washington, DC, 20005.

were the Environmental Protection Agency, health insurance companies, competitors, and, most of all, the Internal Revenue Service (see Figure 1–2).

Insider trading of stocks and bonds, bribery, falsifying documents, deceptive advertising, and defective products are all problems cited as evidence of declining ethical standards. Calvin Klein canceled a provocative advertising campaign, which relied on what appeared to be very young models. Critics called the ads "kiddie porn," but a Justice Department investigation found that the models were all over 18 years of age.[16] Although they did not violate any law, the ads created an ethical debate. Thus the example illustrates the influence of ethical values on business decisions. Such highly publicized cases strengthen the perception that ethical standards in business need to be raised.

Colleges and universities have been put on probation, and in some cases given the "death penalty" — complete suspension of their athletic programs — for illegally recruiting or paying players. In government, various politicians and some high-ranking officials have had to resign in disgrace over ethical indiscretions, including scandals concerning the House of Representatives' bank and post office. And several scientists have been accused of falsifying research data, which could invalidate later research based on those data and jeopardize trust in all scientific research.

But whether made in science or business, most decisions are judged as right or wrong, ethical or unethical. Regardless of what an individual or a business organization believes about a particular behavior, if society judges it to be unethical, whether correctly or not, that judgment directly affects the organization's ability to achieve its business goals. For this reason alone, it is important to understand business ethics and recognize ethical issues.

The Solution

Studying business ethics is valuable for several reasons. The field is not merely an extension of an individual's own personal ethics. Many people be-

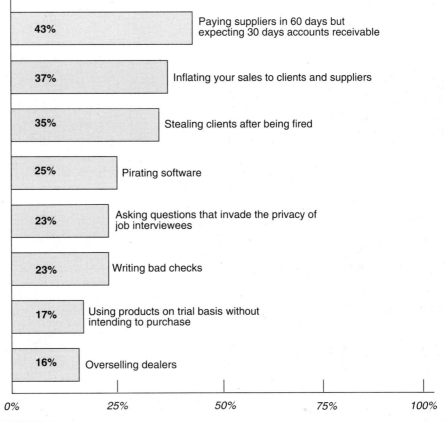

FIGURE 1–1

Percentage of Businesspeople That Judge Questionable Business Practices as Acceptable

Source: Inc., *December 1992, p. 16.*

lieve that if an organization hires good people with strong ethical values, then it will be a good citizen organization. But as we show throughout this text, an individual's personal values and moral philosophies are only one factor in the ethical decision-making process. True, moral rules can be related to a variety of situations in life, and some people do not distinguish everyday ethical issues from business ones. Our concern, however, is with the application of rules and principles in the business context. Many important ethical issues (such as those related to family and sexuality) do not arise very often in the business context, although they remain complex moral dilemmas within one's own personal life. For example, although abortion is a major moral issue in many peoples' lives, it is usually not an issue in a business organization.

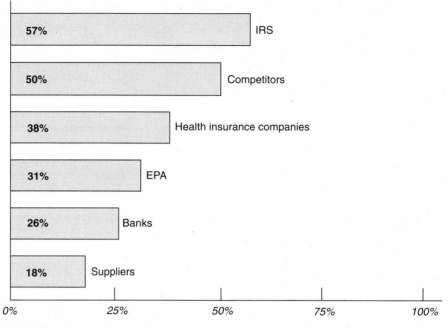

FIGURE 1–2

Percentage of Respondents Who Would Break the Spirit of the Law Against These Entities
Source: Inc., *December 1992, p. 16.*

Professionals in any field, including business, must deal with individuals' personal moral dilemmas as these issues affect a person's ability to function on the job. Normally, a business does not establish rules or policies on personal ethical issues such as sex or the use of alcohol outside the workplace; indeed, in some cases, such policies would be illegal. Only when a person's preferences or values influence his or her performance on the job do an individual's ethics play a major role in the evaluation of business decisions. For example, the captain of the *Exxon Valdez* — which ran aground in Prince William Sound, Alaska, and spilled eleven million gallons of toxic oil — was charged with being drunk at the time of the accident.[17] (The captain was subsequently cleared of these charges.) The captain's drinking was a personal ethical issue, but it became a business ethical issue because of allegations that it affected his ability to perform his duties and caused an accident.

Although a person's racial and sexual prejudices are a concern of individual ethics, racial and sexual discrimination in the workplace create an ethical problem within the business world. Indeed, race, gender, and age discrimination are a major source of ethical and legal debate in the workplace. In the United States, discrimination charges are being filed at the rate of 450 a day, or 150,000 a year.[18] The Equal Employment Opportunity Commission dismisses 66 percent of the discrimination cases it receives. Businesses claim that they are drowning in a sea of frivolous complaints,[19] but most of these cases are ethical disputes about right and wrong behavior.

Just being a good person and, in your own view, having sound personal ethics may not be sufficient to handle the ethical issues that arise in a business organization. It is important to recognize the relationship between legal and ethical decisions. While abstract virtues linked to the high moral ground of truthfulness, honesty, fairness, and openness are often assumed to be self-evident and accepted by all employees, business strategy decisions involve complex and detailed discussions. A high level of personal moral development may not prevent an individual from violating the law in an organizational context, where even experienced lawyers debate the exact meaning of the law. Some business ethics perspectives assume that ethics training is for people who have unacceptable personal moral development, but that is not necessarily the case. Since organizations are culturally diverse and personal values must be respected, a collective agreement on organizational ethics (that is, codes reasonably capable of preventing misconduct) is as vital as other managerial decisions.

Many people who have limited business experience suddenly find themselves making decisions about product quality, advertising, pricing, hiring practices, and pollution control. The values they learned from family, religion, and school may not provide specific guidelines for these complex business decisions. For example, is a particular advertisement deceptive? Should a gift to a customer be considered a bribe, or is it a special promotional incentive? In other words, a person's experiences and decisions at home, in school, and in the community may be quite different from the experiences and the decisions he or she has to make at work. Many business ethics decisions are close calls. Years of experience in a particular industry may be required to know what is acceptable.

Studying business ethics will help you begin to identify ethical issues and recognize the approaches available to resolve them. You will also learn more about the ethical decision-making process and about ways to promote ethical behavior within the organization. By studying business ethics you may begin to understand how to cope with conflicts between your own personal values and those of the organization in which you work.

OUR FRAMEWORK FOR STUDYING BUSINESS ETHICS

We have developed a framework for this text to help you understand how people make ethical decisions and deal with ethical issues. This framework includes an introduction to the concept of business ethics, an overview of major ethical issues that businesses face today, and a discussion of moral philosophy. We also examine a framework that attempts to describe how people make ethical or unethical decisions. We then explore in some detail each of the factors that influence ethical decision making. Finally, we discuss ways of sensitizing business to ethical standards and of applying business ethics on an international scale. Figure 1–3 illustrates how each element in the framework relates to the others and to the decision maker, and where each topic is discussed in this book.

Ethical Issues in Business

Ethical issues, discussed in Chapter 2, are problems, situations, or opportunities that require a person or organization to choose among several actions

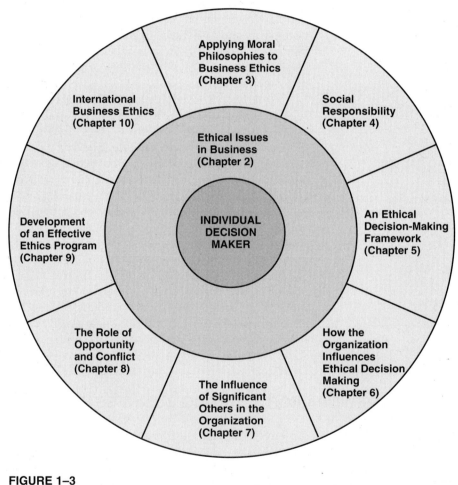

FIGURE 1–3

An Overview of This Book

that must be evaluated as right or wrong. To some extent, the business firm and interested parties define what constitutes an ethical issue. Most ethical issues relate to conflicts of interest, fairness and honesty, communications, or organizational relationships. In general, businesses seem to be more concerned with ethical issues that could hurt the firm, such as bribery, and issues related to consumers and the general public, such as environmental impact. Scandals related to bribes, deceptive communications, and ecological disasters have severely damaged public trust in business institutions and have helped focus attention on activities that could do further harm. Studying ethical issues should help prepare you to identify potential problems within an organization and to understand alternatives and ethical solutions to the problem.

Applying Moral Philosophies to Business Ethics

In Chapter 3 we explore moral philosophies, which are principles or rules that people use to decide what is right or wrong. People learn these principles through socialization by family members, social groups, and formal education. Each moral philosophy has its own concept of rightness or ethicalness and rules for behavior. These rules and concepts of rightness form the basis on which a person decides how to act in a particular situation. We will not make judgments as to which moral philosophy is best to use in business. Instead we present a number of different moral philosophies so you can compare and contrast the usefulness of each in the business environment.

Social Responsibility

Chapter 4 examines major factors that shape social responsibility in business. The concept of social responsibility for business covers four types of responsibilities: *voluntary*, which society desires from business; *ethical*, which society expects from business; and *legal* and *economic*, which society requires of business. The discussion of social responsibility in Chapter 4 also includes environmental factors, such as fluctuations in the economy, laws and regulations, competition among businesses, technological advances, and the attitudes and desires of society. Some of the leading department stores, including Sears, JC Penney, Neiman Marcus, and Dayton Hudson, have been accused of allegedly buying clothing from clandestine sweatshops, which force workers to make clothes under prisonlike conditions. Union leaders charge such companies with hypocrisy, claiming that these stores drive down wages. They urge the companies to check more carefully into the sources of their supplies.[20] Examining how social responsibility and the environment create ethical issues and influence ethical decisions will enrich your understanding of business ethics.

An Ethical Decision-Making Framework

In order to establish policies and rules that encourage employees to behave ethically and in accordance with organizational objectives, business managers must understand how and why people make ethical decisions. Philosophers and social scientists have developed models explaining how factors such as personal moral philosophies, opportunity, organizational culture, and the influence of other individuals contribute to individual ethical decision making. A general framework is discussed in Chapter 5. Although a descriptive framework may not explain how specific individuals make ethical decisions in specific situations, it will help you understand the major factors that influence ethical decision making in business.

How the Organization Influences Ethical Decision Making

How an employee responds to a moral or ethical issue depends in part on the structure and culture of the organization, which are discussed in Chapter 6. A person may learn ethical or unethical behavior while mastering other aspects of the job. Business ethics is a matter not only of understanding moral philosophies but also of recognizing how these moral philosophies are altered or blocked by organizational influence. An organization that actively fosters an ethical climate provides an example of how its employees should behave. The Federal Sentencing Guidelines for Organizations make firms vicariously liable for misconduct by their employees. In other words, the organization has to take responsibility for employee conduct.

The Influence of Significant Others in the Organization

Individuals learn ethical or unethical behavior not only from society in general but also from superiors, peers, and subordinates with whom they associate in the work environment. Chapter 7 discusses the role of these significant others in the decision-making process. The more a person is exposed to unethical decisions by others in the work environment, the more likely he or she is to behave unethically. There may be a conflict between what the organization appears to expect of its workers and managers and what employees' personal ethical standards lead them to expect of themselves. Powerful superiors can directly influence an employee's behavior by putting into practice the company's standard of ethics. The status and power of significant others are closely related to the amount of pressure they can exert on an employee to conform to their expectations. The reporting of misconduct is being encouraged by companies that are appointing ethics directors and enforcing their codes of conduct. Although peers often question the reporting of misconduct, it is clearly on the rise.[21] In organizations where ethical standards are vague and supervision by superiors is limited, peers may provide the most guidance in an ethical decision.

The Role of Opportunity and Conflict

Chapter 8 considers the elements of opportunity and conflict in the decision-making process. Opportunity is a set of conditions that limit unfavorable behavior or reward favorable behavior. An individual who is rewarded or is not punished for unethical behavior is likely to continue to behave unethically, whereas a person who receives no reward or is punished for behaving unethically is less likely to repeat the action. Thus opportunity is an important consideration in understanding ethical decision making. Opportunity sometimes leads to conflicts between the individual and the organization, between the organization and society, or between the individual and society. Understanding ethical conflicts is important to understanding ethical decision making.

Development of an Effective Ethics Program

To encourage ethical behavior, organizations must be responsible for developing an ethics program. As discussed in Chapter 9, a reasonable ethical compliance program for preventing misconduct should include a code of ethics, oversight of the program, employee training, methods for employees to report misconduct, and provisions for monitoring and enforcing the program. Organizations need to analyze potential areas of ethical risk and design a program that addresses problem situations or internal conditions. In addition, they should revise their program on a regular basis in response to misconduct and overall ethical improvement. Finally, organizations have to understand and abide by industry standards of conduct and comply with all legal requirements.

International Business Ethics

Increasingly, businesses are operating across national boundaries and even globally, often in cultures where different moral standards and business ethics prevail. Chapter 10 addresses business ethics on an international scale. Certain international business ethical issues derive from differences in cultures; others relate to discrimination, bribery, pricing, and the impact of multinational corporations. For example, although the U.S. Foreign Corrupt Practices Act prohibits U.S. companies from using bribery in international business dealings, companies from other countries may not be limited by such laws. Some Americans have protested that this law unfairly limits their ability to compete with firms from Japan, Korea, and elsewhere on an international scale.

We hope that this framework will help you develop a balanced understanding of the various perspectives and alternatives in making ethical business decisions. Regardless of your own personal values, the more you know about how individuals make decisions, the better prepared you will be to cope with difficult ethical decisions. Such knowledge will help you improve and control the ethical decision-making environment in which you work.

It is your job to make the final decision in an ethical situation that affects you. Sometimes that decision may be right; sometimes it may be wrong. It is always easy to look back with hindsight and know what one should have done in a particular situation. At the time, the choices may not be so clear. To give you practice in making ethical decisions, a number of cases are provided in Part II of this book. In addition, each chapter begins with a short vignette and ends with a minicase involving ethical problems. We hope they will give you a better sense of the difficulties of making ethical decisions in the real business world.

SUMMARY

This chapter provides an overview of the field of business ethics and introduces the framework through which it will be discussed in this text. Business ethics is a set of moral principles and standards that guide behavior in the world of business. Social responsibility is the obligation a business assumes to maximize its positive effect and minimize its negative effect on society. It can be viewed as a social contract, whereas business ethics relates to moral principles and rules that guide decision makers.

The study of business ethics evolved through five distinct stages. Before 1960, business ethical issues were discussed primarily from a religious perspective. The 1960s saw the rise of many social issues in business and the emergence of a social conscience. Business ethics began to develop as an independent field of study in the 1970s. The field of business ethics developed as a recognized discipline, with academics and practitioners exploring ethical issues and attempting to understand how individuals and organizations make ethical decisions. In the 1980s centers of business ethics provided publications, courses, conferences, and seminars. Many companies established ethics committees and social policy committees. The Defense Industry Initiative on Business Ethics and Conduct was developed to guide corporate support for ethical conduct; its principles had a major impact on corporate ethics in the United States. However, less government regulation and an increase in international operations raised new ethical issues. In the 1990s government has continued to support self-regulation. The Federal Sentencing Guidelines for Organizations have set the tone for organizational ethics programs. These guidelines provided incentives for organizations to take action to prevent organizational misconduct. Companies were encouraged to develop ethics programs and strive to be good citizen corporations.

Studying business ethics is important for many reasons. Recent incidents of unethical activity in business underscore the need for a better understanding of the ethical decision-making process and of the factors that contribute to ethical and unethical decisions. Individuals' personal moral philosophies and decision-making experience may not be sufficient to guide them in the business world.

Finally, the text introduces a framework for studying business ethics. Each chapter of this book addresses some aspect of business ethics and decision making within a business context. The major concerns are ethical issues in business; moral philosophies; social responsibility; ethical decision-making frameworks; organizational structure and culture; the influence of significant others within the organization; the role of opportunity and conflict; development of an effective ethics program; and global business ethics.

A REAL-LIFE SITUATION

Jane paused, told Michelle she had another urgent call, and put her on hold. What was she going to tell her friend Michelle about Ralph? "Why do these things happen to me?" she muttered to herself.

Jane had been a regional sales manager at COBA for almost two years. One of the problems that came with the position was Ralph. Ralph had been with the company for ten years and was a good performer. He always met his quotas and goals and was a team player in every respect. Two years ago, however, Ralph went through a period of depression that severely affected his sales figures as well as his client relationships. Another problem resulting from Ralph's depression was alcohol dependency. COBA had given Ralph the option of either entering a private drug rehabilitation center or being dismissed. Ralph chose the six-week detoxification program.

For about six months all seemed to be going well. Ralph's sales figures went up, and Jane, who was Ralph's boss, had not received any more customer complaints. However, when Ralph started drinking again, Jane confronted him about his alcohol consumption. Ralph justified his actions by telling her that he had to have a few drinks with his clients to keep them happy. "After all, Jane, everyone knows that drinking is something a salesperson does to develop a more personal relationship with the client," he argued. "Besides, my sales figures have not decreased; they've increased." Nevertheless, Jane cautioned Ralph about his behavior.

Several months before Ralph had resumed drinking, a confidential report from the detoxification center had landed on Jane's desk. The center was requesting a blood test from all clients who had gone through the treatment program in the last year. The report discussed a new test that could determine whether alcohol abusers were genetically different from others. The center asked Jane to urge Ralph to submit voluntarily to this blood test.

At about the same time, Jane had received another memo from COBA's insurance carriers. Certain employee illnesses were to be classified industrywide as nonqualifiable if new employees had been diagnosed with them prior to employment. In other words, a new employee who had a preexisting condition named on the list would not be eligible for reimbursement for treatment of that illness. One of the conditions on the list was alcoholism, as defined by the new blood test. Jane worried about her personal liability if she were to use her influence to persuade Ralph to take the blood test, so she said nothing to him.

At a regional sales meeting six weeks after Jane's confrontation with Ralph, he confided in her that he was still having problems with alcohol but that it wasn't affecting his job performance. "You know, Jane, just between you and me, I've been worried that I might be an alcoholic. So I went to a doctor and had a confidential blood test done. It's a new test that determines whether you *really* are an alcoholic. Well, it came up positive, so I know I have to quit. I just wanted to let you know that I appreciate the second chance. Thanks, Jane."

Within a week, another memo from headquarters came across Jane's desk concerning impending litigation against a sales manager. It seems COBA and a manager were being sued by an ex-employee who felt she was fired because of alcoholism. The memo stated that it wanted all regional managers to hear COBA's side of the litigation before questions were asked.

Then the quarterly sales reports came in; Ralph had made his quotas. However, Jane had started to get some negative phone calls about the servicing of some of Ralph's accounts. She believed there was a strong probability that alcohol was affecting his work. That same day, Jane got three phone calls. One was from Chuck, vice president of sales for COBA, asking Jane about Ralph. Jane said tentatively, "Ralph made quota this quarter, but I'm worried about next quarter."

"Well, you know, Jane," Chuck replied, "Ralph is a good salesman. He's had a rough time of it, but I think he'll pull out of it. It's not like he's an alcoholic. Anyway, I just wanted to

see how my nephew is doing. We don't want to lose a good man like Ralph, *do we?* Got to go. Bye."

The next call Jane got was from Michelle, a vice president of EASEL Corporation. Michelle and Jane had worked together at another company and were good friends. EASEL, however, was COBA's main competitor and had been gaining market share on them for the last year. Michelle was calling to check out a salesman she was considering for a regional position. "I know it's unusual for me to ask you to share information about one of your own for a job at the competition, Jane. But it's an important position, so I'm cashing in one of the favors you owe me. I need to know about this guy."

"Well, you know you can count on me, Michelle. Who is it?" asked Jane.

"It's one of your own salespeople, Ralph," Michelle replied.

Jane knew that if she gave a good report on Ralph, he could hurt EASEL's sales and counter its sales strategy.

The third phone call was from the police. The sergeant told Jane that they had just picked up Ralph and if she came down to get him they wouldn't charge him with driving while intoxicated. The sergeant told her that technical problems had invalidated the equipment on Ralph's test, but that didn't change the reality of his condition. The sergeant was calling Jane because they were friends.

Questions

1. What are the ethical issues?
2. Discuss options for Jane and Ralph.
3. Discuss any extra information Jane and Ralph need to make their decision.

IMPORTANT TERMS FOR REVIEW

business ethics
social responsibility
economic responsibilities
legal responsibilities
ethical responsibilities
voluntary responsibilities
Consumers' Bill of Rights
Defense Industry Initiative on Business Ethics and Conduct
Federal Sentencing Guidelines for Organizations

CHAPTER TWO

Ethical Issues In Business

CHAPTER OUTLINE

Foundations of Ethical Conflict

Classification of Ethical Issues

Conflict of Interest
Honesty and Fairness
Communications
Organizational Relationships

Ethical Issues Related to Participants and Functional Areas of Business

Owners
Finance
Employees
Management
Consumers
Marketing
Accounting

Recognizing an Ethical Issue

AN ETHICAL DILEMMA *

DALE GOODIN SAT in his office in Rio de Janeiro and pondered his dilemma. He had been a salesperson with Acme Oil Pumps, Inc., for thirty-five years. He had served in many sales regions and recently had been transferred to Brazil. Dale was an average salesperson, but age and retirement prospects had slowed him down, and his overall sales had gradually declined in the past few years. Dale recognized that, given his age and his recent transfer, if he made too many mistakes, he would be out of a job and could lose his pension.

Three months before, Dale had made a sales presentation to Oscar Garcia, head of all the government oil fields in Brazil. The two men hit it off and became good friends. Over lunch the week before, Oscar had mentioned to Dale that Acme Oil Pumps had a very good chance of getting a $5 million-a-year, five-year contract to supply and install replacement pumps for the Brazilian government's oil fields. However, Oscar also informed Dale that there were three other competitors bidding for the same contract. Because of their friendship, Oscar said, he felt an obligation to tell Dale that Acme's bid was somewhat high and that he should lower it. Dale had thanked Oscar for this information and resubmitted a bid slightly lower than the previous one.

Yesterday Oscar called Dale and said that in all probability Acme Oil Pumps would get the contract for the replacement pumps, but Oscar also requested from Dale a small gift of $50,000 for the contract — in essence, a bribe. At first Dale told Oscar that he would have to think about it. Dale called his superiors in the United States, who told him that it is against U.S. law to offer bribes to anyone in any foreign country to secure business. His superiors also told Dale that he should do what he could to try to secure the contract.

This seemed to be a black-and-white decision, but Dale knew differently. After thirty-five years with the company, he knew that bribes were often given to secure large contracts. He recognized that if he got caught giving Oscar Garcia a bribe, he would probably be fired. But he also knew that if he didn't get the contract, the chances of his remaining with the company would be slim. With retirement only a few years away, Dale needed his pension. He had to make a decision quickly.

Questions

1. Who is affected?
2. What are the ethical and legal issues in this situation?
3. Would your decision change if Dale were younger?

4. Would your decision change if the bribe requested had been larger or smaller and why?

5. In which countries might a bribe be standard procedure?

_____

*This case is strictly hypothetical; any resemblance to real persons, companies, or situations is coincidental.

*P*eople make ethical decisions only when they recognize that a particular issue or situation has an ethical component. For example, if Dale's company had been a company from Germany, it would have been allowed to deduct certain bribes from its income statements. In the People's Republic of China, providing money gifts in order to discuss business with the appropriate buyer or representative is also deemed normal procedure. Thus a first step toward understanding business ethics is to develop ethical-issue awareness. An **ethical issue** is a problem, situation, or opportunity requiring an individual or organization to choose among several actions that must be evaluated as right or wrong, ethical or unethical.

Ethical issues typically arise because of conflicts among individuals' personal moral philosophies and values, the values and attitudes of the organizations in which they work, and those of the society in which they live. The business environment presents many ethical conflicts. A company's efforts to attain its organizational objectives may collide with its employees' endeavors to achieve their own personal objectives. Similarly, consumers' desire for safe and quality products may conflict with manufacturers' desire to earn adequate profits. A manager's wish to hire specific employees that he or she likes may be at odds with the organization's intent to hire the best-qualified candidates and with society's aim to offer equal opportunity to minority group members and women. Characteristics of the work or job and the culture of the organization and society in which one does business can also create ethical issues. Once ethical issues of any sort have been identified, individuals and organizations must decide how to resolve them. Familiarity with the ethical issues that frequently arise in the business world will help you identify and resolve them when they occur.

In this chapter we consider some of the ethical issues that may occur in the business world. We focus first on situations and relationships that may generate ethical conflict. Then we discuss four classifications of ethical issues: conflict of interest, honesty and fairness, communications, and organizational relationships. Specific ethical issues related to the participants and functional areas of business are examined next. Finally, we assess the importance of recognizing ethical issues.

FOUNDATIONS OF ETHICAL CONFLICT

Because ethical issues often emerge from conflict, it is useful to examine the causes of ethical conflict. Business managers and employees often experience some tension between their own ethical beliefs and their obligations to the organizations in which they work.

According to a recent survey, almost one-third of the businesspeople questioned see a difference between their ethical standards at home and at work.[1] This conflict becomes exacerbated when employees feel that their company is encouraging unethical conduct or exerting pressure on them to engage in it. Figure 2–1 and Table 2–1 show that over 25 percent of business employees believe that this pressure is real and that they compromise

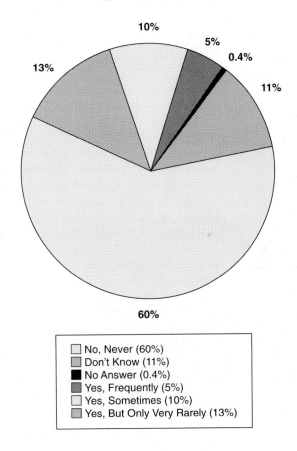

FIGURE 2–1

Employee Beliefs That Their Company Encourages Unethical Conduct from Employees to Meet Business Objectives
Source: Rebecca Goodell, Ethics in American Business: Policies, Programs, and Perceptions *(1994): 20. Permission Provided Courtesy of the Ethics Resource Center, 1120 6th Street, NW, Washington, DC, 20005.*

TABLE 2–1 Principal Causes of Ethical Compromises

%	Senior Mgmt.	Middle Mgmt.	Front Line Supv.	Prof. Non-Mgmt.	Admin. Salaried	Hourly
Meeting schedule pressure	26.5	23.4	25.4	24.9	24.3	28.6
Meeting overly aggressive financial or business objectives	17.7	22.4	18.3	21.6	20.3	13.4
Helping the company survive	21.6	13.8	10.5	9.4	13.4	12.4
Advancing the career interests of my boss	6.1	10.7	11.0	12.2	12.4	11.0
Feeling peer pressure	3.3	5.6	9.6	8.0	8.8	13.4
Resisting competitive threats	13.8	7.7	8.6	8.9	8.8	5.1
Saving jobs	2.7	7.7	8.6	5.2	5.0	7.8
Advancing my own career or financial interests	3.3	4.1	3.7	5.2	3.0	5.1
Other	5.0	4.6	4.6	4.7	4.0	3.2

Source: Adapted from Rebecca Goodell, *Ethics in American Business: Policies, Programs, and Perceptions* (1994): 54. Permission provided courtesy of the Ethics Resource Center, 1120 6th Street, NW, Washington, DC, 20005.

themselves to meet schedules and business objectives and to help the company survive.[2] For example, consider Toshihide Iguchi of Daiwa Bank Ltd. of Japan, who hid $1.1 billion in losses.[3] According to Daiwa insiders, there seems to be no evidence that Iguchi personally profited from his alleged scheme. Rather, he apparently was trying to make more money for his company, but losses exceeded gains.

As mentioned in Chapter 1, lying, stealing, and sexual harassment appear to be high on the ethical infraction list. These common problems also surface when the company interacts with customers, suppliers, and competitors (see Table 2–2). Unethical behavior between such groups usually results in legal problems.

Other surveys have probed the perceptual gap between CEOs and consumers on such issues as the factors considered to be a strong influence on ethical behavior to people's reactions when they discover unethical behavior in the workplace.[4] Table 2–3 shows that although CEO and consumer lists are similar the importance of specific factors can differ. For example, most CEOs (92 percent) believe that the example they set is a strong influencer of ethical behavior, whereas consumers consider a person's own moral code and the behavior of the immediate supervisor to be more important factors. Table 2–4 compares consumer and CEO responses to unethical behavior when it is discovered. The interesting difference is that most CEOs would report the activity to company authorities, but many consumers would not.

TABLE 2–2 Conflicts Between Company Interests and Personal Ethics: Types of Relationships

Percentage of Respondents Reporting Conflicts in Relationships With	Sometimes	Often
Customers	45.6%	4.4%
Suppliers	45.2%	4.3%
Employees	40.0%	1%
Competitors	36.6%	5.3%
The law and government	33.6%	2.7%
Superiors	29.5%	1%
Wholesalers	24.3%	1%
Retailers	18.9%	1%
Potential Investors	7.7%	1%

Source: Scott J. Vitell and Troy A. Festervand, "Business Ethics: Conflicts, Practices and Beliefs of Industrial Executives," *Journal of Business Ethics,* 6 (February 1987), p. 114. Reprinted by permission of Kluwer Academic Publishers, Dordrecht, Holland.

CLASSIFICATION OF ETHICAL ISSUES

Surveys can render a useful overview of the many unsettled ethical issues in business. A constructive next step toward identifying and resolving ethical issues is to classify the issues relevant to most business organizations. In this section we classify ethical issues in relation to conflict of interest, honesty and fairness, communications, and relationships within the organization. Although not all-inclusive, these classifications do provide an overview of some major ethical issues that business decision makers face.

Conflict of Interest

A **conflict of interest** exists when an individual must choose whether to advance his or her own interests, those of the organization, or those of some other group. To avoid conflicts of interest, employees must be able to separate their private interests from their business dealings. In the United States and Canada, it is generally accepted that employees should not accept bribes, personal payments, gifts, or special favors from people who hope to influence the outcome of a decision. However, as discussed later in this text, bribery is an accepted way of doing business in many countries.

Bribes have been associated with the downfall of many managers, legislators, and government officials. For example, in a bribery scandal, Lockheed, finally pleading guilty, admitted making questionable payments of more than $30 million to Egypt. The case also brought to light how Lockheed executives used phony documents to hide the bribes to Egyptian officials. The bribes were classified as "termination" or "other" fees, some of which

TABLE 2–3 Factors Considered to Be a Strong Influence on Ethical Behavior

	Consumer	Corporate CEO
An individual's moral code	59%	82%
Behavior of an employee's immediate supervisor	59%	84%
Example set by CEO or company president	57%	92%
Fear of getting caught or losing one's job	57%	50%
Company's economic situation	46%	26%
Customer opinions	46%	41%
What others would think	46%	56%
Company code of ethics	45%	62%
Company values or culture	45%	88%
Level of ethical behavior of coworkers	40%	72%
Potential harm to firm, stockholders, employees, and customers	39%	44%
Criminal or civil law	37%	38%
Personal religious beliefs	36%	41%

Source: Gene R. Laczniak, Marvin Berkowitz, Russell G. Brooker, and James P. Hale, "The Ethics of Business: Improving or Deteriorating?" *Business Horizons*, 38 (January–February 1995), p. 40. Permission provided courtesy of the Ethics Resource Center.

were $1.8 million and $3.3 million to a husband and wife within the Egyptian government. Lockheed's fines are expected to total $10–$20 million. As a result, other companies, such as Martin Marietta Corp., General Electric, and Teledyne, have agreed to $5.9 million and $13 million settlements for their activities in Egypt, Taiwan, and the Middle East[5] with many company and government employees losing their jobs as well.

When a government official accepts a bribe, it is usually from a business that seeks some favor, perhaps a chance to influence legislation that affects it. Giving bribes to legislators or public officials, then, is a business ethics issue.

The problem of kickbacks exists in private industry as well. In the oil industry, for instance, kickbacks and bribes have become more expensive than theft; they take the form of sports cars, drugs, and prostitutes, as well as large sums of money. According to a *Wall Street Journal* article, one company that services oil rigs gave a supervisor a motor boat, complete with trailer and water skis. A vendor trying to make a sale to another rig boss reportedly was shown forty-two pairs of boots received from other vendors. The rig boss asked, "Can you top that?"[6] Figure 2–2 indicates the problem that business schools and companies have within their own ranks. The data show that business students rank lower than business managers on this honesty poll. These statistics may foreshadow an increase in unethical practices by business in the future. What is more, institutions of higher learning engage in un-

TABLE 2–4
What People Usually Do When They Discover Unethical Behavior in Their Own Company

	Consumer	CEO
Mind their own business	46%	29%
Report it to authorities in the company	36%	63%
Gossip, complain, or talk to coworkers	12%	13%
Talk to the transgressor directly	12%	8%
Fire the transgressor	9%	13%
Report it to the authorities outside the company	8%	7%
Try to right the ethical wrong	7%	7%
Quit	4%	3%
Cover it up	2%	2%

Source: Reprinted from *Business Horizons*, 38–1. Copyright © 1995 by the Foundation for the School of Business at Indiana University.

ethical behavior. Another *Wall Street Journal* article brought to light how universities are inflating Scholastic Aptitude Test (SAT) scores and graduation rates when they supply information for popular guidebooks, such as the *Money's College Guide*. Admission departments were found to be lying to rating agencies, fabricating SAT data, and deliberately misleading alumni and incoming students about their standards.[7] Examples like these demonstrate that the problem of conflict of interest is widespread. Unethical conflicts of interest are of particular concern when they stifle fair competition among businesses.

Honesty and Fairness

Honesty refers to truthfulness, integrity, and trustworthiness; **fairness** is the quality of being just, equitable, and impartial. Honesty and fairness relate to the general moral attributes of decision makers. At a minimum, business-people are expected to follow all applicable laws and regulations. In addition, they should not knowingly harm customers, clients, employees, or competitors through deception, misrepresentation, or coercion. Although people in business often act in their own economic self-interest, ethical business relations should be grounded on fairness, justice, and trust. Buyers should be able to trust sellers; lenders should be able to trust borrowers. Failure to live up to these expectations or to abide by laws and standards destroys trust and makes it difficult, if not impossible, to continue business exchanges.[8]

Ideas of fairness are sometimes shaped by vested interests. One or both parties in the relationship may view an action as unfair or unethical because

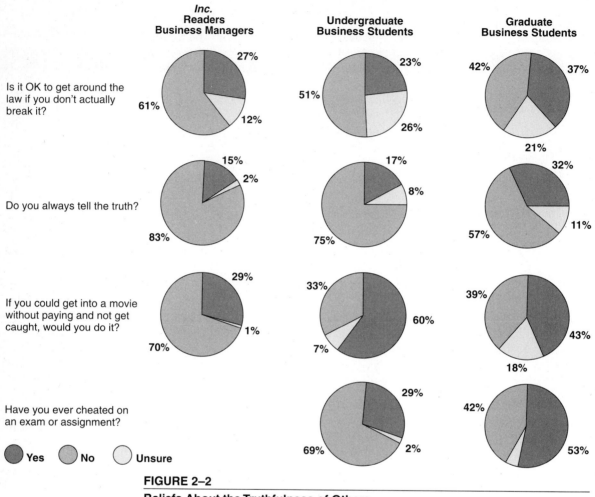

FIGURE 2–2

Beliefs About the Truthfulness of Others

Source: Results of Inc.'s *"Scout's Honor" honesty poll, Ellen E. Spraghs, "Just How Honest Are You?"* Inc. *(February 1992): 104; and the author's survey of business students at a large state university.*

the outcome was less beneficial than expected. For example, in the last few years many hospitals have had a hard time financially, especially as an increasing number of people have found themselves unable to pay for medical care. A federal law enacted early in this decade gives all U.S. citizens the right to such health benefits regardless of their ability to pay. As a result, many hospitals have begun to turn away patients.[9]

Issues related to fairness and honesty also arise because business is sometimes regarded as a "game" governed by its own rules rather than those of society. Eric Beversluis suggests that unfairness is a problem because people often reason along these lines:

1. Business relationships are a subset of human relationships that are governed by their own rules, which, in a market society, involve competition, profit maximization, and personal advancement within the organization.

2. Business can therefore be considered a game people play, comparable in certain respects to competitive sports such as basketball or boxing.

3. Ordinary rules and morality do not hold in games like basketball or boxing. (What if a basketball player did unto others as he would have them do unto him? What if a boxer decided it was wrong to try to injure another person?)

4. Logically, then, if business is a game like basketball or boxing, ordinary ethical rules do not apply.[10]

This type of reasoning leads many people to conclude that anything is fair in sports, war, and business. Indeed, several books have compared business to warfare — for example, Harvey Mackay's *Swim with the Sharks* and Jay Conrad Levinson's *Guerrilla Marketing*. The common theme is that surprise attacks, guerrilla warfare, and other warlike tactics are necessary to win the battle for consumers' dollars. This business-as-war mentality may foster the idea that fairness and honesty are not necessary in business.

Many argue, however, that business is *not* a game like basketball or boxing. Because people are not economically self-sufficient, they cannot withdraw from the game of business. Therefore, business ethics must not only make clear what rules apply in the game of business but must also develop rules appropriate to the nonvoluntary character of participation in the game.[11]

Lack of rules and poor enforcement of the rules that do exist create opportunities for unethical behavior and even encourage it. Table 2–5 shows that in many cases, when employees uncover misconduct, they do not find the corporate response to be either positive or effective. Consequently, many feel that there is no reward for "doing the right thing."

Communications

Communication refers to the transmission of information and the sharing of meaning. Ethical issues in communications relate to advertising messages and information about product safety, pollution, and employee work conditions, as well as other situations. Communications that are false or misleading can destroy customers' trust in an organization. Lying, a major ethical issue within communications, may be a significant problem in the United States. It causes ethical predicaments in both external and internal communications because it destroys trust.

False and deceptive advertising is a key issue in communications. Abuses in advertising can range from exaggerated claims and concealed

TABLE 2–5 Perceived Corporate Response to Reported Employee Misconduct

Nothing happened	13.8%
Corrective action was taken	12.3%
My concerns remained confidential	11.9%
My report was not taken seriously	9.7%
I was not given a prompt or satisfactory response	9.7%
An investigation was launched	8.9%
I never received information on the outcome	7.8%
I was given a prompt or satisfactory response	7.4%
There was a cover-up	5.6%
My concerns did not remain confidential	4.4%
I felt that I was the victim of retaliation or retribution	4.4%
The investigation was not conclusive	4.1%

Source: Rebecca Goodell, *Ethics in American Business: Policies, Programs, and Perceptions* (1994): 24. Permission provided courtesy of the Ethics Resource Center, 1120 6th Street, NW, Washington, DC, 20005.

facts to outright lying. Exaggerated claims are those that cannot be substantiated, as when a commercial states that a certain pain reliever or cough syrup is superior to any other on the market. Sometimes differing interpretations of advertising messages create ethical issues that must be resolved in court. For example, Visa International claimed in ads that seven million merchants that accept Visa cards will not accept American Express. American Express, in turn, bought ads calling Visa a liar and claimed that consumers could save $1.5 billion in annual interest charges if they used American Express's Optima Grace card. The battle of alleged falsehoods extends even to the cost of advertising. American Express's Thomas O. Ryder succinctly explained how competitors feel when their rivals use suspect ads: "There are certain points when you would like to settle this like an old-fashioned schoolyard brawl."[12]

Labeling issues are even murkier. For example, the words *lite* and *super size* have been used in such a variety of ways that the consumer may not know exactly what they mean and what significant differences between product sizes or types they indicate. Companies seem to continue the problem by redefining words. Thus we now have "lite" and "extra lite" products as well as extra large, extra-extra large, super size, and gigantic. This has become a multimillion-dollar headache for clothing manufacturers. For instance, in women's clothing, a size 8 was much smaller in 1942 than it is now; furthermore, one manufacturer's size 8 may differ from another's. The concept of a number being a standardizing measure in the garment industry is no longer true.[13]

Advertising can also mislead by concealing facts within a message. For instance, a salesperson anxious to sell a medical insurance policy might list a large number of illnesses covered by the policy but fail to mention that it does not cover some commonly covered illnesses. To cite another example, in the 1970s Philip Morris Companies came out with the new Merit brand cigarette, touting it as a low-tar cigarette. Many consumers naturally assumed that that also meant lower nicotine levels. Not until 1995, when the Food and Drug Administration began scrutinizing nicotine as a drug, did it come to light that there is not necessarily a direct relationship between tar and nicotine. Modern breeding and filter advances have helped cigarette makers lower the tar content but keep the taste, or nicotine. As Lynn Kozlowski, an addiction expert and professor at Pennsylvania State University, notes, tobacco growers "have learned how to breed more nicotine-rich varieties of tobacco plants."[14] Such behavior creates ethical issues because the communicated messages do not include all the information consumers need to make good purchasing decisions. They frustrate and anger customers, who feel that they have been deceived. In addition, they damage the seller's credibility and reputation.

Another form of advertising abuse involves making ambiguous statements, whose words are so weak that the viewer, reader, or listener must infer the advertiser's intended message. These "weasel" words are inherently vague and enable the advertiser to deny any intent to deceive. The verb *help* is a good example (as in expressions such as "helps prevent," "helps fight," "helps make you feel").[15] Consumers may view such advertisements as unethical because they fail to communicate all the information needed to make a good purchasing decision or because they deceive the consumer outright.

Organizational Relationships

The final category of ethical issues, **organizational relationships,** relates to the behavior of organization members toward customers, suppliers, subordinates, superiors, peers, and others. Ethical employees try to maintain confidentiality in relationships, meet obligations and responsibilities, and avoid putting undue pressure on others that might encourage them to behave unethically. One ethical issue related to relationships is plagiarism: taking someone else's work and presenting it as one's own without providing adequate credit or compensation to the source. Thus an employee responsible for writing a strategic plan for a client might copy a plan written by a peer for another client. Such plagiarism is unfair and dishonest, both to the person who originally wrote the plan and to the client, who is paying for original work tailored specifically to its needs.

ETHICAL ISSUES RELATED TO PARTICIPANTS AND FUNCTIONAL AREAS OF BUSINESS

To help you understand and recognize ethical issues, let us examine the major participants and functions of business from which ethical concerns may arise. Figure 2–3 is a representation of the contemporary business world. The participants are owners, employees, and customers; management, marketing, accounting, and finance are four major functions of any business. In this section we attempt to provide insight into some ethical issues characteristic of each participant type and function.

Owners

Most businesses, large and small, start with the vision of a person or group of people who pool their resources to provide some good or service. The business owners (or stockholders in a corporation), shown at the top of the inner circle in Figure 2–3, generally supply or obtain the resources — usually money or credit — to start and develop the business. The owners may man-

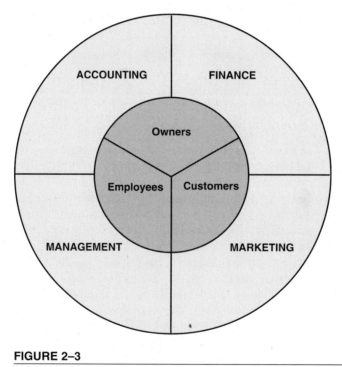

FIGURE 2–3

The Contemporary Business World

age the organization themselves, or they may hire professional managers to run the company.

Owners have an obligation to society. Many owners are concerned about the environment, but some either do not see its relevance in business or choose to ignore or bypass environmental laws because they are perceived as too expensive to follow.

Owners who do not understand the ethical issues that their customers, or society in general, consider important may pay for their lack of understanding in lost sales. Even practices that are considered standard within their industry may be perceived as unethical by outsiders. This was highlighted by several lawsuits brought against law firms accused of overbilling. Among the disputed legal practices that in the past have been defined as ethical by the law profession are the following:

1. *Using a heavy pen:* rounding up when billing for time worked
2. *Claim to a tip:* adding an extra amount to the bill for particularly good work
3. *The smell test:* a crude way of determining how much to charge without seeming to be excessive.[16]

These and other practices such as accepting gifts, giving money to foreign buyers, or accepting trips are being judged as unethical by consumers as gauged by complaints to government. When such events occur, increased legislation is usually the solution.

Finance

Because the owners of a business are responsible for providing financial resources for its operation, owners and finance are in the same segment of Figure 2–3. Owners sometimes have to borrow money from friends or financial institutions to start their business, or they may take on additional owners — partners or stockholders — to obtain money. How financial resources are acquired and deployed can create ethical and even legal issues.

The ethics of money acquisition came into question in the Treasury market. It has been reported that collusion and price fixing have been routine for more than a decade in this $2.3 trillion market. The firm of Salomon Brothers Inc. has already admitted violating several security laws and was subsequently implicated when a number of Japanese companies told of Salomon attempts to collude with them to fix prices and bids.[17]

Other financial issues relate to how companies' financial positions are reported to current and potential investors, government agencies, and other interested parties. Financial documents provide important information on which investors and others base decisions that may involve millions of dollars. If those documents contain inaccurate information, whether intentionally or not, lawsuits and criminal penalties may result.

A recent case shows how people responsible for huge corporations can succumb to such unethical financial practices as embezzlement. Michael I. Monus, former chief executive officer of Phar-Mor Inc., a discount retail chain, and Patrick Finn, Phar-Mor's chief financial officer, were charged with embezzling at least $10 million and funneling it into Monus's pet project, the World Basketball League. Financial books were "cooked," as Monus and Finn overstated company earnings by $340 million and inflated their inventory by $175 million. The two men were fired, and Phar-Mor went into bankruptcy. In 1995 Monus was found guilty of defrauding eighteen banks, in connection with a $600 million line of credit; defrauding eleven insurance companies of $155 million in senior secured notes; and defrauding London-based National Westminster Bank PLC of a $112 million private stock placement. Under current sentencing guidelines, the 48-year-old Monus faces up to 1,246 years in prison and $34 million in fines for fraud, embezzlement, conspiracy, and filing false income returns.[18]

An important issue in the 1990s has been socially responsible investing. As a result, there are at least eleven socially responsible mutual funds (an investment vehicle), with more on the horizon. Managers of these funds avoid buying shares in companies that manufacture nuclear weapons, produce industrial pollution and toxic waste, or fail to promote minorities to positions of authority. This attitude may create ethical issues for firms that manufacture such products when they attempt to obtain additional financial resources.

Another financial issue relates to whether banks should be held responsible for knowing whether large cash deposits are being "laundered" to hide the depositor's involvement in drug trafficking. Society's need to enforce drug-related laws may conflict with banks' desires to maintain the confidentiality of their customers. Although U.S. banks have agreed to tighter controls, unethical and illegal practitioners have sidestepped banks by using wire transfers. Robert Hirsch, a banking and entertainment attorney, favored this type of money laundering method until a woman from the Cali cocaine cartel told him that someone from Colombia would be coming to cut him and his family to pieces unless he turned over $425,000. When Central Intelligence Department agents helped him out, he did not realize that they also knew that he had stolen $2.5 million from members of the cartel.[19]

Employees

Employees, shown in the inner circle in Figure 2–3, carry out the work of the organization. Employees may have to make decisions about assignments that they perceive as unethical. For example, Jeffrey Wigand, a former cigarette executive at Brown & Williamson Tobacco Corporation and now a high school teacher, believed that he could make a safer cigarette. With a doctorate in endocrinology and biochemistry, he felt that a safer cigarette could be made. Unfortunately, Mr. Wigand alleges that Brown & Williamson disagreed with his research and canceled support. He believes that the company is hiding the truth about cigarettes from the public. The company has fired him, but he still believes that what Brown & Williamson is doing is unethical.[20]

Sometimes bosses ask employees to tell lies. Du Pont Co., for instance, has been ordered to pay $115 million in fines or publish a full-page advertisement acknowledging its misconduct concerning a fungicide it produced. Its employees allegedly withheld and misinterpreted test data involving the company's Benlate DF fungicide. Although Du Pont withdrew Benlate DF from the market and paid more than $500 million in settlements, controversy continues in the form of 230 lawsuits.[21]

Bosses may also not want employees to tell them the truth, especially if it would be detrimental to the superior or the company. Albert J. Meyer, an accounting professor who did accounting work for his small college, first became suspicious when he found a $294,000 bank transfer from Spring Arbor College to a foundation called the Heritage of Values Foundation Inc. His superior told him that Heritage of Values was connected to a consultant who had introduced the college to the Foundation for New Era Philanthropy, and that the money was earmarked for New Era.

New Era was the brainchild of John G. Bennett, Jr., who took advantage of churches and philanthropists in a giant **Ponzi scheme.** In a Ponzi scheme, investors are paid with other investors' monies with nothing tangible being produced or supported. Bennett would tell churches that he had other, anonymous, donors that would match their contributions, thus giving the churches a 100 percent return on their investments. But there were no anonymous donors, and Bennett was not investing the money in the traditional way. Even though he reported to the Internal Revenue Service that he drew no salary, the Securities and Exchange Commission has charged that he diverted $4.2 million into personal items, such as a new $620,000 home, which he paid for with cash.[22]

Meyer started probing New Era's activities by amassing financial documents and calling people who had invested. He soon recognized New Era as a Ponzi scheme.[23] Meyer tried repeatedly to warn Spring Arbor, but to no avail. Even though he had no permanent job with the college, he persisted until the IRS and SEC took notice of him and began an investigation which uncovered hundreds of millions of dollars worth of fraud.

Theft and sabotage are other employee issues that companies must deal with occasionally. Employee sabotage is usually a one-time occurrence and the work of an individual who believes that a promotion or raise was unfairly denied. At General Dynamics, Michael Lauffenburger, a programmer, became so disgruntled by not being promoted that he created a logic bomb (a computer program that would destroy the company's parts program and then destroy itself). Lauffenburger quit several months before the program was to be activated and was going to act as a consultant to General Dynamics to rebuild the computer program.[24]

Unlike sabotage, employee theft may be an ongoing, routine occurrence. At Pinkerton Security Investigation Services, Marita Juse, alias Tammy

Gonzalez, was hired by the accounting department to do wire transfers. One day she was delegated to cancel a former superior's approval code, which she instead began to use. Over two years, Juse siphoned off more than $1 million; she was sentenced to twenty-seven months in prison.[25]

There may also be situations where an employee is aware that the boss has been sexually harassing another employee but has no way of proving the offense. Will speaking out make things worse for the employee? And what will it do to the coworker, the victim? Such situations create ethical issues that employees must resolve. One example of how difficult it can be to win a sex bias case is the trauma that Helen L. Walters went through. A trading-room secretary at a California brokerage firm, she said that, among other things, her boss called her a hooker, bitch, and idiot and also left condoms on her desk. One would think that this would be enough evidence for an award of damages. However, there was a complication. As a condition of employment, all registered securities agents must sign an agreement in which they surrender all rights to a trial for virtually any grievance against their employer.[26] Such difficulties are often compounded by employees' fear of losing their jobs if they protest or speak out.

There are other situations where companies understand the importance of ethics and attempt to solve the problem with elaborate systems. However, if such systems are not based on company integrity, they usually become part of the problem. For instance, after several nasty corporate scandals, General Electric created an elaborate ethics program. Yet since then it has paid approximately $70 million to settle charges from a case in which an employee failed to use the program, fearing repercussions. Jay Gourley, editor of a journal that covers the Department of Justice, commented that in the defense industry, where GE has a major stake, employees who complain of wrongdoing or unethical behavior can jeopardize their careers.[27]

Management

Managers of a business have both an ethical and a legal responsibility to manage the business in the interest of the owners. Several ethical issues relate to managers' obligations to owners, especially in the area of corporate takeovers, mergers, and leveraged buyouts. For example, when a business faces the prospect of being bought or taken over by another company or individual, the managers' duties to the current owners may conflict with their own personal interests and objectives (job security, income, and power). Their loyalty to the organization and to the owners and stockholders may be brought into question. A management team may attempt to block a takeover that would benefit shareholders but reduce management's power and perhaps jeopardize their jobs. Managers also have to face decisions about paying "greenmail" to raiders that have acquired a large stake in the firm and will not sell back their shares except at a premium price. If greenmail is not paid, the raider may acquire the company and sell off its assets piece by piece, possibly resulting in the loss of jobs for many employees.

The primary goal of management is to achieve a company's objectives by organizing, directing, planning, and controlling the activities of its employees. Management and employees are in the same segment of Figure 2–3 because managers organize and motivate workers to achieve organizational objectives. Since they guide employees and direct activities, managers influence the ethical issues that evolve within an organization.

Management should also be concerned about ethical issues that relate to employee discipline, discrimination, health and safety, privacy, employee benefits, drug and alcohol abuse in the workplace, the environmental impact of the organization, codes of ethics and self-governance, relations with local communities, plant closings, and layoffs. When such issues are not addressed, employees and communities usually react adversely. For example, Rockwell International was sued by workers at its Denver plant for $30 million because they were not given adequate notice of their plant's closing.[28] General Mills, Bankers Trust of New York, and Brown & Williamson have reported increases in white-collar theft of company secrets, in part because of unethical management.[29] In a case that is being tried about honesty in the real estate industry, Century 21's case will determine whether brokers must double-check client information and whether brokers can intentionally remain ignorant about a property's value. It will also check for deceptive negotiating sales practices.[30]

Managers must carefully balance their duties both to the owners or stockholders, who hired them to achieve the organization's objectives, and to the employees, who look to them for guidance and direction. In addition, managers must comply with society's wishes to have safe working conditions and safe products, to protect the environment, and to promote minorities. For example, amendments to the Civil Rights Act extend punitive damages to the plaintiff for discrimination on the basis of sex, disability, religion, or race. These amendments may encourage the promotion of more women and minorities.

Another area of potential ethical problems for managers is that of the public's concern over privacy issues and data access. Because more data are being stored in computers and the information is being sold, many consumer rights groups worry about the violation of privacy rights. For example, Physician Computer Network Inc. has approached pharmacists and physicians requesting access to patient files. The company states that no names will be retained or disseminated. In return for granting access to these files, the health professionals are given low-cost personal computer hardware and software leases.[31] More and more companies are buying, selling, and manipulating such lists to better target consumers for specific products or services. Some consumers would find it an invasion of privacy to have multiple companies know what items they had purchased at a store, the state of their mental or physical health, or what medications they are taking. Striking an ethical balance among the needs of owners, employees, and society is a difficult task for today's managers.

Consumers

No organization will survive unless consumers purchase its products. Thus the major role of any company is to satisfy its customers. To do so, businesses must find out what consumers want and need, and then create products that will satisfy those wants and needs.

In attempting to satisfy customers, businesses must consider not only consumers' immediate needs but also their long-term desires. For example, although people want efficient, low-cost energy to power their homes and automobiles, they do not want energy generation to pollute the air and water, kill wildlife, or cause disease and birth defects in children. Consumers also expect nutritious food in large quantities at low prices and in convenient form, but they do not want food producers to injure or kill valued wildlife in the process. Thus, because dolphins were often killed in the process used to catch tuna, many consumers boycotted tuna products. Similarly, in response to public protest, several large cosmetics companies have stopped cosmetics testing that involves animals. Consumer protection organizations, like the one led by activist Ralph Nader, have been highly successful in getting businesses to halt activities deemed unethical or harmful to people and the environment. Businesses in general want to satisfy their customers and are usually willing to make requested changes in order to appease concerned consumers and avoid losses from boycotts and negative publicity.

In the last several years, however, some environmental dilemmas have demonstrated the tenuous nature of ethics in business. For example, should acres of forest land be preserved to save the rare spotted owl from extinction? If so, then families in such small towns as Port Angeles and Forks, Washington, would lose their jobs and whole communities might disappear. Suicides, alcohol abuse, and spouse and child abuse might increase. As one picture drawn by a seven-year-old sums up the issue, "An owl needs 2,000 acres to live, why can't I have room to live?"[32] Similar problems exist in relation to other endangered species, such as the sea lion, elk, grizzly bear, and mountain goat.

Such conflicting needs have caused many companies to sidestep environmental issues with the blessing of local townsfolk. For example, a court will determine if Pacific Lumber or the marbled murrelet, a bird that travels at night and nests in the Oak Creek forest in the Northwest, is to survive. Before the case went to court, Pacific Lumber had agreed to cooperate with regulators and minimize harm to the murrelets. Yet over weekends and holidays Pacific cut down trees, arguing that it was not violating the agreement.[33] If business wins this case, and others like it, then the world may lose wildlife and plants that can never be replaced, and the whole ecosystem may become unbalanced. What kind of response to these conflicting priorities will appease concerned consumers and avert negative publicity? You as future businesspeople will be faced by such ethical dilemmas, and there are no easy answers.

Marketing

Marketing and customers are in the same segment of Figure 2–3 because all marketing activities focus on customer satisfaction. Marketing refers to activities designed to provide customers with satisfying goods and services. Marketers first gather information and conduct marketing research to find out what consumers want. Then they develop products, price the products, promote them, and distribute them where and when customers want to buy them. Ethical issues may arise in relation to the safety of products, the advertising and selling of products, pricing, or distribution channels that direct the flow of products from the manufacturer to the consumer. In regard to product safety, for example, breast implants have become suspect, and a $4.2 billion global settlement has been tentatively agreed on. Many scandals have come to light in connection with the implants. To illustrate, it turns out that former Dow Chemical general counsel Wayne M. Hancock knew as early as May 1993 that affidavits concerning the implants were in error, yet he did not correct them.[34]

Some companies take the supply-demand concept to extremes. For instance, Johnson & Johnson's new cancer drug, Ergamisol, costs a patient $1,250 to $1,500 for one year's supply. The ethical problem with the price tag is that Ergamisol is the same thirty-year-old drug Levamisole that has been used as a de-wormer in sheep. Johnson & Johnson claims that the drug's price reflects research costs. Opponents, such as cancer expert and physician Charles G. Moertel of the Mayo Comprehensive Cancer Center, have a different view. Moertel said, "To find a new use for an old drug is a sort of windfall that doesn't justify a price surge. Just because aspirin was found to improve your risk of heart attack should you charge more?" He added, "Cancer drugs are unlike consumer products. It's not like, if you can't afford a Ford, you can buy a Chevy."[35]

More recently, many medical groups have begun to question the benefits of magnetic resonance imaging (MRI) as it relates to any significant differences for the patient, suggesting that the equipment may be only a money generator. To put this in perspective, an MRI costs approximately $1,200 per picture, whereas the older, widely used computed tomography (CT), which it is replacing, costs $500 per picture. According to estimates, more than two thousand MRI machines are in use today.[36] Sonograms — pictures of unborn babies in the mothers' womb — have also raised doubts as to their value. It is estimated that 75 percent of the country's thirty-nine thousand obstetrician-gynecologists have the machines and do the tests themselves. As one physician acknowledged, doing thirty to forty ultrasounds at $150 per test added $60,000 to his annual income.[37]

Accounting

The field of accounting has changed dramatically over the last decade. The profession used to have a club-type mentality: those who became certified public accountants (CPAs) were not concerned about competition. Now CPAs advertise their skills or short-term results in an environment in which competition has increased and overall billable hours have significantly decreased because of technological innovations. Pressures on accountants include the following: time, reduced fees, client requests for altered opinions or for lower tax payments, and increased competition. Because of such pressures, and the ethical predicaments they spawn, some accounting firms have had financial problems. The "Big Eight" accounting firms have been reduced to the "Big Six."

Some of the problems just enumerated were the cause of a $388 million judgment against Price Waterhouse. The story began when a Standards Union Bank subsidiary bought United Bank of Arizona. Price Waterhouse was United's accounting firm and offered to remain its auditor for about half the going rate. Union kept Price Waterhouse, which in turn sent a team that included a 26-year-old staff accountant with very little experience. Normal auditing procedures were not strictly adhered to; there was even failure to ensure that an adequate loan review system was in place. As a result, many large loans did not receive the scrutiny they needed and subsequently went sour.[38] To cite another example, Woolworth Corp. found itself with an accounting problem when investigators discovered irregularities in the company's books.[39]

Other issues that accountants face daily involve complex rules and regulations that must be followed; data overload; contingent fees; and commissions. An accountant's life is filled with rules and data that have to be interpreted correctly. As a result, accountants must abide by a strict code of ethics, which defines their responsibilities to their clients and the public interest. The code also discusses the concepts of integrity, objectivity, independence, and due care. Finally, the code delineates an accountant's scope and the nature of services that ethically should be provided. In this last portion of the code, contingent fees and commissions are indirectly addressed. Since the code provides them with standards, it would be reasonable to assume that accountants have a fairly clear understanding of ethical and unethical practices, but apparently that is not the case. Recently, the American Institute of Certified Public Accountants (AICPA) added a new requirement to the code: that if a company's financial statements are "materially misstated," the accountant should consider reporting the problem to his or her superior. Going along with any type of cover-up would bring loss of license. Robert C.

Reeves, Jr., a former employee of Aetna Life & Casualty Co., reported the misstatements and was subsequently fired. A spokesman for the company denies the allegation that is in the courts and says that Aetna eliminated Reeves's job "as part of the reduction in staff in the mortgage-portfolio management area."[40] There are also different types of issues for different types of accountants, such as those in auditing, tax, and management.

RECOGNIZING AN ETHICAL ISSUE

Although we have described a number of relationships and situations that may generate ethical issues, it can be difficult to recognize specific ethical issues in practice. Failure to acknowledge ethical issues is a great danger in any organization, particularly if business is treated as a game in which ordinary rules of fairness do not apply. Sometimes people who take this view do things that are not only unethical but also illegal in order to maximize their own position or boost the profits or goals of the organization.

One way to determine whether a specific behavior or situation has an ethical component is to ask other individuals in the business how they feel about it and whether they approve. Another way is to determine whether the organization has adopted specific policies on the activity. An activity approved of by most members of an organization, if it is also customary in the industry, is probably ethical. An issue, activity, or situation that can withstand open discussion between many groups, both in and outside the organization, and survive untarnished probably does not pose ethical problems. For instance, when engineers and designers at Ford Motor Co. discussed what type of gas-tank protection should be used in its Pinto automobile, they reached consensus within the organization, but they did not take into account the public's desire for maximum safety. Consequently, even though they might have believed the issue had no ethical dimension, Ford erred in not opening up the issue to public scrutiny. (As it turned out, the type of gas-tank protection in the Pinto resulted in several fires and deaths when the cars were involved in rear-end collisions.)

Once an individual recognizes that an ethical issue exists and can openly discuss it with others, he or she has begun the ethical decision-making process, which is discussed in Chapter 5. When people believe that they cannot discuss what they are doing with peers or superiors, there is a good chance that an ethical issue exists.

In this chapter we have attempted to heighten your awareness of some ethical issues that may develop in a business organization. We have not tried to define whether certain actions are ethical or unethical, but only to show that they are issues worthy of moral discussion and evaluation. Just because an unsettled situation or activity is an ethical issue, the behavior is not necessarily unethical. An ethical issue is simply a situation, a problem, or even an opportunity that requires thought, discussion, or investigation to determine the moral impact of the decision. Because the business world is dynamic, new ethical issues are emerging all the time. In the next chapter, we define and explore various moral philosophies that individuals use to evaluate activities as ethical or unethical and to resolve ethical dilemmas.

SUMMARY

An ethical issue is a problem, situation, or opportunity requiring an individual or organization to choose among several actions that must be evaluated as right or wrong, ethical or unethical. Ethical issues typically arise because of conflicts between individuals' personal moral philosophies and values and the values and attitudes of the organizations in which they work and the society in which they live.

Researchers have found that ethical conflicts arise most often in business relationships with customers, suppliers, employees, and others, and as a result of certain business practices, such as the giving of gifts and kickbacks and pricing discrimination. Business executives and academics acknowledge that these are ethical issues and that they would like to eliminate many unethical practices.

Ethical issues can be classified into four categories: issues of conflict of interest, issues of fairness and honesty, issues of communications, and issues of organizational relationships. A conflict of interest exists when an individual must choose between advancing his or her own personal interests and those of the organization or some other group. Honesty refers to truthfulness, integrity, and trustworthiness; fairness is the quality of being just, equitable, and impartial. Issues related to fairness and honesty often arise in business because many participants believe that business is a game governed by its own rules rather than those of society. Communication refers to the transmission of information and the sharing of meaning. False and misleading communications can destroy customers' trust in an organization. Organizational relationships involve the behaviors of individuals in the organization toward others, including customers, suppliers, subordinates, superiors, and peers.

Ethical issues can also be explored in terms of the major participants and functions of business. Ethical issues related to ownership include conflicts between managers' duties to the owners and their own interests, and the separation of ownership and control of the business. Financial ethical issues include questions of socially responsible investment and the accuracy of reported financial documents. Employees face ethical issues when they are asked to carry out assignments they consider unethical. Managers directly influence the ethical issues that evolve within an organization because they guide and motivate employees. Ethical issues related to consumers and marketing include providing a selection of safe, reliable, high-quality products at reasonable prices without harming the customers or the environment. Accountants are also within the realm of business ethics and face such pressures as competition, advertising, and a shrinking environment. Issues such as data overload, contingent fees, and commissions all place the accounting profession in ethical risk situations.

A good rule of thumb is that an activity approved of by most members of an organization and customary in the industry is probably ethical. An issue, activity, or situation that can withstand open discussion and survive untarnished probably poses no ethical problem. Once an individual recognizes that an ethical issue exists and can openly discuss it and ask for guidance and the opinions of others, he or she enters the ethical decision-making process.

A REAL-LIFE SITUATION

Carla knew something was wrong when Bob got back to his desk. Bob had been with Aker & Aker Accounting for seventeen years. He had started there right after graduation and had progressed through the ranks. He was a strong supporter of the company, which was why Carla had been assigned to him.

Carla had been with Aker & Aker (A&A) for two years. She graduated in the top 10 percent of her class and passed the CPA exam on the first try. She had chosen A&A over one of the Big Six firms because A&A was the biggest and best firm in Smallville, Ohio, where her husband, Frank, managed a locally owned machine tools company. She and Frank had just purchased a new home when things started to turn strange with Bob, her boss.

"What's the matter, Bob?" Carla asked.

"Well, you'll hear about it sooner or later. I've been denied a partner's position. Can you imagine that? Working sixty- and seventy-hour weeks for the last ten years, and all they can say is 'not at this time,'" complained Bob.

Carla asked, "So what else did they say?"

Bob turned red and blurted out, "They said

maybe in a few more years. I've done all that they've asked me to do. I've sacrificed a lot, and now they say a few more years. It's not fair."

"What are you going to do?" Carla asked.

"I don't know," Bob said. "I just don't know."

Six months later, Carla noticed that Bob was behaving in an odd manner. He left early and came in late. One Sunday Carla went into the office for some files and found Bob copying some of the software A&A used in auditing and consulting. A couple of weeks later, at a dinner party, Carla overheard a conversation about Bob doing consulting work for some small firms. At work Monday morning, she asked him if what she had heard was true.

Bob responded, "Yes, Carla, it's true. I have a few clients that I do work for on occasion."

"Don't you think there's a conflict of interest between you and A&A?" asked Carla.

"No," said Bob. "You see, these clients are not technically within the market area of A&A. Besides, I was counting on that promotion to help pay some extra bills. My oldest son decided to go to a private university, which is an extra

$20,000. Plus our medical plan at A&A doesn't cover some problems my wife has. And you don't want to know the cost. The only way I can afford to pay for these things is to do some extra work on the side."

"But what if A&A finds out?" Carla asked. "Won't they terminate you?"

"I don't want to think about that. Besides, if they don't find out for another six months, I may be able to start my own company."

"How?" asked Carla.

"Don't be naive, Carla. You came in on that Sunday; you know."

Carla realized that Bob had been using A&A software for his own gain. "That's stealing!" she said.

"Stealing?" Bob's voice grew calm. "Like when you use the office phones for personal long-distance calls? Like when you decided to volunteer to help out your church and copied all those things for them on the company machine? If I'm stealing, you're a thief as well. But let's not get into this discussion. I'm not hurting A&A and, who knows, maybe within the next year I'll become a partner and can quit my night job."

Carla backed off from the discussion and said nothing more. She couldn't afford to antagonize her boss and risk bad performance ratings. She and Frank had bills, too. She also knew that she wouldn't be able to get another job at the same pay if she quit. Moving to another town was not an option because of Frank's business. She had no physical evidence to take to the partners, which meant that it would be her word against Bob's, and he had ten years of experience with the company.

Questions

1. What are the ethical issues of the case?

2. Assume that you are Carla and discuss your options and what the consequences of each option might be.

3. Assume that you are Bob and discuss your options.

4. Discuss the legal and ethical ramifications of each option for Carla and Bob.

5. Discuss any extra information you feel you need in order to make your decision.

IMPORTANT TERMS FOR REVIEW

ethical issue
conflict of interest
honesty
fairness
communication
organizational relationships
Ponzi scheme

Applying Moral Philosophies to Business Ethics

AN ETHICAL DILEMMA *

ACME MOWERS, INC., had developed a new lawn mower that would out-perform competitive machines currently on the market. The firm's marketing research indicated that there would be a very strong market for the product if it was priced at roughly $130.

Acme's research and development department developed two designs of the product. Version I was a small, easy to handle, lightweight mower, which would retail for $120. Version II was bulky, harder to handle, and would retail for $300. The firm's research indicated that Version I was a virtually perfect product, with one exception: tests showed that after normal use of approximately ten to twenty years, some users would experience hearing loss. Version II, which incorporated noise reduction material in the product, showed no evidence of creating this problem.

Jerry Kelso, Acme's president, had asked the research and development team to find a solution to the problem. The team suggested that a set of high-quality earphones be included with the lawn mower, to be worn when using the machine. However, the earphones would increase the cost of Version I significantly. Market research also found that people rejected the idea of wearing earphones or ear plugs. Jerry concluded that Version I would fail in the market if the use of ear plugs was recommended.

At lunch one day, Jerry overheard a conversation about his main competitor's new lawn mower. The product described sounded almost identical to Acme's Version I, including its lightweight structure. When he got back to the office, Jerry made some phone calls and verified that his competitor was developing a new lawn mower. He knew that the competitive product would encounter the same noise problem. Inside sources also told him that the rival company knew about the problem but was proceeding with production anyway.

Jerry reviewed his options. If he did not make a decision quickly, his competitor might beat him to the market with the product. If Acme launched Version I first, it could capture the market and get out of its current sales slump. But use of the product could lead to deafness for some consumers in ten to twenty years. If Acme marketed Version II, on the other hand, sales would be unacceptable. His competition would introduce its lightweight product in six months, cutting in half any market share Acme might have gained. Jerry considered developing an advertising campaign that might change the nature of demand by calling consumers' attention to the deafness risk. But Acme might then be liable to a lawsuit brought by an angry competitor. Jerry concluded that this was not a viable option.

Before making his decision, Jerry asked his operations manager how a decision not to market the new mower would affect the company. If the new product was not introduced successfully, he learned, Acme would have to lay off two hundred of its one thousand production workers. Jerry also consulted the vice president of finance, who was equally pessimistic. Given the current sales slump, the expense of developing an unsuccessful product could lead the company into bankruptcy, he said.

Questions

1. What are Jerry's options?
2. What consequences might each option have?
3. What are the ethical and legal issues?
4. Who is more important, Acme and its employees or consumers?
5. What pressures are having an impact on Jerry?

_____
*This case is strictly hypothetical; any resemblance to real persons, companies, or situations is coincidental.

oral philosophies have to do with ideas of right and wrong. They help explain why a person believes that one action is right whereas another is wrong; they are often cited to justify decisions or explain actions. Therefore, to understand how people make ethical decisions, it is useful to have a grasp of the major types of moral philosophies.

In this chapter we explore several aspects of moral philosophy. First we define moral philosophy and discuss how it applies to business. Next we describe two broad classifications of moral philosophy: teleology and deontology. Then we consider the relativist perspective from which many ethical or unethical decisions are made in everyday life. Finally, we discuss what is called virtue ethics and how it can be applied to today's multinational business environment.

MORAL PHILOSOPHY DEFINED

When people talk about philosophy, they usually mean the system of values by which they live. **Moral philosophy** refers in particular to the principles or rules that people use to decide what is right or wrong. For example, a production manager may be guided by a general philosophy of management that emphasizes encouraging workers to know as much as possible about the product they are manufacturing. Moral philosophy comes into play when the manager must make decisions such as whether to notify employees in advance of upcoming layoffs. Although workers would prefer advance warning, its side effects might adversely affect production quality and quantity. Such decisions require a person to evaluate the "rightness," or morality, of choices in terms of his or her own principles and values.

Moral philosophies present guidelines for "determining how conflicts in human interests are to be settled and for optimizing mutual benefit of people living together in groups."[1] Moral philosophies guide businesspersons as they formulate business strategies and resolve specific ethical issues. However, there is no single moral philosophy that everyone accepts. Some managers view profit as the ultimate goal of an enterprise and therefore may not be concerned about their firm's impact on the environment or society. In 1994 three such companies were identified as the least admired for community and environmental responsibility: Brooke Group, Gitano, and Food Lion.[2] Other managers believe that it is "right" for the firm to try to contribute to the communities in which it operates. Thus American Express founded Project Access to Computer Training (PACT), a program that prepares qualified physically handicapped people for computer-related jobs; and Honeywell, Ogilvy & Mather Worldwide, Aetna Life and Casualty, and Hewlett-Packard Co. contribute funds, equipment, and personnel to elementary and secondary education reform programs.[3] In fact there are many companies who are very concerned about the communities they reside in. For example, in 1994, out of 404 companies surveyed, the most admired companies for community and environmental responsibility were Rubbermaid, Corning, and Johnson & Johnson.[4] Managers in all these firms have developed strategies for operating their businesses on the basis of personal moral philosophies. They also use these moral philosophies to deal with individual ethical issues.

People base their personal moral philosophies on their concept of right and wrong and act accordingly in their daily lives. Problems arise when they encounter ethical situations they cannot resolve. Sometimes a better understanding of the basic premise of their decision rationale can help them choose the "right" solution. For instance, to decide whether they should offer bribes to customers in the hope of securing a large contract, salespeople need to understand their own personal moral philosophy. If obeying the law is an important motivation, they are less likely to offer a bribe. On the other hand, if the salesperson's ultimate goal is a successful career and if offering a bribe seems likely to result in a promotion, then bribery might not be inconsistent with that person's moral philosophy.

MORAL PHILOSOPHY PERSPECTIVES

There are many moral philosophies, and each one is complex. Because a detailed study of all moral philosophies would be beyond the scope of this book, we will limit our discussion to those that are most applicable to the study of business ethics. Our approach will focus on the most basic concepts needed to help you understand the ethical decision-making process in business. We will not prescribe the use of any particular moral philosophy, for there is no one "correct" way to resolve ethical issues in business.

To help you understand how the moral philosophies discussed in this chapter may be applied in decision making, we will use a hypothetical problem situation as an illustration. Suppose that Sam Colt, a sales representative, is preparing a sales presentation for his firm, Midwest Hardware, which manufactures nuts and bolts. Colt hopes to obtain a large sale from a construction firm that is building a bridge across the Missouri River near St. Louis. The bolts manufactured by Midwest Hardware have a 3 percent defect rate, which, although acceptable in the industry, makes them unsuitable for use in certain types of projects, such as those that may be subject to sudden, severe stress. The new bridge will be located near the New Madrid Fault line, the source of the United States' greatest earthquake, in 1811. The epicenter of that earthquake, which caused extensive damage and altered the flow of the Missouri, is less than two hundred miles from the new bridge site. Earthquake experts believe there is a 50 percent chance that an earthquake with a magnitude greater than 7 on the Richter scale will occur somewhere along the New Madrid Fault by the year 2000. Bridge construction in the area is not regulated by earthquake codes, however. If Colt wins the sale, he will earn a commission of $25,000 on top of his regular salary. But if he tells the contractor about the defect rate, Midwest may lose the sale to a competitor whose bolts are more reliable. Thus Colt's ethical issue is whether to point out to the bridge contractor that, in the event of an earthquake, Midwest bolts could fail, possibly resulting in the collapse of the bridge and the death of anyone driving across it at the time.

We will come back to this illustration as we discuss particular moral philosophies, asking how Colt might use each philosophy to resolve his ethical issue. We will not judge the quality of Colt's decision, and we will not advocate any one moral philosophy as best. In fact, this illustration and Colt's decision rationales are necessarily simplistic as well as hypothetical. In reality, the decision maker would probably have many more factors to consider in making his or her choice, and thus might reach a different decision. With that note of caution, we will introduce four types of moral philosophy: teleology, deontology, the relativist perspective, and virtue ethics (see Table 3–1).

Teleology

Teleology refers to moral philosophies in which an act is considered morally right or acceptable if it produces some desired result, for example, pleasure, knowledge, career growth, the realization of self-interest, or utility. In other words, teleological philosophies assess the moral worth of a behavior by

TABLE 3–1 A Comparison of the Moral Philosophies Discussed in This Text

Teleology	Stipulates that acts are morally right or acceptable if they produce some desired result, such as the realization of self-interest or utility
Egoism	Defines right or acceptable actions as those that maximize a particular person's self-interest as defined by the individual
Utilitarianism	Defines right or acceptable actions as those that maximize total utility, or the greatest good for the greatest number of people
Deontology	Focuses on the preservation of individual rights and on the intentions associated with a particular behavior rather than on its consequences
Relativist	Evaluates ethicalness subjectively on the basis of individual and group experiences
Virtue ethics	Assumes that what is moral in a given situation is not only what conventional morality requires, but also what the mature person with a "good" moral character would deem appropriate

looking at its consequences. Moral philosophers today often refer to these theories as **consequentialism**. Two important teleological philosophies that often guide decision making in business are egoism and utilitarianism.

Egoism　**Egoism** defines right or acceptable behavior in terms of the consequences for the individual. Egoists believe that they should make decisions that maximize their own self-interest, which is defined differently by each individual. Depending on the egoist, self-interest may be construed as physical well-being, power, pleasure, fame, a satisfying career, a good family life, wealth, or something else. In an ethical decision-making situation, an egoist will probably choose the alternative that contributes most to his or her self-interest. The egoist's creed can be generally stated as "Do the act that promotes the greatest good for oneself." Many believe that egoists are inherently unethical, that such people and companies are short-term oriented and will take advantage of any opportunity or consumer. For example, some telemarketers demonstrate this negative egoistic tendency when they prey on elderly consumers who may be vulnerable because of frequent loneliness or the fear of losing financial independence. Margaret Horne, 83, was one of thousands that fall victim to fraudulent telemarketers every year. In less than a year she had lost all her savings and her $187,000 home; she is now residing in a $360-a-month apartment that entitles her to one meal a day.[5]

However, there is also enlightened egoism. **Enlightened egoists** take a long-range perspective and allow for the well-being of others, although their own self-interest remains paramount. Enlightened egoists may abide by professional codes of ethics, control pollution, avoid cheating on taxes, help create jobs, and support community projects. Yet they do so not because these actions benefit others, but because they help achieve some ultimate goal for the egoist, such as advancement within the firm. An enlightened egoist might call management's attention to a coworker who is cheating customers, but only to safeguard the company's reputation and thus the egoist's own job security.

When businesses donate money, resources, or time to specific causes and institutions, their motives may not be purely altruistic either. For example, International Business Machines (IBM) has a policy of donating or reducing the cost of computers to educational institutions. The company receives tax breaks for donations of equipment, which reduce the costs of this policy. In addition, IBM hopes to build future sales by placing its products on campus. When students enter the work force, they may request the IBM products with which they have become familiar. Although the company's actions benefit society in general, in the long run they also benefit IBM.

We now return to the hypothetical case of the salesperson who must decide whether to warn the bridge contractor that 3 percent of Midwest Hardware's bolts are likely to be defective. If Sam Colt is an egoist, he will probably choose the alternative that maximizes his own self-interest. If he defines self-interest as personal wealth, his personal moral philosophy may lead him to value a $25,000 commission more than a chance to reduce the risk of a bridge collapse. An egoist Colt, therefore, might well resolve his ethical dilemma by keeping quiet about the bolts' defect rate, hoping to win the sale and a $25,000 commission.

Utilitarianism   Like egoism, **utilitarianism** is concerned with consequences, but the utilitarian seeks the greatest good for the greatest number of people. Utilitarians believe they should make decisions that result in the greatest total *utility*, that is, achieve the greatest benefit for all those affected by a decision.

Utilitarian decision making relies on a systematic comparison of the costs and benefits to all affected parties. Using such a cost-benefit analysis, a utilitarian decision maker calculates the utility of the consequences of all possible alternatives and then selects the one that results in the greatest utility. Fleet Financial Group Inc., for example, finally decided in 1994 to fund $140 million of an $8 billion loan pool aimed at inner-city, low-income, and small-business borrowers. The probable reason Fleet agreed to aid the Union Neighborhood Assistance Corp. was because of Bruce Marks. For the previous half decade Marks had lobbied members of Congress, filled committee hearing rooms with protesters, and staged a number of outrageous stunts to embarrass Fleet. Ultimately, the damage being done to the company's reputation made Fleet conclude that it had to end the "David-and-Goliath" situation.[6]

In evaluating an action's consequences, many utilitarians consider the effects on animals as well as human beings. This perspective is significant in the controversy surrounding animal research by cosmetics and pharmaceutical companies. Animal-rights groups have protested that such testing is unethical because it harms and even kills the animals and deprives them of their rights. Researchers for pharmaceutical and cosmetics manufacturers, such as Maybelline, however, defend animal testing on utilitarian grounds. The consequences of the research (new or improved drugs to treat disease, safer cosmetics) create more benefit for society, they argue, than would be achieved by halting the research to preserve the animals' rights. Nonetheless, some cosmetics firms, including John Paul Mitchell Systems (a hair-care manufacturer), have responded to the controversy by agreeing to stop animal research.

Now suppose that Sam Colt, the bolt salesperson, is a utilitarian. Before making his decision, he would conduct a cost-benefit analysis to determine which alternative would create the most utility. On the one hand, building the bridge would improve roadways and allow more people to cross the Missouri River to reach jobs in St. Louis. The project would create hundreds of jobs, enhance the local economy, and unite communities on both sides of the river. Additionally, it would increase the revenues of Midwest Hardware, allowing the firm to invest more in research to lower the defect rate of bolts produced in the future. On the other hand, a bridge collapse could kill or injure as many as one hundred people. But the bolts have only a 3 percent defect rate, and there is only a 50 percent probability of an earthquake *somewhere* along the fault line; there might be only a few cars on the bridge at the time of a disaster. After analyzing the costs and benefits of the situation, Colt might conclude that building the bridge with his company's bolts would create more utility (jobs, unity, economic growth, company growth) than would result from telling the bridge contractor that the bolts might fail in an earthquake. If so, the utilitarian Colt would probably not call the bridge contractor's attention to the defect rate.

Utilitarians use various criteria to determine the morality of an action. Some utilitarian philosophers have argued that general rules should be followed to decide which action is best.[7] These "rule utilitarians" determine behavior on the basis of principles, or rules, designed to promote the greatest utility, rather than on an examination of each particular situation. One such rule might be "bribery is wrong." If people felt free to offer bribes whenever they might be useful, the world would become chaotic; therefore, a rule prohibiting bribery would increase utility. A rule utilitarian would not bribe an official even to preserve workers' jobs but would adhere strictly to the rule. Rule utilitarians do not automatically accept conventional moral rules, however. If an alternative rule would promote greater utility, they would advocate changing the convention.

Other utilitarian philosophers have argued that the rightness of each individual action must be evaluated to determine whether it produces the greatest utility for the greatest number of people.[8] These "act utilitarians" examine the action itself, rather than the rules governing the action, to determine whether it will result in the greatest utility. Rules, such as "bribery is wrong," serve only as general guidelines to act utilitarians. They would agree that bribery is generally wrong, not because there is anything inherently wrong with bribery, but because the total amount of utility decreases when one person's interests are placed ahead of those of society.[9] In a particular case, however, an act utilitarian might argue that bribery is acceptable. For example, a sales manager might believe that her firm will not win a construction contract unless a local government official gets a bribe; moreover, if the firm does not obtain the contract, it will have to lay off one hundred workers. The manager might therefore argue that bribery is justified because saving a hundred jobs creates more utility than obeying a law.

Deontology

Deontology refers to moral philosophies that focus on the rights of individuals and on the intentions associated with a particular behavior rather than on its consequences. Fundamental to deontological theory is the idea that equal respect must be given to all persons. Unlike utilitarians, deontologists argue that there are some things that we should *not* do, even to maximize utility. For example, deontologists would consider it wrong to kill an innocent person or commit a serious injustice against a person, no matter how much utility might result from doing so, because such an action would infringe on that person's rights as an individual. The utilitarian, however, might consider as acceptable an action that resulted in a person's death if that action created some greater utility.

Deontological philosophies regard certain behaviors as inherently right, and the determination of rightness focuses on the individual actor, not society. Thus these perspectives are sometimes referred to as **nonconsequentialism, ethical formalism,** and the ethics of *respect for persons.*

Contemporary deontology has been greatly influenced by the German philosopher Immanuel Kant, who developed the so-called categorical imperative: "Act as if the maxim of thy action were to become by thy will a universal law of nature."[10] Simply put, if you feel comfortable allowing everyone in the world to see you commit an act and if your rationale for acting in a particular manner is suitable to become a universal principle guiding behavior, then committing that act is ethical. For example, if a person borrows money, promising to return it but with no intention of keeping that promise, he or she cannot "universalize" borrowing money without any intention of returning it. If everyone were to borrow money without the intention of returning it, no one would take such promises seriously.[11] Therefore, the rationale for the action would not be a suitable universal principle, and the act cannot be considered ethical.

The term *nature* is crucial for deontologists. In general, deontologists regard the nature of moral principles as permanent and stable, and they believe that compliance with these principles defines ethicalness. Deontologists believe that individuals have certain absolute rights:

- Freedom of conscience
- Freedom of consent
- Freedom of privacy
- Freedom of speech
- Due process[12]

To determine whether a behavior is ethical, deontologists look for conformity to moral principles. For example, if a manufacturing worker becomes ill or dies as a result of conditions in the workplace, a deontologist might say that the methods of production must be corrected, no matter what the cost — even if it means bankrupting the company and thus causing all workers to lose their jobs. In contrast, a utilitarian would analyze all the costs and benefits of changing production processes and decide on that basis. This example is greatly oversimplified, of course, but it helps clarify the difference between teleology and deontology. In short, teleological philosophies consider the *ends* associated with an action whereas deontological philosophies consider the *means*.

Returning again to the bolt salesman, let us consider a deontological Sam Colt. He would probably feel obliged to tell the bridge contractor about the defect rate because of the potential loss of life resulting from an earthquake-caused bridge collapse. Even though constructing the bridge would benefit residents and earn the salesman a substantial commission, the failure of the bolts in an earthquake would infringe on the rights of any person crossing the bridge at the time of the collapse. Thus the deontological Colt would probably inform the bridge contractor of the defect rate and point out the earthquake risk, even though doing so could mean the probable loss of the sale.

As with utilitarianism, deontologists may be divided into those who focus on moral rules and those who focus on the nature of the acts themselves. So-called rule deontologists believe that conformity to general moral principles determines ethicalness. Deontological philosophies use reason and logic to formulate rules for behavior. Examples include Kant's categorical imperative and the Golden Rule of Judeo-Christian tradition: Do unto others as you would have them do unto you. Such rules, or principles, guiding ethical behavior override the imperatives emerging from a specific context. The basic rights of the individual, coupled with rules of conduct, constitute rule deontology. For example, a video store owner accused of distributing obscene materials could argue from a rule deontological perspective that the basic right to freedom of speech overrides other aspects of the situation. Indeed, the free speech argument has held up in many courts with the culmination of South Pointe Enterprises Inc., which is one of the first publicly traded explicit sex companies. Its sales in 1994 totaled $9.6 million, and its profits, $507,000.

South Pointe's stock initially came out at 50 cents a share and in 1995 went over $8 a share.[13]

"Act deontologists," in contrast, hold that actions are the proper basis on which to judge morality or ethicalness. Act deontology requires that a person use equity, fairness, and impartiality in making and enforcing decisions.[14] For act deontologists, as for act utilitarians, rules serve only as guidelines, with past experiences being weighted more heavily than rules within the decision-making process. In effect, act deontologists suggest that people simply *know* that certain acts are right or wrong, regardless of the consequences or any appeal to deontological rules. In addition, act deontologists regard the particular act or moment in time as taking precedence over any rule.

As we have seen, ethical issues can be evaluated from many different perspectives. Each type of philosophy discussed here would have a distinct basis for deciding whether a particular action is right or wrong. Adherents of different personal moral philosophies may disagree in their evaluations of a given action, yet all are behaving ethically, *by their own standards*. All would agree that there is no one "right" way to make ethical decisions and no best moral philosophy except their own. The relativist perspective may be helpful in understanding how people make such decisions in practice.

The Relativist Perspective

From the **relativist perspective,** definitions of ethical behavior are derived subjectively from the experiences of individuals and groups. Relativists use themselves or the people around them as their basis for defining ethical standards.

The relativist observes the actions of members of some relevant group and attempts to determine the group consensus on a given behavior. A positive consensus signifies that the action is considered right or ethical. Such judgments may not remain valid forever. As circumstances evolve or the makeup of the group changes, a formerly accepted behavior may come to be viewed as wrong or unethical. Within the accounting profession, for example, it was traditionally considered unethical to advertise. Recently, however, as discussed in Chapter 2, advertising has been gaining acceptance among accountants. This shift in ethical views may have come about by the steady increase in the number of accountants, which has resulted in greater competition. In addition, the federal government has investigated the restrictions accounting groups have placed on their members and has concluded that the restrictions inhibited free competition. Consequently, an informal consensus has emerged in the accounting industry that advertising is now acceptable.

In the case of the Midwest Hardware salesperson, a relativist would attempt to determine the group consensus before deciding whether to tell his prospective customer about the bolts' defect rate. To do so, Sam Colt would look at both his own company's policy and general industry practice. He might also informally survey his colleagues and his superiors and consult industry trade journals and codes of ethics. Such investigations would help him determine the group consensus, which should reflect a variety of moral philosophies. If Colt learns that general company policy, as well as industry practice, is to discuss defect rates with those customers for whom faulty bolts may cause serious problems, Colt may infer that there is a consensus on the matter. As a relativist, he would probably then inform the bridge contractor that some of the bolts may fail, perhaps leading to a bridge collapse in the event of an earthquake. Conversely, if Colt determines that the normal practice in his company and the industry is to not inform customers about defect rates, he would probably not raise the subject with the bridge contractor.

Relativism acknowledges that we live in a society in which people have many different views and many different bases from which to justify decisions as right or wrong. The relativist looks to the interacting group and tries to determine probable solutions based on group consensus. When formulating business strategies and plans, for example, a relativist would try to anticipate the conflicts that will arise between the different philosophies held by members of the organization, its suppliers, its customers, and the community at large.

Virtue Ethics

Some philosophers believe and argue that morality involves more than moral rules and moral reasoning. For them morality is comprised of virtue, which has to do with an individual's character and the type of actions that emanate from that character. This philosophy, termed **virtue ethics,** posits that what is moral in a given situation is not only what conventional morality or moral rules (current societal definitions), however justified, require, but also what the mature person with a "good" moral character would deem appropriate. Virtue ethics assumes that what current societal moral rules require may indeed be the moral minimum for the beginning of virtue. Many that believe in virtue ethics assume a series of transcendental constants that permeate the moral equation. These constants are defined as timeless, without cultural specificity. Some contend that virtue is innate at the beginning of life and that it can be shared but also lost or stolen. Conversely, it can be enhanced by belief, knowledge, and subsequent behavior.

The elements of virtue have been defined as faith, conviction, honesty, truthfulness, and integrity. Its negative attributes would be lying, cheating, stealing, and murder. In their broadest sense, these terms appear to be accepted within all cultures. The problem of virtue ethics comes in the operationalization of its elements within and between cultures. Those who practice virtue ethics go beyond societal norms. For example, if an organization tacitly approves of employees taking some of its supplies for personal use, the employee who adheres to the virtue philosophy would consider it wrong to use company items for noncompany reasons even though approval had been given. Some may call such people moral heroes or saints and rationalize their own behavior in comparison with such people as going beyond what is obligated by society. They may argue that virtue is an unattainable goal and thus one should not be obliged to live up to its standards. To those who espouse virtue ethics, this argument is meaningless, for they believe in the reality of the elements of virtue.

In the case of Sam Colt, he would probably consider the elements of virtue and tell the prospective customer about the defect rate and about his concerns regarding the bridge and the risk of injury, death, and destruction. He would use no puffery in explaining the product or its risks and, indeed, might suggest alternative products or companies that would lower the probability of the bridge collapsing.

SUMMARY

Moral philosophy refers to the set of principles or rules that people use to decide what is right or wrong. In a business context, managers often must evaluate the "rightness," or morality, of alternative actions in terms of their own principles and values. Moral philosophies present guidelines for resolving conflicts and for optimizing the mutual benefit of people living in groups. Businesspeople are guided by moral philosophies as they formulate business strategies and resolve specific ethical issues, but they do not all use the same moral philosophy.

Teleological philosophies stipulate that acts are morally right or acceptable if they produce some desired consequence, such as realization of self-interest or utility. Egoism defines right or acceptable behavior in terms of the consequences for the individual. In an ethical decision-making situation, an egoist will choose the alternative whose consequences contribute most to his or her own self-interest. Utilitarianism is concerned with maximizing total utility, or providing the greatest benefit for the greatest number of people. In making ethical decisions, utilitarians often conduct a cost-benefit analysis, which considers the costs and benefits to all affected parties. Rule utilitarians determine behavior on the basis of rules designed to promote the greatest utility rather than by examining particular situations. Act utilitarians examine the action itself, rather than the rules governing the action, to determine whether it will result in the greatest utility.

Deontological philosophies focus on the rights of individuals and on the intentions associated with a particular behavior rather than on its consequences. In general, deontologists regard the nature of moral principles as permanent and stable, and they believe that compliance with these principles defines ethicalness. Deontologists believe that individuals have certain absolute rights, which must be respected. Rule deontologists believe that conformity to general moral principles determines ethicalness. Act deontologists hold that actions are the proper basis on which to judge morality or ethicalness and that rules serve only as guidelines.

According to the relativist perspective, definitions of ethical behavior are derived subjectively from the experiences of individuals and groups. Consequently, relativists define ethical standards using themselves or the people around them as their base. The relativist observes behavior within a relevant group and attempts to determine what consensus has been reached on the issue in question.

Virtue ethics views every situation and defines alternatives according to a set of constants that do not change in response to dynamic cultural norms, rules, or other people. Those who profess virtue ethics do not believe that the end justifies the means in any situation. Although they may consider cultural norms or rules to be the beginning of virtue, they are convinced that virtue can grow beyond these limits. Virtue comprises such elements as faith, conviction, honesty, truthfulness, and integrity. Its negative attributes are lying, cheating, stealing, and murder.

A REAL-LIFE SITUATION

After three years with the company, Sandy was promoted to assistant plant manager. This was a big step for Unity Welding and Construction, as well as for the industry; Sandy was one of only a handful of women who had broken through the "glass ceiling" and made their way into management. She had proved to the men around her that she deserved the job, and she was now being toasted by assistant managers from other plants across the country. John, her boss, had been her advocate with the company. He had personally lobbied upper management in her behalf.

Unity Welding and Construction is a national firm with twenty fabrication plants, primarily in the South. The company does contract work for other companies that require welding or fabrication of metals into items used in the construction of aircraft, ships, bridges, and component parts for consumer durables. Each plant caters to specific industries. Sandy's plant produces parts primarily for the automotive industry and is located in Arizona. Arizona is perfect for Sandy because of her acute asthma problems. As a teenager, she once visited relatives in Atlanta and had to be hospitalized because of her reactions to the different plants and foliage. Sandy's doctor told her at the time that she would have fewer problems with her asthma if she resided in one of the arid regions of the United States.

Six months had passed since Sandy's promotion, and her first performance rating from John was excellent. John told her that if she continued this type of performance, she would probably be a plant manager in three to six years.

Sandy developed some innovative ways to increase productivity during her six months on the job. For example, she successfully implemented a "team concept," which gave responsibility for certain projects to the workers on the plant floor. She offered incentives if they could decrease job times and increase profitability. John gave Sandy his full support, and the program was working well. Worker salaries on these special projects jumped from an average of $15 per hour to $24 per hour, yet the company's bottom line continued to improve. Workers in the plant began competing to get on special projects.

With the increasing competition, Sandy noticed that the workers were starting to cut corners. Minor worker injuries began to increase, and Sandy was concerned about how some of the workers were disposing of toxic wastes. She informed John about her concerns, and he said he would write the following memo:

Attention: Workers on Special Projects

It has come to management's attention that minor injuries are on the rise. Please review the Occupational Safety and Health Administration guidelines to make sure you are in compliance. In addition, there are rumors of improper disposal of wastes. Please read again the statement from the Environmental Protection Agency. Finally, congrats to Special Project Team Wolf. Profitability on your job increased 8 percent with an increase of $4.50 an hour for each member of the group. Great job!!

Shortly after John sent out his memo, the recession started to hit the automobile industry hard. Some of Sandy's workers were to be laid off. Sandy went through the records and found that her most productive workers had been selected for termination. She went to John with the problem, and he said he'd take care of it. By calling in some favors, John was able to save the workers' jobs, and no pink slips were issued at the plant. Within a week the workers knew John and Sandy had saved them.

Two months later, in November, the special project teams were working especially hard. Sandy noticed that the teams with the highest hourly wages were also the ones that were cutting corners the most. Sandy ran a spot inspection and found major quality problems with the

products, as well as pollution problems. Additionally, she learned that several teams had "procured" software from the competition to reduce their production times. Sandy realized that something needed to be done quickly, so she went to John.

"John, we've got some major problems," she told him. "Quality has decreased below our contract's specifications. I've got workers cutting so many corners that it's just a matter of time before someone really gets hurt. And to top it all off, some of the special project teams have gotten a hold of our competitor's software. What are we going to do?"

John looked at Sandy and said, "Nothing."

"What do you mean, nothing!?" asked Sandy.

"Let me explain something to you," John answered calmly. "We're in a recession. The only reason 20 percent of our workers still have jobs is that our costs are down and our production is way up. I know quality is down; I've doctored some of the quality report forms myself. I also know about the software. Sandy, the only reason we're still working is because of the special projects concept you implemented. And I've got news for you — production orders are going down in December. If we lay off the productive workers, we cut out the lean and save only the lazy workers we can't fire because of their seniority. Plus, have you ever fired someone around Christmas time? It's not a pretty sight.

"So I'll tell you what you're going to do. Sandy, you're going to forget about OSHA, the EPA, and the software, and you're going to doctor up the quality-control reports — because if you don't, we're both out of jobs. Have you ever tried getting a job during a recession? With your health problems, even if you did get a job, insurance would never cover your asthma treatments. You owe me, Sandy. Don't worry. When the recession goes away, we'll straighten things out," said John.

Sandy left John's office and thought about her options.

Questions

1. What are the ethical issues?
2. What are the potential legal issues?
3. Discuss Sandy's options in the situation that has developed.
4. What factors are affecting Sandy's options?
5. Discuss John's behavior relative to the situation.
6. What are the motivators for John?
7. What information is missing that could help you in making a decision?

IMPORTANT TERMS FOR REVIEW

moral philosophy
teleology
consequentialism
egoism
enlightened egoists
utilitarianism

deontology
nonconsequentialism
ethical formalism
relativist perspective
virtue ethics

Social Responsibility

AN ETHICAL DILEMMA *

KAREN BELAMEE FACED a problem that might affect thousands of workers as well as herself. Since graduating from college, she had been in the Investment Banking Division of A. B. Phillips Company. Karen was just getting by before she convinced Don Jones, president of Narco Corporation, to give her some business. Jones has a reputation for acquiring companies and splitting them up for a profit. However, he is also a shrewd corporate raider who can see profit not only from raiding companies, but also from taking them over and turning them around. Because of Jones's business, Karen's yearly commissions have risen into six-digit figures.

About six months ago, Karen's father commented that the management team of his employer, Recreation Products, Inc., was running the company into the ground. Recreation Products produces sporting equipment and employs nearly 40 percent of the work force of the community in which it is located. Karen's father has worked for the company for more than twenty years. "If only someone could buy out Recreation Products and put in a good management team," he mused.

After her conversation with her father, Karen investigated Recreation Products in detail and found that its products were in high demand but that productivity was down because of the present management. She also found that the stock was grossly undervalued. Karen told Don Jones about Recreation Products. He met with the union representatives of the company's workers, and together they worked out a plan to save the company and preserve thousands of jobs. Jones told the union, verbally, that the company would not be broken up. This pleased them and Karen, who had assured the union reps of Jones's sincere wish to save Recreation Products. In return, the union verbally agreed to large concessions that would keep Recreation Products financially sound.

Several weeks later Karen accidentally overheard a disturbing conversation. She discovered that Jones planned to break up Recreation Products, despite his pledge to her and the company's employees that he would not. This meant that thousands of jobs would be lost, just to increase the raider's short-term gains. This change in tactics would, in effect, destroy Karen's credibility with her coworkers, clients, and family.

Recently Karen met Derk Banik, who seemed interested in purchasing Recreation Products to turn it around. Karen recognized that she had two alternatives. She could do nothing and let thousands of workers get laid off, or she could inform the unions and cut a deal with Derk Banik to purchase Recreation Products stock. However, if she provides this information to the unions, Karen might be charged with a breach of confidentiality, similar to insider trading.

Questions

1. If Karen Belamee chooses to provide inside information to the Recreation Products union, what are the ethical issues?

2. What organizational and personal pressures have contributed to Karen's dilemma?

3. What should Karen do?

---

*This case is strictly hypothetical; any resemblance to real persons, companies, or situations is coincidental.

The concepts of business ethics and social responsibility are often used interchangeably, but as we pointed out in Chapter 1, each of these two terms has a distinct meaning. *Business ethics,* as defined in this text, comprises moral principles and standards that guide behavior in the world of business. Specific behavior is usually evaluated in terms of individual and group decisions. A specific action is judged right or wrong, ethical or unethical, by others inside and outside the organization. Although evaluations of ethical behavior are not necessarily accurate, these judgments influence society's acceptance or rejection of individual and group activities within the business environment. *Social responsibility* in business refers to an organization's obligation to maximize its positive impact on society and to minimize its negative impact. There are four kinds of social responsibility: economic, legal, ethical, and philanthropic.[1] Ethics, then, is one dimension of social responsibility. Ethics in the context of social responsibility focuses on issues that influence a firm's positive impact on society and minimize its negative impact.

Business ethics and social responsibility are thus closely linked. Many of the cases, exercises, and vignettes used in this text have both social responsibility and ethical implications. The more you know about social responsibility and its relation to business ethics, the better informed you will be in discussing ethical and social responsibility issues. In this chapter we use a social responsibility framework developed as a pyramid by Archie Carroll, a management professor (see Figure 4–1).[2]

We examine the four components of social responsibility, starting with the first building block, economic responsibilities, as the foundation for all business activities. Next we turn to legal responsibilities. Through its legal system, society enforces acceptable behavior. The third level of the pyramid is that of ethical responsibilities. At this level, firms decide what they consider to be right, just, and fair beyond society's strictly legal requirements.

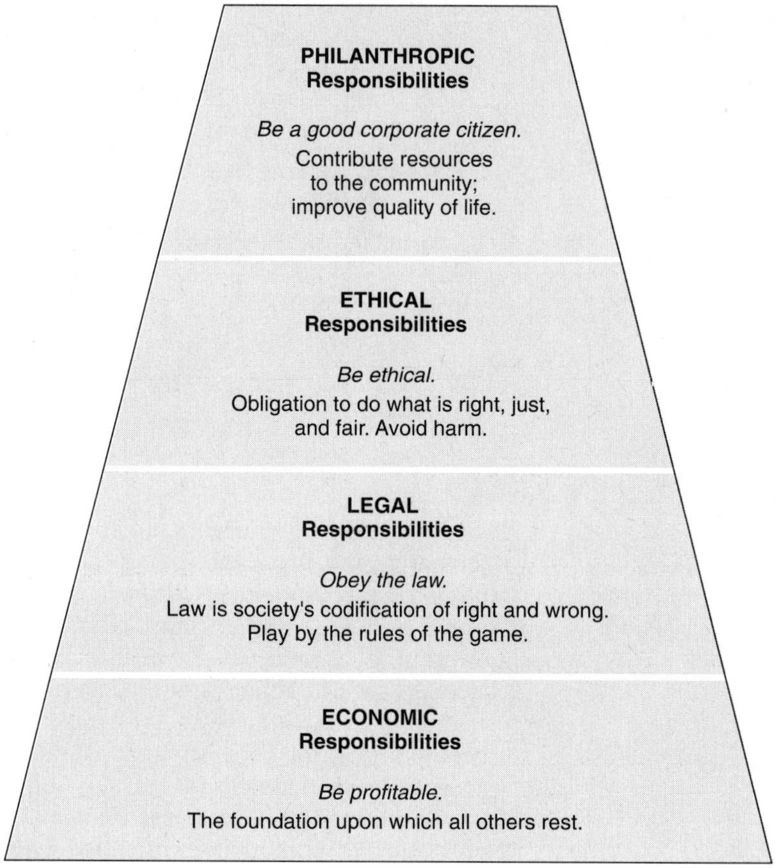

PHILANTHROPIC
Responsibilities

Be a good corporate citizen.
Contribute resources
to the community;
improve quality of life.

ETHICAL
Responsibilities

Be ethical.
Obligation to do what is right, just,
and fair. Avoid harm.

LEGAL
Responsibilities

Obey the law.
Law is society's codification of right and wrong.
Play by the rules of the game.

ECONOMIC
Responsibilities

Be profitable.
The foundation upon which all others rest.

FIGURE 4–1

The Pyramid of Corporate Social Responsibility

Source: Archie B. Carroll, "The Pyramid of Corporate Social Responsibility: Toward the Moral Management of Organizational Stakeholders," adaptation of Figure 3, p. 42. Reprinted from Business Horizons, *July/August 1991. Copyright 1991 by the Foundation for the School of Business at Indiana University. Used with permission.*

Finally, we discuss philanthropic responsibilities, the top of the pyramid. By fulfilling their philanthropic responsibilities, firms contribute financial and human resources to the community and society to improve the quality of life. Each of these four components of social responsibility defines an area in which firms make decisions that result in specific behaviors, which society evaluates.

THE ECONOMIC DIMENSION

The **economic dimension** of social responsibility relates to how resources for the production of goods and services are distributed within a social system. Although the point has not yet been proven, a number of studies support the idea that investors and customers show a preference toward companies exhibiting socially responsible behavior.[3]

Investors, with their financial support, appear to have the primary impact on management's decisions. Therefore, management is faced with the balancing act of keeping customers and employees happy while staying within the boundaries of the law and satisfying investors. Two areas within the economic dimension of social responsibility are considered the foundation of social responsibility: the impact of the economy and competition.

The Economy

When people refer to the "economy," they are generally talking about such factors as inflation and employment rates and how these factors affect their ability to purchase the products they need or want. These economic factors are in continual flux, influencing decisions by both businesses and consumers.

Social responsibility, as it relates to the economy, encompasses a number of issues. How businesses relate to competition, stockholders, consumers, employees, the community, and the physical environment affect the economy. For example, the economy is influenced by the economic power of businesses as it relates to the control of resources and the supply of products. Political power often arises from the size of the business and its ability to control markets and technology and develop an employee skill base as an advantage. Antitrust laws developed out of a fear and mistrust of big business to prohibit contracts or conspiracies that restrain trade and commerce. They specifically dealt with preventing monopolies or attempts to monopolize trade and commerce. They also prohibited price discrimination, unfair competition, and mergers that result in an anticompetitive environment.

The power of large businesses can be seen in complaints that large corporations are forcing small business suppliers out of business. Some corporate department stores are giving apparel makers rules for routing their products that can run as much as fifty pages or more for an order. If the supplier fails to follow them, a penalty such as a deduction from its payment can be made, or the contract may even be cancelled. Some small suppliers say these rules are being used to force them out of business because large retailers only want to deal with one supplier. If many small businesses or suppliers are driven out of business, it will have an effect on the economy in terms of unemployment and the opportunity of smaller businesses to compete.[4]

The relationship between the natural environment and corporations also affects the economy. The Environmental Protection Agency (EPA) was created in 1970 to coordinate environmental agencies involved in enforcing the nation's environmental laws. The major area of environmental concern relates to air pollution, water pollution, and land pollution. Large corporations are being encouraged to establish pollution control and environmental constraints; otherwise these companies could deplete resources and damage the health and welfare of society by focusing only on their own economic interests. There are many tradeoffs in developing a strong economy and a safe environment.

Stockholders, consumers, and employees are important stakeholders that influence the economy. If companies do not provide a customer focus, then it can significantly affect their profitability and ability to compete. For example, in the 1970s American automobile manufacturers failed to make the type of cars that American consumers desired. Japanese companies quickly filled the gap and gained over 25 percent of the U.S. auto market. The result was unemployment and a recession in areas dependent on the automobile industry.

The effect of business activities on the economy as it relates to employees is significant. Issues include equal job opportunity, workplace diversity, job safety and health, as well as employee privacy. In the U.S., the concept of employment-at-will gives companies the right to terminate an employee without just cause and has been used to hire and determine when to terminate employees. Many companies have been involved in corporate downsizing and have terminated millions of employees. IBM's famous no-layoff policy ended in 1993. Since then, almost half of its employees in all work areas have been terminated in its efforts to improve profitability. The layoffs have worked, and now IBM is competitive and profitable. Unemployed persons create a tremendous drain on the economy in addition to the personal hardships and suffering that come from being unemployed.

James Beatty, chief executive officer of NCS International, Inc., of Omaha, Nebraska, exemplifies one way of fulfilling business responsibilities to the community. As one of the nation's few "teleconomic" consultants, he helps small towns and larger cities to develop and market their telecommunications resources. Beatty may be one of the few African-Americans in this business specialty. He has advanced economic development in towns not merely through his telecommunications consulting, but also by striving to build bridges between corporate America and minority communities. He makes his clients understand the needs of minorities and provides ideas for opportunities to employ minority workers. As a result of his efforts, a unit of Lockheed Martin Corp. agreed to open a facility in Madisonville, Kentucky, and hire three hundred workers.[5]

Some communities fight back when major manufacturers lay off employees or close plants. When the Newell Company decided to close a glass plant in West Virginia — eliminating 992 jobs — workers and community leaders filed a $614.6 million breach-of-contract lawsuit against the company to force it to keep the plant open.[6] Because local governments often maintain close ties with business and even offer companies incentives to locate in their areas, citizens may believe that businesses have a social responsibility to the community. Social responsibility problems often center on differences in interpretation of this obligation. In an effort to offset hostile feelings between business and community governments and to protect workers, Congress has enacted legislation requiring a sixty-day notice for all plant closings.

Competition

Issues of competition in social responsibility arise from the rivalry among businesses for customers and profits. When businesses compete unfairly, legal and social responsibility issues can result. Intense competition sometimes makes managers feel that their company's very survival is threatened. In this situation, they may begin to see unacceptable alternatives as acceptable and start engaging in questionable practices in an effort to ensure the survival of their organizations.

Some competitive strategies may focus on weakening or destroying a competitor. These strategies can be injurious to competition and have the potential to reduce consumer welfare. Tactics can include sustained price cuts, discriminatory pricing, and price wars.[7] The primary objective of the antitrust laws is to distinguish competitive strategies that enhance consumer welfare from those that reduce it. The difficulty of this task lies in determining when pricing is directed toward weakening and destroying a competitor.[8]

Intense competition may also lead companies to resort to corporate espionage. Espionage is considered an ethical and legal issue because it gives some companies an unfair advantage over competitors and because it sometimes denies the originator of a product or idea the full benefits of having developed it. General Electric was the victim of a conspiracy to steal drawings and diagrams of its turbine parts. Investigators discovered that, over a period of years, several small manufacturing firms and their executives bribed some GE employees to give them confidential drawings of GE turbine parts, so that the small companies could manufacture spare parts identical to those made by GE. By acquiring these drawings, the companies avoided spending millions of dollars on research and development.[9]

Overly aggressive marketing to sell to vulnerable market segments can also develop competitive pressures, as well as conflict of interest. An R.J. Reynolds Tobacco Co. internal marketing plan allegedly called for a "single-minded focus" on getting young adults, especially 18- to 20-year-olds, to smoke Camels. The confidential business plan, obtained by the *Wall Street Journal*, provided evidence that the cigarette industry uses aggressive marketing to win young smokers.[10] In addition, millions of elementary school children were exposed to tobacco industry views and Joe Camel's image.

Researchers at the University of California at San Francisco analyzed thirty-four articles from the *Weekly Reader*, a children's school magazine, dealing with smoking and found that 68 percent included tobacco industry views and only 38 percent carried a clear message against smoking. Research has shown that Joe Camel is as familiar to children as Mickey Mouse and that Camel cigarettes have increased in popularity among teenagers since the Joe Camel campaign began. A conflict of interest exists in that, at the time, the *Weekly Reader* was owned by K-III Communications, a unit of Kohlberg Kravis Roberts, which was the largest shareholder of RJR Nabisco. Kohlberg Kravis Roberts has since sold its interest in RJR Nabisco.[11]

Although companies have an economic obligation to earn a profit for their investors, this must be done within a business environment that demonstrates responsibility to society. There are rules of acceptable behavior on which most competitors generally agree. When competitors step over the line of acceptable behavior, legal action is taken or ethical concerns are voiced.

THE LEGAL DIMENSION

The **legal dimension** of social responsibility refers to obeying laws and regulations established by governments to set minimum standards for responsible behavior — society's codification of what is right and wrong. Laws regulating business conduct are passed because society — including consumers, interest groups, competitors, and legislators — believes that business cannot be trusted to do what is right in certain areas, such as consumer safety and environmental protection. This lack of trust is the focal point of the legal dimension. Many ethical and economic issues result in lawsuits and legislative debate.

Because public policy is dynamic and often changes in response to business abuses and consumer demands for safety and equality, many laws have been passed to resolve specific problems and issues. But the opinions of society, as expressed in legislation, can change over time, and different courts, or different state legislatures, may take different views. For example, the thrust of most business legislation can be summed up as permitting any practice that does not substantially lessen or reduce competition. Courts differ, however, in their interpretations of what constitutes a "substantial" reduction of competition. Laws can help businesspeople determine what society believes at a certain point in time, but what is legally wrong today may be perceived as acceptable tomorrow, and vice versa. Still, personal views on legal issues may vary tremendously.

Laws are categorized as either civil or criminal. **Civil law** defines the rights and duties of individuals and organizations (including businesses). **Criminal law** not only prohibits specific actions — such as fraud, theft, or securities trading violations — but also imposes fines or imprisonment as punishment for breaking the law. The primary difference between criminal and civil law is that criminal laws are enforced by the state or nation, whereas civil laws are enforced by individuals (generally, in court).

Criminal and civil laws are derived from four sources: the Constitution (constitutional law), precedents established by judges (common law), federal and state laws or statutes (statutory law), and federal and state administrative agencies (administrative law). Federal administrative agencies established by Congress control and influence business by enforcing laws and regulations to encourage competition and to protect consumers, workers, and the environment.

The primary method of resolving conflicts and serious business ethics disputes is through lawsuits, where one individual or organization takes another to court, using civil laws. For example, Compaq Computer has filed suit against Packard Bell, charging the latter with selling computers with used parts as new and even altering serial numbers on components to hide their prior use. Although some personal computer manufacturers recycle good parts from returned PCs into new machines, Compaq, IBM, and other major manufacturers do not; thus Compaq's suit "appears to be an attempt to level the playing field and get everyone to play by the same rules," said one research consultant.[12]

The legal system thus provides a forum for businesspeople to resolve ethical disputes as well as legal ones. The courts may decide when harm or damage results from the actions of others. For example, Figure 4–2 shows an official court notice for a group of consumers who complained (plaintiffs) that they were billed for phone calls made to the *Let's Make a Deal* 900-number game and that cash prizes were less than the amount they were charged for the phone call. In this case, USA Networks, which promoted the 900-number game, denied any wrongdoing or liability but agreed to settle all class action consumer claims against it for $275,000.[13] This is an example of ethical conflict resolution through a civil proceeding within our legal system. Lawsuits like this are usually the way that collective disputes over deception and wrongdoing can be resolved.

The role of laws is not so much to distinguish what is ethical or unethical as to determine the appropriateness of specific activities or situations. In other words, laws establish the basic ground rules for responsible business activities. All businesses must obey these laws. Most of the laws and regulations governing business activities fall into one of five groups: (1) regulation of competition, (2) protection of consumers, (3) protection of the environment, (4) promotion of equity and safety, and (5) incentives to encourage organizational compliance programs to deter misconduct.

LEGAL NOTICE

Official Court Notice

U.S. District Court Southern District of Georgia
Class Action Notice and Notice of Partial Settlement

DID YOU CALL
"LET'S MAKE A DEAL"
USING A 900-NUMBER?

IF YOU DID, THEN YOU MAY QUALIFY AS A CLAIMANT IN A CLASS ACTION SUIT

If you were billed for 900 number calls to the **"Let's Make A Deal"** game, you are part of a class action lawsuit in U.S. District Court in Augusta, Georgia.

The lawsuit seeks **refunds** for people who paid for 1-900 calls to "Let's Make A Deal," a telephone game operated from 1989–December 1992. You may have learned about it by advertisements placed by Teleline, Inc. utilizing Monty Hall and seen on various cable networks and other media outlets.

Plaintiffs in the lawsuit assert that callers were deceived and defrauded. The defendants are AT&T and USA Networks. Another defendant, Teleline, Inc., was dismissed without prejudice. The Court has not yet made any decision on plaintiffs' claims for refunds.

The Court has conditionally certified a class of plaintiffs who were billed for phone calls originating from their homes and made to the Let's Make A Deal game, and whose cash prizes were less than the amount they were charged for the phone call. The Court also has certified a subclass of such callers from Georgia.

What to do: If you are a member of this class and want to remain as a claimant, you do not need to do anything. If you want to exclude yourself from this case, you must write to LMAD, P.O. Box 1707, Augusta, Georgia 30903, by November 15, 1995. Otherwise, you will be bound by any final decision or settlement approved by the Court. You may be represented by your own lawyer.

USA Networks, denying any wrongdoing or liability, has agreed to settle all claims against it for $275,000.00, subject to Court approval at a hearing to be held on December 1, 1995, at the U.S. Courthouse, 985 Broad Street, Augusta, Georgia 30901. The U.S. District Court for the Southern District of Georgia has granted preliminary approval of the settlement. Class members who object to the settlement must file written objections with the Clerk of the Court by November 15, 1995, or appear at the hearing. If the settlement is approved, class members who have not requested exclusion will be bound by any final judgment of the Court and will be deemed to have released USA Networks from all possible causes of action related to this lawsuit. Proceeds of the settlement will be used to finance further proceedings against AT&T.

TO PLACE YOUR NAME AND ADDRESS ON A LIST IF REFUNDS OR OTHER RELIEF BECOME AVAILABLE, OR FOR MORE INFORMATION CALL TOLL FREE:

1-800-511-8740

By Order of the Court,

Henry Crumley, Clerk
U.S. District Court
Southern District of Georgia

DO NOT CALL THE COURT OR
THE CLERK OF COURT

FIGURE 4–2

Court Notice for a Consumer Group with a Legal Complaint
Source: Published in USA Today, *September 22, 1995, p. 4B.*

Laws Regulating Competition

Laws have been passed to prevent the establishment of monopolies, in-equitable pricing practices, and other practices that reduce or restrict competition among businesses. These laws are sometimes called **procompetitive legislation** because they were enacted to encourage competition and prevent activities that restrain trade (see Table 4–1). The Sherman Antitrust Act of 1890, for example, prohibits organizations from holding monopolies in their industry, and the Robinson-Patman Act of 1936 bans price discrimination between retailers and wholesalers.

In law, however, there are always exceptions. Under the McCarran-Ferguson Act of 1944, for example, Congress exempted the insurance industry from the Sherman Antitrust Act and other antitrust laws. Insurance companies were allowed to join together and set insurance premiums at specific industrywide levels. However, a behavior may be viewed as irresponsible if it neutralizes competition and if prices no longer reflect the true costs of insurance protection. This illustrates the point that what is legal is not always considered ethical by some interest groups.

TABLE 4–1 Laws Regulating Competition

Sherman Antitrust Act, 1890	Prohibits monopolies
Clayton Act, 1914	Prohibits price discrimination, exclusive dealing, and other efforts to restrict competition
Federal Trade Commission Act, 1914	Created the Federal Trade Commission (FTC) to help enforce antitrust laws
Robinson-Patman Act, 1936	Bans price discrimination between retailers and wholesalers
Wheeler-Lea Act, 1938	Prohibits unfair and deceptive acts regardless of whether competition is injured
McCarran-Ferguson Act, 1944	Exempts the insurance industry from antitrust laws
Celler-Kefauver Act, 1950	Prohibits one corporation from controlling another where the effect is to lessen competition
Flammable Products Act, 1953	Prohibits the sale of highly flammable clothing or fabrics
FTC Improvement Act, 1975	Gave the FTC more power to prohibit unfair industry practices
Railroad Regulatory Reform Act, 1976	Deregulated the railroad industry
Aviation Deregulation Act, 1978	Deregulated the airline industry
Motor Carrier Reform Act, 1980	Deregulated the trucking industry
Trademark Counterfeiting Act, 1980	Provides penalties against individuals dealing in counterfeit goods

Laws Protecting Consumers

Laws protecting consumers require businesses to provide accurate information about products and services and to follow safety standards (see Table 4–2). The first **consumer protection law** was passed in 1906, partly in response to a novel by Upton Sinclair. *The Jungle* describes, among other things, the atrocities and unsanitary conditions of the meat-packing industry in turn-of-the-century Chicago. The outraged public response to this book and other exposés of the industry resulted in the passage of the Pure Food and Drug Act. Other consumer-protection laws emerged from similar processes.

In recent years, large groups of people with specific vulnerabilities have been granted special levels of legal protection relative to the general population. For example, the legal status of children and the elderly, defined according to age-related criteria, has received greater attention. American society has responded to research and documentation showing that young consumers and senior citizens encounter difficulties in the acquisition, consumption, and disposition of products. Special legal protection provided to vulnerable consumers is considered to be in the public interest.[14]

TABLE 4–2 Laws Protecting Consumers

Pure Food and Drug Act, 1906	Prohibits adulteration and mislabeling of foods and drugs sold in interstate commerce
Wool Products Labeling Act, 1939	Prohibits mislabeling of wool products
Fur Products Labeling Act, 1951	Requires proper identification of the fur content of all products
Federal Hazardous Substances Labeling Act, 1960	Controls the labeling of hazardous substances for household use
Truth in Lending Act, 1968	Requires full disclosure of credit terms to purchasers
Consumer Product Safety Act, 1972	Created the Consumer Product Safety Commission to establish safety standards and regulations for consumer products
Fair Credit Billing Act, 1974	Requires accurate, up-to-date consumer credit records
Magnuson-Moss Warranty Act, 1975	Established standards for consumer product warranties
Energy Policy and Conservation Act, 1975	Requires auto dealers to have "gas mileage guides" in their showrooms
Consumer Goods Pricing Act, 1975	Prohibits price maintenance agreements
Consumer Leasing Act, 1976	Requires accurate disclosure of leasing terms to consumers
Fair Debt Collection Practices Act, 1978	Defines permissible debt collection practices
Toy Safety Act, 1984	Gives the government the power to recall dangerous toys quickly
Nutritional Labeling and Education Act, 1990	Prohibits exaggerated health claims and requires all processed foods to have labels with nutritional information

A legal issue related to consumer protection concerns the regulation of television programs and commercials aimed at children. Many people believe that young children are too impressionable to understand and resist today's sophisticated television advertising. These critics view certain types of advertising as irresponsible because such advertising manipulates children's desires. They argue further that television shows are no longer true entertainment but rather one long commercial that encourages children to ask their parents to buy advertised products. In particular, children's programs such as *Teenage Mutant Ninja Turtles, Barney and Friends, The Simpsons,* and *My Little Pony* have promoted the sales of toys associated with the programs. *Beverly Hills 90210* has generated controversy by promoting dolls, T-shirts, posters, fan clubs, lunch boxes, and other retail items. An especially controversial issue is whether to ban shows in which the viewer participates by using purchased "interactive" toy guns. These guns recognize visual signals emitted by the television show and beep when children fire at the screen and hit certain characters.[15] An unusually strong reaction to issues of children's programming came from the government of the Canadian province of Quebec, which banned all advertising aimed at children under the age of 13.[16]

Laws Protecting the Environment

Environmental protection laws have been largely a response to concerns that began to emerge during the 1960s. Many people have questioned the cost-benefit analyses often used in making business decisions. Such analyses try to take into account all factors in a situation, represent them with dollar figures, calculate the costs and benefits of the proposed action, and determine whether its benefits outweigh its costs. It is difficult, however, to arrive at an accurate monetary valuation of physical pain and injury or environmental damage. In addition, people outside the business world often perceive such analyses as inhuman. From a utilitarian perspective, a company may make decisions that are best for itself or for its consumers, but according to this philosophy, it should make decisions that benefit society as well.

Increases in toxic waste in the air and water, as well as noise pollution, have prompted the passage of a number of laws (Table 4–3). Many environmental protection laws have resulted in the elimination or modification of goods and services. For instance, the Environmental Protection Agency has ordered the phasing out of all leaded gasolines during the 1990s because catalytic converters, which reduce pollution caused by automobile emissions and are required by law on most vehicles, do not work properly with leaded gasolines. Consequently, oil companies have cut back on production of leaded gasolines and have begun to research alternative fuels to maintain their levels of sales. Atlantic Richfield Co. has already developed a new formula of unleaded gasoline that it says performs as well as leaded gasolines in older cars designed to run on leaded gasoline.[17]

In response to a wave of new laws, other companies are changing the

TABLE 4–3 Laws Protecting the Environment

Clean Air Act, 1970	Established air-quality standards; requires approved state plans for implementation of the standards
National Environmental Policy Act, 1970	Established broad policy goals for all federal agencies; created the Council on Environmental Quality as a monitoring agency
Coastal Zone Management Act, 1972	Provides financial resources to the states to protect coastal zones from overpopulation
Federal Water Pollution Control Act, 1972	Designed to prevent, reduce, or eliminate water pollution
Noise Pollution Control Act, 1972	Designed to control the noise emission of certain manufactured items
Toxic Substances Control Act, 1976	Requires testing and restricts use of certain chemical substances, to protect human health and the environment

way they package their products. Most states now have recycling programs in order to stem the nation's garbage crisis. Plastic containers are a particular problem. Because they do not degrade, they are taking up more and more of the limited landfill space. Nearly 50 percent of all garbage is plastic packaging, including Styrofoam containers from fast-food restaurants, plastic soft-drink bottles, plastic carry-out bags, and plastic produce bags.[18] To reduce the amount of plastic garbage, Procter & Gamble, whose products account for 1 percent of all solid waste in the United States, began selling its Spic 'n Span cleaner in recycled plastic bottles.[19] Fabric softeners are now available in concentrated form in smaller plastic bottles and also as refills in cardboard containers. As cities and states regulate the use of plastic and even glass containers more strictly, businesses will be forced to change their packaging to comply with the law and the environmental concerns of society. The recycling of paper has been under way for several years now. We're recycling about half of our paper today, with the marginal cost for extracting more paper from trash increasing substantially.

The harmful effects of toxic waste on water life and on leisure industries such as resorts and fishing have raised concerns about proper disposal of these wastes. Disposal sites meeting EPA standards are limited in number; thus, businesses must decide what to do with their waste until disposal sites become available. Some firms have solved this problem by illegal or unethical measures: dumping toxic wastes along highways, improperly burying drums containing toxic chemicals, and discarding hazardous medical wastes at sea. Congress is considering legislation to increase the penalties for disposing of toxic wastes in this manner. Disposal issues remain controversial because, although everyone acknowledges that the wastes must go somewhere, no community wants them dumped in its own back yard.

Laws Promoting Equity and Safety

Laws promoting equity in the workplace were passed during the 1960s and 1970s to protect the rights of older persons, minorities, women, and persons with disabilities; other legislation has sought to protect the safety of all workers (see Table 4–4). Of these laws, probably the most important to business is Title VII of the Civil Rights Act, originally passed in 1964. Title VII specifically prohibits discrimination in employment on the basis of race, sex, religion, color, or national origin. It also created the Equal Employment Opportunity Commission (EEOC) to help enforce the provisions of Title VII. Among other things, the EEOC helps businesses design affirmative action programs. These programs aim to increase job opportunities for women and minorities by analyzing the present pool of employees, identifying areas

TABLE 4–4 Laws Promoting Equity and Safety

Equal Pay Act of 1963	Prohibits discrimination in pay on the basis of sex
Equal Pay Act of 1963 (amended)	Prohibits sex-based discrimination in the rate of pay to men and women working in the same or similar jobs
Title VII of the Civil Rights Act of 1964 (amended in 1972)	Prohibits discrimination in employment on the basis of race, color, sex, religion, or national origin
Age Discrimination in Employment Act, 1967	Prohibits discrimination in employment of persons between the ages of 40 and 70
Occupational Safety and Health Act, 1970	Designed to ensure healthful and safe working conditions for all employees
Vocational Rehabilitation Act, 1973	Prohibits discrimination in employment because of physical or mental handicaps
Vietnam Era Veterans Readjustment Act, 1974	Prohibits discrimination against disabled veterans and Vietnam War veterans
Pension Reform Act, 1974	Designed to prevent abuses in employee retirement, profit-sharing, thrift, and savings plans
Equal Credit Opportunity Act, 1974	Prohibits discrimination in credit on the basis of sex or marital status
Pregnancy Discrimination Act, 1978	Prohibits discrimination on the basis of pregnancy, childbirth, or related medical conditions
Immigration Reform and Control Act, 1986	Prohibits employers from knowingly hiring a person who is an unauthorized alien
Americans with Disabilities Act, 1990	Prohibits discrimination against people with disabilities, requires that they be given the same opportunities as people without disabilities

where women and minorities are underrepresented, and establishing specific hiring and promotion goals, along with target dates for meeting those goals.

Other legislation addresses more specific employment practices. The Age Discrimination in Employment Act of 1967 prohibits discrimination based on age and outlaws policies that force employees to retire before age 70. The Equal Pay Act of 1963 mandates that women and men who do equal work must receive equal pay for such work. Wage differences are allowed only if they can be attributed to seniority, performance, or qualifications. The Americans with Disabilities Act of 1990 prohibits discrimination against people with disabilities. Despite these laws, inequities in the workplace still exist. According to a report on hourly wages issued by the U.S. Census Bureau, women earn, on average, seventy-four cents for every dollar earned by men.

To date, however, the biggest gains from affirmative action have gone to women. Women now make up over 47 percent of the American work force, up from 35 percent in 1966. Over the last thirty years, women have made great advances within corporations, especially in professional occupations. In the next decade, 39 million workers will enter the U.S. labor force: one-third will be minorities. About 23 million will leave; the majority will be retiring white men. As a result, women and minorities will gradually represent a larger share of the labor force.[20] Today's senior workers are equal parts women and men, and still overwhelmingly white. But entry-level jobs show a multicultural labor force emerging.[21]

Congress has also passed laws that seek to improve safety in the workplace. By far the most significant of these is the Occupational Safety and Health Act of 1970, which mandates that employers provide safe and healthy working conditions for all workers. The Occupational Safety and Health Administration (OSHA), which enforces the act, makes regular surprise inspections to ensure that businesses maintain safe working environments.

Even with the passage and enforcement of safety laws, many employees still work in unhealthy or dangerous environments. Safety experts suspect that companies underreport industrial accidents to avoid state and federal inspection and regulation. The current emphasis on increased productivity has been cited as the main reason for the growing number of such accidents. Competitive pressures are also believed to lie behind the increases in coal-mining injuries.

Despite legislation, then, businesses continue to face legal issues related to competition, protection of consumers and the environment, and safety and equity in the workplace. Society expects businesspeople to take steps to ensure that they compete fairly; to develop, promote, price, and distribute products that are safe for both consumers and the environment; to provide safe working conditions; and to develop programs to hire and promote the most qualified employees, regardless of race, color, sex, religion, and physical ability. Ethical businesses acknowledge obligations that go beyond what is required by law.

Incentives for Compliance: Federal Sentencing Guidelines for Organizations

Legal violations usually begin with businesspersons stretching the limits of ethical standards, as defined by company or industry codes of conduct, then developing identifiable schemes to knowingly or unwittingly violate the law. The **Federal Sentencing Guidelines for Organizations** apply to all felonies and Class A misdemeanors that employees commit in association with their work. The guidelines pertain to those offenses that occurred after November 1, 1991. In general, business activities at the forefront of misconduct in the federal court system are fraud and price fixing/market allocation (antitrust violations).

While many people separate ethical and legal issues, the boundary between these issues is often ambiguous to the business manager who is not ordinarily trained as a lawyer. The manager is trained to make functional business decisions and yet has a responsibility for the management of legal and ethical affairs. When it is suggested that legal and ethical decisions are independent, there is an assumption that the good executive "instinctively" recognizes differences in legal and ethical issues. While there are some legal issues that are obvious, many borderline ethics decisions result in civil litigation. In reality, civil complaints and litigation are a formal procedure resolving ethical disputes between two parties.

With this in mind, three fundamental principles guided the United States Sentencing Commission in designing the organizational guidelines. First, the commission sought to develop a structure or model that organizations could use to define and refine compliance initiatives. Second, the model was designed to provide guidance for determining corporate sentencing and fines when violations occur. Finally, the commission wanted to create an inherent incentive for organizations to comply with the guidelines. As an incentive, organizations that show due diligence in developing an "effective" compliance program minimize their risk for organizational penalties.[22]

The commission developed seven mandatory steps that companies must implement to show due diligence. The steps are based on the commission's determination to emphasize compliance programs and to provide guidance for both organizations and courts regarding program effectiveness. Organizations have flexibility as to the type of program they develop; the seven steps are not a checklist requiring legal procedures for certification of an effective program. The program must be capable of reducing the opportunity that employees have to engage in misconduct.

As a first step, a code of conduct that communicates required standards must be developed. Second, the program must have oversight by high-ranking personnel in the organization who are known to abide by the legal and ethical standards of the industry. Third, no one with a known propensity to engage in misconduct should be put in a position of authority. Fourth, a communications system (ethics training) for disseminating standards and procedures must also be put into place. Fifth, organizational communications should include a way for employees to report misconduct without fearing retaliation, such as an anonymous toll-free hotline or an ombudsman. Monitoring and auditing systems designed to detect misconduct are also required. Sixth, if misconduct is detected, then the firm must take appropriate and fair disciplinary action. Individuals both directly and indirectly responsible for the offense should be disciplined. In addition, the sanctions should be appropriate for the offense. Finally, seventh, after misconduct has been discovered, the organization must take steps to prevent similar offenses in the future. This usually involves modifications to the compliance program, additional employee training, and communications about specific types of conduct. The government expects continuous improvement and refinement of these seven steps for compliance programs.[23]

Managers who define ethics as strictly legal compliance may be endorsing ethical mediocrity for their organizations. An effective compliance program must feature ethics as the driving force of the enterprise. While legal compliance is based on avoiding legal sanctions, organizational ethical integrity is based on guiding values and principles.[24] Making ethical principles an important part of a compliance program is more demanding and requires broader and deeper commitment to appropriate conduct.

THE ETHICAL DIMENSION

Although the economic and legal components of social responsibility are generally accepted, ethical and philanthropic concerns have been receiving more attention recently. The **ethical dimension** of social responsibility refers to behaviors and activities that are expected or prohibited by organizational members, the community, and society, even though these behaviors and activities are not codified into law. Ethical responsibilities from a social responsibility perspective embody standards, norms, or expectations that reflect a concern of major stakeholders, including consumers, employees, shareholders, and the community.[25] In other words, these major stakeholders have a concern about what is fair, just, or in keeping with respect or protection of stakeholders' moral rights.

Companies have a responsibility to fulfill their ethical obligations to various stakeholder groups. Figure 4–3 provides results of a survey of over four thousand employees on how well they thought their companies fulfilled their ethical obligations toward various groups. Respondents rated as *exceptional* their companies' treatment of customers (50 percent) and the public and community (40 percent), followed by stockholders and owners (35 percent), government regulators (33 percent), and management employees (30 percent). The strongest negative assessments, that the company fulfills its obligations *poorly,* were with respect to nonmanagement employees (18 percent) and employees' families (14 percent).

How well does your company fulfill its ethical obligations to the following groups?

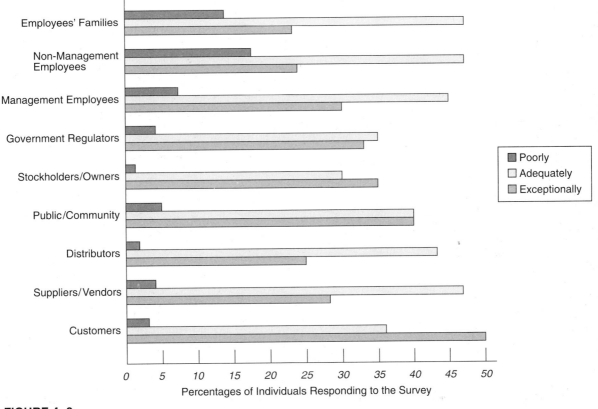

FIGURE 4–3

Fulfilling Obligations to Stakeholders

Source: Rebecca Goodell, Ethics in American Business: Policies, Programs, and Perceptions *(1994): 18. Permission provided courtesy of the Ethics Resource Center, 1120 6th Street, NW, Washington, DC, 20005.*

Ethics as a Force in Social Responsibility

Organizational integrity and ethical compliance go beyond compliance with laws and regulations. Good corporate citizens develop values and principles that are not compromised just to achieve organizational goals. Figure 4–4 delineates some of the ethical components of corporate social responsibility.

Many businesspeople and scholars have questioned the role of ethics and social responsibility in business. The economic and legal dimensions are generally accepted as the most important determinants of performance: "If this is well done," say classical theorists, "profits are maximized more or less continuously and firms carry out their major responsibilities to society."[26] Some economists believe that if firms take care of economic and legal issues, they are satisfying the demands of society and that trying to anticipate and

1. **It is important to perform in a manner consistent with expectations of social norms.**

2. **It is important to recognize and respect new or evolving ethical norms adopted by society.**

3. **It is important to prevent ethical norms from being compromised in order to achieve corporate goals.**

4. **It is important that good corporate citizenship be defined as doing what is expected ethically.**

5. **It is important to recognize that corporate integrity and ethical behavior go beyond mere compliance with laws and regulations.**

FIGURE 4–4

Ethical Components of Corporate Social Responsibility

Source: Archie B. Carroll, "The Pyramid of Corporate Social Responsibility: Toward the Moral Management of Organizational Stakeholders," adaptation of Figure 2, p. 41. Reprinted from Business Horizons, *July/August 1991. Copyright 1991 by the Foundation for the School of Business at Indiana University. Used with permission.*

meet ethical and philanthropic needs would be almost impossible. Milton Friedman has been quoted as saying that "the basic mission of business [is] thus to produce goods and services at a profit, and in doing this, business [is] making its maximum contribution to society and, in fact, being socially responsible."[27] To respond to society, scholars and businesspeople have tried to use the tools and concepts developed over the years by moral philosophers as groundwork for ideal value systems. The concept of corporate social responsiveness has evolved from their efforts.

The concept of social responsiveness is the act of responding to stakeholders and concerned others in society by considering more than just the firm's own wants and needs. Systematic appraisal of the needs of stakeholders can position the firm to be socially responsive. However, if being socially responsive means just responding to ethical issues identified by others, the firm has embraced a form of relativism that may direct managers to take the path of least resistance. It is possible that by being responsive, managers could keep things quiet, appear to be ethical, and focus on maximizing profits.[28]

It should be obvious from this discussion that ethics and social responsibility cannot just be a reactive approach to issues as they arise. Only if firms include ethical concerns in their foundation and business strategy can social responsibility as a concept be embedded in daily decision making. A description of corporate ethical responsibility should include rights and duties, consequences and values, all of which refer to specific strategic factors.[29] The ethical component of business strategy should be capable of providing an assessment of business, work group, and individual behavior as it relates to ethics.

Organizational Direction for Ethics and Social Responsibility

An ethical and socially responsible company depends on the values and moral principles held by the individuals and groups in the organization. From a social responsibility perspective, of course, the values and moral beliefs of organizational members are important, but so are those of key stakeholders — including the investors, employees, and customers. The values and principles of all of these participants are important in understanding a social and economic pattern of interaction. The corporate or overall business strategy determines how the organization will use human and financial resources to achieve its objectives. The value systems of the corporation and stakeholders have a profound effect on the implementation of corporate strategy. Consider these statements.

1. Business strategy must reflect an understanding of the values of organizational members and stakeholders.

2. Business strategy must reflect an understanding of the ethical nature of strategic choice.[30]

If we accept these statements, then ethics becomes a core decision in business strategy.[31] A common criticism of business has been that the role of ethics in business strategy has been systematically ignored; therefore we must respond by attempting to place ethics at the very center of discussions about business strategy.

If business strategies create ethical issues, then top management, as well as stakeholders and society at large, needs to assess and address these ethical issues with meaningful debate and conflict resolution. It is hard to try to address difficult ethical issues, but simply acknowledging that ethics is a component of strategy can change the firm's behavior. Firms that view ethics as a very difficult and personal subject, which should be addressed only at home, may ignore the dimension of social responsibility. Individuals in such organizations are then put into the position of believing that the only way decisions can be made is in accord with their own personal moral philosophies. No coherent ethical policies will emerge unless there is an understanding of the collective morality that evolves through group decision making. This does not mean that individuals should sacrifice their own personal values and ethics, but it does mean that in the resolution of business ethics issues, attempts must be made collectively to bring ethics into the firm's strategy and daily activities.

In the relationship between ethics, social responsibility, and a firm's strategy, the role of top management is crucial. Organizations tend to reflect the norms and values of top managers, and top managers are regarded as role models for socialization and development of the corporate culture, as discussed in Chapter 6. Top managers must avoid verbalizing vague generalities about ethics; instead, they must demonstrate ethical behavior to others in the organization. For example, even written codes of ethics are not by themselves evidence of a business in which executives are socially responsible and have a corporate culture that promotes legal and ethical behavior. Written codes must include specific guidelines, and top managers must demonstrate law-abiding and ethical behavior on a constant, rather than an intermittent, basis.[32]

Successful managers achieve their companies' objectives by influencing their employees' behavior. Employees' perceptions of the ethics of their coworkers and managers are often stronger predictors of behavior than the employees' personal beliefs about right or wrong. Thus the overall ethical climate in an organization sets the standards for employee conduct. Superiors in the organization can affect employees' day-to-day activities and directly influence behavior by implementing the company's standard of ethics. The role of management is extremely important in fostering ethical behavior and social responsibility in an organization.

THE PHILANTHROPIC DIMENSION

The **philanthropic dimension** of social responsibility refers to business's contributions to society. Businesses are expected to contribute to the quality of life and to the welfare of society. Society expects businesses to provide a high standard of living and to protect the general quality of life enjoyed by its members. The philanthropic dimension of social responsibility refers to the expectation that businesses also contribute to the local community.

Quality-of-Life Issues

People want much more than just the bare necessities — shelter, clothing, and food — required to sustain life. Food must not only provide the nutrients necessary for life and good health but also be conveniently available. Consumers want their food free from toxic chemicals, and they want producers of food to avoid environmental pollution. At the same time, they do not want to see endangered wildlife needlessly injured or killed in the process of food production. For example, some environmentally minded consumers stopped buying shrimp to protest Gulf Coast shrimpers' refusal to use devices that would allow endangered sea turtles to escape drowning in their nets. Our society also expects adequate supplies of low-cost healthy grains and livestock. Thus it expects farmers to produce pest-free and disease-free products without using chemicals that are harmful to consumers or to the laborers who get agricultural products to the market.

Consumers want communication systems that allow them to talk to anyone in the world and that quickly provide information from around the globe. At the same time, they do not want the widespread availability of information to infringe on their privacy. They want sophisticated medical services that prolong life and make it more tolerable, and they want cosmetic products that improve physical appearance. They expect education to equip them to improve their standard of living. They also want rapid, convenient, and efficient transportation to take them wherever they want to go, whenever they want to go. They also want clean air, but automobiles are the number one source of air pollution. As a result, the automobile industry is facing increasing pressure to develop inexpensive, fuel-efficient automobiles that do not contribute to air pollution problems — especially since the earth's shielding ozone layer is being depleted.

People want a high quality of life. They do not want to spend all their waking hours working. They seek leisure time for recreation, entertainment, amusement, and relaxation in a pleasant environment. The quality of life is enhanced by leisure time, clean air and water, unlittered earth, conservation of wildlife and natural resources, and security from radiation and poisonous substances. Thus society expects businesses to modify their manufacturing processes to reduce pollutants and wastes.

The environmental responsibility of firms is to avoid the contamination of land, air, and water. Surveys by the Roper Organization Inc. found that 62 percent of Americans believe that pollution is a very serious threat to their health and the environment, and 75 percent say that business should handle the cleanup.[33] Because business activities are a vital part of the total environment, businesspeople have a responsibility to help provide what society wants and to minimize harmful products and conditions that it does not want.

Philanthropic Issues[34]

A final set of issues for businesses concerns their responsibilities to the general welfare of the communities in which they operate. Many businesses simply want to make their communities better places for everyone to live and work in. Although such efforts cover many diverse areas, some of the activities are especially noteworthy. The most common way that businesses exercise their community responsibility is through donations to local and national charitable organizations. In 1994, charitable donations by corporations reached $6.1 billion, falling 2 percent from the previous year and representing a major decline since 1987 when tax reform and downsizing impacted business dramatically.[35] Even small business can participate by sponsoring charitable events — such as Special Olympics meets or a local March of Dimes Walk-a-Thon — or donating to organizations that support community causes.

Many companies have become concerned about the quality of education in the United States, after realizing that the current pool of prospective employees lacked many basic work skills. Recognizing that today's students are tomorrow's employees and customers, firms such as Kroger, Campbell Soup Company, Eastman Kodak, American Express, Apple Computer, Xerox, and Coca-Cola have donated money, equipment, and employee time to help improve schools in their communities and around the nation. The GE Fund, a nonprofit philanthropic foundation established by General Electric, has provided $20 million for high schools in fourteen cities to help improve educational programs. The programs are evaluated based on how many students go to college.[36] Some companies seeking to do good through philanthropy link gifts to marketing activities. For example, Nike, Inc., is sponsoring sports events at local boys' and girls' clubs and then showing these events in their national advertising. This approach has been called "strategic philanthropy," or financially sound goodwill. A Conference Board survey of 463 U.S. companies found that companies are taking a more businesslike approach to charity, resulting in a better image, increased employee loyalty, and improved customer ties.[37] Rather than give cash to causes, some companies donate products. Hewlett-Packard prefers donating computer equipment to schools because it is able to deduct its manufacturing costs and build goodwill in relationships with future consumers.[38] Although some members of the public fear business involvement in education, others believe that if business wants educated employees and customers in the future, it must become involved in the process.

Business is also beginning to take more responsibility for the hard-core unemployed. Some people who want to work do not have job skills or have a history of chronic unemployment that keeps them from getting even low-level jobs. These people have traditionally depended on government welfare programs for survival. Some have mental or physical disabilities; some are chemically dependent; some are homeless. Organizations such as the National Alliance of Businessmen fund programs to train the hard-core unemployed so that they can find jobs and support themselves. Days Inns of America, a hotel chain, hires homeless people as reservations sales agents and allows them to stay in hotel rooms until they can afford their own housing. Some of Days Inns' formerly homeless employees have used the skills they learned there to go on to better, higher-paying jobs.[39] In addition to fostering self-support, such opportunities enhance self-esteem and help people become productive members of society.

SUMMARY

Although the concepts of business ethics and social responsibility are often used interchangeably, each term has a distinct meaning. Social responsibility in business refers to an organization's obligation to maximize its positive impact and minimize its negative impact on society. This chapter described the four dimensions of social responsibilities: economic, legal, ethical, and philanthropic. Economic responsibilities are the foundation of all business activities. The legal responsibilities have been enforced by society to eliminate unacceptable behavior. Ethical responsibilities relate to what firms decide to be right, just, and fair beyond strictly legal requirements. Finally, philanthropic responsibilities relate to the contribution of financial and human resources to the community and greater society to improve the quality of life.

The economic dimension of social responsibility relates to how resources for the production of products are distributed within a social system. The economic dimension also relates to a company's focus on providing employment to sustain growth and profits and returns to investors. Ethical issues in competition arise when businesses do not compete fairly and do not use legal and socially accepted methods of gaining advantage.

The legal dimension of social responsibility refers to laws and regulations established by government to set minimum standards for behavior. Laws regulating business conduct are passed because society — including consumers, interest groups, competitors, and legislators — believes that business must comply with standards established by society. Such laws regulate competition, protect consumers, protect the environment, promote equity and safety, and provide incentives for preventing misconduct.

The ethical dimension of social responsibility refers to behaviors and activities that organizational members, the community, and society expect from business, even though they may not be written into law. Firms need to respond to stakeholders and concerned others in society in an ethical manner. It is important to perform in a manner consistent with social standards and ethical norms. For ethics to be a part of social responsibility, business strategy must reflect an understanding of the values of organizational members and stakeholders and an understanding of the ethical nature of strategic choice.

The philanthropic dimension of social responsibility relates to the structure and dynamics of society and the quality-of-life issues with which it is concerned. Businesses are expected to contribute to the community and to the welfare of society. Companies contribute significant amounts of money to education, the arts, environmental causes, and the disadvantaged. Not only do companies support local and national charitable organizations, they get involved in taking responsibility for helping to train hard-core unemployed.

A REAL-LIFE SITUATION

Sharon had just been hired at Browning and Lakue, a brokerage house in New Orleans, as a financial analyst and stockbroker. Her first assignment was to develop a client base. Having just graduated from East Louisiana State University, she knew that this meant "cold calling" — the practice of calling everyone on a list and attempting to persuade them to purchase stock. Cold calling is extremely ineffective and results in rejection 98 percent of the time. However, as Sharon realized when she decided to go into finance, you start at the bottom and work your way up.

Listening to the other brokers, she developed techniques that helped her create a client base. After three months of calling and some help from friends and relatives, Sharon was surviving as a broker. She also learned that there were some added expenses to being a broker. For example, she was told that brokers need to "look" and "act" successful. "Everyone loves a winner," Gary, her boss, told her. So Sharon bought the appropriate clothes, joined the right clubs, and ate at the right restaurants with the right people.

Gradually, her client base started to grow, but she was still not a stellar performer. When she asked Gary what she was doing wrong, he answered by saying that when she went to parties, she should know who was there. "Identify the 'players' in the large corporations and then listen," he told her.

Sharon took Gary's advice. At the next party, she found out some information about some upcoming mergers by listening to a vice president of finance. The next day she told her clients to buy some specific stocks. Three months later those stocks had increased in value by 50 percent. Sharon continued to use this strategy and found it was very successful. Her client base started to grow. One day Sharon went to visit a sick uncle. She found his finances in desperate shape, so she helped him by sending money.

Six months later her uncle called and said that he wanted to meet with her. At dinner, Uncle Roy told Sharon that his janitorial job gave him access to many law offices, and he gave her some information about several companies that were going to file for bankruptcy. Roy told her it was his way of thanking her for helping him when he needed it. The next day Sharon called her clients who had stock in those companies and told them to sell. Within two months those stocks had lost 75 percent of their value.

By this time Sharon had established herself as a successful broker. She had survived two years in the trenches. One morning Gary suggested to Sharon that she needed to help her clients make more money by taking an aggressive position, meaning that she should look at volatile stocks that fluctuate widely. Gary also suggested that she start getting her clients more "excited" about the stock market by having them buy and sell more frequently. When Sharon did as Gary suggested, her income, as well as her client base, started to increase. However, her clients' overall earnings started to drop. Sharon attributed the dip in part to an overall slowdown in the market, and she drafted a memo explaining her views to some of her clients who had complained.

Several months later Uncle Roy called Sharon to ask a favor. It seems that Uncle Roy had a friend who wanted to invest in the stock market. Uncle Roy explained that Ina, 70 and in poor health, wanted some secure investments. Sharon said she would be happy to help Ina with her little nest egg. To Sharon's surprise, the little nest egg was $750,000. Ina gave Sharon permission to buy and sell stocks for her because she had trouble remembering things and wanted to be sure that she would be able to take care of her expenses at a retirement center. Several months later word had gotten around the retirement center, and Sharon found herself with clients who had large sums to invest in secure stocks and bonds. As a result, Sharon began to be noticed by her managers as a potential "player" for corporate accounts.

In Sharon's fourth year, the market started slowing down, generating client losses. However, Sharon's income increased because of her strategy of getting clients in and out of different stocks and bonds. To help recoup the losses some of her retired clients had suffered, Sharon began to trade in the commodities and precious metals markets. Unfortunately, many of these investments turned sour, and she found herself buying and selling more and more to pull her clients into the black. Things were getting critical. On average, Sharon's clients were losing more than other brokers' clients, and they were turning on her. Sharon herself was losing substantial sums in the futures market and sometimes temporarily borrowed funds from clients to cover short-term losses. She covered these loans within a day or two.

At a recent party, Sharon met a man named Phil, who was known for selling inside information. As the two talked, Phil mentioned several corporations and some information about them that could help Sharon and her investors, but there was one catch. Phil wanted $2,000 for the information.

Questions

1. Identify the social responsibility issues in this case.
2. What are Sharon's options?
3. Discuss the ramifications of these options.
4. How do ethical issues in this situation relate to socially responsible corporate behavior?

IMPORTANT TERMS FOR REVIEW

economic dimension
issues of competition
legal dimension
civil law
criminal law
procompetitive legislation

consumer protection laws
environmental protection laws
Federal Sentencing Guidelines for Organizations
ethical dimension
philanthropic dimension

CHAPTER FIVE

An Ethical Decision-Making Framework

AN ETHICAL DILEMMA*

BILL CHURCH WAS in a bind. A recent graduate of a prestigious business school, he had taken a job in the auditing division of Greenspan & Co., a fast-growing leader in the accounting industry. Greenspan relocated Bill, his wife, and their 1-year-old daughter from the Midwest to the East Coast. On arriving, they bought their first home and a second car. Bill was told that the company had big plans for him. Thus he did not worry about being financially overextended.

Several months into the job, Bill found that he was working late into the night to complete his auditing assignments. He realized that the company did not want its clients billed for excessive hours and that he needed to become more efficient if he wanted to move up in the company. He asked one of his friends, Ann, how she managed to be so efficient in auditing client records.

Ann quietly explained: "Bill, there are times when being efficient isn't enough. You need to do what is required to get ahead. The partners just want results — they don't care how you get them."

"I don't understand," said Bill.

"Look," Ann explained, "I had the same problem you have a few years ago, but Mr. Reed [the manager of the auditing department] explained that everyone eats time so that the group shows top results and looks good. And when the group looks good, everyone in it looks good. No one cares if a little time gets lost in the shuffle."

Bill realized that "eating time" meant not reporting all the hours required to complete a project. He also remembered one of Reed's classic phrases, "results, results, results." He thanked Ann for her input and went back to work. Bill thought of going over Reed's head and asking for advice from the division manager, but he had met her only once and did not know anything about her.

Questions

1. What should Bill do? Describe the process through which Bill might attempt to resolve his dilemma.

2. If anyone is hurt by this company's approach, it would seem to be young accountants, who are expected to work long hours. Why is this an ethical problem?

*This case is strictly hypothetical; any resemblance to real persons, companies, or situations is coincidental.

*T*o improve ethical decision making within a business organization, one must first understand how individuals make ethical decisions. Some philosophers, social scientists, and other academics have attempted to explain the ethical decision-making process in business by examining ethical issue intensity, individual moral philosophy, or corporate culture, including the influence of coworkers. This chapter summarizes our current knowledge of ethical decision-making frameworks for business. While it is impossible to describe exactly how an individual or a work group might make ethical decisions, we can provide generalizations about average or typical behavior patterns within organizations. These generalizations are based on many studies and at least six ethical decision models.[1]

In this chapter we describe a framework for understanding ethical decision making in a business organization context. This framework, shown in Figure 5–1, integrates concepts from moral philosophy, psychology, sociology, and business. It is specific to ethical decisions made in an organization in which a work group environment exists. Too often it has been assumed that individuals make ethical decisions within an organization in the same manner that they make ethical decisions at home in their family or their personal lives. Within the context of an organizational work group, most individuals do not have the freedom to decide ethical issues independently of organizational pressures. The key components of the framework include per-

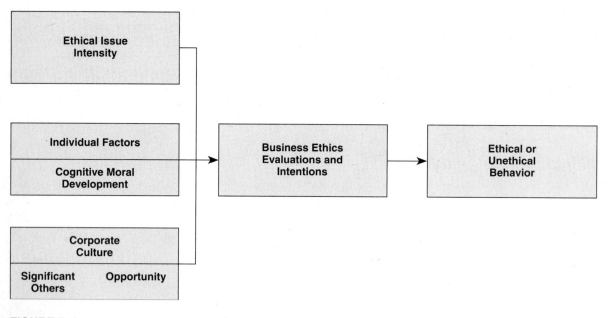

FIGURE 5–1

Framework for Understanding Ethical Decision Making in Business

ceived ethical issue intensity; individual factors, such as cognitive moral development; age and gender; and corporate culture. These factors are all interrelated, and they influence business ethics evaluations and intentions that result in ethical or unethical behavior.

ETHICAL ISSUE INTENSITY

The first step in ethical decision making is to become aware that an ethical issue requires the individual or work group to choose among several actions that must be evaluated as right or wrong. In the context of business, an ethical issue has consequences for others inside the organization and/or external to the organization. The intensity of an ethical issue relates to the perceived importance of the issue to the decision maker.[2] **Ethical issue intensity,** then, can be defined as the perceived relevance or importance of an ethical issue to the individual or work group. It is personal and temporal in character in order to accommodate values, beliefs, needs, perceptions, the special characteristics of the situation, and the personal pressures existing on an ongoing basis or at a particular place and time.[3] Ethical issue intensity is a cognitive state of concern about an issue, which indicates involvement in making choices.

Ethical issue intensity reflects the ethical sensitivity of the individual or work group triggering the ethical decision process. All the other factors in Figure 5–1, including cognitive moral development, corporate culture, and intentions, determine why ethical issues are perceived differently by different individuals.[4] Unless individuals in an organization maintain some common concerns about ethical issues, the stage is set for ethical conflict. The perception of ethical issue intensity can be influenced by management, which can use rewards and punishments, codes of ethics, and values from the corporate culture to this end. In other words, managers can affect the perceived importance of an ethical issue through positive and/or negative incentives.[5]

Ethical issues may not reach the critical awareness level of some employees if management fails to identify and educate employees about problem areas. Employees who have diverse values and backgrounds should be trained on how the organization wants specific ethical issues handled. Identifying ethical issues that employees might encounter is a significant step in developing employees' ability to make ethical decisions. Many ethical issues are identified by industry groups or through general information available to a firm. For example, discrimination based on race, sex, or age is considered an important ethical issue by most firms. Discrimination by businesses often stems from work group attitudes toward a particular group. For example, a 1991 study by the American Bar Foundation revealed that African-Americans, particularly women, paid significantly higher prices for new cars than did whites. Another study, conducted in 1995, yielded similar results:

blacks still pay more for their cars than whites.[6] The ethical issue thus relates to price differences based on race. Employees of auto dealers should be made aware that this is an ethical issue with serious consequences for the firm and society.

Denny's restaurants have experienced discrimination lawsuits many times in the 1990s. For example, Donnette Stahnke, an African-American, claimed that she was passed over in favor of white applicants for jobs at the restaurant. Before suing the restaurant, her lawyer sent three black and three white applicants to the restaurant. The white women were all offered jobs, but the black women were not, even though they had slightly better credentials.[7] Denny's paid $45.7 million in 1994 to settle a class action lawsuit by black customers who said that they were ignored or treated rudely by Denny's workers. It is almost impossible for widespread discrimination and mistreatment to occur without top management, as well as supervisory management, condoning and encouraging discrimination. In the Denny's case, management needed to develop an effective communication and compliance system to identify discrimination as a major ethical problem in its restaurants. Employees in charge of hiring should understand both the ethical and the legal consequences of discrimination.

In order to be in legal compliance with the Federal Sentencing Guidelines for Organizations, discussed in Chapters 1 and 4, firms must assess areas of ethical and legal risk that are, in reality, ethical issues. Issues that are communicated as high in ethical importance could trigger increases in ethical issue intensity. The perceived importance of an ethical issue intensity has been found to have a strong impact on both ethical judgment and behavioral intention. The more likely individuals are to perceive the importance of an ethical issue, the less likely they are to engage in questionable or unethical behavior associated with the issue.[8] Therefore, ethical issue intensity should be considered a key factor in the ethical decision process.

INDIVIDUAL FACTORS: STAGES OF COGNITIVE MORAL DEVELOPMENT

Chapter 3 gives an overview of various moral philosophies that an individual may use as a guide to ethics evaluations. This section provides a well-accepted model that describes the cognitive moral development process — that is, the stages through which people progress in their development of moral thought. Most of the models developed to explain, predict, and control ethical behavior of individuals within a business organization propose that cognitive moral processing is a crucial element in ethical decision making. The theory of cognitive moral development is based on a body of literature in psychology that focuses on studying children and their cognitive development.[9] Psychologist Lawrence Kohlberg developed the six-stage model described in the following pages,[10] though it was not developed specifically for business. According to **Kohlberg's model of cognitive moral develop-**

ment, different people make different decisions in similar ethical situations because they are in different stages of cognitive moral development. Kohlberg proposed that individuals develop through the following six stages:

1. *The stage of punishment and obedience.* An individual in Kohlberg's Stage 1 defines *right* as literal obedience to rules and authority. A person in this stage will respond to rules and labels of "good" and "bad" in terms of the physical power of those who determine such rules. Right and wrong are not associated with any higher order or philosophy but rather with a person who has power. Stage 1 is usually associated with the development of small children, but signs of Stage 1 development are also evident in adult behavior. For example, some companies forbid their buyers to accept gifts from salespeople. A buyer in Stage 1 development might justify a refusal to accept gifts from salespeople by referring to the company's rule that defines accepting gifts as an unethical practice, or the buyer may accept the gift if he or she believes that there is no chance of being caught.

2. *The stage of individual instrumental purpose and exchange.* An individual in Stage 2 defines *right* as that which serves one's own needs. In this stage, the individual no longer makes moral decisions only on the basis of specific rules or authority figures; the person now evaluates behavior on the basis of its fairness to him or her. For example, a sales representative in Stage 2 development doing business for the first time in a foreign country may be expected by custom to give customers "gifts." Although gift giving may be against company policy in the United States, the salesperson may decide that certain company rules designed for operating in the United States do not apply overseas. In the culture of some foreign countries, gifts may be considered part of a person's pay. So, in this instance, not giving a gift might represent an unfair deal for the salesperson. Some refer to Stage 2 as the stage of reciprocity, where, from a practical standpoint, ethical decisions are based on an agreement that "you scratch my back and I'll scratch yours" instead of on principles of loyalty, gratitude, or justice.

3. *The stage of mutual interpersonal expectations, relationships, and conformity.* An individual in Stage 3 emphasizes others rather than himself or herself. Although motivation is still derived from obedience to rules, the individual considers the well-being of others. A production manager in this stage might obey upper management's order to speed up an assembly line if he or she believed that this action would generate more profit for the company and thus maintain employee jobs. The manager not only considers his or her own well-being in terms of following the order, but also tries to put himself or herself in upper management's position, as well as in the employees' situation. Thus Stage 3 differs from Stage 2 in terms of the individual's motives in considering fairness to others.

4. *The stage of social system and conscience maintenance.* An individual in Stage 4 determines what is right by considering his or her duty to society, not just to other specific people. Duty, respect for authority, and maintaining the social order become the focal points. Life or the existence of life is valued in terms of its place in society. For example, a number of years ago an employee of Brown and Root, Inc., discovered that Peruvian safety standards for building highways were inadequate. The standards prescribed no special precautions to be taken when cutting channels through unstable rock formations; as a result, rock slides were likely. The employee felt it was his duty to complain because the rock slides might endanger construction workers or travelers using the highways.[11]

5. *The stage of prior rights, social contract, or utility.* In Stage 5, an individual is concerned with upholding the basic rights, values, and legal contracts of society. Individuals within this stage feel a sense of obligation or commitment, a "social contract," to other groups and recognize that in some cases legal and moral points of view may conflict. To reduce such conflict, Stage 5 individuals base their decisions on a rational calculation of overall utilities. The president of a firm may decide to establish an ethics program because it will provide a buffer to prevent legal problems, and the firm will be a responsible contributor to society.

6. *The stage of universal ethical principles.* A person in this stage believes that right is determined by universal ethical principles that everyone should follow. Stage 6 individuals believe that there are inalienable rights, which are universal in nature and consequence. These rights, laws, or social agreements are valid not because of a particular society's laws or customs, but because they rest on the premise of universality. Justice and equality are examples of principles that are deemed universal in nature. A person at this stage may be more concerned with social ethical issues and not rely on the business organization for ethical direction. For example, a businessperson at this stage might argue for discontinuing a product that has caused death and injury because the inalienable right to life makes killing wrong, regardless of the reason. Therefore, company profits would not be a justification for the continued sale of the product.

Kohlberg's six stages can be reduced to three different levels of ethical concern. Initially, a person is concerned with his or her own immediate interests and with external rewards and punishments. At the second level, an individual defines *right* as conforming to the expectations of good behavior of the larger society or some significant reference group. Finally, at the third, or "principled," level, an individual sees beyond the norms, laws, and authority of groups or individuals. Kohlberg's model implies that a person's level of moral development influences his or her perception of and response to an ethical issue.

Kohlberg's model suggests that people continue to change their decision priorities beyond their formative years. According to his model, as people progress through stages of moral development, and with time, education, and experience, they may change their values and ethical behavior. In the context of business, an individual's moral development can be influenced by corporate culture, especially ethics training. The Ethics Resource Center, in surveying more than four thousand workers, found specific proof that individuals saw improvement in their business ethics over the course of their careers. As Table 5–1 indicates, nearly half (49 percent) saw improvement, while 43 percent saw no change, and about 7 percent reported a decline in their business ethics.[12] More than one-third (34 percent) thought their business ethics had improved because of their personal ethics. Surprisingly, nearly one in eight (13 percent) believed that their personal ethics had improved because of their business ethics.[13]

Experience in resolving moral conflicts accelerates progress in moral development. A manager relying on a specific set of values or rules may eventually come across a situation to which the rules do not apply. For example, suppose Jorge is a manager who has a policy of firing any employee whose productivity declines for four consecutive months. Jorge has an employee, Alisha, whose productivity has suffered because of depression, but Jorge firmly believes that Alisha will be a top performer again within a month or two. Because of the circumstances and the perceived value of the employee, Jorge may bend the rule. Managers in the highest stages of the moral development process seem to be more democratic than autocratic. They are likely to be more aware of the ethical views of others involved in an ethical decision-making situation.

An important question may be whether measures of individual cognitive moral development are the best predictors of ethical behavior in a business organization. A study by the authors found that only 15 percent of a sample of businesspersons maintained the same moral philosophy in both work and nonwork ethical decision-making situations.[14] One explanation may be that cognitive moral development issues that relate to a person's nonwork experiences and home and family situations are not the most significant factors in

TABLE 5–1 Changes in Career Business Ethics over Time

Greatly improved	12%
Modestly improved	37%
Not changed	43%
Modestly declined	6%
Greatly declined	0.6%

Source: Rebecca Goodell, *Ethics in American Business: Policies, Programs, and Perceptions* (1994): 15. Permission provided courtesy of the Ethics Resource Center, 1120 6th Street, NW, Washington, DC, 20005.

organizational ethics issues.[15] Research indicates that perceived ethicalness of the work group, rather than individual cognitive moral development, may be the most important consideration in determining ethical behavior within a business.[16] Nevertheless, most experts agree that a person's cognitive moral development plays a role in how values and actions are shaped in the workplace.

CORPORATE CULTURE

A **corporate culture** can be defined as a set of values, beliefs, goals, norms, and ways to solve problems that members (employees) of an organization share. As time passes, a company or organization comes to be seen as a living organism, with a mind and will of its own. For example, the Walt Disney Company requires all new employees to take a course in the traditions and history of Disneyland and Walt Disney, including the ethical dimensions of the organization. The corporate culture at American Express Company stresses that employees help customers out of difficult situations whenever possible. This attitude is reinforced through numerous company legends of employees who have gone above and beyond the call of duty to help customers. This strong tradition of customer loyalty might encourage an American Express employee to take unorthodox steps to help a customer who encounters a problem while traveling overseas. Employees learn that they can take some risks in helping customers. Such strong traditions and values have become a driving force in many companies, including McDonald's Corp., IBM, The Procter & Gamble Co., and Hershey Foods. Saturn is a division of General Motors but has developed its own corporate culture, including values related to product quality, customer service, and fairness in pricing.

Some corporate cultures support unethical purposes. If the organization makes most of its profit from unethical or illegal activities, then individuals who join this organization will have a hard time surviving unless they participate in these unethical activities. For example, satellite pirates have set up companies to make devices that decode the signals from satellite television and sell these products to customers to obtain programming without paying for it. This undercuts the ownership of proprietary interests of companies such as Direct TV, which provide the satellites for television programming reception. Viewers choose from more than 150 channels for an average monthly payment of $40. If a small decoding device is plugged into the back of a receiver, the fees can be avoided. Companies that manufacture and are currently attempting to sell illegal decoders have developed a corporate scheme to steal satellite television signals. This is an extreme example of a corrupt corporate culture.[17]

As shown in the example just discussed, the ethical climate of the organization is a component of the corporate culture. Whereas corporate culture involves norms that prescribe a wide range of behavior for members of the organization, the ethical climate indicates whether organizations have an ethical conscience. The **ethical climate component** of corporate culture can be thought of as the character or decision processes used to determine whether responses to issues are right or wrong.[18] Factors such as corporate codes of ethics, top management actions on ethical issues, ethical policies, the influence of coworkers, and the opportunity for unethical behavior are all captured by the ethical climate concept. The organizational culture and the resulting ethical climate may be directly related to the recognition of ethical dimensions of decisions, the generation of alternatives, and individual cognitive moral development. In a number of studies, the perceived ethicalness of the immediate work group has been found to be a major factor influencing ethical behavior.[19] The more ethical the perceived culture of the organization, the less likely it is that unethical decision making will occur. This aspect of corporate culture and ethical climate is closely associated with the idea that significant others are a key determinant of ethical decisions within an organization. The concept of ethical climate integrates collective individual cognitive moral development, significant others, and opportunity, as they relate to how the organization perceives and deals with ethics-related issues.

Significant Others

Those who have influence in a work group, including peers, managers, and subordinates, are referred to as **significant others.** Significant others help workers on a daily basis with unfamiliar tasks and provide advice and information in both formal and informal ways. A manager may provide directives about certain types of activities to be performed on the job. Coworkers, such as peers, offer help in the form of comments in discussions over lunch or when the boss is away. Numerous studies conducted over the years confirm that significant others have more impact on a worker's decisions on a daily basis than any other factor in our framework.[20] Work groups also help determine organizational culture and opportunity, which will be discussed later in this chapter.

A worker learns ethical or unethical behavior through interactions with people who are part of his or her intimate personal groups. In other words, a decision maker who associates with others who behave unethically will be more likely to behave unethically too. In a work group environment, employees begin to develop groupthink and feel strength in their ability to conceal information or supply false reports that could affect the company. This happened at Sunrise Medical Inc., where fraudulent financial reporting was found. At least four people concealed the improper accounting through a series of improper entries and falsified computer reports.[21] When the company discovered the fraudulent financial reporting, it reported the activity to the Securities and Exchange Commission. Sunrise stock plunged dramatically after the announcement that its previous profits had been overstated. In fact, many observers believe that peers can change a person's original value system.[22] This value change, whether temporary or permanent, appears to be greater when the significant other is a decision-making superior, especially if the person making the decision is new to the firm.

The role that an individual plays in the organization may depend on such characteristics as age, time with the company, or expertise about the job. Regardless of the assigned job, employees might ask an experienced person for advice on how to ask a superior for a raise or whether to report an incident of unethical activity by a coworker. The distance or number of layers of personnel between the person making the decision and significant others will affect ethical decisions. For example, if there are four layers of management between a decision maker and the regional vice president, the vice president may have only marginal influence on the decision maker. With fewer layers of management between them, the influence would be greater. Of course, some high-ranking managers in an organization may have so much charisma and personal visibility that their suggestions, ideas, and value system may be adopted throughout the organization.

Obedience to authority relates to another aspect of the influence of significant others. Workers usually play a particular role in performing their duties in the company, and obedience to authority can help explain why many people resolve business ethics issues by following the directives of a superior. In organizations that emphasize respect for superiors, for example, employees may feel that they are expected to carry out orders by a superior even if the orders are contrary to the employees' feelings of right and wrong. Later, if a decision is judged to have been wrong, an employee is likely to say, "I was only carrying out orders," or "My boss told me to do it this way."

Superiors can have a negative effect on ethical behavior by setting a bad example and failing to supervise subordinates. Former Kidder Peabody & Co. bond trader Joseph Jett developed a plot to create $350 million in phony bond profits to inflate his bonus and to cover up $100 million in losses. Jett's supervisors, Edward Cerullo and Melvin Mullin, were charged with failing to supervise him. Mullin said that he did nothing wrong in failing to supervise Jett. Cerullo settled a securities fraud charge, agreeing to a one-year suspension from acting as a supervisor in the securities industry; he also paid a fine of $50,000. However, he did not admit wrongdoing.[23] Many supervisors look the other way and do not want to deal with the conflict and other risks associated with handling misconduct.

Workers do not have to be controlled by the company or by their coworkers if they strive to control their own decisions. Individuals who exert such efforts believe they are masters of their own destiny, and they make things happen rather than react to events. For example, a manager who consistently accepts responsibility for his or her decisions is controlling his or her own destiny. The degree of a person's self-esteem and self-confidence may contribute to the decision to either go along with ethical (or unethical) decisions or to refuse to participate in certain decisions. For example, a manager with low self-esteem and a feeling of dependence may go along with a scheme that results in an unethical action. When confronted with the unethical action, the manager may say that he or she was just doing a job. Conversely, a worker with high self-esteem and a feeling of competence may rely more on his or her values and, whether right or wrong, will take responsibility for decisions. This person will be less likely to depend on others in resolving ethical issues.

Stress on the job has been found to be a major factor influencing unethical behavior.[24] **Role stress** is the strain, conflict, or disruptive result of a lack of agreement on certain job-related activities. The role that an individual plays within a business, including the various tasks that have the potential to create conflict, may have a direct bearing on ethical decision-making behavior. Some tasks require a decision maker to make many more tradeoffs and to face many more ethical dilemmas than others. Salespeople, for example, are often confronted by customers who state or imply that they will purchase a product if given extra personal incentives that may be against company policy — that is, a bribe. Accountants who are working on the audit of a company may be called aside and asked not to report information in a way that might disclose discrepancies. A personnel manager may discriminate against a minority. Since there is little doubt that ethical decision making is stressful for decision makers who face conflict, the tendency is for role-stress situations to increase the likelihood of unethical behavior.

Opportunity

Opportunity is a term that describes the conditions that limit or permit ethical or unethical behavior. Opportunity results from conditions that either provide rewards, whether internal or external, or limit barriers to behavior. Examples of internal rewards include feelings of goodness and personal worth generated by performing altruistic activities. External rewards refer to what an individual expects to receive from others in the social environment. Rewards are external to the individual to the degree that they bring social approval, status, and esteem.

An example of a condition that limits barriers to behavior is a company policy that does not punish employees who accept large gifts from clients. The absence of punishment provides an opportunity for unethical behavior because it allows individuals to engage in such behavior without fear of consequences. Opportunity as an aspect of ethical decision making is explored in more detail in Chapter 8.

Opportunity relates to a person's immediate job context — where they work, who they work with, and the nature of the work. The **immediate job context** includes the motivational carrots and sticks that superiors use to influence employee behavior. Pay raises, bonuses, and public recognition are carrots, or positive reinforcers, whereas demotions, firings, reprimands, and pay penalties act as sticks, the negative reinforcers. For example, a salesperson who is given public recognition and a large bonus for making a valuable sale that he or she obtained through unethical tactics will probably be motivated to use unethical sales tactics in the future, even if such behavior goes against the salesperson's personal value system.

Sometimes the corporate culture supports decisions that are made to take advantage of opportunities for maximizing self-interest, usually profits. For example, as retailing has become overly competitive, large stores are taking advantage of their power and often make unfair demands of small suppliers. Many small apparel makers are being pushed out of business because of their inability to comply with details, rules, and regulations — which often run to fifty or more pages — for the delivery of merchandise. Ames Department Stores Inc. lists the following per shipment penalties: "$300 for incorrect labels; $500 for incorrect packing materials; 5 percent of total shipment cost if the shipment arrives early or late."[25] According to apparel makers, small suppliers are also charged for violations that never happened. For example, one supplier, Schwab and Company, was refunded $50,000 of $180,000 in charges when it provided Polaroid photographs of boxes that were shipped according to rules.[26] The ethical issue is this: should large retail stores take advantage of their power and place unrealistic demands on small suppliers and, even worse, charge for violations that never occur? This type of policy is based on the opportunity to use power in the channel of distribution to take advantage of weaker channel members. What is more, policies to exploit small suppliers are based on management policy and not on the actions of a single individual.

The opportunity for unethical behavior in an organization can be eliminated through formal codes, policies, and rules that are adequately enforced by management. For example, financial companies, such as banks, savings and loan associations, and securities companies, have developed elaborate sets of rules and procedures to avoid the opportunity for individuals to manipulate or take advantage of a trusted position. In banks, one such rule requires most employees to take a vacation and stay out of the bank a certain number of days every year so that they cannot be physically present in the bank to cover up embezzlement or other diversion of funds. This rule prevents the opportunity for inappropriate conduct.

The opportunity for unethical behavior cannot be eliminated without aggressive enforcement of codes and rules. A national jewelry store chain president explained to the authors of this text how he dealt with a jewelry buyer in one of his stores who had taken a bribe from a supplier. There was an explicit company policy against taking incentive payments for dealing with a supplier. When the president of the firm learned that one of his buyers had taken a bribe, he immediately traveled to that buyer's office and terminated his employment as a buyer. He then traveled to the supplier (manufacturer) selling jewelry to his stores and terminated his relationship with that particular supplier. The message was clear: taking a bribe is not acceptable for the store's buyers, and salespeople from supplying companies could cost their firm the loss of significant sales by offering bribes to this company. This type of policy enforcement illustrates how the opportunity to commit unethical acts can be eliminated.

BUSINESS ETHICS EVALUATIONS AND INTENTIONS

Ethical dilemmas involve problem-solving tasks in which decision rules are often vague or in conflict. The results of an ethical decision are often uncertain. There is no one who can always tell us whether we have made the right decision. There are no magic formulas, nor is there computer software that ethical dilemmas can be plugged into for a solution. Even if they mean well, most businesspeople will make ethical mistakes. There is no substitute for critical thinking and the individual's ability to take responsibility for his or her decisions.

An individual's intentions and the final decision as to what action to take are the last steps in decision making. When intentions and behavior are inconsistent with ethical judgments, the person may feel guilt. For example, an advertising account executive asked by her client to create an advertisement she perceives as misleading has two alternatives: to comply or to refuse. If she refuses, she stands to lose business from that client and possibly her job. Other factors, such as pressure from the client, the need to keep her job to pay her debts and living expenses, and the possibility of a raise if she develops the advertisement successfully, may influence her resolution of this ethical dilemma. Because of other factors, she may decide to act unethically and develop the advertisement even though she believes it to be inaccurate. Because her actions are inconsistent with her ethical judgment, she will probably feel guilty about her decision.

USING THE ETHICAL DECISION-MAKING FRAMEWORK TO IMPROVE ETHICAL DECISIONS

The ethical decision-making framework presented in this chapter cannot tell you if a business decision is ethical or unethical. We continue to stress that it is impossible to tell you what is right or wrong; instead, we are attempting to prepare you to make informed ethical decisions. Although this chapter does not moralize by telling you what to do in a specific situation, it does provide an overview of typical decision-making processes and factors that influence ethical decisions. The framework is not a guide for how to make decisions but is intended to provide insights and knowledge about typical ethical decision-making processes in business organizations.

Because it is impossible to agree on normative judgments about what is ethical, business scholars developing descriptive models have focused on regularities in decision making and the various phenomena that interact in a dynamic environment to produce predictable behavioral patterns. Furthermore, it is unlikely that ethical problems in an organization will be solved strictly by a thorough knowledge of how ethical decisions are made. By its very nature, business ethics involves value judgments and collective agreement about acceptable patterns of behavior.

We propose that an understanding of typical ethical decision making in a business organization will reveal several ways that decision making could be improved. Chapter 6 explores the impact of organizational culture on ethical decisions and how an understanding of culture can be used to improve the ethical climate of the organization. Chapter 7 provides more detail on the influence of significant others in the organization. Chapter 8 focuses on the role of opportunity and conflict in resolving ethical problems. In Chapter 9, we try to integrate these concepts and explain how managers can use this knowledge to improve ethical decision making in their organizations.

With more knowledge about how the decision process works, you will be better prepared to critically analyze ethical dilemmas and to provide ethical leadership regardless of your role in the organization. One important conclusion that should be developed from this framework is that ethical decision making within an organization does not rely strictly on the moral philosophies of individuals. Organizations take on an ethical climate of their own, which may have a significant influence on business ethics.

SUMMARY

The key components of the ethical decision-making framework provided in this chapter include ethical issue intensity, individual cognitive moral development, corporate culture, significant others, and opportunity. These factors are interrelated and influence business ethics evaluations and intentions, which result in ethical or unethical behavior.

Ethical issue intensity is defined as the perceived relevance or importance of an ethical issue to the individual or work group. It reflects the ethical sensitivity of the individual or work group triggering the ethical decision process. All the other factors in ethical decision making, including cognitive moral development, corporate culture, and intentions, influence this sensitivity. Hence ethical issues can be perceived differently by different individuals.

According to Kohlberg's model of cognitive moral development, individuals make different decisions in similar ethical situations because they are in different stages of moral development. Kohlberg proposed that everyone is in one of six stages of moral development: (1) the stage of punishment and obedience; (2) the stage of individual instrumental purpose and exchange; (3) the stage of mutual interpersonal expectations, relationships, and conformity; (4) the stage of social system and conscience maintenance; (5) the stage of prior rights, social contract, or utility; or (6) the stage of universal ethical principles. Kohlberg's six stages can be further reduced to three levels of ethical concern. The first two correspond to immediate self-interest. Stages 3 and 4 deal with social expectations, and the last two stages focus on general ethical principles. This model may help us understand individual ethical decision making in business because it explains why some people may change their beliefs or moral values. In addition, it explains why, given the same situation, individuals may make different decisions.

A corporate culture can be defined as a set of values, beliefs, goals, norms, and ways to solve problems that members (employees) of an organization share. The ethical climate of the organization is a component of the corporate culture. Whereas corporate culture involves norms that prescribe a wide range of behavior for organization members, the ethical climate indicates whether organizations have an ethical conscience. The organizational culture and the resulting ethical climate may be directly related to the recognition of ethical dimensions of decisions, the generation of alternatives, and individual cognitive moral development. Significant others and opportunity are two important parts of the corporate culture.

Significant others, people such as peers, managers, and subordinates who influence the work group, have been shown to have more impact on an employee's decisions on a daily basis than any other factor in the decision-making framework. Ethical or unethical behavior is learned through interactions with people who are part of a worker's intimate personal groups. Obedience to authority may explain why many business ethics issues are resolved by following the directives of a superior. The individual's own degree of self-esteem and self-confidence also contributes to decisions in some cases. Role stress, which is the strain, conflict, or disruptive result of a lack of agreement on certain job-related activities, has been found to be a major factor influencing unethical behavior.

Opportunity results from conditions that either provide rewards, whether internal or external, or limit barriers to ethical or unethical behavior. Included in opportunity is a person's immediate job context, which includes the motivational techniques superiors use to influence employee behavior. The opportunity for unethical behavior in an organization can be eliminated through formal codes, policies, and rules that are adequately enforced by management.

Ethical dilemmas involve problem-solving tasks in which decision rules are often vague or in conflict. There is no substitute for critical thinking and the individual's ability to accept responsibility for his or her decision.

The ethical decision-making framework provided in this chapter is not a guide for making decisions; it is intended to provide insights and knowledge about typical ethical decision-making processes in business organizations. Ethical decision making within an organization does not rely strictly on the moral philosophies of individuals. Organizations take on an ethical climate of their own, which may have a significant influence on business ethics.

A REAL-LIFE SITUATION

Kent was getting pressure from his boss, parents, and wife about the marketing campaign for Broadway Corporation's new video game called "Lucky." He had been working for Broadway for about two years, and the Lucky game was his first big project. Kent and his wife, Amy, had graduated from the same college and had decided to go back to their home town of Tablerock, Texas, near the Mexican border. Tablerock's population is ten thousand, and the nearest U.S. town is forty miles away. Kent's father knows the president of Broadway, which enabled Kent to get a job in its marketing department. Broadway is a medium-size company with about five hundred employees, making it the largest employer in Tablerock. Broadway develops, manufactures, and markets video arcade games.

Within the video arcade industry, competition is fierce. Games typically have a life cycle of only eighteen to twenty-four months. One of the key strategies in the industry is providing unique, visually stimulating games by using color graphics technology, fast action, and participant interaction. The target markets for Broadway's video products are children aged 5 to 12 and teenagers from 13 to 19. Males constitute 75 percent of the market.

When Kent first started with Broadway, his task was to conduct market research on the types of games desired. His research showed that the market wanted more action (violence), quicker graphics, multiple levels of difficulty, and sound. Further research showed that certain tones and types of sound were more pleasing than others. As part of his research, Kent also observed people in video arcades, where he found that many became hypnotized by a game and would quickly put in quarters when told to do so. Research suggested that many target consumers exhibited the same symptoms as compulsive gamblers. Kent's research results were very well received by the company, which developed several new games using the information. The new games were instant hits with the market.

In his continuing research, Kent had found that the consumer's level of intensity increased as the game's intensity level increased. Several reports later, Kent suggested that target consumers might be willing, at strategic periods in a video game, to insert multiple coins. For example, a player who wanted to move to a higher level of difficulty would have to insert two coins; to play the final level, three coins would have to be inserted. When the idea was tested, Kent found it did increase game productivity.

Kent had also noticed that video games that gave positive reinforcements to the consumer, such as audio cues, were played much more frequently than others. He reported his findings to Brad, Broadway's president, who asked Kent to apply the information to the development of new games. Kent suggested having the machines give candy to the game players when they attained specific goals. For the teen market, the company modified the idea; the machines would give back coins at certain levels during the game. Players could then use the coins at strategic levels to play a "slot-type" chance opening of the next level. By inserting an element of chance, these games generated more coin input than output, and game productivity increased dramatically. These innovations were quite successful, giving Broadway a larger share of the market and Kent a promotion to product manager.

Kent's newest assignment was the Lucky game — a fast-action scenario in which the goal was to destroy the enemy before being destroyed. Kent expanded on the slot-type game for the older market, with two additions. First, the game employed virtual reality technology, which gives the player the sensation of actually being in the game. Second, keeping in mind that most of the teenage consumers were male, Kent incorporated a female character who, at each level, removed a piece of her clothing and taunted the player. A win at the highest level left her nude. Test market results suggested that the two additions increased profitability per game dramatically.

Several weeks later, Brad asked about the Lucky project. "I think we've got a real problem, Brad," Kent told him. "Maybe the nudity is a bad idea. Some people will be really upset about it." Brad was very displeased with Kent's response.

In Tablerock, word got around fast that the Lucky project had stalled. During dinner with his parents, Kent mentioned the Lucky project and his dad said something that affected Kent. "You know, son, the Lucky project will bring in a great deal of revenue for Broadway, and jobs are at stake. Some of your neighbors are upset with your stand on this project. I'm not telling you what to do, but there's more at stake here than just a video game."

The next day Kent had a meeting with Brad about Lucky. "Well," Brad asked, "what have you decided?"

Kent answered, "I don't think we should go with the nudity idea."

"What if we just give the illusion but show no nudity?" suggested Brad. "In fact, I just got a call from our Mexican clients, and if we tone down the violence, we can market it to them as is."

Questions

1. What are the ethical issues?

2. What are Kent's options?

3. Which is more acceptable in the United States — sex or violence? Why?

4. What are the ethical climate organizational issues?

IMPORTANT TERMS FOR REVIEW

ethical issue intensity
Kohlberg's model of cognitive moral development
corporate culture
ethical climate component
significant others
obedience to authority
role stress
opportunity
immediate job context

How the Organization Influences Ethical Decision Making

AN ETHICAL DILEMMA *

JIM LAMPAD KNEW he would have to make this decision alone. Since the night before, he had been trying to call his boss, Craig Mona, to find out what he should do. Jim had been with Cedar Construction Co. for five years and had earned satisfactory performance reviews in three of those years. The last two had been somewhat negative.

Jim's job was to research and bid on large contracts for Cedar. His current assignment had taken him out of the country. Through private talks, Jim had discovered that his proposed bid on a contract was too high and would not be accepted if submitted. The $10 million contract would represent a significant amount of business for Cedar. Before he left on this assignment, he had been told by Craig that his career hinged on securing this project.

As Jim pored over the specifications of the bid, he realized that the client had not clearly spelled out the grade of steel to be used. By following the letter and not the spirit of the requirements of the project, Jim could submit a lower bid based on using a cheaper grade of steel in the project; such a bid would be low enough to be accepted. Jim knew that using the cheaper steel could result in a long-term weakening of the structure. On the other hand, he also knew that this practice was occasionally followed in the construction industry.

Because Cedar Construction's organization was extremely centralized, all deviations from planned proposed bids had to be cleared with one's immediate supervisor. Changing the bid without authorization would not only violate Cedar's centralized decision-making hierarchy; it would also go against the company's cultural requirement of respect for authority and rules. Jim had not been able to reach Craig, who was preoccupied by another emergency situation. So Jim called Craig's superior, Janet Darnell, a Cedar vice president and daughter of the company's founder. She told him that she was not familiar enough with the project to make a decision and advised him to continue trying to contact Craig, the only person who could properly authorize a change in the bid. She reminded Jim that it was improper to go over his superior's head, regardless of the situation.

At 11:55 A.M., Craig still could not be reached. Jim's bid for Cedar Construction had to be faxed to the project coordinator by noon.

Questions

1. What should Jim do?
2. Discuss how Cedar's organizational structure and culture have influenced this dilemma and its resolution.

3. What is Jim's ethical dilemma?

4. Are there any legal issues?

5. If the contract was for $10 million, would your decision change?

---

*This case is strictly hypothetical; any resemblance to real persons, companies, or situations is coincidental.

*O*rganizations are much more than structures in which we work. Although they are not alive, we attribute human characteristics to them. When times are good, we say the company is "well"; when times are not so good, we may try to "save" the company. Understandably, people have feelings toward the place that provides them with income and benefits, challenge and satisfaction, self-esteem, and often lifelong friendships. In fact, excluding the time spent sleeping, we spend almost 50 percent of our lives in this second home with our second "family." It is important, then, to examine how the organizational structure and culture influence the ethical decisions made within the organization.

In the decision-making framework described in Chapter 5, we discuss how organizational factors such as corporate culture and significant others influence the ethical decision-making process. In this chapter we describe two organizational structures and examine how they may influence ethical decisions. Next we discuss organizational, or corporate, culture and how the values and traditions of a business affect employees' ethical behavior. Then we consider the impact of groups within organizations. Finally, we examine the implications of organizational relationships for ethical decisions.

ORGANIZATIONAL STRUCTURE AND BUSINESS ETHICS

The structure of an organization can be described in many ways. For simplicity's sake, we discuss two broad categories of organizational structures: centralized and decentralized. Table 6–1 compares some strengths and weaknesses of the two types of structure.

Centralized Organizations

In a **centralized organization,** decision-making authority is concentrated in the hands of top-level managers, and little authority is delegated to lower levels of the organization. Responsibility, both internal and external, rests with top-level managers. This structure is especially suitable for organiza-

TABLE 6–1 Structural Comparison of Organizational Types

Characteristic	Emphasis	
	Decentralized	*Centralized*
Hierarchy of authority	Decentralized	Centralized
Flexibility	High	Low
Adaptability	High	Low
Problem recognition	High	Low
Implementation	Low	High
Dealing with changes in environmental complexity	Good	Poor
Rules and procedures	Few and informal	Many and formal
Division of labor	Ambiguous	Clear-cut
Use of managerial techniques	Minimal	Extensive
Coordination and control	Informal and personal	Formal and impersonal

tions that make high-risk decisions and whose lower-level managers are not highly skilled in decision making. It is also suitable for organizations in which production processes are routine and efficiency is of primary importance. Centralized organizations stress formal rules, policies, and procedures, backed up with elaborate control systems. Their codes of ethics may specify the techniques for decision making. These organizations are usually extremely bureaucratic. The division of labor is typically unambiguous. Each worker knows his or her job and what is specifically expected, and each has a clear understanding of how to carry out assigned tasks. General Motors and the U.S. Army are examples of centralized organizations.

Among the ethical issues that may arise in centralized organizations, where authority is concentrated at the top, is blame shifting, or "scapegoating." People may try to transfer blame for their actions to others who are not responsible. For example, First Community Corp. of Boston had an apparent practice of hiring inexperienced brokers and encouraged them to use high-pressure sales tactics. The Commodity Futures Trading Commission (CFTC) received numerous complaints that the young brokers had been guilty of fraud. First Commodity Corp. responded by firing those brokers rather than retraining them or changing its hiring procedures.[1] Instead of accepting responsibility, the company placed blame on lower-level personnel. In contrast, when Chrysler had a regional problem with dealers "rolling back" the mileage on demo cars, then Chairman Lee Iacocca took full responsibility for the actions and established more visible policies for dealers to follow.

Other ethical concerns in centralized structures may arise because there is very little upward communication. Top-level managers may not be aware of problems and unethical activity. For example, when the *Exxon Valdez* spilled eleven million gallons of oil into Prince William Sound off the coast of Alaska, it took more than four days before Exxon officials fully understood the magnitude of the disaster and could react appropriately. Early directives were to give the appearance of doing something even if the action did not clean up the oil spill. A significant problem was poor communication between high-level decision makers and those on the scene.[2]

The problem of poor communication between the company and a subcontractor in centralized organizations can also result in allegations of unethical activity. For example, the spread of illegal home-sewing networks in the United States has hurt the garment unions. The reason these home-sewing networks are illegal is that workers usually do not report their income and those that employ them usually pay below minimum wage levels. Estimates of the home-sewing population range from twenty thousand to eighty thousand, with many of the home-sewn garments ending up in department stores such as J C Penney, Sears, and Dayton Hudson. These companies deny any knowledge of such activities and point to contracts with suppliers or company policies that forbid the use of illegal labor; yet the Labor Department has documents to the contrary.[3]

Decentralized Organizations

In a **decentralized organization,** decision-making authority is delegated as far down the chain of command as possible. Such organizations have relatively few formal rules, and coordination and control are usually informal and personal. They focus instead on increasing the flow of information. As a result, one of the main strengths of decentralized organizations is their adaptability and early recognition of external change. With greater flexibility, managers can react quickly to changes in their ethical environment. A parallel weakness of decentralized organizations is the difficulty of responding quickly to changes in policy and procedures established by top management. In addition, independent profit centers within a decentralized organization may deviate from organizational objectives. Domino's Pizza maintains a fairly decentralized organization; local managers' ability to generate the thirty-minute-delivery policy not only affects performance but also has ethical implications. Some stores have been accused of permitting careless driving, which resulted in accidents. Other firms may look no farther than the local community for ethical standards. If a firm that produces toxic wastes leaves decisions on disposal to lower-level operating units, those managers may feel that they have solved their problem as long as they find a way to dump wastes outside their immediate community.

Compared with decentralized companies, centralized organizations tend to be more ethical in their practices because they have and enforce more rigid controls, such as codes of ethics and corporate policies on ethical practices.[4] Centralized organizations may also exert more influence on their employees because they have a central core of policies and codes of ethical conduct. However, it is also true that decentralized organizations may be able to avoid ethical dilemmas by tailoring their decisions to the specific situations, laws, and values of a particular community. Unethical behavior is possible in either type of structure, arising from specific corporate cultures that permit or encourage workers to deviate from accepted standards.

THE ROLE OF CORPORATE CULTURE IN ETHICAL DECISION MAKING

Another influence on ethical decision making in business, as discussed briefly in Chapter 5, is organizational, or corporate, culture. A **corporate (or organizational) culture** can be defined as a set of values, beliefs, goals, norms, and rituals that members or employees of an organization share.[5] It includes the behavioral patterns, concepts, values, ceremonies, and rituals that take place in the organization.[6] Culture gives the members of the organization meaning and provides them with rules for behaving within the organization.[7] When these values, beliefs, customs, rules, and ceremonies are accepted, shared, and circulated throughout the organization, they represent its culture. All organizations, not just corporations, have some sort of culture.

Organizational culture is a broad and widely used concept. There are a multitude of definitions, none of which has achieved universal acceptance. Definitions range from highly specific to generically broad. For example, *culture* has been defined as "the way we do things around here,"[8] "the collective programming of the mind,"[9] and "the social fiber that holds the organization together."[10] Culture is also viewed as "the shared beliefs top managers in a company have about how they should manage themselves and other employees, and how they should conduct their business(es)."[11]

Business leaders have had similar definitions. William F. Kieschnick, president of Atlantic Richfield Co., defined corporate culture as "a company's business style and sometimes also . . . its values."[12] Similarly, W. Brooke Tunstall, assistant vice president of AT&T, described corporate culture as "a general constellation of beliefs, mores, customs, value systems, behavioral norms, and ways of doing business that are unique to each corporation, that set a pattern for corporate activities and actions, and that describe the implicit and emergent patterns of behavior and emotions characterizing life in the organization."[13]

A company's history and unwritten rules are a part of its culture. Thus for many years IBM salespeople adhered to a series of unwritten standards for dealing with clients. The history or stories passed down from employee generations within an organization are like the traditions that are propagated within society. However, not only good traditions are passed on. When it comes to the effect of history, centralized companies may have a harder time uprooting unethical activity than decentralized organizations. The latter have a more fluid history, which is prone to changes that may affect only a small portion of the company. The following analogy can help clarify the dynamics of organizational structures and culture. In a country with a benevolent king (centralization) who is "good," ethical rules, laws, and traditions can quickly be implemented, and the overall ethics of the culture can be increased. However, if the king is an immoral, corrupt despot, who establishes a tradition of evil, overall ethicalness within the culture decreases. In a country where a democratic structure (decentralization) is in place, the "good" or "bad" contribution of one official will not change the people (organization) significantly.

Some cultures are so strong that they come to represent the character of the entire organization to outsiders. For example, Levi Strauss, Ben and Jerry's Homemade (the ice cream company), and Apple Computer are widely perceived as casual organizations, whereas IBM, Procter & Gamble, and Texas Instruments are perceived as more formal ones. The culture of an organization may be explicitly articulated or unspoken.

Explicit statements of values, beliefs, and customs usually come from upper management. Memos, written codes of conduct, handbooks, manuals, forms, and ceremonies are all formal expressions of an organization's culture. As an illustration, consider the case of the Gitano empire, which unraveled because of the practices of the founding Dabah family. In 1977 Morris Dabah, a former low-level Israeli bureaucrat, started the business with his sons and close friends and established the Gitano label, which in 1992 peaked at $827 million in sales. Although the company appeared to have a strong ethical background, the culture was somewhat different. For example, Gitano's foreign contractors would habitually make substitutions when filling orders, such as shipping snap-front instead of button-front jeans. As inventories grew, the Dabah family decided to falsify country-of-origin documents to get less expensive products into their markets. In addition, in 1994 accountants began to uncover problems with financial statements, such as more than $15 million booked as profit, yet unverified. This glaring discrepancy became known within the company as "the black hole." When Customs arrested Gitano, the Securities and Exchange Commission (SEC) also discovered falsified earnings (Gitano took a $28 million write-off and labeled it "related party" receivables when the Children's Place retail chain reneged on payments). It found, too, that the Dabah family had been dipping into company funds for personal loans. In this example much of the formal culture was not consistent with actual practice.

As a result of upper management's behavior, the whole company suffered. Since leaving Gitano, the Dabah family has declared personal bankruptcy. Morris Dabah has retired and Issac Dabah, his son, is running Gloria Vanderbilt Apparel Inc. and awaiting sentencing for his actions.[14]

Corporate culture is often expressed informally — for example, through comments, both direct and indirect, that communicate the wishes of management. In some companies, shared values are expressed through informal dress codes, working late, and participation in extracurricular activities. Corporate culture can even be expressed through gestures, looks, labels, promotions, and legends (or the lack of these). For example, one way that former

Simon & Schuster head Richard Snyder would get results was to tell employees that he would cut off their hands or tear out their throats if they failed to perform. "I would only say that as a joke, and with a grin on my face," Snyder explained. Yet he admitted that in his younger days he must have been impossible: "My mother tells me so, and my first wife tells me so."[15] At American Airlines, Robert L. Crandall's management style also communicated something about corporate values. By his aggressive handling of meetings, Crandall conveyed to his subordinates, and ultimately to the whole company, the value of being fiercely competitive.[16] In contrast, Nike has a very loyal group of employees but the mood and culture are more relaxed. Phil Knight, president of Nike, is notorious for walking the hallways and borrowing lunch money from new employees with no intention of paying them back. This usually occurs only once per employee — they learn their lesson, but feel more a part of the company. Thus even subtle expressions of organizational values indicate behavior expectations to employees.

Ethics as a Component of Corporate Culture

R. Eric Reidenbach and Donald P. Robin point out in *Ethics and Profits* that top management provides the blueprint of what the corporate culture should be.[17] If the desired behaviors and goals are not expressed by upper management, a culture will evolve on its own and, in so doing, will still reflect the goals and values of the company. If ethical behaviors are not valued by the organization, unethical behaviors may be rewarded and sanctioned.

Therefore, the organization's ethical decisions will have a strong impact on the organization's culture. For example, in the history of college sports, university teams have often violated National Collegiate Athletic Association (NCAA) regulations by paying or otherwise compensating college athletes; as a result, many of these teams became nationally ranked. University officials were sometimes aware of the cheating but overlooked it because they wanted national recognition and alumni support. Thus the values embedded within these universities become strong indicators of an organizational culture that sanctions illegal and unethical activity in collegiate athletics. In many cases, only the deterrent of NCAA sanctions such as the "death penalty" (not allowing the team to play) have changed the universities' orientation toward ethics.

An organization's failure to monitor or manage its culture may foster questionable behavior. Management's sense of the organization's culture may be quite different from the values and ethical beliefs that are actually guiding the firm's employees. Ethical issues may arise because of conflicts between the cultural values perceived by management and the ones actually at work in the organization. For example, management may believe that the culture encourages respect for peers and subordinates. On the basis of the rewards or sanctions associated with various behaviors, however, the firm's employees may believe that the organization encourages competition between its members. As a result, employees may intentionally or unintentionally sabotage others' work in order to win organizational rewards. Thus it is very important for top management to determine what the organization's culture is and to monitor the firm's values, traditions, and beliefs to ensure that they represent the desired culture. The rewards and punishments imposed by an organization need to be consistent with the actual corporate culture. As Reidenbach and Robin state, "Employees will value and use as guidelines those activities for which they will be rewarded. When a behavior that is rewarded comes into conflict with an unstated and unmonitored ethical value, usually the rewarded behavior wins out."[18]

Ethical Framework and Audit for Corporate Culture

Corporate culture has been conceptualized in many ways. N. K. Sethia and M. A. Von Glinow presented two basic dimensions to determine an organization's culture: concern for people (the organization's efforts to care for its employees' well-being) and concern for performance (the organization's efforts to focus on output and employee productivity). A two-by-two matrix represents the general organizational cultures (see Figure 6–1).[19]

As shown in Figure 6–1, the four organizational cultures can be classified as apathetic, caring, exacting, and integrative. The apathetic culture shows minimal concern for either people or performance. In this culture, individuals focus on their own self-interests. Apathetic tendencies can occur in almost any organization. For example, firms such as IBM, Scott Paper, Merck, and American Express have started policies of cutting longevity-reward

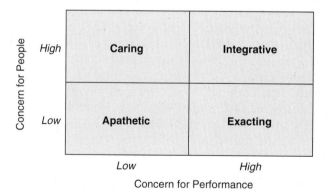

FIGURE 6–1

A Framework of Organizational Culture Typologies

Source: N. K. Sethia and M. A. Von Glinow, "Arriving at Four Cultures by Managing the Reward System," *Gaining Control of the Corporate Culture* (San Francisco, CA: Jossey-Bass, Inc.), 1985, p. 409. Reprinted by permission.

programs.[20] Simple gestures of gratitude, such as anniversary watches, rings, dinners, or birthday cards for family members, are being dropped. Many companies view long-serving employees as deadwood and do not take into account past performance. This attitude demonstrates the companies' apathy.

The caring culture exhibits high concern for people but minimal concern for performance issues. From an ethical standpoint, the caring culture seems to be very appealing. However, even good intentions can go bad, as happened at Orange & Rockland Utilities Inc. (O&R). Several key personnel there have been arrested for grand larceny. The alleged larceny was not discovered for a while because most of the board of directors were friends of the CEO, James F. Smith. Some of the items in Smith's indictment are as follows: September 1990, the company reimbursed him $1,750 to buy paintings he gave as wedding gifts; November 1992, O&R spent over $3,000 for him and his wife to tour Russia and Eastern Europe; September 1993, $7,300 of O&R money was used to rent vehicles by his son's film production company to shoot a film, entitled *Kiss It Goodbye.* Because of the caring environment, safeguards were forgotten and ethical problems occurred. The Orange & Rockland board "was one big, happy family," says Kenneth Gribetz, the district attorney for O&R's county. People were just concerned about people and not about the bottom line.[21]

In contrast, the exacting culture shows little concern for people but a high concern for performance; it focuses on the interests of the organization. Recent changes at United Parcel Service of America Inc. (UPS) underscore the strength of this culture in the company. UPS has always been very exacting. It knows precisely how many workers it needs to deliver its 10 million packages a day. With increased competition, drivers are working harder than ever, carrying more and heavier packages, driving faster, and working more overtime to justify their $40,000-plus salaries, generous benefits, and profit sharing. As a result, the Occupational Safety and Health Administration (OSHA) has targeted the company for more frequent safety checks. Also, UPS was ordered by a Seattle court to pay $12 million to two thousand drivers because it forced them to work through lunch. As one driver commented about UPS and its strict culture, "You just wonder how much they can squeeze out of us before something breaks."[22]

The integrative culture combines high concern for people and for performance. An organization becomes integrative when superiors recognize that employees are more than interchangeable parts — that employees have an ineffable quality that helps in the firm's performance criteria. Many companies — among them Johnson & Johnson Co., Novell, and NorthWestern Mutual Life Insurance Co. — have such cultures. That does not mean, however, that they are impervious to ethical problems. For example, although Johnson & Johnson (J&J) has an excellent reputation, it recently shredded thousands of documents related to a federal investigation into whether the company illegally promoted its Retin-A acne drug as a wrinkle remover. Fines and court costs total approximately $7.5 million, and three senior employees have been fired. Will this revelation affect the culture of J&J so that this type of activity is not repeated? Given Retin-A sales of more than $100 million in 1994 — out of J&J total sales of $14.1 billion — and the statement from a J&J spokesman that the company does not believe its activities violated FDA marketing rules, one might be led to wonder.[23]

An organization's culture — its values, norms, beliefs, and customs — can be identified by conducting a cultural audit. A cultural audit is an assessment of the organization's values. It is usually conducted by outside consultants but may be performed internally. Table 6–2 illustrates some of the issues that an ethics audit of a corporate culture should address. These issues can help identify a corporate culture that creates ethical conflict.

As indicated in the framework in Chapter 5, corporate culture is a significant factor in ethical decision making. If the culture encourages or rewards unethical behavior, employees may act unethically. Sears' automotive division in California was investigated for auto repair fraud. Employees stated that the only way they could achieve their sales objectives, as established by top management, was to unnecessarily replace certain car parts. The rewards they received were for achieving their sales goals. If an organization's culture dictates hiring people who have specific, similar values, and if those values are perceived as unethical by society, society will view the organization and its members as unethical. Such a pattern often occurs in certain areas of marketing. For example, salespeople may be seen as unethical because they sometimes use aggressive selling tactics to get people to buy things they do not need or want. If a company's primary objective is to make as much profit as possible, through whatever means, its culture may foster behavior that conflicts with society's ethical values.

GROUP DIMENSIONS OF ORGANIZATIONAL STRUCTURE AND CULTURE

In discussing corporate culture we focus on the organization as a whole. But corporate values, beliefs, patterns, and rules are often expressed through smaller groups within the organization. In addition, individual groups within the organization often adopt their own rules and values. Thus we look next at several types of groups, group norms, and conflicts between individual and group norms.

Types of Groups

There are two main categories of groups that affect ethical behavior in business. A **formal group** is defined as an assembly of individuals that has an organized structure accepted explicitly by the group. An **informal group** is defined as two or more individuals with a common interest but without an explicit organizational structure.

TABLE 6-2 Organizational Culture Ethics Audit

Answer YES or NO for each of the following questions.*

YES	NO	1. Has the founder or top management within the company left an ethical legacy to the organization?
YES	NO	2. Does the company have methods for detecting ethical concerns within the organization and in the external environment?
YES	NO	3. Is there a shared value system and understanding of what constitutes appropriate behavior within the organization?
YES	NO	4. Are there stories and myths embedded in daily conversations with others about appropriate ethical conduct when confronting ethical situations?
YES	NO	5. Are there codes of ethics or ethical policies communicated to employees?
YES	NO	6. Are there ethical rules or procedures in training manuals or other company publications?
YES	NO	7. Are there penalties that are publicly discussed for ethical transgressions?
YES	NO	8. Are there rewards for good ethical decisions even if they don't always result in a profit?
YES	NO	9. Does the company recognize the importance of creating a culture concerned about people and their self-development as members of the business?
YES	NO	10. Does the company have a value system of fair play and honesty toward customers?
YES	NO	11. Do employees treat each other with respect, honesty, and fairness?
YES	NO	12. Do people in the organization spend their time on what is valued by the organization in a cohesive manner?
YES	NO	13. Are there ethically based beliefs and values about how to succeed in the company?
YES	NO	14. Are there heroes or stars in the organization that communicate a common understanding about what is important in terms of positive ethical values?
YES	NO	15. Are there day-to-day rituals or behavior patterns that create direction and prevent confusion and mixed signals on ethics matters?
YES	NO	16. Is the firm more focused on the long run than on the short run?
YES	NO	17. Are employees satisfied or happy, with low employee turnover?
YES	NO	18. Do the dress, speech, and physical setting of work prevent an environment of fragmentation, inconsistency, and the lack of a coherent whole about what is right?
YES	NO	19. Are emotional outbursts with role conflict and role ambiguity very rare?
YES	NO	20. Has discrimination and/or sexual harassment been eliminated?
YES	NO	21. Is there an absence of open hostility and severe conflict?
YES	NO	22. Do people act in a way on the job that is consistent with what they say is ethical?
YES	NO	23. Is the firm more externally focused on customers, the environment, and the welfare of society than internally focused in terms of its own profits?
YES	NO	24. Is there open communication between superiors and subordinates to discuss ethical dilemmas?
YES	NO	25. Have there been instances where employees have received advice on how to improve ethical behavior or were disciplined for committing unethical acts?

*Add the number of yes answers. The greater the number of yes answers, the less ethical conflict will be experienced in the organization.

Formal Groups

Committees   A committee is a formal group of individuals assigned to a specific task. Often a single manager could not complete the task, or management may believe that a committee can represent different constituencies and improve coordination and implementation of decisions. Committees may meet regularly to review performance, develop plans, or make decisions about personnel. Most formal committees in organizations operate on an ongoing basis, but membership may change over time. A committee is an excellent example of a situation in which coworkers and significant others within the organization can influence ethical decisions. Committee decisions are to some extent legitimized because of agreement or majority rule. In this context, minority views on issues such as ethics can be pushed aside with authority. Committees bring diverse personal moral values into the ethical decision-making process, which may expand the number of alternatives considered. The main disadvantage of committees is that they typically take longer to reach a decision than an individual would. Committee decisions are generally more conservative than those made by individuals and may be based on unnecessary compromise, rather than on identification of the best alternative.

Although many organizations have financial, problem-solving, personnel, or social responsibility committees, only a very few organizations have committees devoted exclusively to ethics. An ethics committee might raise ethical concerns, resolve ethical dilemmas in the organization, and create or update the company's code of ethics. At Motorola, for example, the Business Ethics Compliance Committee is charged with interpreting, classifying, communicating, and enforcing the company's ethics code.[24] An ethics committee can gather information on functional areas of the business and examine manufacturing practices, personnel policies, dealings with suppliers, financial reporting, and sales techniques to find out whether the company's practices are ethical.[25] Whereas much of the corporate culture operates on an informal basis, an ethics committee would be a highly formalized approach for dealing with ethical issues.

Ethics committees can be misused if they are established for the purpose of legitimizing management's ethical standards on some issue. In such cases, ethics committees may be quickly assembled for political purposes, to make a decision on some event that has occurred within the company. If the CEO or manager in charge selects committee members who will produce a predetermined outcome, the ethics committee may not help the organization solve its ethical problems in the long run.

It is also possible for ethics committee members to fail to understand their role or function. If members of ethics committees attempt to apply their own personal ethics to complex business issues, resolving ethical issues may be difficult. Since most people differ in their personal ethical perspectives, the committee may experience conflict. Even if the committee members reach a consensus, they may enforce their personal beliefs rather than the organization's standards on certain ethical issues.

Ethics committees should be organized around professional, business-related issues that occur within the organization. In general, the ethics committee should formulate policy, develop standards, and then assess the compliance with these requirements for ethical behavior. Ethics committees should be aware of industry codes of ethics, community standards, and the organizational culture in which they work. Although ethics committees do not always succeed, they can provide one of the best organizational approaches to fairness in resolving ethical issues within the organization. Pacific Bell has established a successful ethics advisory committee. In addition, the firm has six full-time employees helping the company in ethics training seminars and answering twelve hundred calls a year on an ethics hotline.[26]

Work Groups, Teams, and Quality Circles   Work groups are used to subdivide duties within specific functional areas of a company. For example, on an automotive assembly line, one work group might install the seats and interior design elements of the vehicle while another group installs all the dashboard instruments. Production supervisors then can specialize in a specific area and provide expert advice to work groups.

Whereas work groups operate within a single functional area, teams bring together the functional expertise of employees from several different areas of the organization — for example, finance, marketing, and production — on a single project, such as developing a new product. Many manufacturing firms, including General Motors, Westinghouse, and Procter & Gamble, are using the team concept to improve participative management within their organizations. Ethical conflicts may arise because team members come from different functional areas. Each member of the team has a particular role to play and has probably had limited interaction with other members of the team. Members may have encountered different ethical issues within their own functional areas and may therefore have different viewpoints when an ethical issue arises in the team effort. For example, a production quality-control employee might believe that antilock brakes should be standard equipment on all automobiles for safety reasons. A marketing member of the team may reply that the cost of adding antilock brakes would force the company to raise prices beyond the reach of some consumers. The production employee might then argue that it is unethical for an automobile maker to fail to include a safety feature that could save hundreds of lives. Such conflicts often occur when members of different organizational groups must interact. However, bringing up viewpoints representative of all the functional areas helps provide more options from which to choose.

The use of quality circles — small groups of volunteers who meet regularly to identify, analyze, and solve problems related to their work relationships — originated in Japan but has become popular in the United States. Quality circles have been used successfully by Texas Instruments and

Campbell Soup Company. Quality circles give their members, and ultimately the entire organization, an opportunity to discuss solutions to ethical problems and to improve product quality, communication, and work satisfaction. Employees usually receive no extrinsic reward for joining quality circles; they participate because they want to contribute to the organization and help improve its efficiency or the quality of its products. The Japanese have extended the concept of quality circles by creating a work environment in which everyone works together and the small groups working together constitute a large group. This approach creates a well-defined corporate culture, based on cooperation and trust between labor and management.

Work groups, teams, and quality circles provide the organizational structure for group decision making. One of the reasons individuals cannot implement their personal beliefs about what should be ethical in the organization is that so many decisions are reached collectively in the work group. Persons with legitimate power are in a position to perform ethics-related activities. The work group, team, and quality circle relationships often sanction certain activities as ethical or define unethical activities for their members.

Informal Groups

In addition to the groups organized and recognized by the business — such as committees, work groups, and teams — most organizations have a number of informal groups. These groups are usually composed of individuals, often from the same department, who have similar interests and who band together for companionship or for other purposes that may or may not be relevant to the goals of the organization. For example, four or five persons who have similar tastes in outdoor activities and music may discuss their interests while working, and they may meet outside work for dinner, concerts, games, or other activities. Other informal groups may evolve with the purpose of forming a union, getting a manager fired, or protesting work practices they view as unfair. Informal groups may generate disagreement and conflict, or they may enhance morale and job satisfaction.

Informal groups help develop informal channels of communication, sometimes called the "grapevine," which are important in every organization. Informal communication flows up, down, diagonally, and horizontally through the organization, not necessarily following the communication lines shown on an organization chart. Information passed along the grapevine may relate to the job, the organization, or an ethical issue, or it may be simply gossip and rumors. The grapevine can act as an early warning system for employees. If employees learn informally that their company may be sold or that a particular action will be condemned as unethical by top management or the community, they have time to think about what they will do. Since many people love to gossip, the information passed along the grapevine is not always accurate. Managers who understand how the grapevine works can use it to spread acceptable values, beliefs, and anecdotes that reinforce those beliefs throughout the organization.

The grapevine is also an important source of information that individuals can use to assess ethical behavior within their organization. One way an employee can determine acceptable behavior is to ask friends and peers in informal groups about the consequences if certain actions are taken. Usually, informal information is passed along the grapevine about what will happen if, for example, an employee lies to a customer about a product safety issue. The corporate culture may provide a general understanding of the patterns and rules that govern the behavior of an organization, but informal groups make this culture come alive and provide direction for employees' daily activities. For example, if a new employee finds out through the grapevine that the organization does not punish ethical violations, he or she may seize the next opportunity for unethical behavior if it accomplishes the organization's objectives. The grapevine has clearly communicated that the organization rewards those who break the ethical rules to achieve desirable objectives.

Group Norms

Group norms are standards of behavior that groups expect of their members. Just as corporate culture establishes behavior guidelines for members of the entire organization, so group norms help define acceptable and unacceptable behavior within a group; in particular, group norms define the limit on deviation from group expectations. Most work organizations, for example, develop norms governing their rate of production and communication with management, as well as a general understanding of behavior considered right or wrong, ethical or unethical, within the group. For example, an employee who reports to a supervisor that a coworker has covered up a serious production error may be punished by other group members for this breach of confidence. Other members of the group may glare at the informant, who has violated a group norm, and refuse to talk to or sit by him or her.[27]

Norms have the power to enforce a strong degree of conformity among group members. At the same time, norms may prescribe different roles for different group members.[28] Thus, a low-ranking member of a group may be expected to carry out an unpleasant task, such as accepting responsibility for an ethical mistake of the organization.

Sometimes group norms conflict with the values and rules prescribed by the organization's culture. For example, the organization overall may value hard work done at a fast pace, and management may use rewards and punishments to encourage this culture. In a particular informal group, however, norms may encourage doing only enough work to meet quotas and avoid drawing attention from management. Issues of equity may arise in this situation if other groups believe they are unfairly forced to work harder to make up for the underperforming group. These other employees may complain to management or to the offending group. If they believe management is not taking corrective action, they too may slow down and do only enough work to get by, thus hurting the whole organization's productivity. Management therefore must carefully monitor not only the corporate culture, but also the norms of all the various groups within the organization. Sanctions may be necessary to bring in line a group whose norms deviate sharply from the overall culture.

IMPLICATIONS OF ORGANIZATIONAL RELATIONSHIPS FOR ETHICAL DECISIONS

Regardless of whether an organizational structure is centralized or decentralized, employees learn ethical behavior from group members and coworkers within their organizational environment. Individual decisions about how to react to daily problems are fundamentally influenced by observing other employees' behavior. As we indicated, centralized organizations stress formal rules, policies, and procedures with elaborate control systems. This type of organization makes sure that workers know how to carry out assigned tasks. Since ethical decisions are made on a daily basis in centralized organizations, ethics is learned from supervisors and coworkers.

Perceived Ethicalness of the Work Group Affects Ethical Decisions

Even though in the decentralized organization decision-making authority is delegated as far down the chain of command as possible, groups within such organizations have a strong impact on ethical behavior. In fact, research has shown that the perceived ethicalness of work groups has the greatest effect on daily ethical decisions.[29] In addition, high levels of conflict among employees may directly or indirectly influence the amount of unethical behavior within the organization.[30] The more conflict within a group, the lower its perceived ethicalness. Because coworkers are so important in accomplishing daily business activities, it is crucial for both workers and management to support ethics among coworkers.

Young businesspeople in particular indicate that they often support their superiors to demonstrate loyalty in matters related to ethical judgments. In a national Roper poll, 38 percent of young adults under the age of 30 indicated that they believed deceit and corruption was the best way to get ahead. If this national survey is representative, it means that most work groups, teams, or informal groups will have a few people who are willing to bend the rules to gain some advantage. This also means that as some people gain a supervisory role they may attempt to manipulate others or to encourage others to take actions that will cause conflict. Employees will experience conflict when what is expected of them as members of organizational groups contradicts their own personal ethical standards.

A manager in a position of authority can exert strong pressure to ensure compliance on ethically related issues. Alternatively, a manager can avoid ethical issues and be very vague, providing almost no guidance on how to handle tough ethical issues. In these cases, the organization's structure may become very important in the decision-making process. Research indicates that the more a person is exposed to unethical activity by others in the organization, the more likely it is that he or she will behave unethically.[31] Many ethical issues in an organization are resolved by the group, not by the individual.

Can People Control Their Own Ethical Actions Within an Organization?

Many people find it hard to accept the fact that an organization's culture can exert such a strong influence on behavior within the organization. In our society, we want to believe that individuals control their own destiny. Therefore, a popular way of viewing business ethics is to see it as reflections of the alternative moral philosophies that individuals use to resolve their personal moral dilemmas. As this chapter has shown, however, ethical decisions within the organization are often made by committees and formal and informal groups, not by individuals.

Decisions related to advertising, product design, sales practices, and pollution-control issues are often beyond the influence of one individual. In addition, these decisions are frequently based on business rather than personal goals. For example, between 1973 and 1987 General Motors mounted the fuel tanks of some pickup trucks outside the frame. This location allowed truck owners to travel long distances without refueling — a customer desire. In 1992 the federal government was asked to investigate charges that GM trucks with tanks mounted outside the frame may catch fire in collisions. GM built more than 10 million pickup trucks between 1973 and 1987; about half remain on the road. The company faces more than a hundred liability lawsuits regarding these trucks. An Insurance Institute for Highway Safety study indicated that fires occurred twice as often in crashes involving GM trucks as in those involving Ford and Chrysler pickup trucks. GM has called these crash tests unfair and still refused to recall these trucks as of 1995, although $1,000 rebate coupons were offered to all owners of these trucks who would buy a new GM truck.[32] It is doubtful that one person at GM decided to mount the gas tanks in the allegedly more vulnerable location; many teams and committees worked on the design of the truck. But in 1983, the company did discover that changing the design would make the trucks less vulnerable to fires.[33]

Most new employees in highly bureaucratic organizations have almost no input into how things will be done in terms of basic operating rules and procedures. Along with sales tactics and accounting procedures, employees may be taught to ignore a design flaw in a product that could be dangerous to users. Although many personal ethics issues may seem straightforward and easy to resolve, individuals entering business will usually need several years of experience within a specific industry to understand how to resolve close calls. For example, what constitutes false claims about a product? When Kellogg's introduced Heartwise cereal, the Federal Trade Commission insisted that the name be changed to Fiberwise because there was no conclusive evidence that the cereal benefited the heart. The branding of the cereal was a complex decision that required the judgment of many professional people in terms of the cereal's benefits. And some professional health experts do believe a high-fiber diet is related to good health, including a strong heart. There is no way to avoid ethical problems. The only thing that is certain is that one person's opinion is usually not sufficient. Group decisions are used when complex issues must be resolved.

It is not our purpose to suggest that you ought to go along with management or the group on matters of ethics within the business. Honesty and open discussion of ethical issues are important to successful ethical decision making. We believe that most companies and business people try to make ethical decisions. However, because of so many individual differences, ethical conflict is inevitable.

Regardless of how a person or the organization views the acceptability of a particular activity, if society judges that activity to be wrong or unethical, then this view directly affects the organization's ability to achieve its goals. Not all activities deemed unethical by society are illegal. But if public opinion decries or consumers protest against a particular activity, the result may be legislation that restricts or bans a specific business practice. For example, when America's number one brand of home computer for children, Nintendo, announced that it was entering the gambling business, the public was morally outraged. When the company sent ten thousand computers and modems to Minnesota families so that they could play the state lottery on their living room television sets, Nintendo was condemned in an editorial in the Twin Cities daily, the *Star Tribune.* Minnesota State Senate Majority Leader Roger Moe called the test "not only unethical but insidiously destructive to society."[34] When public opinion supports a particular viewpoint, such as opposition to state-sponsored gambling on home television sets, legislation can follow. Similarly, building on the baseball card craze, a company decided to develop bubble gum cards depicting convicted felons. When parents saw their children trading Bo Jackson cards for a well-known felon card, public outrage began and eventually the cards were discontinued.

If a person believes that his or her personal ethics severely conflict with the ethics of the work group and of superiors within an organization, the only alternative may be to exit the organization. In the highly competitive employment market of the 1990s, quitting a job because of an ethical conflict requires a strong commitment and, possibly, the ability to survive without a job. Obviously, there are no easy answers to resolving ethical conflicts between the organization and the individual. Our goal is not to tell you what you should do. But we believe that the more you know about how ethical decision making within an organization occurs, the more opportunity you will have to influence decisions in a positive manner and resolve ethical conflict more effectively.

SUMMARY

In a centralized organization, decision-making authority is concentrated in the hands of top managers, and little authority is delegated to lower levels of the organization. Ethical issues associated with centralized organizations relate to scapegoating and lack of upward communication. In a decentralized organization, decision-making authority is delegated as far down the chain of command as possible. Research has shown that centralized organizations tend to be more ethical in their behavior than decentralized ones because centralized organizations enforce more rigid controls, such as codes of ethics and corporate policies on ethical practices. However, this does not hold true if the centralized organization is inherently corrupt.

Corporate culture refers to the patterns and rules that govern the behavior of an organization and its employees, particularly their shared values, beliefs, customs, concepts, ceremonies, and rituals. These shared values may be formally expressed or unspoken. A cultural ethics audit is conducted to identify an organization's corporate culture. Before the audit is conducted, it is helpful to have a framework for assessing the corporate culture. This chapter presents such a framework, delineating the organizational culture as caring, integrative, apathetic, or exacting. The corporate culture ethical audit can help identify traits that create ethical conflict. If the culture rewards unethical behavior, people within the company are more likely to act unethically.

In addition to the values and customs that represent the culture of an organization, individual groups within the organization often adopt their own rules and values. The main types of groups are formal groups — which include committees, work groups, teams, and quality circles — and informal groups. Informal groups often feed an informal channel of communication, called the "grapevine." Group norms are standards of behavior that groups expect of their members. They help define acceptable and unacceptable behavior within a group, especially defining the limit on deviation from group expectations. Sometimes group norms conflict with the values and rules prescribed by the organization's culture.

The perceived ethicalness of the work group has been found to be a predictor of daily ethical decisions. In addition, high levels of conflict between employees may directly or indirectly influence the amount of ethical behavior within an organization. Employees experience conflict between what is expected of them as members of an organization and its corporate culture and their own personal ethical standards — especially since organizational ethical decisions are often resolved by committees, formal groups, and informal groups, rather than by individuals. When such ethical conflict is severe, the individual may have to decide whether to stay with the organization or leave it.

A REAL-LIFE SITUATION

Denise was an international tax accountant with the Aikeo Corporation of Japan. Her job at the U.S. company headquarters in Los Angeles was to take advantage of all tax credits and incentives allowed by law within the U.S. tax system and to monitor exchange and tariff rates among different countries. She also monitored and fixed transfer prices, that is, the prices set on products manufactured and transferred to other units within the company. Most of Aikeo's products (VCRs) were made in Taiwan and Japan and shipped to a free trade zone in Esenada for assembly by Mexican workers.

Over the years the VCR industry had become extremely competitive, with most companies striving to make the lowest-cost products with the highest quality possible. Many companies, including Aikeo, closed older production facilities in favor of facilities in countries with cheaper labor. Consequently, many Taiwanese and Japanese firms were having difficulty competing with low-wage-rate countries such as the Philippines, Malaysia, and China. The plant closings in Japan and Taiwan resulted in some demonstrations against Aikeo. In addition, there had been allegations that convicts had been used to make some lines of Aikeo's VCRs. Aikeo has officially denied the allegations. However, Denise knew from the location of the plants and their actual production costs that the allegations were probably true. A letter and phone call from Japan directed her to avoid discussing this internal matter with anyone.

Denise's six-month appraisal was excellent,

and she was put in charge of all U.S. transactions. One day while Denise was looking at some computer printouts, she discovered that there was a significant difference between the prices of Aikeo VCRs going to Japan and those being sold in the United States. It appeared that Aikeo was dumping VCRs in the United States. Denise spoke to her counterpart in Japan and found out that the company was indeed dumping VCRs. In other words, the company was selling VCRs in the United States for less than it sold them in Japan, even though its actual costs were higher for the U.S. market than for Japan. Denise warned that Aikeo could be in violation of the U.S. Sherman Antitrust and Robinson-Patman Acts if its intent was to reduce competition in the United States. Her superior in Japan phoned and listened to her concerns, then asked Denise to have her department calculate the approximate cost of penalties associated with the violations. He also spoke to Ron Jones, Aikeo's U.S. attorney, and asked him to calculate a time range of when such a tactic might be discovered and how long it might take to get an injunction that would halt Aikeo's sales.

A week later, Denise sent her findings to her Japanese counterpart. Several weeks went by before she received a reply, which read that Aikeo would continue the practice and wait. In the meantime, the U.S. marketing department was told to start selling Aikeo's low-end VCRs to unauthorized dealers. When Denise asked why, she was told that a newer line would replace the old one and the company wanted to clear out inventory. Several months later a new line was introduced, but it was at the highest, not the lowest, end of Aikeo's product line. Six months later, Japanese management requested that Denise instruct the marketing department to use the same strategy with the middle-range line of VCRs.

Denise received an exceptional rating in her next evaluation. Although she anticipated a promotion from the review, one was not forthcoming. Another six months went by, with another exceptional review of her work but still no mention of a promotion. When she questioned her counterpart in Japan, he had no clear answers. When Denise questioned others in the company, there was no response.

After another six months had elapsed and her performance was again rated exceptional, Denise called Japan and asked for a clear answer about her status in the company. She was told to be patient. Several weeks later Denise received a fax from Japan requesting that she visit Aikeo corporate headquarters. When she arrived, her itinerary had been planned for the next week. Finally, after many sightseeing tours and dinners, she was ushered into her counterpart's office. He was very gracious but did not really say anything of substance.

At this point Denise lost her self-control and demanded to know why she was talking to her counterpart rather than to his superior. He appeared frustrated and upset with Denise's reaction. He tried to explain to her that in Japanese culture things were done differently. Denise didn't accept that explanation and replied, "I've been patient for over two years concerning my promotion. I would like to understand why I haven't received one and why I can't see your superior."

He explained that his superiors had assigned Denise to him and that *he* was her superior. Moreover, his superiors still found a woman in such a high position "uncomfortable." "You see," he said, "they have not been westernized, and they find American ways of dealing with people unconventional relative to Japanese ways. It may be many more years before my superiors can accept a woman having so much authority. But Denise, please be patient. In time, they will change."

Questions

1. What are the ethical issues?
2. Are there any legal issues?
3. Discuss how Aikeo's corporate culture influenced Denise's decisions.
4. What did Denise learn from her trip to Japan?
5. What are Denise's alternatives?

IMPORTANT TERMS FOR REVIEW

centralized organization
decentralized organization
corporate (organizational) culture
formal group
informal group
group norms

CHAPTER SEVEN

The Influence of Significant Others in the Organization

AN ETHICAL DILEMMA*

TOM JENKINS WAS just starting out as a salesman with the Acme Corporation. His boss, Melanie Carter, an aggressive, no-nonsense, get-the-job-done type of person, had been promoted to manager several months earlier. Melanie had assigned Tom a very important client, Bob Hillman, the buyer for Thermocare, a national hospital bedding manufacturer. The two men first met in Bob's office, where he suggested to Tom that they go to lunch. Tom, of course, was expected to pay the check. During lunch, Bob agreed to purchase $100,000 worth of equipment from Tom. This deal represented a significant portion of Acme's overall sales. In addition to his usual commission, Tom received a bonus of $1,000.

Tom called on Bob again some months later, seeking a new sale of $150,000. In passing, Bob mentioned that he greatly enjoyed attending baseball games and hinted he would like some season tickets, which both men knew Acme had purchased. Tom thought it over for a moment and then offered some tickets to Bob, who signed a contract for a $150,000 sale. Tom got a healthy bonus and a letter of achievement from his boss.

Six months later, Tom, now one of the top producers in his division, tried to interest Bob in buying another $200,000 worth of merchandise. Bob suggested that he and his wife would enjoy a vacation in Acapulco; if Acme could arrange the trip, he would place the $200,000 order. Tom's boss, Melanie, advised him to pay for the trip out of the miscellaneous "slush fund" for such activities. When Tom reported that Acme would be happy to send Bob and his wife to Acapulco, Bob bought another $200,000 worth of goods from Acme; Tom got a raise and a bonus.

Some time later Melanie Carter announced to her division that they would take their best clients to Las Vegas for a celebration. One of the participants was Bob Hillman. When they arrived in Las Vegas, Bob indicated an interest in adult entertainment, and Melanie once again told Tom to do whatever was needed to make Bob happy. Because prostitution is legal in some Nevada counties, Tom had no trouble making the necessary arrangements. He then excused himself from the night's activities. Much later, however, in Tom's motel room, the phone rang. It was Bob's wife, wanting to locate her husband.

Questions

1. What type of authority does Tom's boss wield? What type of power does Bob wield?

2. What role relationships are at work in this situation? How does Tom's role in the organization affect his perception of the situation?

3. What should Tom do?

_____

*This case is strictly hypothetical; any resemblance to real persons, companies, or situations is coincidental.

*B*usinesspeople learn ethical or unethical behavior not only from society and culture, but also from people with whom they associate in work groups and in the business organization. The outcome of this learning process depends on the strength of individuals' personal values, opportunity, and their exposure to others who behave ethically or unethically. Organization members often make ethical decisions jointly with significant others with whom they associate in informal groups and in formal relationships within the work environment. **Significant others** include superiors, peers, and subordinates in the organization who influence the ethical decision-making process. Although persons outside the organization, such as family members and friends, also influence decision makers, we focus here on the influence of significant others within the organization.

In this chapter we discuss how organizational structure and culture operate through significant others in the ethical decision-making process. First we examine interpersonal relationships, including a view of employee conduct, role relationships, socialization, role-sets, and differential association. Then we explore the impact of leadership, power, and motivation. Finally, we consider why significant others have such an important influence on ethical decision making.

INTERPERSONAL RELATIONSHIPS IN ORGANIZATIONS

Organizations consist of individuals and groups of people working together to achieve one or more objectives. Getting people to work together efficiently and ethically, while coordinating the skills of diverse individuals, is a major challenge for business managers. Relationships among these individuals and within groups are an important part of the proper functioning of a business organization. In fact, interpersonal relations play a key role in business ethics. To understand how interpersonal relations influence persons making decisions about ethical issues, we first consider variation in employee conduct. Then we examine the role relationships within the organization, including socialization and role-sets, and differential association.

Variation in Employee Conduct

A substantial amount of research and survey data indicate significant differences in values and philosophies that influence how individuals make ethical decisions.[1] When people have been asked in surveys what they would do in specific situations, their answers have supported a wide variation in employee conduct.

As Table 7–1 shows, approximately 10 percent of employees indicate that they take advantage of situations to further their own personal interests. A study of 4,000 workers by the Ethics Resource Center found that 10 percent indicated they had engaged in acts within the past year that they were ashamed to tell about.[2] They are more likely to manipulate, cheat, or be self-serving if the penalty is less than the benefit received from the misconduct. For example, employees may make personal long-distance telephone calls from work if the only penalty is having to pay for these calls, if caught. Therefore, the lower the risk of being caught, the more likely it is that the 10 percent most likely to take advantage will be involved in unethical activities.

Approximately 40 percent of workers go along with the work group on most matters. These employees are concerned about mutual interpersonal expectations, relationships, and conformity; they are most concerned about the social implications of their actions and want to fit into the organization. Although they may have their own personal opinions, they are very easily influenced by what people around them are doing. Thus an individual may know that using work telephones for personal long-distance calls is improper, yet view it as acceptable because others are doing it. These employees rationalize by saying that such telephone use must be one of the benefits of working at the particular business, and since the company does not enforce a policy preventing such activity, it must be acceptable. Coupled with this philosophy is the belief that by doing what everybody else is doing no one will get in trouble, for there is safety in numbers.

About 40 percent of a company's employees always try to follow company

TABLE 7–1 Variation of Employee Conduct

10 Percent	40 Percent	40 Percent	10 Percent
Follow their own values and beliefs Believe that their values are superior to others in the company	Try to always follow company policies and rules	Go along with the work group	Take advantage of situations if: — penalty is less than the benefit — low risk of being caught

Source: Ferrell Gray, Inc., 4148 Southwestern, Houston TX 77005, ph. (713) 661-3131. © 1996 Ferrell Gray, Inc.

policies and rules. These workers not only have a strong grasp of the corporate culture regarding acceptable behavior, but they also attempt to comply with codes of ethics, ethics training, or other communications about appropriate conduct. The employees in this group would probably not make personal long-distance calls from work if their company had a policy prohibiting this activity. However, they would not be outspoken about the 40 percent that go along with the work group, for they prefer to focus on their jobs and stay clear of any misconduct within the organization. If the company fails to communicate standards of appropriate behavior, members of this group devise their own. Because people are culturally diverse and have different values, they interpret situations differently and vary in their ethical decisions concerning the same ethical issue.

The final 10 percent of employees try to maintain formal ethical standards that focus on rights, duties, and rules. They embrace values that assert certain inalienable rights and actions that are always ethically correct. In general, members of this group believe that their values are the right values and are superior to other values in the company, or even to the company's value system, if there is an ethical conflict. This group has a tendency to report the conduct of others or to become confrontational when it views activities within the company as unethical. Consequently, members of this group would tend to report fellow workers who make personal long-distance calls.

The significance of the variation in the ethical behavior of individuals in a company is that employees use different approaches to making ethical decisions. Since a large percentage of any work group will either take advantage of situations or go along with the work group, it is important that the organization provide communication and control mechanisms to maintain an ethical climate. Companies that fail to monitor activities and penalize for unethical behavior are guaranteeing a low-risk environment for those who want to take advantage of situations to accomplish their personal, and sometimes unethical, objectives.

Good business practice and concern for legal compliance requires the recognition that there is much variation in employees' desire to be ethical in the workplace. The percentages cited in this section are only estimates of the variation in ethical behavior. The important point is not the actual percentages but the fact that most evidence indicates that these variations exist in most organizations. Particular attention should be paid to managers who oversee day-to-day operations of employees within the company. Ethical compliance training is necessary to make sure that the business is operated in an ethical manner and that the company does not become the victim of fraud, theft, or other misconduct committed by people who have a pattern of unethical behavior. However, human resource managers must make sure that they do not violate individual privacy rights and that background checks and control activities are conducted in a legal manner.[3]

There are many examples of employees who have a background of misconduct but are hired and placed in positions of trust. For instance, a seemingly endless number of gullible business owners hired Donald Peterson as a bookkeeper to manage their financial affairs. He was entrusted with company money and stole millions. Peterson recounted that he had been lying and stealing since he was a teenager. He began writing checks for more than he had in his account, then began the scam of working as a bookkeeper for small companies and writing company checks to himself under a different name. After scamming a number of companies, he was arrested and pleaded guilty to fraud and related offenses. He is serving a 105-month federal prison sentence.[4]

Role Relationships

Much like a part in a movie, a **role** is a part that a person plays in an organization. All the roles a person plays in an organization constitute a position and prescribe the behavior others expect because of that position. For example, a supermarket cashier plays a role involving the receipt of payment for products. The cashier is expected to behave professionally and courteously while assisting customers for the benefit of the supermarket. Another role the cashier may play is as a member of a committee that deals with minimizing coupon fraud at the checkout and making certain that each product is registered at the appropriate price. Each person in an organization has a specialized task or role in helping the organization achieve its goals. Some work on the assembly line; some do clerical work; some are managers who direct the work of others. Other members, such as foremen or department heads, have broader tasks, to keep all the groups in the organization working toward the common goal. The work group has potentially the greatest effect on daily ethical decisions. High levels of role conflict between employees may directly or indirectly influence the amount of unethical behavior within the organization. The more conflict there is within the organization, the lower are the perceptions of ethicalness of the work group.[5] Because coworkers are so important in accomplishing daily business activities, it is vital to support the ethics of the work group. In addition to carrying out the assigned tasks, each person is expected to act according to the role he or she occupies. New employees learn through socialization how to act in their roles, including what is acceptable ethical behavior.

Socialization   **Socialization** refers to the process through which a person learns the values and behavior patterns considered appropriate by an organization or group. Through socialization, employees are taught how to behave in accordance with their roles within the organization. For example, new employees are usually socialized to accept the principle of accountability — that they are answerable to a superior or to peers for the outcome of a project. The socialization process is a powerful influence on ethical behavior. Ethical issues such as lying, cheating, and the payment of bribes may be defined through socialization of organizational values and norms.

As an example, consider a company that provides office supplies to a university. Over the years the members of this company have developed expectations as to how salespeople will carry out their assigned tasks. The current members want new recruits to accept their standards and ethical beliefs for proper behavior and therefore try to socialize them to do so.

Ethical conflict can arise when the values and norms taught through the socialization process contradict the new employee's personal values. Suppose that an experienced salesperson tells the new recruit that the supplies company obtained the university account because it gave the university the lowest estimates on some specified products. However, to make up for the low prices, it was now providing lower-quality grades of paper and charging high rates on products for which no price had been negotiated. The new employee may find this practice deceitful and unethical. But the senior salesperson could explain that the company is providing a fair product for the price and that such a practice is common in the industry. These discussions may convince the newcomer to accept the company's views on this ethical issue. Similar situations, in which going along with coworkers and managers may conflict with a personal standard of morality, are not uncommon in business.

Role-sets   A **role-set** is the total of all role relationships in which a person is involved because of his or her position in an organization. For example, an account executive in an advertising agency has relationships with immediate superiors, upper-level managers, peers (other account executives), advertising copy writers and artists, and employees and managers from other departments, as well as clients and media personnel. He or she has a different role relationship with each of these persons in connection with the account executive position. A role-set, then, explains all the role relationships with significant others and includes their location, authority, perceived beliefs, and behaviors. Understanding a person's role-set may help predict his or her ethical behavior.

Persons in the same department are socialized within the same immediate organizational context and often share the same specialization and knowledge base. Even when they work in different departments, members of an organization tend to be more similar to one another than to people who are not members of the organization. Boundaries between (and within) departments and organizations limit the individual's knowledge of attitudes and behaviors beyond the immediate group. Significant others outside the individual's group probably differ in orientation, goals, and interests. The greater the distance between the decision maker and a significant other, the less likely the other is to influence ethical behavior.

Within the organization, peers and top managers are likely to have a major influence on the ethical decisions of individuals. Top management will have more influence on the individual than peers because of its authority. This, however, does not hold when there is little interaction between top management and the individual.[6] In fact, the perceived actions of peers and top management are better predictors of unethical behavior than an individual's own personal belief system or opportunity for engaging in unethical behavior.[7] Figure 7–1 illustrates this relationship.

Because research has found that perceived actions of peers and top management are predictors of unethical behavior does not mean that individuals are not responsible for the consequences of their behavior. Sometimes the consequences of any individual's ethical actions within the group are not that easy for the individual to see. Ethical decisions do not just happen in the group; obviously, they are made through human choice. Personal values do play a role in the final decision, but on business matters, group decisions are often used to resolve ethical dilemmas.

Consider the ethical problems of Sears, Roebuck and Co. auto centers. An investigation concluded that thirty-three Sears centers in California overcharged consumers by an average of $223 in nearly 90 percent of the cases investigated. The deception and overcharges were caused by a quota system that had been established for service advisers. The quota set a minimum of parts, services, and repair sales for every eight-hour shift. Service advisers were instructed to sell a certain number of shock absorbers or struts per hour worked.

Sears acknowledged responsibility, and its president promptly concluded that the incentive compensation and goal-setting program inadvertently created an environment in which mistakes occurred. The president quickly dealt with the ethical problem and stated that "we have eliminated incentive compensation and goal-setting systems for automotive advisers — the folks who diagnose problems and recommend repairs to you."[8] It is obvious in this case that service advisers were accountable to managers and that impossible goals were set for every eight-hour shift. Service advisers were forced to sell a certain number of products whether customers needed the products or not.

This example illustrates how employees can be influenced by supervisors who control whether they will keep their jobs. These findings should be

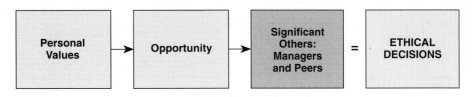

FIGURE 7–1

Significant Others Are the Most Influential Factor in Ethical Organizational Decision Making

alarming to individuals who feel that one's personal ethics should be a major consideration when occupying business roles. Conflicts between what you are asked to do by superiors and your personal ethics create many ethical dilemmas, as well as opportunities to improve business ethics. Because our findings show that managers went along with peers or superiors does not mean that we suggest this is the way you ought to behave.

Managers who are in supervisory positions should take responsibility for the actions of their subordinates, including unethical behavior. A survey of managers from *Fortune* 500 companies indicates that managers need to get closer to their employees to develop a successful relationship. Openness, trust, and friendship were most often cited as the key factors in building such a relationship. These factors seem important in communicating ethical values and encouraging responsible conduct.[9]

Differential Association

Differential association refers to the idea that people learn ethical or unethical behavior while interacting with others who are part of their role-sets or other intimate personal groups.[10] The learning process is more likely to result in unethical behavior if the individual associates primarily with persons who behave unethically. Association with others who are unethical, combined with the opportunity to act unethically oneself, is a major influence on ethical decision making as described in the decision-making framework in Chapter 5.[11]

For example, two cashiers work different shifts at the same supermarket. Kevin, who works in the evenings, has seen his cashier friends take money from the bag containing the soft-drink machine change, which is collected every afternoon but not counted until closing time. Although Kevin personally believes that stealing is wrong, he has often heard his friends rationalize taking the money by saying that the company owes them free beverages while they work. During his break one evening, Kevin discovers that he has no money to buy something to drink. Because he has seen his friends take money from the bag and has heard them justify the practice, Kevin does not feel guilty about taking 50 cents from the bag. However, Sally, who works the day shift, has never seen her friends take money from the bag. When she discovers that she does not have enough money to purchase a beverage for her break, it does not occur to her to take money from the change bag. Instead, she borrows from a friend. Although both Sally and Kevin view stealing as wrong, Kevin has associated with others who say the practice is justified. When the opportunity arose, Kevin used his friends' rationalization to justify his theft.

A variety of studies have supported the notion that differential association influences ethical decision making; in particular, superiors have a strong influence on the ethics of their subordinates. A study of marketing managers revealed that differential association with peers and opportunity are better predictors of ethical or unethical behavior than is the respondent's own ethical belief system.[12] Several research studies have found that employees, especially young managers, tend to go along with their superiors to demonstrate loyalty in matters related to moral judgments.[13] Hopefully, we have made it clear that learning how people typically make ethical decisions is not necessarily the way they should make ethical decisions. But we believe you will be able to help improve ethical decisions after you understand the potential influence of interacting with others who are part of intimate work groups.

When employees think they know the right course of action in a situation, yet their work group or company promotes or requires unethical decisions, interpersonal conflict will ensue and whistle-blowing may occur. **Whistle-blowing** means exposing an employer's wrongdoing to outsiders such as the media or government regulatory agencies. If employees conclude that they cannot discuss with their coworkers or superiors what they are doing or what should be done, they may go outside the organization for help. To provide an in-house channel for reporting misconduct and voicing objections, many companies are now installing anonymous reporting services, usually toll-free numbers, for employees to express their concerns and gain internal company assistance. In fact, the Federal Sentencing Guidelines for Organizations include rewards (reductions of organizational penalties) for companies that detect and address unethical or illegal activities on a systematic basis. As for whistle-blowers, they often lose their jobs. Some, however, turn to the courts and obtain substantial settlements if their grievances are determined to be valid. An engineer with General Electric was awarded $1.7 million as a part of GE's $7.18 million payment to the U.S. government to resolve a suit filed by the employee. He had charged the company with selling to the military jet engines that did not comply with contract terms. The case is controversial because GE maintains that the engines were safe and considers itself vindicated by the settlement. Still, the settlement shows that the legal system does provide rewards for reporting misconduct.[14]

ORGANIZATIONAL PRESSURES AND SIGNIFICANT OTHERS

Because ethics is a series of perceptions of how to act in terms of daily issues, organizational success is determined by an employee's everyday performance in achieving company goals. Middle managers may be subject to particularly intense pressure to perform and increase profits. The Sears quota system in which employees were required to sell a certain number of auto parts per hour even if customers did not need the repairs exemplifies such pressure. Internal organizational pressure stemming from role-set relationships and differential association is a major predictor of unethical behavior. Although individuals can overcome this pressure, they may risk losing their jobs.

A former employee of Dartmouth College's prestigious Amos Tuck School of Business Administration alleged in a lawsuit that she was fired after complaining that the school was altering data it provided to magazines for guidebooks ranking colleges. Dartmouth maintained that the employee saw only preliminary data, which were later revised and verified. According to the employee's attorney, however, the employee suffered such intense criticism from her supervisor that she had to take a stress-related disability leave. Obviously, this specific ethical matter will be resolved through a civil lawsuit. But the larger ethical issue of disseminating inaccurate information remains. Business school officials across the United States have long acknowledged privately that cheating goes on in the data reported to magazines.[15] Yet questioning the way information is reported or the accuracy of released information can generate conflict and pose a personal risk to the individual within an organization.

Knowing when to report a supervisor or boss who is committing perceived unethical activities is very difficult. Many companies are establishing ethics codes and ethics departments. As noted earlier, they are also setting up anonymous hotlines and encouraging employees to use them to report misconduct. But having recourse to a mechanical process such as a hotline does not solve the problem of when to report a supervisor. For instance, two of three brokers at NationsBank quit their jobs because they considered the company guilty of high-pressure sales tactics and other infractions. When the third broker went public with the charges by filing a complaint with the National Association of Securities Dealers, the two former employees joined him in the complaint. NationsBank filed a counterclaim against all three, charging defamation, and the matter is in arbitration. If they lose, the three may have to pay large fines and legal fees.[16]

Even when an organization agrees with the employees reporting misconduct and takes appropriate action, those employees may still suffer consequences: an emotional fallout. At Honeywell, for example, a small group of workers anguished for weeks before reporting a boss for misdeeds. After the offender was dismissed, the group felt a lingering sense of guilt along with relief.[17]

Top management and superiors play crucial roles in developing the environment that influences ethical decisions. Most experts agree that the chief executive officer and other top managers at the executive level set the ethical tone for the entire organization.[18] Lower-level managers take their cues from the top, yet their personal value systems also have an influence on the business. This interplay between corporate culture and executive leadership helps determine the ethical value system of the firm. We now take a closer look at the concepts of leadership, motivation, and power.

LEADERSHIP

Leadership, the ability or authority to guide and direct others toward achievement of a goal, has a significant impact on ethical decision making because leaders have power to motivate others and enforce the organization's rules and policies as well as their own viewpoints. In this section we explore aspects of leadership that influence ethical decision making, including motivation and power.

In the long run, if group members are not reasonably satisfied with their leader, he or she will not retain a leadership position. A leader must not only have followers' respect but must also provide a standard of ethical conduct to group members. For example, when it became known that some Chrysler Corp. managers had been disconnecting odometers or altering their readings, the company's chairman acknowledged that the practice was wrong and said that it would not be tolerated.[19] This statement sent a message to both employees and the public that Chrysler would not condone unethical behavior.

The leadership style of an organization influences how employees act. For example, the management philosophy of John F. Welch, Jr., chairman of General Electric Co., is summed up as follows by one of his group heads: "The Welch theory is those who do, get, and those who don't, go."[20] Taken at face value, this statement tells managers that they can carry out tasks his way or find employment elsewhere. Studying the leadership styles and attitudes of an organization can also help pinpoint where future ethical issues may arise. For instance, although age discrimination is against the law, Welch's philosophy is that "some people past a certain age aren't trainable, and they do better to leave GE."[21] By virtue of his leadership position, Welch could contribute to the practice of age discrimination, although GE's formal hiring policies do not discriminate against older potential employees. Even concerning actions that may be against the law, employees often look to their organizational leaders to determine how to resolve an ethical issue.

Leadership is also important because managers can use rewards or punishments to encourage employee behavior that supports organizational goals. Rewards and punishment are part of the concept of opportunity in the ethical decision-making framework discussed in Chapter 5. Researchers have identified four dimensions of leader behavior relating to reward and punishment.

1. *Performance-contingent reward behavior.* The leader gives positive reinforcements, such as recognition and praise, for subordinates' good performance. For example, a subordinate might be praised for doing the "right," or "ethical," thing even though profits were not maximized.

2. *Contingent punishment behavior.* The leader uses negative reinforcements, such as reprimands, for subordinates' poor performance. Thus a sales

manager may punish a salesperson who used an unethical sales technique by docking the subordinate's pay or withholding the commission.

3. *Noncontingent reward behavior.* The leader gives positive reinforcement regardless of subordinates' performance. A production manager, for instance, might ignore unethical behavior or poor-quality work and be a "nice guy" to everyone.

4. *Noncontingent punishment behavior.* The leader gives negative reinforcement regardless of subordinates' performance. For example, a finance manager might punish a worker who pointed out that some financial documents required by a government regulatory agency were inaccurate.

Performance-contingent behaviors are most productive in encouraging ethical behavior. As discussed in previous chapters, positive reinforcement for ethical behavior usually encourages that behavior. When employees who behave ethically are rewarded, they will continue to do so; when they are punished for behaving unethically, they are unlikely to repeat the unethical behaviors. In addition, performance-contingent reward behavior is generally associated with higher levels of employee performance and satisfaction. Noncontingent-punishment behavior is generally believed to have a negative effect on performance and satisfaction, with the remaining behaviors delivering mixed results.

Motivation

A leader's ability to motivate subordinates is a key consideration in maintaining an ethical organization. **Motivation** is a force within the individual that focuses his or her behavior to achieve a goal. To create motivation, an organization offers incentives to encourage employees to work toward organizational objectives. Understanding motivation is important in the management of others, and it helps explain their ethical behavior. For example, a person who aspires to higher positions in an organization may sabotage a coworker's project to make that person look bad. This unethical behavior is directly related to the first employee's ambition (motivation) to rise in the organization.

As businesspeople move into middle management and beyond, higher-order needs (social, esteem, and recognition) tend to become more important relative to lower-order needs (salary, safety, and job security).[22] Research has shown that career stage, age, organization size, and geographic location vary the relative importance of respect, self-esteem, and basic physiological needs.

From an ethics perspective, needs or goals may change as a person progresses through the ranks of the company. This shift may cause or help solve problems, depending on the current ethical status of the person relative to the company or society. For example, junior executives might inflate purchase or sales orders, overbill time worked on projects, or accept cash gratuities if they are worried about providing for their families' basic physical necessities. As they continue up the ladder and are able to fulfill these needs, such concerns may become less important. Consequently, these managers may go back to obeying company policy or culture.

It is possible that an individual's hierarchy of needs may influence motivation and ethical behavior. After basic needs such as food, working conditions (existence needs), and survival are satisfied, resources are available for relatedness needs and growth needs, which may become important. **Relatedness needs** are satisfied by social and interpersonal relationships, and **growth needs** are satisfied by creative or productive activities.[23] Consider what happens when a new employee, John Taylor, joins a company. At first John is concerned about working conditions, pay, and security (existence needs). After some time on the job, he feels he has satisfied these needs and begins to focus on developing good interpersonal relations with coworkers. When these relatedness needs have been satisfied, John wants to advance to a more challenging job. However, he learns that a higher-level job would require him to entertain clients with alcoholic beverages, which is against his religious beliefs. He decides, therefore, not to work toward a promotion (need frustration) and to focus instead on furthering good interpersonal relations with coworkers (frustration-regression — focusing on an area not related to the main problem to reduce anxiety). John would continue to emphasize high performance in his present job. In this example, John's need for promotion has been modified by his values. To feel productive, John goes back and attempts to fill his needs. Thus John's frustration level may not lead him to seek other employment.

Examining the role of motivation in ethics is an attempt to relate business ethics to the broader social context in which workers live and the deeper moral assumptions on which society depends. Workers are individuals, and they will be motivated by a variety of personal interests. While we keep emphasizing that managers are positioned to exert pressure and obtain compliance on ethically related issues, we also acknowledge that an individual's personal ethics and needs will significantly affect ethical decisions.

Power

A second dimension of leadership is power and influence. Power refers to the influence leaders and managers have over the behavior and decisions of subordinates. An individual has power over others when his or her presence causes them to behave differently. Exerting power is one way to influence the ethical decision-making framework described in Chapter 5 (especially significant others and opportunity).

The status and power of significant others are directly related to the amount of pressure they can exert on employees to conform to their expectations. A superior in an authority position can put strong pressure on employees to comply, even when their personal ethical values conflict with the superior's wishes. For example, a manager might say to a subordinate, "I want the confidential data about our competitor's sales on my desk by Monday morning, and I don't care how you get it." A subordinate who values his or her job may feel pressure to do something unethical to obtain the data.

Professors John French and Bertram Ravin have defined five power bases from which one person may influence another: (1) reward power, (2) coercive power, (3) legitimate power, (4) expert power, and (5) referent power.[24] These five bases of power can be used to motivate individuals either ethically or unethically.

Reward Power   **Reward power** refers to a person's ability to influence the behavior of others by offering them something desirable. Typical rewards might be money, status, or promotion. Consider, for example, a retail salesperson who has two watches (a Timex and a Casio) for sale. Let us assume that the Timex has a higher level of quality than the Casio but is priced about the same. Without any form of reward power, the salesperson would logically attempt to sell the Timex watch. However, if Casio gave him an extra 10 percent commission, the salesperson would probably focus his efforts on selling the Casio watch. This "carrot dangling" has been shown to be very effective in getting people to change their behavior in the long run. In the short run, however, it is not as effective as coercive power.

Coercive Power   **Coercive power** is essentially the opposite of reward power. Instead of rewarding a person for doing something, coercive power penalizes actions or behavior. As an example, suppose a valuable client asks an industrial salesperson for a bribe and insinuates that he will take his business elsewhere if his demands are not met. Although the salesperson believes bribery is unethical, she has been told by her boss that she must keep the client happy or lose her chance at promotion. The boss is imposing a negative sanction if certain actions are not performed.

Coercive power relies on fear to change behavior. For this reason, it has been found to be more effective in changing behavior in the short run than in the long run. Coercion is often employed in situations of extreme imbalance in power. However, people who are continually subjected to coercion may seek a counterbalance by aligning themselves with other, more powerful persons or simply leaving the organization. In firms that use coercive power, relationships usually break down in the long run.

Power is an ethical issue not only for individuals, but also for work groups that establish policy for large corporations. Small, independent pharmacies have won a $600-million settlement from thirteen big drug makers, which the pharmacies accused of overcharging for drugs. The settlement came from a class action lawsuit by some forty thousand pharmacy owners who objected to the manufacturers' practice of offering big discounts to bulk buyers, such as health maintenance organizations and pharmaceutical mail-order firms.[25] In this case, the large pharmaceutical companies attempted to charge higher prices to smaller firms that were dependent on their products but did not have the power to demand fair market prices.

Legitimate Power   **Legitimate power** stems from the belief that a certain person has the right to exert influence and that certain others have an obligation to accept it. The titles and positions of authority that organizations bestow on individuals appeal to this traditional view of power. Many people readily acquiesce to those who wield legitimate power, sometimes committing acts that are contrary to their beliefs and values.

Such staunch loyalty to authority figures can also be seen in corporations with strong charismatic leaders and centralized structures. In business, if a superior tells an employee to increase sales no matter what it takes and if that employee has a strong affiliation to legitimate power, he or she may try anything to fulfill that order. For example, when a senior marketing executive of ITT Corp. entertained air force employees in exchange for inside information on two defense contracts valued at $180 million, he may have felt that he was conforming to his superior's vague instructions about getting the contracts.[26] That is, the vagueness of the superior's instructions may have served as an unstated cue to acquire the information at whatever cost. Because his superior had legitimate power, the executive considered all options, ethical, unethical, and illegal. In this case the use of legitimate power may have created an ethical issue.

Expert Power   **Expert power** is derived from a person's knowledge (or the perception of knowledge). Expert power usually stems from a superior's credibility with subordinates. Credibility, and thus expert power, is positively related to the number of years a person has worked in a firm or industry, the person's education, or the honors received for performance. Expert power can also be conferred on a person by others who perceive the individual as an expert on a specific topic. A relatively low-level secretary may have expert power because he or she knows specific details about how the business operates.

Expert power may cause ethical problems when it is used to manipulate others or to gain an unfair advantage. Medical doctors, lawyers, or consultants can take unfair advantage of unknowing clients. Accounting firms may gain extra income by ignoring concerns about the accuracy of financial data provided in an audit.

Referent Power   **Referent power** may exist when one person perceives that his or her goals or objectives are similar to another's. The second person may attempt to influence the first to take actions that will lead both to achieve their objectives. Thus, when referent power is used, one person's attempts to influence another's decision will be seen as beneficial. For this power base to be effective, however, some sort of empathy must exist between the individuals. Identification with others helps boost the decision maker's confidence when making a decision, thus providing an increase in referent power.

Consider the following situation: Lisa Jones, a manager in the accounting department of a manufacturing firm, has asked Michael Wong, a salesperson, to speed up the delivery of sales contracts, which usually take about one month to process after a deal is reached. Michael protests that he is not to blame for the slow process. Rather than threaten to slow delivery of Michael's commission checks (coercive power), Lisa makes use of referent power. She invites Michael to lunch, and they discuss some of their work concerns, including the problem of slow-moving documentation. They agree that if document processing cannot be speeded up, both will be hurt. Lisa then suggests that Michael start faxing contracts instead of mailing them. He agrees to give it a try, and within several weeks the contracts are moving faster. Lisa's job is made easier, and Michael gets his commission checks a little faster.

The five bases of power are not independent. People typically use several power bases to effect change in others. Although power in itself is neither ethical nor unethical, its use can raise ethical issues. Sometimes power is used to manipulate a situation or a person's values in a way that provokes a conflict that relates to the value structure. For example, a manager who forces an employee to choose between staying home with his sick child and keeping his job is using coercive power, which creates conflict directly linked to the employee's values.

SIGNIFICANT OTHERS AND ETHICAL BEHAVIOR IN BUSINESS

As we have emphasized, personal values, significant others, and opportunity all affect ethical behavior. One study concerning the values of corporate managers concluded that personal values are involved in ethical decisions but are not the central component that guides an organization's decisions, actions, and policies. This study found that personal values make up only one part of an organization's total value system.[27] Ethical behavior depends on the organization's values and traditions, and the pressures exerted by significant others, as well as the personal values of the individuals who actually make the decisions. Some people, for instance, will not consider employment with an organization unless it maintains a certain level of ethical values. A high standard of ethics will not necessarily motivate such employees to work harder, but it may keep them from changing their own values or being swayed by peers (significant others) or money (opportunity).

Consequently, ethical behavior may be a function of several different dimensions of an organization's system: the embedded organizational value system (or corporate culture), significant others, and the personal value preferences of the organization's groups and individual members. An individual member of an organization assumes some measure of moral responsibility by agreeing in general to abide by an organization's rules and standard operating procedures. Significant others help in the socialization process that transforms the employee from an outsider to an insider. This process results in cohesiveness within the organization, with members maintaining loyalty, support, and trust.

If managers and coworkers can provide direction and encourage ethical decision making, significant others become a force to help individuals make better ethical decisions. When workers have greater participation in the design and implementation of assignments, conflict within work groups is reduced, and ethical behavior may increase.

Businesses with an organizational culture that results in managers and employees acting contrary to their individual ethics need to understand the costs of unethical behavior. Some employees succumb to organizational pressures rather than follow their own values, rationalizing their decisions by maintaining that they are simply agents of the corporation. According to Gene R. Laczniak and Patrick E. Murphy, this rationalization has several weaknesses, including the following:[28]

1. People who work in business organizations can never fully abdicate their personal, ethical responsibility in making business decisions. Claiming to be an agent of the business organization is not accepted as a legal excuse and is even less defensible from an ethical perspective.

2. It is difficult to determine what is in the best interest of the business organization. Short-term profits earned through unethical behavior may not be in the long-run interest of the company.

3. A person in a business has a responsibility to parties other than the business organization. Stakeholders, any group or individual who can be affected by the firm, and other concerned publics must be considered when making ethical decisions.

Understanding the influence of significant others and the interpersonal relations within the organization provides insights into the ethical decision-making process. For business-related decisions, significant others have been found to be the most influential variable affecting ethical decisions. In extreme situations — for instance, if asked to break into a competitor's office to obtain trade secrets — employees may abide by their own personal value systems. But in most day-to-day decisions, they tend to go along with the group on issues that appear to be defined and controlled by the work group. Hence understanding how significant others influence the ethical decision-making process helps explain why unethical decisions may be made in business.

SUMMARY

Significant others include superiors, peers, and subordinates within the organization who influence the ethical decision-making process. Relationships among these individuals and within groups, or interpersonal relations, are an important part of the functioning of a business organization, strongly influencing ethical behavior.

There is a substantial amount of research and survey data indicating significant variation in how individuals make ethical decisions. Approximately 10 percent of employees may take advantage of opportunities to be unethical — that is, they take advantage of situations to further their own personal interests. Some 40 percent of workers go along with the work group on most matters, and another 40 percent try to follow company policies and rules. The final 10 percent of employees believe their value system is superior to that of their coworkers and the organization.

A role is the part that a particular person plays in an organization; it refers to that person's position and the behavior others expect from someone holding the position. Each person in an organization has a specialized task or role in helping the organization achieve its goals. Socialization refers to the process through which a person learns the values and appropriate behavior patterns of an organization or group and the behavior expected of his or her role within the organization. Ethical issues such as lying, cheating, and the payment of bribes may be defined through socialization, which instills organizational values and norms in employees. A role-set is the total of all role relationships in which a person is involved because of his or her position in an organization. Differential association refers to the idea that people learn ethical or unethical behavior while interacting with others who are part of their role-sets or other intimate personal groups. The learning process will encourage ethical or unethical behavior, depending on the behavior of the person's associates.

Pressure to perform and increase profits may be particularly intense in middle management. This organizational pressure stems from role-set relationships and differential association and is a major predictor of unethical behavior. The roles of top management and superiors are extremely important in developing the environment that influences ethical decisions.

Leadership, the ability or authority to guide others toward achievement of a goal, has a significant impact on the ethical decision-making process because leaders have power to motivate others and enforce the organization's rules and policies, as well as their own viewpoints. A leader must not only gain the respect of his or her followers but also provide a standard of ethical conduct. In addition, leadership is important because managers have the power to reward or punish employees and to encourage behavior that supports organizational goals. Performance-contingent rewards and contingent punishments are most productive in encouraging ethical behavior.

Motivation is an internal force that focuses an individual's behavior to achieve a goal; it can be created by the incentives an organization offers employees. Motivation can be used to influence the ethical behavior of others.

Power refers to a leader's influence over the behaviors and decisions of subordinates. Reward power is exercised by providing something desirable to others so that they will conform to the wishes of the power holder. Coercive power, in contrast, penalizes actions and uses fear to change behavior. Legitimate power stems from the belief that someone has the right to exert influence, whereas others have an obligation to accept it. Expert power is derived from a person's knowledge. Referent power may exist when one person perceives that his or her goals or objectives are similar to another's. These five power bases can be used to motivate individuals either ethically or unethically.

Ethical behavior may be a function of several dimensions of an organization's system: the embedded organizational value system or corporate culture, significant others, and the personal value preferences of the organization's groups and individual members. Significant others have been found to be the most influential variable affecting ethical decisions in business-related matters.

If managers and coworkers provide positive role models, significant others become a force to help individuals make better ethical decisions. But when there is severe role conflict and pressure to commit unethical acts, unethical behavior in the organization may increase. Some employees may rationalize their decisions by maintaining that they are simply agents of the corporation. This is not acceptable as a legal excuse and is even less defensible from an ethical perspective. From a normative perspective, there is general agreement that a businessperson has a responsibility to parties other than just the business organization.

A REAL-LIFE SITUATION

Jim had been with Cinco for about four years and had completed the company's management-training program. He had been a plant manager for about three months. Cinco Corporation owned pulp-processing plants that produced various grades of paper from fast-growing trees. Jim's plant, the smallest and oldest of Cinco's plants, was located in upstate New York near a small town. It employed between 100 and 175 workers, most from the nearby town. In fact, the plant boasted about workers whose fathers and grandfathers also worked there. Every year, Cinco held a Fourth of July picnic for the entire town.

Cinco's policy was to allow each manager a free hand in dealing with employees, the community, and the plant itself. Its main measure of performance was the bottom line. The employees were keenly aware of this fact.

Like all pulp-processing plants, Cinco's plant was located near the local river. Because of the plant's age, much of its equipment was outdated. Consequently, it took more time and money to produce paper at Jim's plant than at Cinco's newer plants. Cinco had a long-standing policy of starting new people at this plant to see if they could manage a work force and a mill efficiently and effectively. Tradition had it that a manager who did well with the upstate New York plant would be transferred to a larger, more modern one. As a result of this strategy, the plant's workers had experienced many managers and were hardened and insensitive to change. In addition, most of the workers were older and more experienced than their managers, including Jim. Many of the older workers called him "Jimmy" or "Little Jim."

In his brief tenure as plant manager, Jim had learned a great deal from his workers about the business. Jim's secretary, Ramona, made sure that reports were done right, that bills were paid, and that Jim learned how to perform these tasks. Ramona had been at the plant for so many years that she had become a permanent, and often immovable, fixture. Jim's three foremen were all in their late 40s and kept things running smoothly. Jim's wife, Elaine, was having a very difficult time adjusting to New York. Speaking with other managers' wives, she learned that the "prison sentence," as she called Jim's current assignment, typically lasted no longer than two years. She kept a large calendar in the kitchen and crossed off each day they were there.

One morning as Jim came into the office, Ramona didn't seem her usual stoic self. "What's up?" Jim asked her.

"You need to call the EPA," she replied. "It's not real important. Ralph Hoad from the EPA said he wanted you to call him."

When Jim made the call, Ralph told him the mill's waste disposal into the river exceeded EPA guidelines, and he would stop by next week to discuss the situation. Jim hung up the phone and asked Ramona for the water sample results for the last six months upstream, downstream, and at the plant. After inspecting the data and comparing them with EPA standards, he found no violations of any kind. He then ordered more tests to verify the original data. The next day Jim compared the previous day's tests with the last six months' worth of data and found no significant differences and no EPA violations. As he continued to look at the data, something stood out on the printouts that he hadn't noticed before. All the tests had been done on the first or second shifts. Jim called the foremen of the two shifts to his office and asked if they knew what was going on. Both men were extremely evasive with their answers and referred him to the third-shift foreman. When Jim phoned him, he, too, was evasive and said not to worry — that Ralph would explain it to him.

That night, Jim decided to make a spot inspection of the mill and test the waste water. When he arrived at the river, he knew by the smell that something was wrong. Jim immediately went back to the mill and demanded to know what was happening. Chuck, the third-shift foreman, took Jim down to the lowest level of the plant. In one of the many rooms stood four large storage tanks. Chuck explained to Jim that when the pressure gauge reached a certain level, a third-shift worker opened the valve and allowed the waste to mix with everything else. "You see," Chuck told Jim, "the mill was never modernized to meet EPA standards so we have to divert the bad waste here; twice a week it goes into the river."

"Who knows about this?" asked Jim. "Everyone who needs to," answered Chuck.

When Jim got home, he told Elaine about the situation. Elaine's reaction was, "Does this mean we're stuck here? Because if we are, I don't know what I'll do!" Jim knew that all the other managers before him must have had the same problem. He also knew that there was no budget for new EPA-approved equipment for at least another two years.

The next morning Jim checked the EPA reports and was puzzled to find that the mill had always been in compliance. There should have been warning notices and fines affixed, but he found nothing. That afternoon Ralph Hoad stopped by. Ralph talked about the weather, hunting, and fishing, and then he said, "Jim, I realize you're a new manager. I apologize for not coming to you sooner and introducing myself, but I saw no reason for it because your predecessor had taken care of me up until this month."

"What do you mean?" Jim asked.

"Ramona will fill you in. There's nothing to worry about. I know no one in town wants to see the old mill close down, and I don't want it to either. There are lots of memories in this old place. I'll stop by to see you in another couple of months."

With that, Ralph left. Jim asked Ramona about what Ralph had said. She showed Jim the financial ledger and pointed to an item indicating "Miscellaneous expense, $100." "We do this every month," she told him.

"How long has this been going on?" asked Jim.

"Since the new EPA rules," Ramona replied. She went on to clarify Jim's alternatives. Either he could continue paying Ralph, which didn't amount to a whole lot, or he could stop paying Ralph, which would mean payment of EPA fines and a potential shutdown of the plant. As Ramona put it, "Headquarters only cares about the bottom line. Now, unless you want to live here the rest of your life, the first alternative is the best for your career. The last manager who bucked the system lost his job. The rule in this industry is that if you can't manage Cinco's New York plant, you can't manage. That's the way it is."

Questions

1. What are the ethical issues?

2. What significant others are affecting Jim's decisions?

3. What is Jim's power structure and leadership position in New York?

4. What should Jim do?

IMPORTANT TERMS FOR REVIEW

significant others
role
socialization
role-set
differential association
whistle-blowing
leadership
motivation

relatedness needs
growth needs
reward power
coercive power
legitimate power
expert power
referent power

CHAPTER EIGHT

The Role of Opportunity and Conflict

AN ETHICAL DILEMMA*

ANN KAUFMAN, 33, an energetic single woman with an 8-year-old son, had just been promoted to administrator of a hospital. South Haven Hospital, a very large institution in an urban district, was one of many owned by the A. H. Corporation. The patients who used the facilities at South Haven Hospital were primarily blue-collar, semiskilled factory workers from several large industrial complexes located in and around the city. South Haven had a long-standing policy of accepting all patients who needed care, whether or not they had insurance or were able to pay their bills.

Ann was, of course, very excited about her new job. She had previously been administrator of a very small A. H. Corporation hospital in a small community. Thus this promotion was a signal that Ann was on the fast track at A. H. Corporation.

Six months after Ann's promotion, however, the local economy collapsed. Several of the largest plants in the city closed; in some cases the parent company moved production to other areas with more promising economies. Several thousand employees in the city were laid off or fired. In the first month after the plant closings, South Haven Hospital experienced a dramatic drop in billables (accounts on which the hospital actually expects to receive payment). A. H. Corporation executives sent Ann a memo telling her that if billables did not increase, she would need to cut expenses if she wished to keep her position. Ann responded by reducing her office staff and the hospital's nursing staff, despite an already chronic shortage of nurses. Even though the quality of care might suffer, Ann firmly believed that these were only temporary measures.

In the second quarter after the plant closings, billables continued to decline. Ann tried to explain to her superiors that this trend reflected the plant closings, but her bosses believed otherwise. They suspected that the problem was due to Ann's inadequate performance, perhaps to her lack of experience in managing a large urban hospital. Consequently, they reminded her either to increase billables or to reduce costs. In response, Ann slowed down payments to the hospital's creditors and increased the pressure for collection of bills from insurance companies and patients. These actions helped, but only for a short while.

The next quarter was a disaster for Ann and South Haven Hospital. Billables continued to decline, and a new government regulation concerning the proper disposal of medical wastes came into force. To comply with the law, waste disposal companies were forced to raise their fees dramatically. Ann was now in a real bind. She took the problem to her superiors, who informed her that they did not care what actions she took as long as the hospital remained profitable.

The following day Ann met with John Macke, owner of Macke Disposal, which had been handling disposal of all the hospital's wastes. Macke informed Ann that he knew about the new regulation but that he would continue to dispose of the hospital's wastes at the same costs as before. Ann asked him if his company was going to obey the new federal law. Macke again replied that he would continue to dispose of the hospital's wastes for the same amount of money. Ann knew that what Macke really meant was that the wastes would not be disposed of properly in accordance with the new law. Later that day the home office told Ann that she was dangerously close to losing her job because of the profit problems at South Haven.

Ann considered her options for making the hospital profitable and keeping her own job. She could obey the new law and face rising costs for waste disposal (and ultimately lose her job); she could disobey the law by employing Macke Disposal, which could have legal consequences for the hospital and could hurt her own career, if the decision was later discovered; or she could cancel South Haven Hospital's policy of accepting indigent patients. The last option was extremely distasteful to Ann, who had been brought up to believe that the purpose of a hospital is to take care of all people with health needs. On the other hand, she also believed that the law of the land should be obeyed.

Questions

1. How, do you think, will the opportunity to dispose of the hospital's wastes improperly affect Ann's decision?
2. What other aspects of opportunity exist in this scenario?
3. Describe the various conflicts that exist in this situation: personal-organizational, personal-societal, and organizational-societal.
4. Would your decision change if Ann could automatically get another job? If so, why?
5. Would your decision change if this was the only hospital in the area?

---

*This case is strictly hypothetical; any resemblance to real persons, companies, or situations is coincidental.

*O*pportunity is a key influence on the ethical behavior of members of a business organization and a source of conflict regarding ethical action. It has been found to be a better predictor of unethical behavior than one's own personal moral beliefs.[1] It can also give rise to conflict between the decision maker's personal interests and the firm's interests. Conflicts generally occur when an individual's values differ from those of others in the work and social environment.

In this chapter we examine opportunity and conflict as two major influences on the ethical content of decisions made in business. We first consider the impact of opportunity on ethical decision making and then explore three dimensions of conflict.

OPPORTUNITY

One's circumstances, which may preclude or encourage ethical or unethical behavior, constitute the opportunity dimension. Once opportunistic circumstances are discovered, an ethical dilemma often arises involving the exploitation of the opportunity. **Opportunity** is a set of conditions that limit unfavorable behavior or reward favorable behavior. It often is a situation that has the potential for a positive outcome or reward. Rewards may be internal: the feelings of goodness and self-worth one experiences after doing something beneficial without expecting anything in return. For example, if a factory worker reports to management that another employee is drinking on the job, he may feel good because he has called the coworker's problem to the attention of someone who can help and because he has also acted to reduce danger to others. Rewards may also be external — such as a raise or praise for a job well done. A salesperson who has refused a bribe, for instance, may be praised by her superiors and might even be offered a promotion.

A person who behaves unethically and is rewarded (or not punished) for the behavior is likely to continue to act unethically, whereas a person who is punished (or not rewarded) for behaving unethically is less likely to repeat the behavior. Thus an accountant who receives a raise after knowingly preparing financial documents that are not completely accurate is being rewarded for unethical behavior and may continue to use such tactics in the future. On the other hand, both companies and society at large often punish transgressions. For example, Donald Peterson is serving a prison sentence and was fined $1.8 million for embezzlement. Still, he had escaped punishment for a series of white-collar crimes for some twenty years. Peterson would lure small companies into hiring him by his exceptional bookkeeping proficiency scores, willingness to work for a low salary, and rejection of company-paid insurance. He would also inform his employers of ways to reduce costs. But his aim was to siphon off their funds. One of his tactics was to cash quarterly IRS monies into his personal accounts. Because of the slowness of the IRS, Peterson was almost guaranteed success. When he was interviewed in prison and asked if he had any remorse, he responded, "Not really."[2] If they are not caught early on, those who engage in misconduct tend to rationalize their decisions. Prison terms and fines can send clear messages that society views certain actions as unacceptable and, if enforced early on, can reduce actual and potential white-collar crimes.

For many businesses, opportunity means the chance to market a product that will earn large profits and benefit customers, sometimes even saving lives. Ethical issues may arise, however, when businesses hurry those products to the marketplace without adequate testing or with dangerous flaws. Shiley, Inc., a subsidiary of Pfizer Inc., is currently facing lawsuits and negative publicity because of problems and deaths resulting from defects in its C-C mechanical heart valve. Nearly four hundred of the valves have broken after being installed in patients, who face only a one-in-three chance of survival after a rupture. Although some independent experts state that the valves broke because of a design flaw, other experts and some former Shiley employees say that welds inside the valves were defective. The former employees claim that the company knew about the defects and at first tried to cover them up. After problems emerged and were publicized, sales fell and Pfizer withdrew the product from the market. Shiley and Pfizer now face lawsuits from families of victims who died after a valve malfunctioned, as well as from living patients who fear that their mechanical heart valves will break. Federal investigations are also under way to determine if Shiley misled federal agencies and the public about the riskiness of the device.[3] Although Shiley's intentions in developing the product were good, the company may not have exercised adequate caution in the manufacture of the product in order to begin earning profits as soon as possible.

Because of opportunity, some companies may knowingly either bring a product to market prematurely or modify others to existing markets. Premature product introduction may have been the case with Intel's Pentium chip. Intel says that it discovered a floating-point processor problem (an arithmetic miscalculation) approximately six months before introducing the Pentium chip but had "fixed it." When customers started calling about the problem, Intel dismissed it as a rare, random occurrence and not a serious matter for the average person. Eventually, Intel set up a toll-free number for complaints but would only replace the chip if the caller made a convincing case. That did not satisfy customers. As one buyer of the flawed chip said, "I paid out my hard-earned dollars for a chip and I want it to operate 100 percent or I want my money back."[4] Ultimately, Intel replaced all chips that were called in. Sandoz Pharmaceuticals Corp.'s drug Parlodel may be a case where an existing product got into trouble when its sales were directed to a secondary market. Parlodel was first approved for endocrine disorders and Parkinson's disease. One of its other effects is to lower hormone levels that make milk production possible in women. This lactation suppressant was marketed to doctors who, in turn, prescribed it to a 1.8-million-women market. As the drug was being used, side effects such as seizures, strokes, and heart attacks were reported. As a result, at least six lawsuits have been filed, and the FDA requested that Sandoz stop selling Parlodel and several other drugs as lactation suppressants. Sandoz agreed to this but argues that the drug is safe.[5]

As all the examples illustrate, several elements within the business environment help to create opportunities. The two most critical ones are knowledge and an individual's status within an organization.

Knowledge

A person who has an information base, expertise, or information about competition has the opportunity to exploit this knowledge. An individual can be a source of information because of familiarity with the organization. Individuals long employed by one organization become "gatekeepers" of its culture, unwritten traditions, and rules. They help socialize newer employees to abide by the rules and norms of doing business both inside and outside the company. They may function as mentors or supervise managers in training. Like drill sergeants in the army, these trainers mold the new recruits into what the company wants.

Trainers and mentors influence a new employee's decision process in two ways. First, by providing information, the trainer can determine whether the new employee will identify a certain kind of situation as posing an ethical choice. For example, one study found that salespeople do not consider it unethical to pad an expense account by less than 10 percent.[6] Such attitudes are influenced in part by those who trained the salespeople. Second, by virtue of their title and its associated power, trainers can lead new employees to replace their own value systems with those of the trainer and the organization. Opportunity is lost or gained by the way trainers of new employees use their knowledge base.

Individual Status

Opportunity can also come from the status of individuals within an organization. Title and status may give a person more opportunities to behave unethically. As we discuss in Chapter 7, a person's title or status is associated with the legitimate power base. For example, a regional vice president's status within the organization allows this executive to formulate policy that defines whether certain acts are condoned or condemned as unethical.

Persons outside the organization can also have an impact on opportunity. Thus financial auditors, though external to the organization, encounter many ethically laden situations as a result of their profession. The primary responsibility of an auditor is to determine the financial soundness of an organization by reviewing accounting data and presenting these data in an objective manner. Opportunity for ethical conflict exists because the auditor is hired and paid by the company requesting the audit. What happens if the company screens potential auditors until it finds one that will provide a favorable statement? The auditor's credibility as an impartial reporter then comes into question because of the selection process. The auditor is under implicit pressure to give a positive judgment. The opportunity to become involved in potentially unethical situations results from the status given to the independent auditor. Recently, several accounting firms that had audited troubled savings and loan associations have had to face criminal charges resulting from inaccurate statements about the financial soundness of those institutions.

CONFLICT

Opportunity sometimes leads to or results from conflict between the values of the decision maker and significant others, the organization, or society. **Conflict** occurs when it is not clear which goals or values take precedence — those of the individual, the organization, or society. (Remember that an individual's values relate directly to his or her moral philosophy.) There has been major conflict over executive pay in recent years. Even poorly performing companies often pay executives millions of dollars in salary and benefits. Although the executives receiving high levels of compensation may feel that they deserve it, other stakeholders might prefer seeing some portion of the funds invested in other ways. The Securities and Exchange Commission has proposed a total overhaul in the compensation disclosure system so that stockholders will understand how much executives are really getting paid.[7]

When individuals must choose between two equally good goals, particularly if one may result in more positive rewards than the other, they experience conflict. A choice between two bad alternatives can also cause conflict. As noted above, conflict can occur along several dimensions: personal, organizational, and societal.

Individuals' goals start with basic food and shelter and culminate in a search for new experiences and intellectual growth. Organizations also pursue goals, such as earning a profit, capturing a certain portion of a market, or completing a certain program of activity. All these goals relate in some way to surviving and being successful. Society is not concerned with the specific goals of any one organization, but rather with the betterment of the whole. In addition to this main goal, a subgoal within American society is the protection of individual rights, such as the rights of privacy and freedom of speech.

Conflict occurs when interactions of these dimensions raise questions as to which goals or values are most important. In such situations, there is no one clear-cut good or bad alternative or solution. In this section we examine the three primary types of conflicts: personal-organizational, personal-societal, and organizational-societal.

Personal-Organizational Conflict

Personal-organizational conflict occurs when a person's individual philosophies and methods for reaching a desired goal differ from those of the organization or a group within the organization. For example, suppose that a convenience store manager has strong views against the distribution of magazines such as *Playboy* and *Penthouse,* but the company's policy is to sell these products. In this case the organizational philosophy conflicts directly with the individual's personal philosophy. The manager has two options: to comply with the company's policy or to refuse to sell the magazines. Conceivably, refusal could mean getting fired. On the other hand, it would also bring feelings of self-esteem that come from acting in accordance with one's own values. Compliance with company policy would maintain the individual's employment and income status, but at the price of guilt.

Employees often find themselves in such situations, especially before they have been fully socialized into the organization. Many people try so hard to land their first job in business that they fail to consider the corporate values that will govern them. A person may not share the values that are characteristic of other members of his or her profession. Attitudes and values related to drinking, gambling, sex, and religion are personal moral issues and are not universal. A person who believes drinking is wrong, for example, might feel uncomfortable working in an organization in which some after-hours business is conducted over drinks in a nearby bar. In such a situation, the new employee typically decides either to fight the system or to find a job in a more compatible organization. Those who choose to fight usually fail because they lack the power and support to change the values of the company.

But failure and lack of support are not always the case. For example, Herbert Schulte of Prudential Insurance Co. was facing dismissal for low production when his manager printed out a list of customers and handed him sales material that repeatedly referred to a Prudential life insurance policy as nursing home coverage. Schulte believed that the material was deceptive and promoted "churning" (having customers buy unneeded policies). The manager told Schulte to "trust him" and do what he was told. When Schulte refused and made inquiries higher up in the company, he found that the material was unauthorized and "a serious violation of company policy." His boss was fired and Schulte helped Prudential identify a serious ethical flaw.[8]

One common source of conflict has to do with working conditions. In recent years changing technology has caused workers to become more concerned about their environment, and they are demanding that management, or the government, investigate and correct physical hazards that result in illness or injury. Health issues are raised by new carcinogenic chemicals, such as polychlorinated biphenyls (PCBs), and by frequent repetitive movements required in work on assembly lines or at computer keyboards, which give rise to an occupational condition known as cumulative trauma disorder. Cumulative trauma disorders are especially prevalent in the meatpacking and data-processing industries. Employees today take the attitude that their employers should not treat them as pieces of private property, but instead as individuals with ideas, skills, and goals and with bodies that can be damaged.

Employees are also sensitive about their rights to privacy and free speech. For example, many employees believe that their activities outside work are of no concern to their employers and that random testing for drug and alcohol use is thus a violation of their personal privacy (unless, of course, the substances are being consumed in the work environment and may result in injury to the abusers or others). Other employees are concerned about their employers monitoring their behavior on the job. Monitoring activities — such as listening in to see how telephone operators handle calls or using electronic devices to keep track of the number of keystrokes per hour — may be construed as an invasion of privacy. Finally, free speech issues may be relevant when employees accuse their company of deceit or fraud. As noted in Chapter 7, whistle-blowing refers to an employee reporting illegal or unethical activities by an organization to some outside party, such as the press or a government agency.

For example, as a result of whistle-blowing, Teledyne, a defense contractor, has been charged with a pattern of corrupt activities. The defense contractor kept two sets of books, one for the official cost estimates for the Pentagon and another for the company. The company has been charged with improper testing, overbilling, selling defective components, using unskilled labor, false billing, and bribery of a foreign official. A number of Teledyne employees felt so much conflict that they became whistle blowers, telling the government about Teledyne's corrupt activities. One whistle-blower suit, filed by Steven C. Reddy, a program manager for Teledyne Electronics in the Middle East, charged that the company paid a $1.5 million bribe in cash to obtain a $23 million Egyptian air force contract.[9] And in another example, John M. Gravitt, a former machinist foreman at General Electric, "blew the whistle" when he reported that company executives altered employees' time cards so the company would receive more money from the government on defense contracts.[10]

Personal-Societal Conflict

Personal-societal conflict occurs when an individual's values deviate from those of society. Societal values are often stated in the form of laws and regulations established by federal and local governments. Values, such as the desire for clean air and water, can be translated into regulations on behavior. Communities may differ in their values, however. For example, all vehicles in Arizona and California must meet strict pollution emission standards to operate. But nearby Utah, New Mexico, and Idaho set no such standards. Apparently, people in these states do not consider such strict guidelines to be necessary. As a result, a car that is legal to drive in Utah may become illegal as it crosses the border into Arizona. The ethics conflict has been created by two societies imposing their differing values. Alcohol consumption, certain types of entertainment, and Sunday business activities are other examples of behaviors treated differently by different communities.

People whose values conflict with those of society are often regarded as deviants. If they flagrantly defy society's value system, they may be ostracized or even imprisoned. For example, in 1989 Pete Rose was banned for life from the game of baseball because of allegations that he gambled on baseball games. Society may not regard gambling itself as unethical, but gambling on baseball games, and especially on one's own team, violates the rules of the major baseball leagues, which reflect society's views. Although Rose neither denied the gambling charges nor admitted guilt, nearly 67 percent of the persons surveyed in a *USA Today* poll believed that he did bet on baseball games.[11]

When society believes that a particular activity is unethical although currently legal, new laws may be enacted to help define the minimum level of ethical behavior. In the realm of business, this pattern began as early as the railroad monopolies of the 1800s, which prompted passage of the Sherman Antitrust Act. In the early twentieth century, society responded to Upton Sinclair's novel *The Jungle* by raising standards for food processing. More recently, after CEO Frank Lorenzo used bankruptcy laws to break union control at Continental Airlines, Inc., legislation was passed to restrict this use of bankruptcy laws. Because the United States is a pluralistic democracy, personal-societal conflicts will continue to evolve and be redefined.

Organizational-Societal Conflict

When the norms and values of an organization contravene those of society in general, organizational-societal conflict occurs. As companies strive to develop and produce goods and services that satisfy the desires of specific markets, they share many but not all of society's values. In one such instance, the U.S. Department of Agriculture notified nine hundred convenience stores that they could no longer accept food stamps because they sell too many sodas and snacks and not enough milk and bread. For stores to be eligible to take food stamps, at least half the sales must be staples. The balance can be foods such as candy, soft drinks, coffee, tea, condiments, and spices. Since these stores did not focus on selling staple products to food-stamp customers, they came in conflict with societal goals.[12] Toys 'R' Us is one example of a company that has shown sensitivity to societal changes by announcing that it will not sell "realistic" toy guns.[13]

The marketing of new products often brings business into conflict with society, especially when the products have moral overtones for certain groups. When the automobile was introduced, for instance, many felt that human beings were not meant to travel at such high speeds. There was a moral outcry against the new vehicles, in part because they were considered more dangerous than traditional forms of transportation, such as horses. Similar concerns have been voiced about air and space travel.

Advertising of products may also result in conflict when society believes that advertising wrongly appeals to certain groups. In recent years, many consumer groups have expressed concerns about alcoholic-beverage advertising that appeals to teenagers and young college students not legally allowed to consume alcohol. RJR Nabisco, Inc., was sharply criticized by various interest groups for targeting its Dakota brand of cigarettes at poorly educated, blue-collar women between the ages of 18 and 24. Many antismoking groups say that it is wrong for the company to aim its product directly at uneducated women, who may not realize that smoking cigarettes is associated with lung cancer, now the leading cause of death among women. The company was forced to abandon another cigarette product, called Uptown, that was to have been targeted at blacks. Many consumers believe that it is wrong to promote cigarette smoking at all, because of its health effects, but they have been especially critical of tobacco marketers that aim their products at specific disadvantaged groups and at the young.[14] There is evidence that tobacco companies are reaching out even to children by showing Joe Camel along with promotional items in the *Weekly Reader* and *Scholastic News.* As Edith Balbach, a University of California researcher points out, some of the materials had "no negative markings on the photos, such as the international 'no' symbol. In effect, they were not that different from actual ads."[15]

The World Health Organization is trying to calculate how many people now living will be killed by tobacco-caused diseases if current smoking patterns persist. The United States is the leading cigarette exporter, and U.S. tobacco companies are becoming more aggressive in advertising and promoting cigarettes to Asia and other Third World regions. Senator Edward Kennedy of Massachusetts has stated that we should not "let the legality of the product protect us from feeling any moral obligation to protect health and life."[16]

Other types of products and services have also drawn criticism. For example, many groups are now opposing the use of certain chemicals and herbicides often applied to fruits and vegetables. (One such chemical, Alar, which is used on apples and might cause cancer, has been targeted.) Critics have argued that the increased probability of cancer exceeds the benefits provided by use of the chemical. Although the Food and Drug Administration says that Alar is not harmful, many apple growers have yielded to public sentiment and stopped using the chemical.

Another conflict between companies and society relates to oil exploration and drilling in environmentally sensitive areas such as Alaska and in the ocean off the coasts of California, New England, Florida, and Texas. Environmentalists believe that wildlife and their habitats are more important than the oil that could be extracted from these areas. Their concerns were heightened in recent years by major oil spills — in Alaska, Delaware, Rhode Island, and Texas — that caused the deaths of many sea birds and mammals, fouled beaches, and threatened national parks and vital industries

When company goals or values conflict with those of society, businesses have three options: fight, flee, or compromise. Some companies that choose to fight establish **political action committees (PACs),** which lobby the government. PACs try to influence legislatures to take actions that will favor their industry or business. As recently as 1994 such groups as the Pacific Legal Foundation, the Aluminum Trade Group, and the Idaho Farm Bureau have used to their benefit legislation that was intended to restrict companies and have tied up, bypassed, or forced changes in state and federal laws.[17] Another way some companies fight is by building support for policies favorable to their purposes and thus trying to alter the business environment. For example, if a chemical firm pollutes the air but employs many members of a community, citizens may tolerate the pollution problem. If the issue is raised, the company may orchestrate community support for its position. In this instance, a company's goal of profitability and society's need for jobs and income supersede a societal value — the desire for clean air. In addition, the company's goal conflicts with the social desire for clean air but *not* with the social desire for jobs.

When a business concludes that it can no longer afford to operate within the social constraints imposed on it by a particular community, it may take its operations elsewhere. Conflict over the ethical issue of fair wages, for example, has led many companies to flee to less developed countries, such as Mexico and China, where prevailing wage rates are lower.

One company, Nike, Inc., was accused of exploiting Indonesian laborers by paying them less than poverty-level wages to work in unsafe factories. A series of articles in the *Portland Oregonian* claimed that Indonesian workers, without protective clothing, operate hot molds, presses, and cutting machines for 15 cents an hour.[18]

In some cases, societal constraints such as laws requiring cleaner water and air, less noise pollution, and better health insurance, have left firms unable to earn a profit. All these problems are ethical in nature, in that they involve issues of fairness, health, and safety for individuals in a societal setting.

Many companies choose to compromise, perhaps by moving some aspects of their operations to another country while keeping others in the original country. American businesses often follow a compromise strategy for reasons of public relations. For example, profitable products that generate toxic waste can create ethical problems in a society concerned with its own environment, as are the United States and Canada. Some companies compromise by moving the hazardous aspects of production out of the concerned society into a cash-poor developing country, where employment opportunities are greatly valued. The first society continues to have access to needed products, and the society in which production is located receives an economic boost. The problem of toxic waste disposal still exists, but it has been transferred to a society in which that issue is less pressing than the fundamental need for economic development.

A similar situation is occurring in the United States. Several Native American reservations have agreed to store garbage, toxic waste, and even nuclear waste on their land in exchange for hundreds of millions of dollars.[19] Some impoverished tribes believe that allowing the dumps on their sacred lands is a necessary tradeoff by which they will gain funds for desperately needed social programs and job development. Recently, Native Americans have come up with an alternative revenue source: gambling.

A FINAL NOTE ON OPPORTUNITY AND CONFLICT

As we have stressed earlier, a businessperson whose unethical behavior is rewarded and not punished is likely to repeat the behavior, whereas the one who receives no reward or is punished will probably not repeat the behavior. At Caterpillar, for example, an employee caught violating the company's ethical standards as detailed in its code of ethics may be reprimanded, placed on probation, suspended, or even fired. Such sanctions send a message to the employee that unethical or illegal behavior will not be tolerated and make it less likely that it will recur. The greater the reward and the less severe the punishment for unethical behavior, the greater is the likelihood that unethical behavior will continue.

Other elements in the business environment also serve to control opportunities. Ethics-related corporate policies, as well as professional and company codes of ethics, influence opportunity by prescribing what behaviors are acceptable. The corporate culture provides the framework for patterns of acceptable behavior, and dealing with opportunity is part of this system.

We do not want to leave the impression that the only way to prevent unethical behavior is for the company to eliminate opportunity situations for company or personal gain. The relationships in a business are based on trust and responsible behavior. Just as the majority of the people who go into retail stores do not try to shoplift at each opportunity, so most businesspersons do not try to take advantage of every opportunity for unethical behavior. Differences in personal moral philosophies may have a major impact on whether an individual becomes opportunistic and attempts to take advantage of situations, regardless of the circumstances. Since a variety of individual moral philosophies are represented in every organization, the company must develop policies and codes to prevent certain individuals from taking advantage. As discussed in Chapter 7, besides individuals' moral philosophies, significant others greatly influence a person's tendency to exploit opportunity.

SUMMARY

Both opportunity and conflict affect the ethical content of decisions made in business. Opportunity is a set of conditions that limit unfavorable behavior or reward favorable behavior. Rewards may be internal or external. An unethical individual who is rewarded or not punished is likely to continue to act unethically, whereas a person who is punished or not rewarded for behaving unethically is less likely to repeat the behavior. An individual who has an information base, expertise, or information about competition has the opportunity to exploit this knowledge unethically. Status within an organization may also bring opportunities to behave unethically.

Conflict occurs when there is a question as to which goals or values take precedence in a situation: those of the individual, the organization, or society.

A personal-organizational conflict arises when an individual's philosophies or methods for reaching a desired goal differ from those of the organization. Such situations occur frequently, especially for new employees who have not yet been socialized into the organization. Persons whose values do not coincide with those of others in their profession may fight or leave the organization. Before the employees leave, however, they should find out from experienced managers whether their perceptions are accurate.

Personal-societal conflict develops when the values of an individual differ from those of society. Such individuals are usually classified as deviants. When society feels that a particular activity is unethical yet at that point legal, laws may be enacted to help define the minimum level of ethical behavior.

Organizational-societal conflict occurs when the norms and values of the organization are opposed to those of society in general. The marketing of new products often brings business into conflict with society, especially when the products raise moral issues for certain groups. When such conflicts occur, companies have three options: fight, flee, or compromise. Some companies fight by establishing political action committees — organizations that lobby the government for specific legislative purposes — or otherwise attempting to influence government policy so that their own goals and objectives can be fulfilled. When a business believes that it can no longer afford to operate within the social constraints imposed on it, it may flee that society and take its operations somewhere else. Many companies compromise by moving some aspects of the company's operations to another country, while maintaining others within the original country.

Besides rewards and punishments, or their absence, other elements in the business environment help control opportunities. Ethics-related corporate policy, as well as professional and company codes of ethics, influence opportunity by prescribing acceptable behaviors. However, most people in business organizations do not try to exploit every opportunity. Differences in personal moral philosophies cause some to take advantage of situations, regardless of the circumstances. Companies should be aware of the need for policies and codes to prevent individuals from taking advantage in a way that creates ethical conflict.

A REAL-LIFE SITUATION

Things had been going poorly for Wendy over the last couple of months. She had been with Tarco Systems for three years and was hoping for a promotion to district sales representative. Tarco Systems sold computer software and developed information systems for various clients in the United States. The company was young and aggressive and had moved into third place in a competitive industry. Wendy had graduated with an engineering degree and an MBA in information systems. She was engaged to Doug, an accountant at one of the major firms in the New York metropolitan area. Last year they purchased a home in one of the boroughs of New York.

For the last three years Wendy had worked sixty- and seventy-hour weeks developing her clientele and sharpening her skills as a consultant. She had progressed from being a member of a consulting team to director of a consulting team and then area representative. Tarco's corporate structure brought people in as team members and moved them through the ranks all the way to vice president, as in the following promotional structure:

Vice-President, Sales
↑
Regional Representative
↑
District Representative
↑
Area Representative
↑
Team Director
↑
Team Member

Wendy now wanted the district job in the New York area. Her boss, Chuck, was being promoted from the New York district to the East Coast regional position, and Wendy felt the time was right for her own promotion. However, she had problems with Chuck.

Chuck had been a fair boss, but he was a little eccentric. He was also famous for his parties. Someone once asked him how he could afford to give such expensive parties, and he said he didn't pay for them. Tarco was paying for his parties, as well as for his car. "Do you think I could afford a car like this? I write it off on the books as entertainment expenses," Chuck said.

Chuck also had a reputation for promoting employees he liked the most. Rumor was that Sally had been made a team director after a trip to Buffalo even though she wasn't qualified. When Wendy congratulated Sally on her promotion, Sally responded that she did what she had to do to get promoted.

Wendy asked, "What do you mean?"

Sally responded, "In this company, the higher up you want to go, the more they require of you. At least with Chuck, he says it up front so there's no question about it."

Wendy remembered that when she made team director, Chuck had made some sexual overtures to her. She had reminded him that she was engaged and that was the end of it, and three months later she was promoted. He had made advances again when she went up for her area promotion. This time, however, Chuck had been more persistent.

As area manager, Wendy had discovered that some of Chuck's practices were against company policy. In addition, she felt that the company was shortsighted in promoting people like Chuck, who had such eccentricities.

Some months ago Wendy received a phone call from a "headhunter," a person who identifies quality talent in companies and tries to hire them for other companies. The offer was from a competing company within the metro area, which was closer to her home. Wendy had listened, but at the time she was not interested.

Meanwhile, Sally continued to climb the corporate ladder. Another district position had opened and Sally was promoted to it. Chuck had commented sarcastically to Wendy that Sally had gotten the promotion on her "merits." Wendy knew that her own options with the company depended on "other" variables. At about this time the New York housing market became depressed. Wendy had considered transferring to another region, but she would have to take a huge loss on the sale of her home, so moving would not be an acceptable option for at least another year. At work Chuck was becoming more aggressive, and Wendy knew her career was about to come to a dead end if she did not play Chuck's "game."

Last week the headhunter called again and offered Wendy a district position at a higher salary. However, the competing company making the offer would expect Wendy to bring sensi-

tive information about Tarco and her clients to the new position. Wendy's contract with Tarco stipulated that she could not work for any of the competition within a 150-mile radius. Violating the contract would result in large fines but no jail time. Some employees had challenged the legality of such contracts as undue restraint.

The same afternoon the headhunter called, Chuck also called Wendy. He told her he was about to evaluate her relative to the New York district opening. Then he asked if she could help him with some business in Buffalo over the weekend.

Questions

1. Discuss the ethical issues.
2. What are Wendy's options?
3. What types of opportunity exist for Wendy and Chuck in the Tarco Systems organization?
4. How could Tarco control the opportunity to be unethical?
5. Where are the conflict points in this case?

IMPORTANT TERMS FOR REVIEW

opportunity
conflict
political action committees (PACs)

CHAPTER NINE

Development of an Effective Ethics Program

AN ETHICAL DILEMMA*

BILL DUNHAM, AGE 26, had been the assistant manager of the Manhattan region for Thor Environmental Management Systems for two years. During his four years with Thor, Bill had come up through the ranks to his current position in the biggest cash-generating region of the company. His superior, Francine Williams, was a very friendly, likable, but aggressive manager. She had made many influential friends in her twelve years with Thor Systems. As a result, she was slated for promotion to vice president.

Six months ago Francine went through a divorce, which Bill knew had affected her deeply. In fact, Bill had heard that Francine was abusing alcohol. He also noticed that her behavior had become very erratic. For example, one day Francine fired four people because she underbid on a small project, and they had told her that her figures were wrong. Sales had been slipping recently, and Thor's executives were pressuring Francine to bring them back up. Francine was confident that Thor would make up for the decline by winning a very big contract.

Last week Bill had given Francine the materials she needed to prepare the company's bid on a project. Francine returned the materials to Bill yesterday, along with her bid, which he also had to approve. But Bill found a problem. The bid Francine had prepared was inaccurate. In fact, the bid was so low that, if accepted, Thor would lose a substantial amount of money over the next three years.

Thor's recently established code of ethics said, "No employee of Thor Environmental Management Systems will knowingly prepare, submit, or report false information in order to obtain business." As far as Bill knew, however, no one had ever been reprimanded or fired for violating any of the code's provisions, although certain employees had broken these rules. If Bill explained the problem to Francine and suggested that she modify the bid, he would risk losing his favorite-son status and perhaps his job. Bill thought about taking the problem to Francine's superior. However, the company culture dictated respect for the chain of command. Employees who bypassed their immediate supervisors were often branded as undesirable and tended to be fired or laid off for some reason eventually or to find their careers at a dead end.

Questions

1. What role does the company's culture play in the decision-making process?
2. What role does Thor's code of ethics play in Bill's decision-making process?
3. What should Bill do?

---

*This case is strictly hypothetical; any resemblance to real persons, companies, or situations is coincidental.

*O*ur goal in this book is to encourage you to think about the impact of your ethical decisions on business and society. Although there is no universally accepted approach for dealing with business ethics, companies should establish organizational structures and corporate cultures that foster ethical behavior and should pursue ethical business strategies. In Chapter 1, we indicated that the Federal Sentencing Guidelines for Organizations had set the tone for organizational ethics programs in the 1990s. These guidelines broke new ground by codifying into law incentives for organizations that take action by developing effective internal ethical compliance programs to prevent employee misconduct. Therefore, this chapter uses the framework established by the Federal Sentencing Commission to prevent misconduct. This framework for developing an effective ethics program is consistent with current research on how to improve ethical decision making and with the ethical decision-making process described in Chapter 5. Businesses and managers must assume responsibility and ensure that ethical standards are properly implemented on a daily basis.

In this chapter we provide an overview of how managers can develop an organizational ethics program. First we define an effective ethical compliance program. Then we consider the factors that are crucial for the development of such a program: codes of ethics and compliance standards; high-level personnel's responsibility for the ethical compliance program and the delegation of authority; effective communications and ethical training programs; systems that monitor, audit, and enforce ethical standards in the organization; and efforts needed to keep improving the ethical compliance program. (See Table 9–1 for a list of the minimum requirements for compliance with the Federal Sentencing Guidelines for Organizations.) Next we discuss the

TABLE 9–1 Minimum Requirements for Ethical Compliance Programs

1. Standards and procedures, such as codes of ethics, reasonably capable of detecting and preventing misconduct
2. High-level personnel responsible for ethics compliance programs
3. No substantial discretionary authority given to individuals with a propensity for misconduct
4. Effective communication of standards and procedures via ethics training programs
5. Establishment of systems to monitor, audit, and report misconduct
6. Consistent enforcement of standards, codes, and punishment
7. Continuous improvement of the ethical compliance program

Source: Adapted from U.S. Sentencing Commission, *Federal Sentencing Guidelines Manual* (St. Paul, Minn.: West Publishing, 1994), Chapter 8.

role of personal values in the organization and provide an ethical compliance audit that could be used to assess the company's effectiveness in ethical compliance.

We use the term *compliance* in this chapter from the business perspective of establishing and enforcing company policies on ethics. We do not intend to imply an objective of controlling the personal ethics and moral beliefs of individuals in the business organization. When companies attempt to assess personalities and personal beliefs that might influence ethical decisions on the job, great care must be taken to avoid infringing on employees' personal freedoms and ethical beliefs. In cases where individuals' personal beliefs and activities are inconsistent with company policies on ethics, conflict can develop. If the individual feels that ethical compliance systems in the organization are deficient or directed in an inappropriate manner, some type of open conflict resolution may be needed to deal with the differences.

AN EFFECTIVE ETHICAL COMPLIANCE PROGRAM

Throughout this book, we have emphasized that ethical issues are at the forefront of organizational concerns as managers and employees face increasingly complex decisions. Often these decisions are made in a group environment comprising employees with different value systems, competitive pressures, and political concerns that contribute to the possibility of misconduct. Nearly one-third of the four thousand employees surveyed nationally by the Ethics Resource Center felt pressure to engage in misconduct to achieve business objectives.[1] In addition, nearly one-third of employees are seeing misconduct, but less than half are reporting it to their companies.[2] When opportunity to engage in unethical conduct abounds, companies are vulnerable not only to ethical problems, but also to legal violations if employees do not know how to make the right decision. Legal issues are often attempts to resolve gray areas or borderline ethical disputes.

An organizational ethics program should help reduce the possibility of penalties and negative public reaction to misconduct. The accountability and responsibility for appropriate business conduct is in the hands of top management. A company has to have an effective ethics program to ensure that all employees understand the values of the business and comply with policies and codes of conduct that create the ethical climate of the business.

If the corporate culture provides rewards or opportunity to engage in unethical conduct through lack of managerial concern or failure to comply with the minimum requirements of the Federal Sentencing Guidelines for Organizations (Table 9–1), then the company may face penalties and loss of public confidence. The main objective of these federal guidelines is to encourage companies to assess risk, then self-monitor and aggressively work to deter unethical behavior, by punishing members or stakeholders who engage in it.

At the heart of the Federal Sentencing Guidelines for Organizations is the carrot-and-stick philosophy. Companies that act to prevent organizational misconduct may receive a "carrot" and avoid penalties should a violation occur. The ultimate "stick" is organizational sentencing with fines and even organizational probation. Organizational probation involves on-site consultants observing and monitoring a company's ethical compliance efforts and reporting to the Federal Sentencing Commission on the company's progress in avoiding misconduct.

The sentencing of organizations is governed by four considerations. First, the court orders the organization to remedy any harm caused by the offense. Second, if the organization operated primarily with a criminal purpose, fines are set sufficiently high to divest the firm of all assets. Third, fines levied against the organization are based on the seriousness of the offense and the culpability of the organization. Fourth, probation is deemed an appropriate sentence for an organizational defendant when it will ensure that the firm will take action to reduce further misconduct.[3] The Federal Sentencing Guidelines for Organizations require federal judges to increase fines for organizations that continually tolerate misconduct and to reduce or eliminate fines for firms with extensive ethics compliance programs. A firm cannot succeed solely through a legalistic approach to ethics and compliance with the sentencing guidelines; top management must seek to develop high ethical standards that serve as a barrier to illegal conduct. The company must want to be a good corporate citizen and recognize the importance of ethics to successful business activities.

Until the Federal Sentencing Guidelines for Organizations were formulated, courts were inconsistent in holding corporations responsible for employee misconduct. Even with the best ethics program, there were no specific benefits for extensive compliance efforts, including effective supervision of employees. Now organizations gain credit for ethical compliance programs that meet a rigorous standard. The effectiveness of a program is determined by its design and implementation: it must deal effectively with the risk associated with a particular business and has to become part of the corporate culture.

An effective ethical compliance program can help a firm avoid civil liability, but the company bears the burden of proving that such a program exists. An ethics program developed in the absence of misconduct will be much more effective than a code of conduct imposed as a reaction to misconduct. To rule a company not guilty in civil liability cases, the court must conclude that an employee's unethical actions or behavior were outside the scope of assigned duties and responsibilities. According to the principle of vicarious liability, an organization is responsible for the conduct of its employees in their daily execution of duties.

The legal test of a company's ethical compliance program is possible when an individual employee is charged with misconduct. The court system or the U.S. Sentencing Commission evaluates organizational responsibility for the individual's behavior in the process of an investigation. If the organization contributed to the misconduct or did not show due diligence in preventing misconduct, then organizational sentencing may occur. The ethical test of a compliance program can be evaluated as it relates to industry standards, community standards, or the acceptance of the firm's conduct by important publics, including employees and customers.

CODES OF ETHICS AND COMPLIANCE STANDARDS

Ethical behavior can be encouraged through the establishment of organizational standards of conduct. These standards may take the form of codes of ethics or policy statements on certain questionable practices. A code of conduct should be specific enough to be reasonably capable of preventing misconduct. Very general codes that communicate at the level of "do no harm" or "be fair and honest" are not enough. The company must give enough direction for employees to avoid risks associated with their particular business.

Employees may have different moral philosophies and come from different cultures and backgrounds. Without uniform policies and standards, they are likely to have difficulty in determining what is acceptable behavior in the company. **Codes of ethics,** formal statements of what an organization expects in the way of ethical behavior, let employees know what behaviors are acceptable or improper.

Many organizations have established strong codes of ethics or policies related to ethics, as well as strategies for enforcing them. Codes of ethics will not solve every ethical dilemma, but they do provide rules and guidelines for employees to follow. These codes may address a variety of situations, from internal operations to sales presentations and financial disclosure practices.

A code of ethics has to reflect senior management's desire for organizational compliance with the values, rules, and policies that support an ethical climate. Development of a code of ethics should involve the president, board of directors, and senior managers who will be implementing the code. Legal staff should be called upon to ensure that the code has correctly assessed key areas of risk and that potential legal problems are buffered by standards in the code. A code of ethics that does not address specific high-risk activities within the scope of daily operations is inadequate for maintaining standards that can prevent misconduct. For example, some small retailers are involved in food stamp fraud totaling over $1 billion a year. The government is investigating food stamp fraud; therefore, the redemption of food stamps should be a high-risk issue for retail food chains.[4] A code of ethics could address the need to maintain strict compliance with food stamp redemption policies.

Walter W. Manley II has developed six steps for implementing the code

TABLE 9–2 Code of Ethics Implementation

Six Steps to Effective Implementation of a Code of Ethics

1. Distribute the code of ethics comprehensively to employees, subsidiaries, and associated companies.
2. Assist employees in interpreting and understanding the application and intent of the code.
3. Specify management's role in the implementation of the code.
4. Inform employees of their responsibility to understand the code and provide them with the overall objectives of the code.
5. Establish grievance procedures.
6. Provide a conclusion or closing statement, such as this one from Cadbury Schweppes:

    The character of the company is collectively in our hands. Pride in what we do is important, and let us earn that pride by the way we put the beliefs set out here into action.

Source: Adapted from Walter W. Manley II, *The Handbook of Good Business Practice* (London: Routledge, 1992), p. 16.

of ethics; they are listed in Table 9–2. Since Texas Instruments has gained recognition as having one of the leading ethics programs in the United States, we describe in detail how it implemented its code.

Texas Instruments' Code of Ethics

A large multinational firm, Texas Instruments (TI) manufactures computers, calculators, and other high-technology products. Its code of ethics resembles that of many other organizations. The code addresses issues relating to policies and procedures; government laws and regulations; relationships with customers, suppliers, and competitors; gifts and entertainment; political contributions; business payments; conflicts of interest; investment in TI stock; handling of proprietary information and trade secrets; relationships with government officials and agencies; and enforcement of the code. TI's code emphasizes that ethical behavior is critical to maintaining a profitable enterprise.

> The trust and respect of all people — fellow workers, customers, stockholders, government employees, elected officials, suppliers, competitors, neighbors, friends, the media, and the general public — are assets that cannot be purchased. They must be earned every day. This is why all of TI's business must be conducted according to the highest ethical, moral, and legal standards.

Like most codes of ethics, TI's requires employees to obey the law. In many instances, moreover, TI expects its employees to adhere to ethical standards more demanding than the law. For example, although some local laws permit companies to contribute to political candidates or elected officials, TI's code states that "no company funds may be used for making political contributions of any kind to any political candidate or holder of any office of any government — national, state or local. This is so even where permitted by local law." TI also goes beyond the federal law prohibiting discrimination against minorities, and expects its employees to treat all fellow workers with dignity and respect. "The hours we spend at work are more satisfying and rewarding when we demonstrate respect for all associates regardless of gender, age, creed, racial background, religion, handicap, national origin, or status in TI's organization."

This code of ethics is not just lip service paid to societal concerns about business ethics; the company enforces the code through audits and disciplinary action where necessary. TI's corporate internal audit function measures several aspects of business ethics, including compliance with policies, procedures, and regulations; the economical and efficient use of resources; and the internal controls of management systems. In addition, the code states that "any employee who violates TI's ethical standards is subject to disciplinary action which can include oral reprimand, written reprimand, probation, suspension, or immediate termination."

To ensure that its employees understand the nature of business ethics and the ethical standards they are expected to follow, TI has published a booklet called "Cornerstone." This pamphlet uses a question-and-answer format to explore a number of possible ethical issues and how employees should resolve them. "Cornerstone" includes an "ethics quick test" to help employees when they have doubts about the ethics of specific situations and behaviors:

> Is the action legal?
> Does it comply with our values?
> If you do it, will you feel bad?
> How will it look in the newspaper?
> If you know it's wrong, don't do it!
> If you're not sure, ask.
> Keep asking until you get an answer.

Finally, the booklet provides a toll-free number for employees to call, anonymously, to report incidents of unethical behavior or simply to ask questions.[5]

Texas Instruments explicitly states what it expects of its employees and what behaviors are unacceptable. By enforcing the codes wholeheartedly, TI has taken logical steps to safeguard its excellent reputation for ethical and responsible behavior. When such standards of behavior are not made explicit, employees sometimes base ethical decisions on their observations of the behavior of peers and management. The use of rewards and punishments to enforce codes and policies controls the opportunity to behave unethically and increases employees' acceptance of ethical standards.

HIGH-LEVEL MANAGERS' RESPONSIBILITY
FOR ETHICAL COMPLIANCE PROGRAMS AND
THE DELEGATION OF AUTHORITY

An ethical compliance program can be significantly enhanced if a high-level manager or a committee is made responsible for its administration and oversight. The ethical compliance program should involve senior management or the owner of the organization, although each officer, manager, or employee has to be responsible for supporting and complying with the program. The high-level manager in charge of the program is often called the compliance coordinator, ethics officer, or compliance officer. In large corporations, usually one or more senior managers are appointed to serve as compliance or ethics officers, but the entire senior management is required to support and be involved in the ethical compliance process. Sometimes the structure includes a special committee of senior managers and/or the board of directors to oversee the company's ethical compliance program.[6] Many of the *Fortune* 1000 firms in the United States have established the post of ethics officer. The vast majority of these positions have been created in the last five years. Ethics officers usually have the following responsibilities:

■ Coordinating the ethical compliance program with top management, the board of directors, and senior management

■ Developing, revising, and disseminating a code of ethics

■ Developing effective communication of ethical standards

■ Establishing audit and control systems to determine the effectiveness of the program

■ Developing consistent means of enforcing codes and standards

■ Reviewing and modifying the ethics program to improve its effectiveness

Regardless of how the oversight of the ethics program is managed, it is important that the managers in charge of the program tailor it to the scope, size, and history of the organization. Just as important is reviewing the need for special compliance components based on the organization's legal history, industry standards, and regulatory concerns. If there is high risk due to the nature of the business, then special attention should be given to these matters and preventive measures included in the program. Furthermore, without an effective manager in charge of the ethics program, it will be impossible to develop organizational learning and records that document the company's steps in managing the program.

The high-level managers who oversee the ethics program must be responsible for avoiding delegation of substantial discretionary authority to people who are known to engage in misconduct. Information in the personnel files, the results of company audits, managers' opinions, and other available information should be used to ascertain the likelihood that managers will engage in misconduct. An adequate search must also be performed be-

TABLE 9–3   Keys to Successful Ethics Training

1. Help employees identify the ethical dimensions of a business decision.
2. Give employees a means to address ethical issues.
3. Help employees understand the ambiguity inherent in ethical situations.
4. Make employees aware that their actions define the company's ethical posture both internally and externally.
5. Provide direction for finding managers or others who can assist in ethical conflict resolution.
6. Eliminate the belief that unethical behavior is *ever* justifiable by stressing that

   ▪ stretching the ethical boundaries results in unethical behavior.
   ▪ whether discovered or not, an unethical act is just that.
   ▪ an unethical act is *never* in the best interests of the company.
   ▪ the firm is held responsible for the misconduct of its members.

Source: Adapted from Walter W. Manley II, *The Handbook of Good Business Practice* (London: Routledge, 1992), p. 87.

fore the company hires individuals who have been convicted of offenses, if the firm knows — or should know — about these convictions. When past wrongdoing is uncovered — for instance, if the individual in question had been convicted of a felony or fired for misconduct in another organization — then the firm must take responsibility for delegating authority. Those in charge of ethical oversight within the organization have the obligation to prevent unethical people from holding positions of authority.

EFFECTIVE COMMUNICATION OF ETHICAL STANDARDS

Managers cannot motivate employees or coordinate their efforts without proper communication. Communication by top executives keeps the firm on its ethical course, and top executives must ensure that the ethical climate is consistent with the company's overall objectives. Communication is important in providing guidance for ethical standards and activities that provide integration between the functional areas of the business. A vice president of marketing, for example, must communicate and work with regional sales managers and other marketing employees to make sure that all agree on what constitutes certain unethical activities, such as bribery, price collusion, and deceptive sales techniques. Top corporate executives must also communicate with managers at the operations level (in production, sales, and finance, for instance) and enforce overall ethical standards within the organization. Table 9–3 lists the factors crucial to successful ethics training. It is most important

TABLE 9–4 Citicorp's Basic Principles of Ethical Standards and Conflict of Interest Policy — Committee on Good Corporate Practice

Citicorp has earned a reputation for excellence and integrity while achieving outstanding business success. In order to safeguard our record of integrity, we should be careful to deal with customers who also have high standards of integrity. We should not accept any business plan or individual proposition that might impair Citicorp's reputation.

Committee on Good Corporate Practice

The Committee on Good Corporate Practice is part of Citicorp's continuing program to avoid situations in which our personal interests may conflict or appear to conflict with either Citicorp's or its customers' interests.

The Committee members determine whether or not a conflict of interest exists in a given situation, and advise and assist us whenever questions arise. If we have any doubt as to whether a conflict of interest exists, or whether a situation raises a reasonable question of conflict, we should report the facts to a supervisor and seek guidance. If the supervisor is in doubt, he or she should, in turn, request the Committee's guidance. Questions should be forwarded to the Committee chairman or the Committee secretary through the Corporate Secretary's Office.

There is no wish to inquire into any individual's personal affairs beyond the point that will keep the name of Citicorp above reproach and prevent censure of its people. Each of us must do his or her part in maintaining our high standards by promptly disclosing or submitting for review any situation that could develop into a possible conflict of interest.

Source: *Ethical Choices*, Citicorp, p. 6. Reprinted by permission.

to help employees identify ethical issues and give them the means to address and resolve such issues in ambiguous situations. In addition, employees must be offered direction on seeking assistance from managers or other designated personnel in resolving ethical problems.

Recognizing that the world is composed of many different cultures and value systems, Citicorp has developed ethical principles to guide the company and create open communications. In order to promote communication at different levels of the organization, Citicorp has instituted a committee on good corporate practice whose aim is to implement ethical standards and eliminate conflict of interest. Table 9–4 offers an excerpt from Citicorp's handbook *Ethical Choices* and provides an illustration of how an ethics committee can help resolve conflicts of interest.

Companies can implement ethical principles in their organizations through training programs. Discussions conducted in ethical training programs sometimes break down into personal opinions about what should or should not be done in particular situations. To be successful, business ethics programs need to educate employees about formal ethical frameworks and models for analyzing business ethics issues. Employees would then be able to base ethical decisions on some knowledge of choices, rather than on emotions.

ESTABLISHING SYSTEMS TO MONITOR, AUDIT, AND ENFORCE ETHICAL STANDARDS

Compliance involves comparing employee performance with the organization's ethical standards. Ethical compliance can be measured through the observation of employees and a proactive approach to dealing with ethical issues. An effective ethical compliance program uses investigatory and reporting resources. Sometimes external auditing and review of company activities is helpful in developing benchmarks of compliance.

The existence of an internal system for employees to report misconduct is especially useful in monitoring and evaluating ethical performance. A number of firms have set up ethics hot lines, often called help lines, to offer support and give employees an opportunity to register ethical concerns. While there is always some worry that people may misreport a situation or misuse the hot line to retaliate against another employee, hot lines have become widespread and employees do utilize them. For example, when NYNEX Corporation set up an ethics hot line, it received over 2,700 calls in one year; only 10 percent dealt with alleged misconduct.[7]

To determine whether a person is performing his or her job adequately and ethically, observation might focus on how the employee handles an ethically charged situation. For example, many businesses use role playing in the training of salespeople and managers. Ethical issues can be introduced into the discussion, and the results can be videotaped so that both the participant and the superior can evaluate the results of the ethical dilemma.

Questionnaires that survey employees' ethical perceptions of their company, their superiors, coworkers, and themselves, as well as ratings of ethical or unethical practices within the firm and industry, can serve as benchmarks in an ongoing assessment of ethical performance. Then, if unethical behavior is perceived to increase, management will have a better understanding of what types of unethical practices may be occurring and why. A change in the ethics training within the company may be necessary. Thus when General Dynamics Corp. was caught overbilling the government on defense contracts, the company issued a twenty-page statement entitled "Standards of Business and Conduct" to all 100,000 employees. In addition, General Dynamics created a committee of board members to review ethics policy and a corporate steering group to supervise policy execution.[8]

Corrective action involves rewarding employees who comply with company policies and standards and punishing those who do not. When employees comply with organization standards, their efforts may be acknowledged and rewarded through public recognition, bonuses, raises, or some other means. Conversely, when employees deviate from organizational standards, they may be reprimanded, transferred, docked, suspended, or even fired.

If a company is to maintain ethical behavior, its policies, rules, and standards must be worked into its compliance system. Reducing unethical behavior is a business goal no different from increasing profits. If progress is not being made, the company needs to determine why and take corrective action, either by enforcing current standards more strictly or by setting higher standards. If the code of ethics is aggressively enforced and becomes part of the corporate culture, it can be effective in improving ethical behavior within the organization. If a code is merely window dressing, and not genuinely part of the corporate culture, it will accomplish very little.

Efforts to deter unethical behavior are important to companies' long-term relationships with their employees, customers, and community. If corrective action is not taken against behavior that is organizationally or socially defined as unethical, such behavior will continue.

Consistent enforcement and necessary disciplinary action are essential to a functional ethical compliance program. The ethics or compliance officer is usually responsible for companywide disciplinary systems, implementing all disciplinary actions the company takes for violations of its ethical standards. Many companies are including ethical compliance in employee performance appraisals. During performance appraisals, employees may be asked to sign an acknowledgement that they have read the company's current guidelines on its ethical policies. The company must also promptly investigate any known or suspected misconduct. The appropriate company official, often the ethics officer, needs to make a recommendation to senior management on how to deal with a particular ethical infraction. In some cases, the company is required to report substantiated misconduct to a designated governmental or regulatory agent in order to receive credit under the Federal Sentencing Guidelines for Organizations for having an effective compliance program.[9]

CONTINUOUS IMPROVEMENT OF THE ETHICAL COMPLIANCE PROGRAM

Improving the system that encourages employees to make more ethical decisions is not very different from implementing other types of business strategies. **Implementation** means putting strategies into action. Implementation in ethical compliance means the design of activities to achieve organizational objectives, using available resources and given existing constraints. Implementation translates a plan for action into operational terms and establishes a means by which organizational ethical performance will be monitored, controlled, and improved.

A firm's ability to plan and implement ethical business standards depends in part on the organization structuring resources and activities to achieve its ethical objectives in an effective and efficient manner. For example, ever since its founding in 1850, apparel manufacturer Levi Strauss & Co. has communicated company values — what it stands for and what its people believe in, as well as its tradition of always treating people fairly and caring about their welfare.[10] The firm's "Mission Statement" and "Aspiration Statement" (see Table 9–5) tell how the business should be run. People's attitudes and behavior must be guided by a shared commitment to the business instead of by obedience to traditional managerial authority. Encouraging diversity of perspectives, disagreement, and the empowerment of people within the organization helps to align the company's leadership with its employees.

If a company determines that its performance has not been satisfactory in ethical terms, that company's management may want to reorganize the way certain kinds of ethical decisions are made. For example, a decentralized organization may need to centralize key decisions, if only for a time, so that top-level managers can ensure that the decisions are ethical. Centralization may reduce the opportunity for lower-level managers and employees to make unethical decisions. Top management can then focus on improving the corporate culture and infusing more ethical values throughout the organization by providing rewards for positive behavior and sanctions for negative behavior. In other companies, decentralization of important decisions may be a better way to attack ethical problems, so that lower-level managers, familiar with the forces of the local business environment and local culture and values, can make more decisions. Whether the ethics function is centralized or decentralized, the key need is to delegate authority in such a way that the organization can achieve ethical performance.

THE INFLUENCE OF PERSONAL VALUES IN BUSINESS ETHICS PROGRAMS

Corporate values tend to dominate most organizational cultures, particularly in the absence of individual ethical values. Although personal values are involved in ethical decisions, they are only one of the central components that guide the decisions, actions, and policies of organizations. An organization's values, as derived from its procedures and policies, tend to drive the company toward certain goals and along certain pathways. Thus the burden of ethical behavior relates to the organization's values and traditions, not just to the individuals who make the decisions and carry them out.[11]

The **"bad apple–bad barrel" theory** may help explain the relationship between personal values and organizational culture in business ethics. The "bad apple" argument — the notion that blame for unethical behavior rests with a few unsavory individuals — assumes that people are either ethical or unethical, depending on personal moral development, and implies that organizations can do little to influence ethical behavior. If the bad apple principle

TABLE 9–5 Levi Strauss's Statement of Mission and Aspirations

Levi Strauss & Co. Mission Statement

The mission of Levi Strauss & Co. is to sustain profitable and responsible commercial success by marketing jeans and selected casual apparel under the Levi's brand.

We must balance goals of superior profitability and return on investment, leadership market positions, and superior products and service. We will conduct our business ethically and demonstrate leadership in satisfying our responsibilities to our communities and to society. Our work environment will be safe and productive and characterized by fair treatment, teamwork, open communications, personal accountability and opportunities for growth and development.

Aspiration Statement

We all want a Company that our people are proud of and committed to, where all employees have an opportunity to contribute, learn, grow and advance based on merit, not politics or background. We want our people to feel respected, treated fairly, listened to and involved. Above all, we want satisfaction from accomplishments and friendships, balanced personal and professional lives, and to have fun in our endeavors.

When we describe the kind of LS&CO. we want in the future what we are talking about is building on the foundation we have inherited: affirming the best of our Company's traditions, closing gaps that may exist between principles and practices and updating some of our values to reflect contemporary circumstances.

What Type of Leadership is Necessary to Make Our Aspirations a Reality

New Behaviors: Leadership that exemplifies directness, openness to influence, commitment to the success of others, willingness to acknowledge our own contributions to problems, personal accountability, teamwork and trust. Not only must we model these behaviors but we must coach others to adopt them.

Diversity: Leadership that values a diverse workforce (age, sex, ethnic group, etc.) at all levels of the organization, diversity in experience, and a diversity in perspectives. We have committed to taking full advantage of the rich backgrounds and abilities of all our people and to promote a greater diversity in positions of influence. Differing points of view will be sought; diversity will be valued and honesty rewarded, not suppressed.

Recognition: Leadership that provides greater recognition — both financial and psychic — for individuals and teams that contribute to our success. Recognition must be given to all who contribute: those who create and innovate and also those who continually support the day-to-day business requirements.

Ethical Management Practices: Leadership that epitomizes the stated standards of ethical behavior. We must provide clarity about our expectations and must enforce these standards through the corporation.

Communications: Leadership that is clear about Company, unit, and individual goals and performance. People must know what is expected of them and receive timely, honest feedback on their performance and career aspirations.

Empowerment: Leadership that increases the authority and responsibility of those closest to our products and customers. By actively pushing responsibility, trust and recognition into the organization we can harness and release the capabilities of all our people.

Source: Levi Strauss & Co. Reprinted by permission.

is true, then organizations should attempt to identify unethical individuals and avoid hiring them or remove them from the organization.[12]

The idea of the bad barrel is that something in the bad barrel poisons otherwise good apples; in other words, the corporate culture poisons otherwise ethical people. This view assumes that people are not inherently ethical or unethical but are influenced by the corporate culture surrounding them, including peers, superiors, and the reward system.[13] The organization can influence individual behavior by providing conditions that encourage ethical and discourage unethical behavior. This approach would support the use of codes of ethics and training programs.

People who have high cognitive moral development and are principled tend to act more ethically than others. Thus hiring people with high ethical standards can raise the ethical tone of the organization and improve daily ethical decision making. It is also true that employees with higher expectations of punishment behave more ethically. This finding implies that corporate culture has a major impact on ethical decision making. A company that wants to foster ethical behavior may pursue both approaches. It may try to hire people with socially accepted ethical standards and to develop an ethical corporate culture. In other words, the system will work best if there are both good apples and good barrels. Either bad apples or bad barrels are likely to lead to ethical problems.

THE ETHICAL COMPLIANCE AUDIT

In Chapter 5, we presented a framework that described the ethical decision-making process. Although this model does not explain exactly how ethical decision making occurs, it does provide a good overview that could be helpful in implementing an ethical compliance audit within a company. An **ethical compliance audit** is a systematic evaluation of an organization's ethics program and/or performance to determine its effectiveness. In particular, it is useful to focus on the key factors that influence how ethical decisions are made. The corporate culture, including peers, superiors, and formal systems of reward and punishment, exerts an important influence on the ethical behavior of employees. Understanding the ethical issues in an audit can help in establishing codes of ethics and other programs to control ethical behavior in business organizations.

The ethical compliance audit in Table 9–6 offers examples of items that could be used to assess an organization's ethical concerns and control mechanisms. An audit should provide a systematic and objective survey of the ethical condition of the organization. Like an accounting audit, an ethics audit may be more helpful if someone with expertise but from outside the organization conducts the audit. Note that the questions under "Organizational Issues" in the audit in Table 9–6 do not prescribe specific normative ethics actions; rather, they check for mechanisms that promote an ethical organization.

TABLE 9–6 The Ethical Compliance Audit

Organizational Issues*

YES   NO   1. Does the company have a code of ethics that is reasonably capable of preventing misconduct?

YES   NO   2. Is there a person with high managerial authority responsible for an ethical compliance program?

YES   NO   3. Are there mechanisms in place to avoid delegating authority to individuals with a propensity for misconduct?

YES   NO   4. Does the organization have effective communication of standards and procedures via ethics training programs for its employees?

YES   NO   5. Does the organization communicate its ethical standards to suppliers, customers, and significant others that have a relationship with the organization?

YES   NO   6. Do the company's manuals and written documents guiding operations contain ethics messages about appropriate behavior?

YES   NO   7. Is there formal or informal communication within the organization about procedures and activities that are considered acceptable ethical behavior?

YES   NO   8. Does top management have a mechanism to detect ethical issues relating to employees, customers, the community, and society?

YES   NO   9. Is there a system for employees to report unethical behavior?

YES   NO   10. Is there consistent enforcement of standards and punishments in the organization?

YES   NO   11. Is there an ethics committee, department, team, or group that deals with ethical issues in the organization?

YES   NO   12. Is there an attempt to provide continuous improvement of the ethical compliance program within the organization?

*A high number of yes answers indicates that ethical control mechanisms and procedures are in place within the organization.

Examples of Specific Issues That Could Be Monitored in an Ethics Audit**

YES   NO   1. Are systems and operational procedures for individual employees to safeguard ethical behavior absent?

YES   NO   2. Is it necessary for employees to break company ethical rules in order to get the job done?

YES   NO   3. Is there an environment of deception, repression, and cover-ups concerning events that would be embarrassing to the company?

YES   NO   4. Are participatory management practices that allow the discussion of ethical issues absent?

YES   NO   5. Are compensation systems totally dependent on performance?

YES   NO   6. Is there sexual harassment?

YES   NO   7. Is there any form of discrimination — race, sex, or age — in hiring, promotion, or compensation?

YES   NO   8. Are the only concerns about environmental impact those that are legally required?

YES   NO   9. Is concern for the ethical value systems of the community with regard to the firm's activities absent?

YES   NO   10. Are there deceptive and misleading messages in promotion?

YES   NO   11. Are products described in a misleading manner, with negative impact or limitations uncommunicated to customers?

YES   NO   12. Are the documents and copyrighted materials of other companies used in unauthorized ways?

YES   NO   13. Are expense accounts inflated?

YES   NO   14. Are customers overcharged?

YES   NO   15. Is there unauthorized copying of computer software?

**The number of yes answers indicates the number of possible ethical issues to address.

The specific issues to monitor in an ethics audit are given as an example, and the questions contain normative evaluations of behavior. Organizations should participate in the development of their ethics audit instrument to make sure that the key issues they confront are included in the audit. Top management should get involved in determining which normative issues to evaluate, based on the company's desired ethical perspective. Where ethical concerns are found, the ethics audit can help management establish codes of ethics and policies as guidelines for employee actions.

SUMMARY

An effective organizational compliance program involves the following: codes of ethics and compliance standards; high-level personnel responsible for the ethical compliance program and the delegation of authority; effective communications and ethical training programs; systems that monitor, audit, and enforce ethical standards; and efforts needed to keep improving the ethical compliance program.

An organizational ethics program should help reduce the possibility of legally enforced penalties and negative public reaction to misconduct. Top management is accountable and responsible for appropriate business conduct. A company must have an effective ethics program to ensure that all employees understand the values of the business and comply with policies and codes of conduct that create the ethical climate of the organization.

The main objective of the Federal Sentencing Guidelines for Organizations is to encourage companies to assess risk, then self-monitor and aggressively work to deter unethical acts and punish organizational members or stakeholders who engage in unethical behavior. The sentencing of organizations is governed by four considerations. First, any harm caused by the organizational offense must be remedied. Second, if the firm operated primarily with a criminal purpose, fines are to be set sufficiently high to divest it of all assets. Third, organizational fines are based on the seriousness of the offense and the culpability of the organization. Fourth, probation is an appropriate sentence for an organizational defendant when it will ensure that the firm will take action to reduce further misconduct.

Ethical behavior can be encouraged by establishing organizational standards of conduct, particularly codes of ethics. Many companies have adopted codes of ethics: formal statements regarding the behavior that the organization expects of its employees. Without uniform policies and standards, employees will have difficulty determining acceptable behavior in the company. A code of ethics must be developed as part of senior management's desire for organizational compliance with values, rules, and policies that support an ethical climate.

There are six steps to the effective implementation of a code of ethics: comprehensive distribution; assisting in the interpretation and understanding of the code's application and intent; specifying management's role in the implementation; informing employees about the code's objectives and their responsibility to understand them; establishing grievance procedures; and providing a conclusion statement.

An ethical compliance program can be significantly enhanced by having a high-level manager or committee responsible for the administration and oversight of the program. Each officer, manager, and employee is responsible for supporting and complying with the ethics program. The managers who oversee the ethics program are responsible for avoiding delegation of substantial discretionary authority to people with a propensity for misconduct.

Effective communication by top executives keeps the firm on its ethical course, and top executives must ensure that the ethical climate is consistent with the company's overall objectives. Communication is important in any attempt to set ethical standards that provide integration between the functional areas of the business.

Successful ethics training is important in helping employees identify ethical issues and providing the means to address such issues and resolve them. Employees should seek help in the resolution of ethical problems from managers or other designated personnel.

Compliance involves comparing employee performance with the organization's ethical standards. Ethical compliance can be measured through the observation of employees and a proactive approach to addressing ethical issues. Corrective action involves rewarding employees who comply with company policies and standards and punishing those who do not. Consistent enforcement and disciplinary action are necessary to have a functioning ethical compliance program.

A firm's ability to plan and implement ethical business standards depends in part on the organization structuring resources and activities to achieve its ethical objectives in an effective and efficient manner.

Although personal values are involved in ethical decision making, they are only one of the components that guide the decisions, actions, and policies of organizations. The burden of ethical behavior relates to the organization's values and traditions, not just the individuals who make the decisions and carry them out. The "bad apple–bad barrel" theory may help explain the relationship between personal values and organizational culture in business ethics.

An ethical compliance audit provides a systematic and objective survey of the ethical condition of an organization and may be more objective if conducted by someone from outside the organization.

A REAL-LIFE SITUATION

At the Dun and Ready Company, Sid was responsible for monitoring the Japanese stock exchange to determine patterns and identify stocks that could become active. Sid was fluent in Japanese, and the company had sent him to Tokyo, where he joined ten other people from the company. Because he was relatively new to the firm and his Japanese was good, Sid was told to gather information for his boss, Glenna. Glenna had been with Dun and Ready for ten years. She was not excited about being assigned to Japan because of the cultural barriers. Glenna encouraged Sid to get to know the Japanese brokers, traders, and other key people in the business. Because Sid had a Japanese background, he found that he blended easily into the culture.

In Japan, ceremony and favor giving is a way of life. Sid learned that by observing Japanese customs and perfecting his Japanese he became not only an information resource on the Japanese stock market and its players for his company, but also a resource for Japanese who wanted to invest in the U.S. market. He found that the locals would talk to him about important investments rather than coming into the office to see Glenna.

One of his assignments was to take key customers to bars, restaurants, and vacation spots for entertainment purposes. One day when he was entertaining some government officials, one of them hinted that he would like to play golf on some of the famous U.S. courses. Sid understood what was wanted and relayed the requested favor to Glenna. She told Sid that granting such a favor would normally be against policy, but that since such favors seemed to be the custom in Japan, they could do some "creative" accounting. Glenna told Sid to invite the gentleman to the United States, and by pulling some strings,

she managed to have the client play at ten of the most exclusive U.S. golf courses. Later, several such excursions were set up for selected clients and key customers in the Japanese government.

Six months later Glenna was transferred back to the States. Rumor was that the transfer was made because expenses were too high and revenue too low. Her replacement was Ron Lemon. Like Glenna, Ron didn't want to be in Japan. He told the staff the first week that the way he was getting out was by slashing expenses and increasing productivity levels. Ron was a "by-the-book" person. Unfortunately, company rules did not take into account cultural differences. After two months of Ron, seven of the original ten people had quit or were fired. None were transferred.

Sid was barely surviving. One day one of his contacts in the government repaid a favor by suggesting several stocks to buy and several to sell. Sid told all his clients about the stock and had the company buy and sell them as well. The insider information paid off, and Sid gained some breathing room from "the Lemon," as Ron was called behind his back. Around the same time some of Sid's Japanese clients lost a considerable amount of money in the U.S. markets and wanted a "discount" — the term used for a practice of some large Japanese brokerage houses that informally pay off part of some of their best clients' losses. Several times when Glenna was still with the company she used some of the company's assets to fund such "discounts." Because everything went through Ron, Sid and the others believed their situation was hopeless. However, late one afternoon Sid and a few others provided the proper forms, and Ron signed them without noticing.

Several months passed, and the survivors at

the office had resorted to lowering their expenses by using their own funds. This, in turn, led to Sid's "churning" some of his accounts — that is, he bought and sold to gain personal revenue rather than profits for the investor. Churning is moderately tolerated in Japan, but it is unacceptable in the United States. Ron failed to notice what Sid was doing because he was interested solely in reducing expenses and increasing revenues.

Last month a group of key clients in the market gave a party for a few of the top brokers in the office, including Sid. After the customary toasts and small talk, it was suggested that a Japanese cartel might be interested in Dun and Ready. More toasts and small talk ensued, and the following week the Japanese cartel asked if Sid and a few others could join them for drinks. At the party, cartel members hinted that for the buyout to take place they would need certain sensitive information. If they got this information and if all went well, the cartel would reward the brokers with positions in the new, reorganized company.

That week Ron had announced that headquarters was pleased with the productivity of the office. "It's only a matter of time now before I get transferred out, and I *want* to go back to the States. Because of this, there will be some changes next week," said Ron with a tight smile. Sid recognized that this meant fewer people would be working even harder. If they were going to gather the information the cartel wanted, they would have to act quickly before someone in the group was fired.

Questions

1. What are ethical issues?

2. Assume that being fired is an unacceptable option to you. What would you do and why?

3. What moral philosophies might have been used by Sid, Glenna, and Ron in this case?

4. What are some control options that Dun and Ready could have used to create an ethical climate?

IMPORTANT TERMS FOR REVIEW

codes of ethics
implementation
"bad apple–bad barrel" theory
ethical compliance audit

CHAPTER TEN

International Business Ethics

AN ETHICAL DILEMMA*

KATHY WANG, OPERATIONS manager of the CornCo plant in Phoenix, had a dilemma. She was in charge of buying corn and producing corn chips marketed by CornCo in the United States and Third World countries. Several months earlier her supervisor, CornCo Vice President Bob Stevens, called to tell her that corn futures were on the rise, which would ultimately increase overall production costs of corn chips. In addition, a new company called Abco Snack Foods had begun marketing corn chips at very competitive prices, which had eroded CornCo's share of the market. Bob was concerned that Kathy's production costs would rise, and therefore CornCo's profitability would decline. Bob asked Kathy to find ways to cut her costs.

But Kathy's problem was more complicated. Recently, there had been a large increase in aflatoxin — a naturally occurring carcinogen that induces liver cancer — in the U.S. corn crop. Once corn has been ground into corn meal, the aflatoxin is virtually impossible to detect in the final product. In effect, no one could tell the difference if CornCo decided to use the contaminated corn to manufacture corn chips. U.S. laws stated that corn contaminated with aflatoxin could not be used for U.S. production, but no law prohibited shipping corn contaminated with aflatoxin to other countries.

Since CornCo could not afford higher production costs because of the competition, Bob told Kathy to buy the contaminated corn and use it in the production of corn chips shipped to Third World markets. Although this action was perfectly legal, it would increase the likelihood of liver cancer in those who consumed the corn chips.

To help make her decision, Kathy decided to consult with operations managers in other divisions of CornCo that made products with a corn base. One of them, Lee Garcia, an operations manager for CornCo's breakfast cereals division, told Kathy that he was using the contaminated corn in both the U.S. and the Third World markets. He defended his decision by saying that he had to support his family and that Bob had told him that if his profitability declined he would be looking for another job. Lee pointed out that the aflatoxin could not be detected in the final product, so everything was okay.

Kathy now had to decide whether to hold costs down by using the contaminated corn. If her decision was affirmative she also had to decide whether to use the contaminated corn in corn chips destined for the U.S. market, which would be illegal, or only in Third World markets, which would be legal although harmful to consumers. Because aflatoxin could not be detected in the final product, her use of the contaminated corn would probably not be discovered. Moreover, Kathy knew that she would probably lose her job if her production costs went up. Because the chip industry was intensely competitive, any increase in production costs could result in a dramatic decrease in market share. In addition, Kathy knew that a new job in her field would be hard to get, particularly if people knew that CornCo's production costs had increased under her management.

Questions

1. What product-related ethical issues are raised by this scenario?
2. What cultural norms and values (those of the United States and of the Third World countries) might influence Kathy's decision?
3. What laws might have an impact on the decision?
4. Which corporate rights or duties might be affected by each alternative decision?
5. What should Kathy do?

*This case is strictly hypothetical; any resemblance to real persons, companies, or situations is coincidental.

Advances in communication, technology, and transportation have shrunk the world, resulting in a new global economy. More countries are attempting to industrialize and compete internationally. Because of these trends, more companies are doing business outside their home countries. These activities and all business transactions across national boundaries are defined as global business. Global business brings together people and countries that have different cultures, values, and ethical standards. The international businessperson must not only understand the values, culture, and ethical standards of his or her own country but also be sensitive to those of other countries. Hence the multinational corporation becomes more complex in the way it must define and handle ethical situations. We first consider the different perceptions of corporate ethics, cultural differences, and cultural relativism. Then we examine multinational corporations and the ethical problems they face. We also discuss a universal, or common, set of ethical principles that is being accepted around the world. Finally, we highlight some of the major global ethical issues. As before, we do not offer absolute answers to the ethical issues. Rather, our goal is to help you understand how international business activities can create ethical conflict.

TABLE 10–1 Comparison of the Corporate Ethics of American Companies with Foreign Competitors

Country Compared to U.S. Corporations	Group	Better Than	Similar To	Worse Than	Don't Know
Japanese	Consumer	27%	33%	32%	8%
businesses	CEO	51%	28%	10%	8%
German	Consumer	26%	41%	17%	16%
businesses	CEO	31%	50%	3%	13%
Other industrialized	Consumer	37%	44%	9%	9%
countries	CEO	38%	45%	6%	9%
Third World	Consumer	63%	15%	10%	11%
countries	CEO	74%	4%	7%	12%

Source: Gene R. Laczniak, Marvin W. Berkowitz, Russell G. Brooker, and James P. Hale, "The Ethics of Business: Improving or Deteriorating?" *Business Horizons*, 38 (January–February 1995): 42.

ETHICAL PERCEPTIONS AND INTERNATIONAL BUSINESS

When businesspeople travel, they sometimes perceive different modes of operation abroad. For example, doing business in Russia may entail dealing with the local mafia. When Nikolai Lisai started to be successful in the computer software business, the mob offered to provide all the funds needed for a world-class operation. However, there was one catch: if he failed, they would kill him.[1]

Current research reveals that there is at least the perception in the United States that American companies are different from "them." Table 10–1 compares the perception regarding the corporate ethics of American companies with foreign competitors. Other research shows that Australian, Canadian, Chinese, and Thai companies differ in their ethics from U.S. ones.[2] In business, the perception that "we" differ from "them" is called the **self-reference criterion (SRC).** The SRC is an unconscious reference to one's own cultural values, experiences, and knowledge. When confronted with a set of facts, we react on the basis of knowledge that has accumulated over a lifetime and is usually grounded in the culture of our origin. Our reactions are based on meanings, values, and symbols that relate to our culture but may not have the same relevance to people of other cultures.

CULTURE AS A FACTOR IN BUSINESS

To examine the complexities of ethical decision making in the global arena, we must focus on the causes of conflict among people and organizations. One of the most difficult concepts to understand and apply to the business environment is culture. Because customs, values, and ethical standards vary from person to person, company to company, and even society to society, ethical issues that arise from international business activities often differ from those that evolve from domestic business activities. Distinctively international issues are often related to differences in cultures. Thus it is important to define and explore the concept of culture as it relates to the global setting.

Culture is defined as everything in our surroundings made by people, both tangible items and intangible concepts and values. Language, religion, law, politics, technology, education, social organization, general values, and ethical standards are all included in this definition. Each nation has a distinctive culture and, consequently, distinctive beliefs about what business activities are acceptable or unethical. Thus, when conducting international business, individuals encounter values, beliefs, and ideas that may diverge from their own because of cultural differences.

Cultural differences include differences in speech and body language. Problems of translation into another language often make it difficult for businesspeople to express exactly what they mean. For example, when a marketing research firm requested information on the annual German production of washers, it was surprised to receive figures on the production of small metal disks used in construction and plumbing. What it wanted was information about washing machines. Similarly, PepsiCo, Inc., experienced problems with translations of one of its advertising slogans, "Come Alive with Pepsi. " In Germany, the phrase was translated literally as "Come out of the grave"; in Asia it became "Bring your ancestors back from the dead."[3] Although blunders in communication may have their humorous side, they frequently offend or anger others, derail important business transactions, and even damage international business relations. For example, when an American bank was given a thirty-day option to purchase a Middle Eastern bank, the American buyer suggested in French that the loans be put into an escrow account, a common American practice. However, in French *escrow* translates to a gyp, or cheater. The local bank officials, insulted and upset, left the negotiating table and ultimately sold the bank to another group.[4]

Cultural differences in body language can also lead to misunderstandings. Body language is nonverbal, usually unconscious, communication through gestures, posture, and facial expressions. Americans, for instance, nod their heads up and down to indicate "yes," but in Albania this means "no," and in Britain it indicates that they hear, not that they agree. A commonplace gesture among Americans, pointing a finger, is considered very rude in Asia and Africa.[5] Personal space — the distance at which one person feels comfortable when talking with another — also varies from culture to culture. American and British businesspeople prefer a larger space than do South American, Greek, and Japanese. This difference can make people from different countries ill at ease with each other in their negotiations. Table 10–2 contains examples of gift giving behavior that may be construed as impolite or even unethical in certain regions of the world.

TABLE 10–2 It's Not the Gift That Counts, but How You Present It

Japan

■ Do not open a gift in front of a Japanese counterpart unless asked and do not expect the Japanese to open your gift.

■ Avoid ribbons and bows as part of gift wrapping. Bows as we know them are considered unattractive and ribbon colors can have different meanings.

■ Do not offer a gift depicting a fox or badger. The fox is the symbol of fertility; the badger, cunning.

Europe

■ Avoid red roses and white flowers, even numbers, and the number 13. Do not wrap flowers in paper.

■ Do not risk the impression of bribery by spending too much on a gift.

Arab World

■ Do not give a gift when you first meet someone. It may be interpreted as a bribe.

■ Do not let it appear that you contrived to present the gift when the recipient is alone. It looks bad unless you know the person well. Give the gift in front of others in less personal relationships.

Latin America

■ Do not give a gift until after a somewhat personal relationship has developed unless it is given to express appreciation for hospitality.

■ Gifts should be given during social encounters, not in the course of business.

■ Avoid the colors black and purple; both are associated with the Catholic Lenten season.

China

■ Never make an issue of a gift presentation — publicly or privately.

■ Gifts should be presented privately, with the exception of collective ceremonial gifts at banquets.

Source: Originally appeared in "International Business Gift-Giving Customs," previously published by the Gillette Company Stationery Products Group. Out of print.

Perceptions of time may likewise differ from country to country. Americans value promptness, but businesspeople from other lands approach negotiations in a more relaxed manner. An American firm lost a contract in Greece after it tried to impose its customs on the local negotiators by setting time limits for meetings. Greeks deem such limits insulting and lacking in finesse.[6] Americans, on the other hand, may view the failure to meet contractual obligations on a timely basis as an ethical issue.

When firms transfer personnel, cultural variations can turn into liabilities. Consequently, large corporations such as General Motors spend thousands of dollars per family to make sure that the employees they send abroad are culturally prepared. Seemingly innocuous customs of one country can be offensive or even dangerous in others. For example, one GM employee stationed in Kenya invited his managers to a business dinner at a local Nairobi restaurant and expected their wives to attend as well. However, married women in Kenya view restaurants as places frequented by prostitutes and marked by loose morals.[7]

Divergent religious values can also create ethical issues in international business. For instance, before a British fast-food hamburger chain entered the Indian market, its market research indicated a problem. The ruling class in India is predominately Hindu, and its members abstain from eating beef for religious reasons. Even though other Indian religions permit consumption of beef, the British firm decided to avoid giving offense and not use beef for its hamburgers. However, companies are not always so considerate of other cultures' values and mores.

One of the critical ethical issues linked to cultural differences is the question of whose values and ethical standards take precedence in negotiations and business transactions. When conducting business outside their own country, should businesspeople impose their own values, ethical standards, and even laws on members of other cultures? Or should they adapt to the values, ethical standards, and laws of the country in which they are doing business? As with many ethical issues, there are no easy answers to these questions.

ADAPTING ETHICAL SYSTEMS TO A GLOBAL FRAMEWORK: CULTURAL RELATIVISM

When asked how one succeeds in China, a senior salesperson from a German firm replied that he regularly pays up to $30,000 in order to get to see a decision maker. A Japanese company allegedly won a $320 million Middle Eastern contract by paying government officials $3 million. And in Indonesia, businesspeople complain that a payment to officials of $1,800 is needed to correctly process foreign work permits.[8] "When in Rome do as the Romans" or "You must adapt to the cultural practices of the country you are in" are the explanations businesspeople offer for straying from their own ethical values when doing business abroad. By defending the payment of bribes or "greasing the wheels of business" and other questionable practices in this fashion, they are resorting to **cultural relativism:** the concept that morality varies from one culture to another since business practices are defined as right or wrong by the particular culture. For instance, in Japanese business the custom has been to discriminate against women. "I had no chance to become an officer" or "It's the businessmen who have the power" are common remarks by Japanese women. In a 1995 survey of female job seekers in Japan, common reasons for rejection ranged from gender to leg size.[9] Cultural relativists feel that since sexual discrimination is within the Japanese tradition, it is ethical. In Hong Kong, a senior buyer explains that within the Chinese culture monetary gifts of 3 percent of sales are customary in some industries and hence deemed ethical. But when a buyer asked for 6 percent and this information was passed on to the company's president, the buyer was fired — not because he took the money, but because he had asked for more than was culturally acceptable, or ethical.

As with all philosophies, relativists ride a continuum. Some profess **ethical relativism:** the belief that only one culture defines ethical behavior for the whole globe, without exceptions. For the business relativist there may be no ethical standards except for the one in the transaction culture. The advantage of this belief is that those who hold it can always adjust to the ethics of the particular foreign culture. The disadvantage is that they may be in conflict with their own individual moral standards and perhaps with their own culture's values and legal system. As business becomes more global and multinational corporations proliferate, the chances of ethical conflict increase.

THE MULTINATIONAL CORPORATION

Multinational corporations (MNCs) are corporate organizations that operate on a global scale without significant ties to any one nation or region. It is not uncommon, for instance, to find a Mexican-based MNC, which operates in Venezuela, Puerto Rico, and the United States, dominating the markets with its products. MNCs represent the highest level of international business commitment and are characterized by a global strategy of investment, production, and distribution.[10] Examples of multinational corporations include Shell Oil Company, General Electric Co., Siemens, International Business Machines Corp., Lever Bros., Renault, and Exxon Corporation. As Table 10–3 shows, the United States is losing MNCs and Japan and Germany are creating them.

Because of their size and financial power, MNCs have been the subject of much ethical criticism, and their impact on the countries in which they do business has been hotly debated. Thus, U.S. labor unions argue that it is unfair for MNCs to transfer jobs overseas, where wage rates are lower. Other critics have charged that MNCs use laborsaving devices that increase unemployment in the countries where they manufacture. MNCs have also been accused of increasing the gap between rich and poor nations and of misusing and misallocating scarce resources. Their size and financial clout enable MNCs to control money supplies, employment, and even the economic existence of less-developed countries. In some instances, MNCs have controlled entire cultures and countries. Several Central American countries and the rubber economies of Malaysia and Liberia were almost totally dependent on companies such as Firestone Tire & Rubber Co. and United Fruit Company. On occasion, companies have even tried to redraw political boundaries, as when the Belgian mining company Union Minière S.A. helped finance the attempted breakaway of Katanga soon after Zaire (formerly Belgian Congo) at-

TABLE 10–3 The Nationalities of the World's 100 Largest Industrial Corporations (by country of origin)

	1963	1979	1984	1990	1993
United States	67	47	47	33	32
Germany	13	13	8	12	14
Britain	7	7	5	6	4
France	4	11	5	10	6
Japan	3	7	12	18	23
Italy	2	3	3	4	4
Netherlands–United Kingdom	2	2	2	2	2
Netherlands	1	3	1	1	1
Switzerland	1	1	2	3	3
Argentina	—	—	1	—	—
Belgium	—	1	1	1	—
Brazil	—	1	—	1	1
Canada	—	2	3	—	—
India	—	—	1	—	—
Kuwait	—	—	1	—	—
Mexico	—	1	1	1	1
Venezuela	—	1	1	1	1
South Korea	—	—	4	2	4
Sweden	—	—	1	2	1
South Africa	—	—	1	1	—
Spain	—	—	—	2	2
Turkey	—	—	—	—	1

Source: Adapted from "The World's 500 Largest Industrial Corporations," *Fortune*, July 25, 1994, pp. 137–144.

tained independence.[11] Joint-venture problems have also occurred, such as those between Borden and Japan's Meiji Milk Products company or between the Italian family conglomerate of the Agnellis and the French mineral-water company, Perrier, which the Agnellis sought to control. While the Perrier buyout was being attempted, the French public became aware of the Italian venture and found it culturally unacceptable.[12]

Critics believe that the size and power of MNCs create ethical issues related to the exploitation of both natural and human resources. One question is whether MNCs should be able to pay a low price for the right to remove minerals, timber, oil, and other natural resources and then sell products made from those resources for a much higher price. In many instances, only a small fraction of the ultimate sale price of such resources comes back to benefit the country of origin. This complaint led many oil-producing countries to form the Organization of Petroleum Exporting Countries (OPEC) in the 1960s to gain control over the revenues from oil produced in those lands.

Critics also charge that MNCs exploit the labor markets of host countries. Although some MNCs have been accused of paying inadequate wages, the ethical issue of fair wages is complicated. Sometimes MNCs pay higher wages than local employers can afford to match; then local businesses complain that the most productive and skilled workers go to work for multinationals. Measures have been taken to curtail such practices. For example, many MNCs are trying to help organize labor unions and establish minimum wage laws. In addition, host governments have levied import taxes to increase the price MNCs charge for their products and reduce their profits; they have also imposed export taxes to force MNCs to share more of their profits. Import taxes are meant to favor local industry as sources of supply for an MNC manufacturing in the host country. If such a tax raises the MNCs' costs, it might lead them to charge higher prices or accept lower profits, but such effects are not the fundamental goal of the law.

The activities of multinational corporations may also raise issues of unfair competition. Because of their diversified nature, MNCs can borrow money, using up all local capital resources so that little is left for local firms. MNCs have also been accused of not carrying an appropriate share of the cost of social development. They frequently apply advanced technologies that local companies cannot afford or cannot implement because of a lack of qualified workers. The MNCs thus become more productive and can afford to pay higher wages to workers. Because of their advanced technology, however, they hire fewer people than would be hired by the local firms that produce the same product. And, given their economies of scale, MNCs can also negotiate lower tax rates; by manipulating transfer payments among affiliates, they may pay little tax anywhere. The overall result is the claim that MNCs compete unfairly. For example, many heavy-equipment companies in the United States try to sell construction equipment to foreign companies that build major roads, dams, and utility complexes. They argue that this equipment will make it possible to complete these projects sooner, to the benefit of the country. Some less-developed countries counter that such equipment purchases remove hard currency from their economies and increase unemployment. Certain nations, such as India, believe that it is better in the long run to hire laborers to do construction work than to buy a piece of heavy equipment. The country keeps its hard currency in its own economy and creates new jobs, which increases the quality of life more than having a project completed sooner.

Although MNCs are not inherently unethical, their size and power often seem threatening to less-developed countries. The ethical problems that MNCs face arise from the conflicting demands made from opposing points of view. Differences in cultural perspectives may be as important as differences in economic interests. Because of their size and power, multinational corporations must take extra care to make ethical decisions that not only achieve their own objectives but also benefit the countries in which they manufacture or market their products. Even IBM and other premier MNCs

TABLE 10–4 Global Management Ethics

1993 Parliament of the World's Religions *The Declaration of a Global Ethic*	State of California *Handbook on . . . Moral and Civic Education . . .*	Michael Josephson *Character Counts, Ethics: Easier Said Than Done*
Nonviolence (love)	Morality	Trustworthiness
Respect for life	Truth	Honesty
Commitment	Justice	Integrity
Solidarity	Patriotism	Promise keeping
Truthfulness	Self-esteem	Loyalty
Tolerance	Integrity	Respect for others
Equal rights	Empathy	Responsibility
Sexual morality	Exemplary conduct	Fairness
	Reliability	Caring
	Respect for family, property, law	Citizenship

William J. Bennett *The Book of Virtues*	Thomas Donaldson *Fundamental International Rights*	Rushworth W. Kidder *Shared Values for a Troubled World*
Self-discipline	Physical movement	Love
Compassion	Property, ownership	Truthfulness
Responsibility	No torture	Fairness
Friendship	Fair trial	Freedom
Work	Nondiscrimination	Unity
Courage	Physical security	Tolerance
Perseverance	Speech and association	Responsibility
Honesty	Minimal education	Respect for life
Loyalty	Political participation	
Faith	Subsistence	

Source: Andrew Sikula, Sr., *Applied Management Ethics* (Irwin, Burr Ridge, Ill, 1996), p. 127. Reprinted by permission.

sometimes find themselves in ethical conflict. For example, IBM's reputation has been tarnished in Argentina by alleged kickbacks to government officials to obtain a $250 million contract to modernize the country's banking system.[13] If the allegations are true, IBM would be subject to prosecution under the Foreign Corrupt Trade Practices Act. Hence in the United States the practice becomes a societal instead of just a business ethics decision.

A UNIVERSAL SET OF ETHICS

Many theorists have tried to establish a set of global or universal ethical standards. Table 10–4 lists six books and documents that show a pattern of shared values — such as truthfulness, integrity, fairness, and equality — within the world. When applied to global business, these values constitute a universal set of ethics. From these lists William Frederick, a business ethicist, has developed five areas, which he calls the Moral Authority of Transnational Corporate Codes.[14] This global corporate code (see Table 10–5) mirrors what many governments are now attempting to coordinate with MNCs and others. The code's five universal business areas are employee practices and policies; basic human rights and fundamental freedoms; consumer protection; environmental protection; and political payments and involvement. Finally, the Caux Round Table in Switzerland, in collaboration with business leaders in Europe, Japan, and the United States, has created an international ethics code (see Table 10–6). By reviewing many of the laws enacted around the world, it becomes apparent that many of the values described have been codified. Fraud, for instance, has a universal definition. In 1996, when Mexican banking regulators found that Carlos Cabal Peniche was making millions of dollars of loans to himself from his bank, they too considered the action fraudulent. Before Cabal left the country, he had built for himself a $2 billion banking and fruit empire and was putting together a $1 billion bid for the Del Monte Foods Corporation.[15] The shared values assume that we all have basic rights and responsibilities that must be adhered to when doing business.

If there is a universal set of ethics, why then do businesses have problems understanding what is ethical and unethical? The answer lies partially in how these basic rights and responsibilities are operationalized, or put into use. When someone from another culture mentions integrity or democracy, listeners look reassured. However, when these concepts are explained, differences surface. For example, in both Japan and the United States honesty is valued. Part of honesty is operationalized, or made tangible, by trust. In Japan's banking industry, people demonstrated that trust by hiring retired Japanese bureaucrats to become auditors, directors, executives, and presidents. The practice is known as *amakudari,* or "descent from heaven." The rationale was that because these men were so trusted, nothing bad or unethical would happen to the banks. The relationship between regulated and regulator became fuzzy because the regulators implicitly trusted their former superiors. In the United States, businesspeople may trust former superiors, but they also understand that there should always be a separation between those who regulate and those who are regulated. The Japanese implementation of trust may have been proved erroneous as the country tries to deal with a $356 billion bad-loan problem, which many believe had been caused by these former governmental officials.[16] Although honesty, charity, virtue, and doing good to others may be qualities that are universally agreed on, the differences in implementing them can cause problems.

In the next section we discuss some common global ethical issues that arise when companies do business internationally. Our list should not be taken as complete, but only as a sampling of the complexity of ethical decision making in the global arena.

TABLE 10–5 The Moral Authority of Transnational Corporate Codes

I. Employment Practices and Policies

1. MNCs should not contravene the manpower policies of host nations. [ILO]
2. MNCs should respect the right of employees to join trade unions and to bargain collectively. [ILO; OECD; UDHR]
3. MNCs should develop nondiscriminatory employment policies and promote equal job opportunities. [ILO; OECD; UDHR]
4. MNCs should provide equal pay for equal work. [ILO; UDHR]
5. MNCs should give advance notice of changes in operations, especially plant closings, and mitigate the adverse effects of these changes. [ILO; OECD]
6. MNCs should provide favorable work conditions, limited working hours, holidays with pay, and protection against unemployment. [UDHR]
7. MNCs should promote job stability and job security, avoiding arbitrary dismissals and providing severance pay for those unemployed. [ILO; UDHR]
8. MNCs should respect local host-country job standards and upgrade the local labor force through training. [ILO; OECD]
9. MNCs should adopt adequate health and safety standards for employees and grant them the right to know about job-related health hazards. [ILO]
10. MNCs should, minimally, pay basic living wages to employees. [ILO; UDHR]
11. MNCs' operations should benefit lower-income groups of the host nation. [ILO]
12. MNCs should balance job opportunities, work conditions, job training, and living conditions among migrant workers and host-country nationals. [Helsinki]

II. Basic Human Rights and Fundamental Freedoms

1. MNCs should respect the rights of all persons to life, liberty, security of person, and privacy. [UDHR; ECHR; Helsinki; ILO; TNC Code]
2. MNCs should respect the rights of all persons to equal protection of the law, work, choice of job, just and favorable work conditions, and protection against unemployment and discrimination. [UDHR; Helsinki; ILO; TNC Code]
3. MNCs should respect all persons' freedom of thought, conscience, religion, opinion and expression, communication, peaceful assembly and association, and movement and residence within each state. [UDHR; ECHR; Helsinki; ILO; TNC Code]
4. MNCs should promote a standard of living to support the health and well-being of workers and their families. [UDHR; Helsinki; ILO; TNC Code]
5. MNCs should promote special care and assistance to motherhood and childhood. [UDHR; Helsinki; ILO; TNC Code]

III. Consumer Protection

1. MNCs should respect host-country laws and policies regarding the protection of consumers [OECD; TNC Code]
2. MNCs should safeguard the health and safety of consumers by various disclosures, safe packaging, proper labelling, and accurate advertising. [TNC Code]

IV. Environmental Protection

1. MNCs should respect host-country laws, goals, and priorities concerning protection of the environment. [OECD; TNC Code; Helsinki]
2. MNCs should preserve ecological balance, protect the environment, adopt preventive measures to avoid environmental harm, and rehabilitate environments damaged by operations. [OECD; TNC Code; Helsinki]
3. MNCs should disclose likely environmental harms and minimize risks of accidents that could cause environmental damage. [OECD; TNC Code]
4. MNCs should promote the development of international environmental standards. [TNC Code; Helsinki]
5. MNCs should control specific operations that contribute to pollution of air, water, and soils. [Helsinki]
6. MNCs should develop and use technology that can monitor, protect, and enhance the environment. [OECD; Helsinki]

V. Political Payments and Involvement

1. MNCs should not pay bribes nor make improper payments to public officials. [OECD; TNC Code]
2. MNCs should avoid improper or illegal involvement or interference in the internal politics of host countries. [OECD; TNC Code]
3. MNCs should not interfere in intergovernmental relations. [TNC Code]

Key

The United Nations Universal Declaration of Human Rights (1948) [Abbreviated as UDHR]

The European Convention on Human Rights (1950) [ECHR]

The Helsinki Final Act (1975) [Helsinki]

The OECD Guidelines for Multinational Enterprises (1976) [OECD]

The International Labor Office Tripartite Declaration of Principles Concerning Multinational Enterprises and Social Policy (1977) [ILO]

The United Nations Code of Conduct on Transnational Corporations (Not yet completed nor promulgated but originating in 1972.) [TNC Code]

Source: Reprinted with permission from Business Ethics Magazine, 52 S. 10th St. #110, Minneapolis, MN 55403

TABLE 10–6 The Caux Round Table Business Principles of Ethics

PRINCIPLE 1. The Responsibilities of Businesses: Beyond Shareholders Toward Stakeholders

The value of a business to society is the wealth and employment it creates and the marketable products and services it provides to consumers at a reasonable price commensurate with quality. To create such value, a business must maintain its own economic health and viability, but survival is not a sufficient goal.

Businesses have a role to play in improving the lives of all their customers, employees, and shareholders by sharing with them the wealth they have created. Suppliers and competitors as well should expect businesses to honor their obligations in a spirit of honesty and fairness. As responsible citizens of the local, national, regional, and global communities in which they operate, businesses share a part in shaping the future of those communities.

PRINCIPLE 2. The Economic and Social Impact of Business: Toward Innovation, Justice, and World Community

Businesses established in foreign countries to develop, produce, or sell should also contribute to the social advancement of those countries by creating productive employment and helping to raise the purchasing power of their citizens. Businesses also should contribute to human rights, education, welfare, and vitalization of the countries in which they operate.

Businesses should contribute to economic and social development not only in the countries in which they operate, but also in the world community at large, through effective and prudent use of resources, free and fair competition, and emphasis upon innovation in technology, production methods, marketing, and communications.

PRINCIPLE 3. Business Behavior: Beyond the Letter of Law Toward a Spirit of Trust

While accepting the legitimacy of trade secrets, businesses should recognize that sincerity, candor, truthfulness, the keeping of promises, and transparency contribute not only to their own credibility and stability but also to the smoothness and efficiency of business transactions, particularly on the international level.

PRINCIPLE 4. Respect for Rules

To avoid trade frictions and to promote freer trade, equal conditions for competition, and fair and equitable treatment for all participants, businesses should respect international and domestic rules. In addition, they should recognize that some behavior, although legal, may still have adverse consequences.

PRINCIPLE 5. Support for Multilateral Trade

Businesses should support the multilateral trade systems of the GATT/World Trade Organization and similar international agreements. They should cooperate in efforts to promote the progressive and judicious liberalization of trade, and to relax those domestic measures that unreasonably hinder global commerce, while giving due respect to national policy objectives.

PRINCIPLE 6. Respect for the Environment

A business should protect and, where possible, improve the environment, promote sustainable development, and prevent the wasteful use of natural resources.

PRINCIPLE 7. Avoidance of Illicit Operations

A business should not participate in or condone bribery, money laundering, or other corrupt practices; indeed, it should seek cooperation with others to eliminate them. It should not trade in arms or other materials used for terrorist activities, drug traffic, or other organized crime.

PRINCIPLE 8. Customers

We believe in treating all customers with dignity, irrespective of whether they purchase our products and services directly from us or otherwise acquire them in the market. We therefore have a responsibility to:

- provide our customers with the highest quality products and services consistent with their requirements;
- treat our customers fairly in all aspects of our business transactions, including a high level of service and remedies for their dissatisfaction;
- make every effort to ensure that the health and safety of our customers, as well as the quality of

their environment, will be sustained or enhanced by our products and services;

- assure respect for human dignity in products offered, marketing, and advertising; and
- respect the integrity of the culture of our customers.

PRINCIPLE 9. Employees

We believe in the dignity of every employee and in taking employee interests seriously. We therefore have a responsibility to:

- provide jobs and compensation that improve workers' living conditions;
- provide working conditions that respect each employee's health and dignity;
- be honest in communications with employees and open in sharing information, limited only by legal and competitive restraints;
- listen to and, where possible, act on employee suggestions, ideas, requests, and complaints;
- engage in good faith negotiations when conflict arises;
- avoid discriminatory practices and guarantee equal treatment and opportunity in areas such as gender, age, race, and religion;
- promote in the business itself the employment of differently abled people in places of work where they can be genuinely useful;
- protect employees from avoidable injury and illness in the workplace;
- encourage and assist employees in developing relevant and transferable skills and knowledge; and
- be sensitive to serious unemployment problems frequently associated with business decisions, and work with governments, employee groups, other agencies and each other in addressing these dislocations.

PRINCIPLE 10. Owners/Investors

We believe in honoring the trust our investors place in us. We therefore have a responsibility to:

- apply professional and diligent management in order to secure a fair and competitive return on our owners' investment;

- disclose relevant information to owners/investors subject only to legal requirements and competitive constraints;
- conserve, protect, and increase the owners/investors' assets; and
- respect owners/investors' requests, suggestions, complaints, and formal resolutions.

PRINCIPLE 11. Suppliers

Our relationship with suppliers and subcontractors must be based on mutual respect. We therefore have a responsibility to:

- seek fairness and truthfulness in all of our activities, including pricing, licensing, and rights to sell;
- ensure that our business activities are free from coercion and unnecessary litigation;
- foster long-term stability in the supplier relationship in return for value, quality, competitiveness, and reliability;
- share information with suppliers and integrate them into our planning processes;
- pay suppliers on time and in accordance with agreed terms of trade;
- seek, encourage, and prefer suppliers and subcontractors whose employment practices respect human dignity.

PRINCIPLE 12. Competitors

We believe that fair economic competition is one of the basic requirements for increasing the wealth of nations and, ultimately, for making possible the just distribution of goods and services. We therefore have a responsibility to:

- foster open markets for trade and investment;
- promote competitive behavior that is socially and environmentally beneficial and demonstrates mutual respect among competitors;
- refrain from either seeking or participating in questionable payments of favors to secure competitive advantages;
- respect both tangible and intellectual property rights; and

TABLE 10–6 The Caux Round Table Business Principles of Ethics (continued)

- refuse to acquire commercial information by dishonest or unethical means, such as industrial espionage.

PRINCIPLE 13. Communities

We believe that as global corporate citizens, we can contribute to such forces of reform and human rights as are at work in the communities in which we operate. We therefore have a responsibility in those communities to:

- respect human rights and democratic institutions, and promote them wherever practicable;
- recognize government's legitimate obligation to the society at large and support public policies and practices that promote human development through harmonious relations between business and other segments of society;

- collaborate with those forces in the community dedicated to raising standards of health, education, workplace safety, and economic well-being;
- promote and stimulate sustainable development and play a leading role in preserving and enhancing the physical environment and conserving the earth's resources;
- support peace, security, diversity, and social integration;
- respect the integrity of local cultures; and
- be a good corporate citizen through charitable donations, educational and cultural contributions, and employee participation in community and civic affairs.

Source: Caux Round Table in Switzerland, "Principles for Business," special advertising supplement contributed as a public service by Canon, *Business Ethics* (May–June, 1995): 35.

ETHICAL ISSUES AROUND THE GLOBE

Major ethical issues that complicate international business activities include sexual and racial discrimination, price discrimination, bribery, harmful products, prison labor, the Foreign Corrupt Practices Act, cartels, and telecommunications.

Sexual and Racial Discrimination

As noted in Chapter 4, various U.S. laws prohibit American businesses from discriminating on the basis of sex, race, religion, or disabilities in their hiring, firing, and promotion decisions. However, the problem of discrimination is certainly not limited to the United States. In the United Kingdom, East Indians have traditionally been relegated to the lowest-paying, least-desired jobs. Australian aborigines have long been the victims of social and economic discrimination. In many Southeast Asian and Far Eastern countries, employees from particular ethnic backgrounds may not be promoted. In Japan, although women are beginning to make inroads into the business and political worlds, they are seldom promoted to high-level positions.[17] For example, Yuka Hashimoto had been hired by Fuji Bank and put on a fast track in bond trading. However, she also has to wear a bright pink suit and serve tea to office guests, something her male colleagues never do. Although Japan now has made sex discrimination illegal, there are no penalties for violations.[18]

In many Middle Eastern nations, businesswomen are a rarity. Often Middle Eastern women must wear special clothing and cover their faces; in public, they may be physically separated from men. Since many Middle Eastern countries prescribe only nonbusiness roles for women, companies negotiating with Middle Eastern firms have encountered problems in using women sales representatives. Indeed, a Middle Eastern company may refuse to negotiate with saleswomen or may take an unfavorable view of foreign organizations that employ them. The ethical issue in such cases is whether foreign businesses should respect Middle Eastern values and send only men to negotiate sales transactions, thus denying women employees the opportunity to further their careers and contribute to organizational objectives. The alternative would be to try to maintain their own ideas of social equality, knowing that the women sales representatives will probably be unsuccessful because of cultural norms in those societies.

Racial discrimination has been a much-discussed issue in the United States. For example, a few years ago the city of Los Angeles reversed itself on a $115 million contract for high-technology trolley cars. Initially the contract was awarded to the Sumitomo Corporation of Tokyo. However, through an "America First" campaign, partly instigated by the Morrison Knudsen Corporation, anti-Japanese sentiment was inflamed so much that Los Angeles rescinded its order and added a stipulation that all transit cars must now be built in the community. Meanwhile, Morrison Knudsen gained contracts in other cities, amounting to more than $255 million. Many industry observers believe Knudsen was chosen over Japanese competition to avoid the furor that arose in Los Angeles.[19] Racial discrimination is also apparent in Germany, which will not grant citizenship to Turkish workers, even though some of them are second-generation German residents. It can also be seen in the glass ceiling that exists in Japan for Japanese Koreans in business.

Price Discrimination

The pricing of products sold in other countries also creates ethical issues. A frequently debated issue in international business is **price discrimination,** which occurs when a firm charges different prices to different groups of consumers. Price differentials are legal if they do not substantially reduce competition or if they can be justified on the basis of costs — for example, the costs of taxes and import fees associated with bringing products into another country. However, price discrimination may be an ethical issue, or even be illegal, under the following conditions: (1) the practice violates either country's laws; (2) the market cannot be divided into segments; (3) the cost of segmenting the market exceeds the extra revenue from legal price discrimination; and (4) the practice results in extreme customer dissatisfaction.

When a market is artificially divided into segments that are charged different prices, an inequality can emerge that cannot be explained by added costs, thus creating an ethical concern. In some cases, such pricing policies may be judged illegal when courts rule that they substantially decrease competition. In the United States, price discrimination that harms competition is prohibited under the Robinson-Patman Act. In other countries, judgments of illegality result from precedent or fairness rulings.

When companies market their products outside their own countries, the costs of transportation, taxes, tariffs, and other expenses can raise the prices of the products. However, when the price increase exceeds the costs of these additional expenses, an ethical issue emerges. Increasing prices in this way is sometimes referred to as **gouging.** For example, Hoffman LaRoche Inc. was asked to explain why it charged very high prices for its drugs Librium and Valium in Germany. Authorities in Australia, New Zealand, Canada, the Netherlands, South Africa, and Sweden also complained about the prices of the drugs.[20] Most countries have laws forbidding companies to charge exorbitant prices for lifesaving products, which include some pharmaceuticals. However, these laws do not apply to products that are not lifesaving, even if they are in great demand and have no substitutes, as was the case with Librium and Valium.

In contrast, when companies charge high prices for products sold in their home markets while selling the same products in foreign markets at low prices that do not cover all the costs of exporting the products, the practice is known as **dumping.** Dumping is unethical if it damages competition or hurts firms and workers in other countries. It becomes illegal under many international laws if it substantially lessens or reduces competition. For example, Mitsui & Co., Ltd., was convicted of falsifying documents and using kickbacks to dump steel in the United States. Mitsui attempted to mask its dumping by importing wire rope from the United States and putting that label on its steel. It then gave its U.S. customers a $1.3 million rebate that was equal to the difference between the nominal and actual exchange rates. Hitachi, Ltd., Melix of Poland, Sanyo Mfg. Corp., Toshiba Corporation, and many other companies have also been accused of dumping.[21]

Dumping may occur for several reasons. Charging low prices allows a company to enter a market quickly and capture a large market share. Sometimes dumping occurs when the domestic market for a firm's product is too small to support an efficient level of production. In other cases, technologically obsolete products that are no longer salable in the country of origin are dumped overseas. Dumping is difficult to prove, but even the suspicion of dumping can lead to the imposition of import quotas, which can hurt innocent firms.

Price differentials, gouging, and dumping create ethical issues because some groups of consumers have to pay more than a fair price for products. Pricing is certainly a complicated issue in international marketing because of the additional costs imposed by tariffs, taxes, customs fees, and paperwork. Nonetheless, corporations should take care to price their products to recover legitimate expenses and earn a reasonable profit while competing fairly.

TABLE 10–7 Major Types of Bribes

Facilitating payments	Disbursements of small amounts in cash or kind as tips or gifts to minor government officials to expedite clearance of shipments, documents, or other routine transactions. Examples: In India, not a single product can move if the clerk's palm is not greased with cash. In Italy, distribution of *bustarella* (an envelope containing a small amount of money) helps to move products into and out of the country more efficiently.
Middlemen commissions	Appointments of middlemen (agents and consultants) to facilitate sales in a nonroutine manner, and payment of excessive allowances and commissions to them, not commensurate with the normal commercial services they perform. Often, the middlemen may request that part or all of their commissions be deposited in a bank in a third country. Example: Northrop Corporation's payment of $30 million in fees to overseas agents and consultants, some of which was used for payoffs to government officials to secure favorable decisions on government procurement of aircraft and military hardware.
Political contributions	Contributions that take the form of extortion because they violate local law and custom. Also payments that, while not illegal, are made with the specific intent of winning favors directly or indirectly. Example: Gulf Oil Corporation's payment of $3 million in 1971 to South Korea's Democratic Republican party under intimidation and threat.
Cash disbursements	Cash payments made to important people through slush funds or in some other way, usually in a third country (i.e., deposit in a Swiss bank) for different reasons, such as to obtain a tax break or a sales contract, or to get preferential treatment over a competitor. Example: United Brands' payment of $2.5 million to Honduran officials for the reduction of export tax on bananas via Swiss bank accounts.

Source: Peter J. LaPlaca, ed., *The New Role of the Marketing Professional* (American Marketing Association, 1978), pp. 138–145.

Bribery

In many cultures, giving bribes — also known as **facilitating payments** — is an acceptable business practice. In Mexico, a bribe is called *la mordida*. South Africans call it *dash*. In the Middle East, India, and Pakistan, *baksheesh*, a tip or gratuity given by a superior, is widely used. The Germans call it *schimengeld*, grease money, and the Italians call it *bustarella*, a little envelope. Table 10–7 describes the major types of bribes and what one might see them called in the global business community. Companies that do business internationally should be aware that bribes are an ethical issue and that the practice is more prevalent in some countries than in others. Bribes or payoff requests are frequently associated with large construction projects, turnkey capital projects, and large commodity or equipment contracts. Northrop Corporation, for example, was under investigation for employing a secret lobbyist,

TABLE 10–8 Factors Responsible for Bribes

Home Country Factors

Costs of doing business in certain countries
An established practice in certain countries, no other way to get around
Encouragement by Pentagon to buy "influence" to pursue Atlantic Alliance
Importance of hiring middlemen services in certain countries — to bridge gap
   between medieval aristocracies and modern corporations
Increasing competition in international markets
Pressure from top management to achieve results
Opportunity to protect undercover operations via Swiss banks

Host Country Factors

Lure of easy money
Political involvement in decision making
Token of appreciation
Friendly gesture
Fair "business" deal
Pressure from vendors

Source: Peter J. LaPlaca, ed., *The New Role of the Marketing Professional,* American Marketing Association, 1978, pp. 138–145.

who allegedly bribed Korean officials in an effort to obtain a sales contract for the company's F-20 fighter planes. Some $6.25 million was deposited in a Hong Kong bank. Northrop executives claimed that the money was intended to help build a Korean hotel.[22]

Table 10–8 describes several factors that help explain why people give or accept bribes and groups them into two categories: home and host country. Many businesspeople view bribes as a necessary cost of conducting business in certain countries. A study commissioned by Pitney Bowes Inc. revealed that one out of every five executives surveyed believed that bribes should be paid if they are the practice in the host country; others disagree.[23] IBM has been accused of providing bribes to Argentinian officials, which, it says, headquarters knew nothing about. As one of those under suspicion commented, "Our honesty was always a tremendous plus and now our reputation for honesty has been destroyed."[24] Once a company starts paying bribes in one country, other countries will expect the same, regardless of the culture.

Harmful Products

In the advanced industrialized nations, governments have banned the sale of certain products that are considered harmful. However, some companies based in advanced nations continue to sell such products in other countries where they are still legal. For example, several pesticides, such as Velsic Phosvel and 2 4-D (which contains dioxin), have been banned in the United States but are still sold directly or indirectly to other countries. These chemicals are suspected carcinogens or mutagens. The manufacturers of these products argue that, given the food shortages in some nations, the benefits of using the pesticides to increase crop yields outweigh the health risk. Profits are a further motivation, of course. When American Vanguard Corporation was barred from selling the pesticide DBCP directly to American companies, it continued to export it to other nations, explaining its decision as follows:

> Notwithstanding all the publicity and notoriety surrounding DBCP, it was [our] opinion that a vacuum existed in the marketplace that [we] could temporarily occupy, [and we] further believed that with the addition of DBCP, sales might be sufficient to reach a profitable level.

According to a former executive, American Vanguard would have gone bankrupt if it had not been able to sell DBCP in other countries.[25]

A similar ethical issue relates to the exportation of tobacco products to less-developed countries. Cigarette sales in the United States are declining in the face of stricter tobacco regulations and increasing evidence that smoking causes a number of illnesses and medical problems. In addition, there are signs that cigarette smoking is becoming socially unacceptable in the United States. As U.S. sales decline, tobacco companies have increased their efforts to sell cigarettes and other tobacco products in other countries, particularly the less-developed ones. The overseas sales volume of Philip Morris Company Inc., the leading U.S. cigarette marketer, is 65 percent larger than the volume of domestic sales and is growing nearly 8 percent annually.[26] The ethical issue becomes whether tobacco marketers should knowingly sell in other countries a product that is considered harmful in their home country. Recent testimony has linked Brown and Williamson Tobacco Corporation to empirical knowledge about the addictive properties of cigarettes and even revealed that the company had added coumarin (an active compound in rat poison and a lung-specific carcinogen) to pipe tobaccos.[27]

Many consumers in underdeveloped countries view tobacco as good, both physically and economically. They argue that the tobacco industry provides jobs and stimulates economies and that cigarette consumers enjoy smoking. Many also cite low longevity rates as a reason to discount the health hazards of tobacco. In the long run, however, as industrialization raises the standard of living in less-developed countries, in turn increasing longevity rates, those countries may change their views on tobacco. As people live longer and the health hazards begin to cost both the people and government more in time and money, ethical issues will increase.

The dumping of waste materials into less-developed countries is also becoming an issue, especially when countries and communities do not know the contents of the trash. Although Africa and Latin America have banned the trade in trash, the People's Republic of China has not. Its companies supposedly purchase the garbage for its residual metals, plastics, and other useful material. By using cheap labor, they are able to make a profit. But when one deals in garbage, things happen. For example, when the Jiangsu Province imported wastes, they poisoned the public water supply until a 150-square-kilometer "black tide" passed downriver.[28] With cheap labor in Cambodia, Vietnam, and Laos, the global garbage business will continue to inflict long-term harm on other peoples. ·

At times products that are not harmful in some countries become harmful to consumers in others because of illiteracy, unsanitary conditions, or cultural values. For example, products marketed by the Nestlé Corporation include infant formulas, which are used in the supplemental feeding of infants and have been tested as safe when used correctly. When the company introduced its product into African countries as an alternative to breast-feeding, local mothers quickly adopted the product. However, as time passed, infant mortality rates rose dramatically. Investigators found that, because of high illiteracy rates, many mothers were not able to follow instructions for using the formula correctly. In addition, the water used for mixing with the powdered formula was often unsafe, and poor mothers also diluted the formula to save money, which reduced the nutritional value of the feeding. Nestlé was further criticized for its aggressive promotion of the infant formula; the company employed so-called milk nurses to discourage mothers from breast-feeding by portraying the practice as primitive, and to promote Nestlé's infant formulas instead. Under heated pressure from international agencies and boycotts by consumer groups, Nestlé agreed to stop promoting the infant formula; it also revised its product labeling and educational materials to point out the dangers of using the formula incorrectly and the preferability of breast-feeding.[29] After a period of time, however, the company reverted to its previous practices, and as of 1996 the World Health Organization has renewed the boycott. Thus even traditionally safe and adequately tested products can create ethical issues when a marketer fails to evaluate foreign markets accurately or to maintain adequate responses to health problems associated with their products in certain markets.

The Foreign Corrupt Practices Act

Since 1977 the U.S. **Foreign Corrupt Practices Act (FCPA)** has prohibited American corporations from offering or providing payments to officials of foreign governments for the purpose of obtaining or retaining business abroad. Violators of the FCPA face corporate fines of up to $1 million, while company executives face a maximum of five years in prison or $10,000 in fines, or both. The FCPA does permit small "grease" payments to foreign ministerial or clerical government employees. Such payments are exempted because of their size and the assumption that they are used to persuade the recipients to perform their normal duties, not to do something critical to the distribution of new goods and services.

Between 1977 and 1980 only ten cases were brought to trial. No prison sentences resulted, and only one $50,000 fine has been levied. Some critics of the FCPA say that although the law was designed to foster fair and equal treatment to all, it places American firms at a disadvantage in the international business arena. The FCPA applies only to American businesses; other nations have not imposed such restraints on their companies doing business abroad. For example, if three companies — from the United States, France, and Korea — were bidding on a dam-building project in Egypt, the French and Korean firms could bribe Egyptian officials in their efforts to acquire the contract, but it would be illegal for the American firm to do so. Thus the issue of bribery sets the values of one culture — the U.S. disapproval of bribery — against those of other cultures.

When the FCPA was enacted, the Securities and Exchange Commission (SEC) established a voluntary disclosure program. As a result of the program, more than 400 corporations, including 117 of the *Fortune* 500, reported making more than $300 million in facilitating payments and other types of bribes. In 1988 the **Omnibus Trade and Competitiveness (OTC) Act** reduced FCPA legislation in the following ways: lobbying, "reason to know," facilitating payments, affirmative defenses, and the repeal of the Eckhardt Amendment. The Eckhardt Amendment prevented senior managers from using agents or employees as scapegoats when bribes were given. The new act makes prosecution even more difficult, thus decreasing the power and applicability of the FCPA in global business settings.

Telecommunications

With the advent of satellites, e-mail, and the Internet, information can be accessed in a matter of seconds instead of weeks. Information overload and Internet slowdowns are becoming more common around the globe. With the ease of information access come ethical issues, which can differ by country, and no geographic or time barriers exist. For example, copyright laws were established to protect originators of products and services. However, as use of the Internet and electronic bulletin boards spread, it has become difficult to enforce country-specific laws. Electronic bulletin boards commonly display copyrighted material. Walt Disney, H & R Block, and most of the news corporations are already finding it hard to protect their materials. Lawyers representing these companies point out that litigation is effective only against large on-line services such as America Online. "Cyberspace is so vast that there is a risk-reward ratio," said one attorney.[30] Many companies, such as Viacom and Time Warner, worry that enhanced technology will have an even greater impact on copyright infringement. For example, the motion-picture industry fears that new devices that make digital copies of movies will give rise to some who market the films via the Internet's 3.2 million computers.

The speed of global communications has also affected the fashion industry. Imitations have always been a problem, with "knockoffs" usually entering the market a few months behind the originals and then by way of a few retailers. The situation has changed dramatically. For example, a fashion show by the Italian designer Gianni Versace in Milan featured a $1,232 rubberized-silk minidress and a $1,370 pink "safety-pin" dress. Months before these dresses were made available by the designer, Macy's and other large retailers had ordered and received look-alikes at less than 25 percent of Versace prices.[31] A photograph can be taken at a fashion show in Milan and faxed overnight to a Hong Kong factory; the next day a sample garment is sent by Federal Express to a New York showroom for retail buyers. Stores order these lower-priced "interpretations" for their own private-label collections and sometimes even show the costlier designer versions at the same time. Since competition in the malls is fierce and fashion merchandise is highly perishable, the industry has become very competitive. Some designers are countering these imitations by suing and by bringing out affordable knock-off versions before anyone else can.

Questionable financial activities, such as money laundering, have been made easier by global telecommunications. **Money laundering** means that illegally received funds are transferred or used in a financial transaction so as to conceal their source or ownership or facilitate an "illegal" activity. Money laundering can be legal depending on the countries involved and their interpretations of each other's statutes. A decade ago actual paper currency such as dollars, francs, or British pounds would have to be converted by smuggling. Now drug traffickers and others move funds through wire transfers and checks that are sent to other countries. Money laundering has grown so extensive that when a drug sale is completed in the United States a "controller" auctions the money to "brokers," who bid about 85 cents on the dollar for $10 to $20 million bundles. Brokers have two weeks to return 85 percent of the cash to their clients. In a number of instances, law firms have been used because of the legal limitations on their records, i.e., the courts cannot subpoena their records. One such case in the United States involved a banking and entertainment person, who received a phone call from the Cali cocaine cartel threatening to cut him and his family to pieces unless he cooperated. His testimony helped uncover a $100 million money-laundering scheme and implicated a former law professor.

SUMMARY

Global business involves the development, promotion, pricing, and distribution of goods and services across national boundaries. The global businessperson must not only understand the values, culture, and ethical standards of his or her own country but also be sensitive to those of other countries. Culture is defined as everything in our surroundings made by people, both tangible items and intangible concepts, including language, law, religion, politics, technology, education, social organizations, and general values and ethical standards. Each nation has a different culture, and hence different beliefs about what business activities are acceptable or unethical. Cultural differences that create ethical issues in international business include differences in language, body language, time perception, and religion.

According to cultural relativism, morality varies from one culture to another, and business practices are defined as right or wrong by the particular culture. Ethical relativism, on the other hand, assumes that only one culture defines ethical behavior for the whole world.

Multinational corporations (MNCs) are companies that operate on a global scale without significant ties to any one nation or region. Because of their size and financial power, MNCs can have a serious impact on the countries where they do business, which may create ethical issues.

When applied to global business, certain shared values — such as truthfulness, integrity, fairness, and equality — constitute a universal set of ethics. From it a global corporate code, called the Moral Authority of Transnational Corporate Codes, has been developed. It covers five universal business areas: employee practices and policies; basic human rights and fundamental freedoms; consumer protection; environmental protection; and political payments and involvement. The Caux Round Table has also created an international ethics code.

Major global ethical issues range from sexual and racial discrimination, price discrimination, and bribery (also known as facilitating payments) to harmful products and telecommunications. Although U.S. laws prohibit American companies from discrimination in employment, discrimination in other countries is often justified on the basis of cultural norms and values. Price discrimination creates an ethical issue and may be illegal when the practice violates either country's laws; when the market cannot be segmented or the cost of segmenting exceeds the extra revenue from legal price discrimination; or when the practice results in customer dissatisfaction. When companies market their products outside their own countries, the costs of transportation, supplies, taxes, tariffs, and other expenses can raise the prices of the products. However, when the foreign price of a product exceeds the full costs associated with exporting, the ethical issue of gouging exists. When companies sell products in their home markets at high prices while selling the same products in foreign markets at low prices that do not cover the full costs of exporting, the practice is known as dumping. Price differentials, gouging, and dumping create ethical issues because some groups of consumers have to pay more than a fair price for products.

The U.S. Foreign Corrupt Practices Act (FCPA) prohibits American businesses from offering or providing payments to officials of foreign governments for the purpose of obtaining or retaining business. The Omnibus Trade and Competitiveness (OTC) Act reduced FCPA legislation and has made prosecution and applicability of the FCPA in global business settings nonthreatening.

Advances in telecommunications have intensified such ethical issues as copyright infringement and unauthorized duplication of fashion designs. They have also made it easier to carry out questionable financial activities — notably, money laundering, which involves transferring illegally received money or using it in financial transactions so as to conceal the source or ownership or to facilitate an "illegal" activity.

A REAL-LIFE SITUATION

David's job at B&B Pharmaceutical was to recycle or find new markets for prescription medications that had reached the maturity phase of their product life cycle. The maturity phase is reached when sales begin to peak and then decline because of newer medications introduced into the marketplace. David was in charge of five drugs, including Cholerend, a drug used to prevent cholera in chickens. Cholera, a bacterial disease, results in severe gastrointestinal symptoms and can be fatal. B&B was replacing Cholerend with a new, lower-cost drug with fewer side effects. David was also responsible for Predicort, a human health drug, which had been used in England but was rejected by the Food and Drug Administration for use in the United States because of its side effects (loss of body hair, nausea, and double vision).

David had been extremely fortunate in landing a job with B&B. With a degree in business and several medical course electives to his credit, he convinced B&B that it would be more practical to hire a person like himself, who had more interpersonal and managerial skills than technical knowledge, than to train a nurse or other medically skilled person in business skills. After three and a half years at B&B, David was an up-and-coming star and had recently gained his new position. His job demanded that he work sixty-hour weeks and be away from his family two weeks a month.

David began to look for new markets for Cholerend. After much research and contacting various agricultural departments, he learned that several countries — Mexico, Argentina, Iran, and Brazil — had chicken production facilities similar to U.S. facilities. Consequently, the chicken growers in these countries had some of the same problems with chickens dying of cholera. If he could penetrate these markets, it would boost sales for the company and also save about a thousand U.S. jobs. Getting into Brazil and Argentina was just a matter of red tape. Even if 10 percent of all shipments would be confiscated and resold by government officials — which was likely — Cholerend would still produce a healthy profit. In Mexico, however, the Ministry of Agriculture used a different approach. David realized that not only would part of each shipment (approximately 5 percent) be held for testing and then resold by the government, but that he also would have to pay several government officials small sums of money (less than $1,000 each) to ensure that each shipment arrived at its destination on time. In Iran, the company would have to ship through a Moslem country and have the drug repackaged with the country-of-origin label changed to that particular country. These procedures were due, in part, to trade sanctions between the United States and Iran. Although shipping and handling costs would be higher, sales of Cholerend to Iran would still net B&B a large profit.

While David was developing his distribution strategies, he was given data that showed that a drug derived from Cholerend was safe for humans and had been used successfully in the treatment of obesity; taken before meals, the drug decreased the appetite. David submitted the appropriate paperwork on the Cholerend derivative to the FDA and, six months later, the derivative was approved for the treatment of obesity and eating disorders. With millions of obese people as potential customers, David followed a skimming pricing strategy — that is, he charged the highest price possible relative to the drug's demand. As a result of David's pricing strategy and some foreign market penetration, manufacturing capacity for Cholerend and the Cholerend derivative doubled, which created two thousand new U.S. jobs.

David's other drug, Predicort, was a different matter. After doing some research, he developed a two-tier strategy. First, the drug would be sold to countries that had lower quality standards than those of the United States — countries such as India, China, and many African countries. For sales to the African countries, the drug was discounted relative to the available funds of each nation. In China and India, B&B would sell the rights to manufacture Predicort and receive a small percentage of sales. The result of this sec-

ond strategy would, however, lower the quality of the drug, thereby increasing the risk of each side effect proportionately.

Everything was going well until David was called into the office of B&B's president. Bob Evans had managed B&B for the last ten years and had risen through the ranks. The meeting was one of "damage control." David didn't understand what the problem was.

"Well," Bob said, "Some of our target clientele for the Cholerend derivative have discovered that it costs no more to make than the Cholerend we've been manufacturing for years, and they want to know why it's costing them $1,020 a year to use it."

David responded, "As you know, Mr. Evans, the strategy I chose was a skimming one. It reflects the demand/supply equation to yield optimal profitability."

"I know," said Bob. "But now we've got some special-interest groups complaining. They want to know why it costs 25 cents a year to treat a chicken and $1,020 a year to treat a human. I want you to develop a strategy that keeps profits up but gives the public the perception that we are an ethical drug company."

Questions

1. Discuss the ethical issues.

2. What type of ethical climate or ethical corporate culture exists at B&B?

3. What moral philosophies might David and Bob hold?

4. What pricing strategy would you develop for the Cholerend derivative for human use?

5. Identify social responsibility issues, if any exist.

IMPORTANT TERMS FOR REVIEW

self-reference criterion
(SRC)
culture
cultural relativism
ethical relativism
multinational corpora-
tions (MNCs)
price discrimination

gouging
dumping
facilitating payments
Foreign Corrupt Practices Act
(FCPA)
Omnibus Trade and Competitiveness
(OTC) Act
money laundering

PART TWO

Cases

Hershey Foods' Ethics and Social Responsibility

ershey Foods Corporation is the number-one confectioner in North America. The Hershey Chocolate U.S.A. Division, the nation's largest chocolate producer, makes up approximately 44 percent of the U.S. chocolate industry. In 1995 Hershey had record sales and profits: $3.7 billion and $282 million, respectively.

Hershey manufactures more than fifty-five brands of confectionery products, including such familiar brands as Hershey's milk chocolate bar, Hershey's syrup, Hershey's cocoa, Almond Joy, Mr. Goodbar, Hershey's Kisses, Kit Kat, and Reese's peanut butter cups. In its Confectionery Division, Hershey sells ready-to-eat puddings in four candy-bar flavors. The Hershey Pasta group, the second largest pasta producer in the United States, manufactures regionally distributed brands of pasta, including San Giorgio, Skinner, and Ronzoni. The confectionery companies Mars and Nestlé are Hershey's major competitors.

Milton Hershey was born in 1857 and was of Pennsylvania Dutch descent. He became an apprentice to a candy maker in 1872, at age 15. By age 30, Hershey had begun the Lancaster Caramel Company. He visited the Chicago Exhibition in 1893 and became interested in a new chocolate-making machine. He sold the caramel factory and built a large chocolate factory in Derry Church, Pennsylvania, in 1905, and the city was renamed Hershey in 1906. Hershey pioneered modern confectionery mass-production techniques by developing much of the machinery for making and packaging his milk chocolate products.

From the beginning, Milton Hershey was concerned about doing what was right. His firm was built with high standards of fairness, integrity, honesty,

This case was prepared by O. C. Ferrell for classroom discussion rather than to illustrate either effective or ineffective handling of an administrative, ethical or legal decision by management.

and respect. Hershey also believed in fairness to consumers, and he provided the highest-quality mass-market product. Everything he did was based on what he believed to be the highest ethical standards. These standards influenced his relationship with his community, customers, and employees.

COMMUNITY FOCUS

An example of his concern for the community was the founding of an orphanage, the Hershey Industrial School (now called the Milton Hershey School), in 1909. Many of the children who attended the school became Hershey employees, and former Hershey chairman, William Dearden (1976–1984), was one of them. Today the ten-thousand-acre school houses and provides education for nearly twelve hundred socially disadvantaged children. Although Hershey is now a public company, the school is supported by a trust that owns 42 percent of Hershey Foods. This stock ownership provides substantial dividends to offset the costs of operating the school. In addition, the Hershey trust owns 77 percent of the Hershey Foods' voting shares and 100 percent of the Hershey Entertainment and Resort Company, a theme park developed by Milton Hershey.

Another example of the company's commitment to youth is its sponsorship of the Hershey's National Track and Field Youth Program. Hershey Foods also supports the Children's Miracle Network, a national program benefiting children's hospitals across the United States. Furthermore, employees may have their gifts to institutions of higher learning matched via an employee gift-matching program. Hershey contributes more than $6 million in cash, products, and services to a variety of charities every year.

It is often said that Milton Hershey was more concerned with benevolence than with profits. He put people to work when they were unemployed and did everything possible to treat his employees fairly. During the Great Depression of the 1930s, Hershey hired people to construct a hotel, golf courses, a library, theaters, a museum, a stadium, and other facilities in Hershey, Pennsylvania. In 1995 the U.S. Postal Service announced that it had agreed to issue a commemorative stamp to honor Milton Hershey for his many philanthropic deeds. Hershey joins Thomas Jefferson, Jack London, Margaret Mitchell, Buffalo Bill Cody, and Sitting Bull among those honored in the "Great American" stamp series.

HERSHEY'S VALUES AND ETHICS PROGRAM

The strong value system put in place by Milton Hershey is still the guiding philosophy of Hershey Foods today. His system dictates that all employees conduct their business in an ethical manner. Whereas some companies mount codes of ethics on the wall or display other outward appearances of ethical standards, Hershey's ethical values are an integral part of the corporate culture. Employees know that their company will support them as long as they focus on quality, integrity, and honesty. All Hershey employees are made aware of specific policies that provide guidance for handling ethical issues. Specific policies also exist for relationships with stakeholders, suppliers, employees, and customers. The following statements are Hershey Foods' corporate philosophy:

- Honesty, integrity, fairness and respect must be key elements in all dealings with our employees, shareholders, customers, consumers, suppliers and society in general.

- Our operations will be conducted within regulatory guidelines and in a manner that does not adversely affect our environment.

- Employees will be treated with respect, dignity and fairness.

- Our ongoing objective is to provide quality products and services of real value at competitive prices that will also insure an adequate return on investment.

Each year the company distributes the "Key Corporate Policies" booklet to all employees. The booklet consists of the organization's statement of corporate philosophy and policies regarding the use of corporate funds, resources, and conflict of interest; the antitrust law prohibition on price fixing; trading in Hershey Foods and other related securities; and the personal responsibilities of employees. Employees are asked to review the policies carefully, then sign, date, and return a certification card, which states that the employee has read, agrees with, and "will adhere to Hershey Foods Corporation's 'Key Corporate Policies.'"

Hershey employees with questions concerning proper policy or conduct are instructed to consult their supervisor first, but if the supervisor is deemed a problem, there are alternatives. Antitrust questions are referred to the legal department. Questions about ownership or stock purchases are directed to the corporate secretary's office. The human resources office handles personnel problems. Employees also have the right to go to any corporate or division officer. In addition, employees can call an 800 number, which has the following message:

> You have reached the Hershey Foods' employee concern line. This forum is provided for Hershey Foods' employees without fear of retribution or reprisal as long as this call is made in good faith. If you choose to remain anonymous, please provide specific and detailed information pertaining to your concern. If you would like your call returned, please leave your name and number and you will be contacted by . . . within forty-eight hours. If you would feel more comfortable expressing your concern in writing, address your letter to. . . . Your concern will be reviewed and, if warranted, a confidential investigation will be conducted. Please begin speaking after you hear the tone. You will have three minutes to deliver your message. Thank you for calling the concern line.

CONCERN FOR CUSTOMERS AND EMPLOYEES

Hershey has always emphasized quality products and good relationships with consumers. Today Hershey's Quality Assurance Division makes certain that customers get full value for their money. By using the highest-quality ingredients and numerous quality-control checks, the firm even ensures that the right number of almonds go into each Almond Joy.

The company values employee cultural diversity and is able to attract and retain the most qualified employees. Hershey is a corporate sponsor of the National Minority Supplier Development Council, which seeks to expand business opportunities for minority-owned businesses. The company was also recently cited for an innovative program to promote healthier employee lifestyles.

Ethics and social responsibility are not just words at Hershey; they are an important part of the corporate culture and the way business is conducted on a daily basis. All managers go through ethics-training programs to make sure that they understand how to handle the many complex issues they deal with in operating the company. Employees have a clear idea of the company's ethical values and know they will be supported in following them. The company continues to be the most profitable company in the confectionery market; it has outperformed the stock market over the last ten years.

Questions

1. What impact did Milton Hershey's personal moral philosophies have on the Hershey corporate philosophy of ethics in use today?

2. How has social responsibility at Hershey helped the company attain success?

3. Identify what you believe to be the most significant ethics or social responsibility program at Hershey today. Why do you believe it is so significant to the company?

4. What can other firms learn from Hershey's ethical and social responsibility actions?

These facts are from "Hershey Foods Announces Fourth Quarter Results," *PR Newswire,* January 26, 1996; "'Hershey Boys' Push for Postal Stamp," *Charleston Daily Mail,* October 2, 1995, p. 10A; Karen Riley, "Harmful Pleasures Put You at Risk of Paying More for Health Coverage," *Washington Times,* April 22, 1995, p. C1; "The Business Week 1,000," *Business Week,* Special Bonus Issue, 1992, p. 128; Gary Hoover, Alta Campbell, and Patrick J. Spain, *Hoover's Handbook* (Austin, Tex.: California Publishers Group West, 1991), p. 287; "Hershey Foods Philosophy and Values," Hershey Foods Corporation videotape (1990); "A Tradition of Excellence," Hershey Foods Corporation, August 1990; and Steven S. Ross, "Green Groceries," *Mother Jones,* 14 (February–March 1989): 48–49.

R.E.M. and Hershey Foods Corporation Resolve a Conflict

Hershey Foods Corporation, in an effort to promote its Kit Kat candy bar, offered a sweepstakes contest for which the prizes were either a trip for two to the R.E.M. concert at Hershey Park Stadium, or a new compact disc by R.E.M. However, it has long been a tradition of the alternative music group R.E.M. to avoid corporate sponsorship or endorsements of any kind, citing that this type of crass commercialism is entirely inappropriate and inconsistent with their philosophy. R.E.M. filed a civil action lawsuit against Hershey and its agents, citing violations of trademark infringement and fraudulent misrepresentation.

R.E.M.: ITS MUSIC AND ITS REPUTATION

R.E.M. formed as a group while the four members were students at the University of Georgia in Athens, playing their first gig at a party in April 1980. During the past several years R.E.M. has developed a national and international reputation and has grown into one of the premier musical groups in the world. R.E.M. has released nine albums, which have worldwide sales in excess of 30 million units. Their first album, *Murmur,* was given four stars by *Rolling Stone* and described as intelligent, enigmatic, deeply involving, and revealing a depth and cohesiveness of the band. *Rolling Stone,* in fact, named *Murmur* its album of the year and R.E.M. Best New Artist in 1989. Subsequent releases from the band garnered similar praise from the music world, as well as from other sources. The *Christian Science Monitor* in June 1995

This case was prepared by Phylis Mansfield for classroom discussion rather than to illustrate either effective or ineffective handling of an administrative, ethical, or legal decision by management.

described R.E.M. as "America's hottest rock band . . . the patriarch of alternative rock . . . admired by other bands since the 1980s." R.E.M. has received a significant number of awards in the United States, including Grammy Awards and MTV Music Awards, as well as international awards, including multiple Brit Awards for best international band. The group has won other professional awards throughout the world.

While other bands of similar talent have gone by the wayside, R.E.M. has prevailed by focusing on what is important to them as individuals and as a collective group. At least some of the band's longevity and popularity is related to its music. R.E.M. seems to focus on its work, the music, rather than on the band members themselves or on the latest fad. Concentrating on being leaders in the music world rather than followers, at least one band member, Peter Buck, cites their individuality and resolve as a group to do what they feel is right, as a contributing factor to their success. "R.E.M. have insisted on retaining creative control over every aspect of their careers, from concert dates to album-cover designs to videos. . . . It's not like we're asking for the brown M&M's to be taken out of the dish. We want the power of our lives in our own hands. We made a contract with the world that says: 'We're going to be the best band in the world; you're going to be proud of us. But we have to do it our way.'"

R.E.M.'S VIEW ON CORPORATE SPONSORSHIP

Part of doing it their way is avoiding corporate sponsorship and product endorsements, which they have managed to do since their inception as a group in 1980. While other bands have provided endorsements for tours, appearances, songs, and albums, R.E.M. has refused to participate in what could be extremely lucrative agreements, citing their personal views of the action as offensive and inappropriate. *Billboard* in 1994 commented that "through the years, R.E.M. has been able to find success while retaining its artistic integrity." In the *Los Angeles Times,* Robert Hilburn noted that "after eight studio albums R.E.M. stands with its original independence and vision intact."

This independence is partly due to R.E.M.'s credibility, or "cred."* Credibility in the music-world sense is the "widespread perception that an artist, band or individual has the respect of the population at large, as well as its peers. In rock and roll, credibility has always been a desirable quality." Credibility doesn't end with the musical performance, however; it includes integrity in attitude, integrity in regard to the audience, and remaining true to one's beliefs. Alternative rock bands such as R.E.M., Pearl Jam, and Nirvana have sold as many records as mainstream groups partly because of their credibility.

---

*Gina Arnold, "Cashing in on Cred," *San Francisco Chronicle,* January 22, 1995.

It is difficult to determine the amount of money that R.E.M. has turned down from commercial endorsements over the years since it does not track such information. Recently R.E.M. refused an offer from Microsoft to use R.E.M.'s song "It's the End of the World as We Know It" in Microsoft's worldwide brand campaign. Instead, Microsoft settled on the Rolling Stones' song "Start Me Up," reportedly for a fee of close to $12 million.

R.E.M. has continued to reject corporate sponsorship for its tours. *Amusement Business* quotes R.E.M.'s booking agent as saying that it is the only band to go to Singapore, Taiwan, and Hong Kong without any sponsor affiliation, including airlines and hotels. In addition, the band has a detailed contractual agreement with the concert promoter, which requires prior written approval for the use of the name, logo, photograph, or likeness of the group in connection with any commercial enterprise. Even the concert tickets have specific language that is subject to prior approval. These limitations, which appear in every R.E.M. agreement, have been enforced since the band's inception in 1980. At that time R.E.M. acquired rights to a federal trademark and servicemark for its own use for entertainment, services, recordings, and clothing. The public knows that R.E.M. is the source of the goods and services bearing its name and mark. And the public accords this mark additional value because of the band's credibility.

HERSHEY'S ADVERTISING BACKGROUND

Hershey's sales exceed $3 billion in the United States and approach $4 billion worldwide. Hershey's Kit Kat wafer bar is one of the best selling candy bars in this country and is currently third behind Snickers (M&M/Mars) and Reese's peanut butter cups (Hershey). Founded in 1893 by Milton Hershey, the company was one of the first chocolate manufacturers in the United States. Milton Hershey lived until 1945, and during his lifetime refused to let the firm advertise, believing that quality would speak for itself. The company continued his no-advertising policy after his death, until 1970.

In 1992, largely due to the strength of a spirited advertising campaign tied to its sponsorship of the Olympics, Hershey pulled out in front of M&M/Mars. Now it is an experienced advertiser; it spent more than $120 million on advertising in 1994. Hershey directs a significant portion of its promotional expense to sponsorships. In 1995 it sponsored the NCAA Final Four tournament, marketing with a multibrand promotion linked to the NCAA games. As a new NCAA corporate partner in 1995, Hershey promoted special offers on all Hershey loose candy bars, and it launched in-store promotions giving customers a shot at a trip to the annual college hoop championship. The Hershey and Reese's lines, along with other Hershey brands such as Kit Kat, Mounds, and Almond Joy, were flagged in-store with displays. As part of store giveaways, retailers received basketballs and jackets with Final Four logos, as well as tickets to the Final Four games. In 1994

Hershey had activated its existing sponsorship of the NFL with a similar retail promotion. Its other sports tie-ins include a NASCAR sponsorship and a figure-skating package for its Hershey Kisses product line.

Promotional tie-ins are typical in modern advertising. Such tie-ins suggest to consumers an affiliation between the corporate sponsor and the object of the tie-in. Consumer perception of an association between sponsor and event or group is valued by the company because it can benefit from the goodwill possessed and generated by the other party. Recently, sponsorship has turned to rock concert events in order to tap the lucrative high school and college-age markets. Advertisers use celebrity endorsements to promote their products, realizing that the greater the number of people who recognize the celebrity, the greater the visibility for the product. This onslaught of advertisers on the music industry was featured in a front-page story in *Billboard* entitled "Madison Avenue Eyes Modern Rock, But Acts Remain Wary."

HERSHEY'S KIT KAT PROMOTION

In August 1995 Hershey was promoting its Kit Kat candy bar and advertising on rock music stations. In Atlanta, the radio advertisement included the following:

> Kit Kat wants to give you a chance to win a trip for two to the September 30th R.E.M. concert at Hershey Park Stadium or one of 25 copies of R.E.M.'s latest CD. Be among the first 10,000 people to call 1-800-[number] with your name and complete address and you'll be in the running for the Kit Kat concert trip to Hershey, Pennsylvania. That's 1-800-[number]. Phone lines close August 18th. No purchase necessary. Continental U.S. residents, eighteen plus. For details send a self-addressed, stamped envelope to: Kit Kat Rules, Box 535, Seaford, New York, 11783.

The radio commercial was aired on stations that played a generic rock music piece, which sounded like R.E.M.'s; but no R.E.M. music was used. The generic piece, along with the text of the radio commercial, suggested a link with R.E.M. It may have implied R.E.M.'s involvement and possibly sponsorship or affiliation with Hershey's Kit Kat contest. The message that callers heard on the 800 number may well have reinforced this impression. It began with "Welcome to the Kit Kat R.E.M. concert at Hershey Park Stadium sweepstakes line" and continued with the same specifics about the prizes as the radio ad.

THE CONFLICT BETWEEN R.E.M. AND HERSHEY

R.E.M. considered Hershey's actions an infringement of its trademark and servicemark, a dilution of and injury to the R.E.M. business reputation, and misappropriation of identity under the Lanham Act. Citing that among the major elements of R.E.M.'s success are its credibility with fans and its integrity in conducting its business affairs, R.E.M. reiterated that its name and music were not for sale. It charged Hershey with exploiting the magnetism of the R.E.M. name for commercial purposes and thus tarnishing the name and the band's artistic integrity. According to R.E.M., Hershey did not seek authorization for use of the R.E.M. name because it was aware that such authorization would not be granted for product endorsements. R.E.M. also claimed that, because of its public stance against doing product endorsements, the strong suggestion of a link between Kit Kat and R.E.M. in Hershey's ad would lead the public to believe that the band's members are hypocrites.

LEGAL IMPLICATIONS

R.E.M.'s lawsuit charged that Hershey's false and misleading representations created a likelihood of confusion and caused damage to R.E.M.'s business, reputation, and the goodwill extended to it by the public. According to the lawsuit, Hershey's actions violated Section 43(a) of the Lanham Act, U.S. Code 1125.

R.E.M. asserted that Hershey also misappropriated the name and likeness of R.E.M. for its own gain. Unlike other causes of action for an invasion of privacy, a corporation may have similar rights and remedies as a private individual under misappropriation. R.E.M. asserted that Hershey appropriated the goodwill and reputation, commercial standing, and corporate identity of the R.E.M. name — as well as the personal identity of the band's members — for its own use. Since, according to R.E.M., Hershey's conduct was causing and was likely to cause substantial injury to R.E.M., R.E.M. considered itself entitled to injunctive relief and to recover damages, including the fair market value of its services and injury to its goodwill, professional standing, and future publicity value, as well as Hershey's profits, and reasonable attorneys' fees.

In its suit, R.E.M. asked that Hershey and its agents be restrained from engaging in any of these activities:

1. Using the mark "R.E.M." in commercial advertising
2. Expressly or by implication representing to the public that Hershey is in any way connected or associated with R.E.M., including sponsorship
3. Passing off its goods as endorsed or approved by R.E.M.
4. Distributing any promotional materials bearing the R.E.M. name or mark
5. Diluting the distinctive quality of the R.E.M. name or reputation
6. Engaging in violations of Section 43 of the Lanham Act and state statutes against false advertising

7. Otherwise infringing on the R.E.M. mark or unfairly competing in any manner whatsoever.

R.E.M. also asked that Hershey be required to deliver up for destruction all inventory, literature, brochures, or other materials that bear the R.E.M. name or likeness.

CONFLICT RESOLUTION

The lawsuit did not proceed, however, because all the parties involved decided to settle the matter out of court. The settlement included the following points:

1. R.E.M. and Hershey would issue a joint press release announcing that the dispute between them had been amicably resolved.

2. Hershey and its agents, including its advertising agency, agreed not to use the R.E.M. name in connection with any commercial endorsement or promotion without prior written approval.

3. Although the prizes offered in the promotional contest would be awarded, neither Hershey nor its agents would make use of the list of names obtained through the contest 800 number or of any other information obtained in connection with the promotion.

4. Westwood One, the radio affiliate, would contribute $50,000 for distribution to ten charitable entities designated by R.E.M.

Questions

1. Do you think that celebrities should own their "identities" and be able to protect them from the promotional activities of others?

2. Discuss the difference between the legal issues and the ethical issues in this case.

3. Discuss any ethical concerns about the technique used by Hershey and its agents to gain R.E.M. contest entrants.

4. Hershey Food Corporation has an excellent ethical compliance program and has a history of being a model ethical and socially responsible company (see Case One). What organizational factors and/or relationships with its agents caused this ethical conflict? How can Hershey prevent this type of conflict in the future?

These facts are from Debbie Gilbert, "R.E.M.: Why They're Still Around," *The Memphis Flyer,* November 2, 1995, p. 13; Gina Arnold, "Cashing in on Cred," *San Francisco Chronicle,* January 22, 1995; Robert Sandall, "Sponsorship's Rocky Road," July 2, 1995, p. 16; *Amusement Business,* November 1994; Linda Corman, "All About Chocolate," *New York Times,* February 21, 1993, sec. 3, p. 10; and *R.E.M./Athens, Ltd., Plaintiff* v. *Hershey Foods Corporation, Defendant,* August 1995, verified complaint (civil action court document obtained through America Online).

Dow Corning's Breast Implants

Dow Corning Corp., a fifty-fifty joint venture between Dow Chemical Co. and Corning, Inc., has long been viewed as a pioneer in corporate ethics. Dow recognized the importance of moral issues early and was among the first businesses to develop an ethics program, described by some as the most elaborate in corporate America. The program performs audits to monitor company compliance with rules and regulations and communicates with its employees about ethics. Despite its emphasis on ethics, Dow Corning came under fire in 1992 for problems related to its silicone breast-implant product. As of early 1996, the company was still dealing with the aftermath of its breast implant problems.

THE HISTORY OF SILICONE BREAST IMPLANTS

During the Second World War, Corning Glass and Dow Chemical developed liquid silicone as a substitute for rubber for use as an insulator in transformers. From that research, a revolutionary idea emerged. During the war, Japanese prostitutes allowed the injection of liquid silicone directly into their breasts to increase their bustline. By the 1960s silicone injections had spread to the United States, but the trend slowed when the long-term results of the silicone injections became known: The silicone liquid migrated to other parts of the body, causing lumpy breasts, scars, and, in extreme cases, death.

After the health risks became apparent, the U.S. Food and Drug Admin-

This case was prepared by John Fraedrich, Dawn Yoshizumi, and Terry Gable for classroom discussion rather than to illustrate either effective or ineffective handling of an administrative, ethical or legal decision by management. Research assistance was provided by Gwyneth M. Vaughn.

istration (FDA) outlawed silicone injections. Doctors at Dow Corning continued to research the process in an effort to find a safer alternative. In 1962 two doctors at Dow Corning, Frank Gerow and Thomas Cronin, developed a new technique, using a silicone gel wrapped in a thin silicone polymer envelope; the envelope was then implanted into the breast. Dow Corning began marketing the new product in 1963. Initial reactions to breast implants were positive, and the "silicone gel in the sandwich bag" was implanted in over 2 million American women by 1992. About 80 percent of women with implants had them done for cosmetic reasons; the other 20 percent, as reconstructive surgery after mastectomies. However, the procedure was not risk free, and complications soon emerged. Many health problems are now being blamed on the silicone implants, and the FDA placed a moratorium on them in January 1992.

HEALTH HAZARDS

The health risks associated with breast implants are still coming to light and raising concern among women who have them. The dangers include adverse reactions to the silicone gel; rupturing gel sacs, which allow the gel to flow to other parts of the body; and the role implants play in preventing early detection of breast cancer. An estimated 10 percent of the women with implants have experienced a condition called capsular contracture, in which the body reacts to the silicone by producing a fibrous tissue around the implant, causing the breast to harden. If the silicone gel migrates to other parts of the body and interacts with bodily organs and fluids, it can affect the body's immune system and connective tissues, causing immune system disorders, arthritis, debilitating fatigue, swollen lymph nodes, or lupus. Some studies have found that silicone used in other medical products, such as tubes, valves, clips that close fallopian tubes in sterilization surgeries, penile prostheses, intraocular lenses, and tubing for blood oxygenators and dialysis machines, also presents health hazards.

The subject of silicone implants is so sensitive and controversial that some doctors are reluctant to do breast surgery to remove the silicone sacs from women who are not yet experiencing any immediate detrimental side effects from their implants. And many women are filing lawsuits against Dow Corning because they believe the breast implants are endangering their health.

TESTING ETHICS

While preparing for one of those lawsuits, Attorneys Nancy Hersh and Dan Bolton of the firm Hersh & Hersh researched Dow Corning's testing process and found evidence suggesting that Dow knew of the potential health hazards of its silicone gel products. Patient files contained complaints of gel envelopes rupturing and silicone migrating to other parts of the body. The envelope used to contain the gel was permeable and allowed the gel to bleed out, and the migrating silicone often affected the body's immune system.

Bolton claims to have found evidence that Dow Corning knew the silicone gel had an adverse effect on the immune system when conflicting reports over the same testing process emerged. Dow Corning had tested the effect of the silicone gel implants in dogs. One version of reports presented to the FDA indicated that the implants did not affect the future health of the dogs and that their lives were normal. A second set of scientific reports that Dow Corning did not present to the FDA stated that all thirty-eight dogs faced chronic inflammation after receiving the silicone implants.

Internal memos from Dow Corning further suggest concerns about the safety of the silicone gel. A Dow Corning engineer, Thomas D. Talcott, who helped develop the silicone gel used in the implants, warned that the polymer sac could rupture and leak the silicone gel, thereby posing serious health threats. His warnings went unheeded, however, and in 1976 he resigned in protest from Dow Corning. In 1977 another employee addressed his concerns in a memo claiming that fifty-two of four hundred implants had resulted in ruptures. There is no evidence that Dow Corning took any corrective actions following these warnings. On the contrary, it has been suggested that Dow Corning conducted few safety studies, and the studies that were done were not comprehensive.

Testing the effects of silicone on the body's immune system is not easy because each body is different and reacts differently to various situations. Furthermore, it is difficult to determine what a representative sample is when testing the effects of silicone on the human body.

One scientist who questioned Dow Corning's testing claimed he had found a direct linkage between the silicone in breast implants and disorders of the immune system. But Dow Corning rebuffed his efforts to continue researching the linkage in order to determine the safety of the implant procedure. Studies done by Dr. John Paul Heggers of the University of Texas at Galveston suggested that the human body reacts to the silicone in breast implants by producing antibodies against it, and the antibodies attack not only the silicone, but also the body's own tissues associated with the silicone.

Further evidence against silicone implants came from Dr. Steven Weiner of the School of Medicine at the University of California at Los Angeles (UCLA). He has treated women with implants who have experienced immune disorders. He reported that there is no solid evidence to prove that the implants cause any health hazards, but that a majority of his patients' conditions improved after their implants were removed. A UCLA colleague, Dr. Nir Kossovsky, claimed that silicone is not the direct cause of the immunal disorders but that the body reacts to the silicone by producing proteins resulting in an autoimmune reaction. That reaction then spills over to the rest of the body, indirectly causing other health problems.

Dow Corning countered these findings by arguing that its own research results disagreed with those that found a link between the immune system and the silicone. Dow said that medical studies support the safety of the silicone gel, and the company specifically stated that it "disagreed with Dr. Heggers' scientific approach to the problem."

MORE PROBLEMS FOR DOW CORNING

When Dow Corning was deluged with implant lawsuits in 1992, more than forty insurers balked at paying claims for liability coverage policies sold to the company between 1962 and 1985; they argued that Dow Corning had misrepresented the litigation risks posed by the implants. They also cited previous allegations made against Dow Corning regarding inadequate implant testing procedures and the firm's production and marketing of the product in spite of evidence questioning its safety.

In March 1995 Dow Corning announced that it was contributing $2 billion to a lawsuit settlement fund designed to end massive litigation against it and other implant marketers. In May 1995 it filed for bankruptcy court protection, partly on the basis that it could not pay the billions of dollars in outstanding consumer claims against it without the money it felt it was owed from its insurers. As a result of the filing, more than nineteen thousand outstanding lawsuits against the company were put on hold until Dow Corning's problems regarding its financial and legal capabilities and responsibilities could be resolved. The bankruptcy filing also brought into question the status of the $4.25 billion industry lawsuit settlement fund.

Dow Corning eventually sued the insurance companies for their refusal to pay claims related to the lawsuits against it. After a three-month trial, in February 1996 a Michigan jury returned a verdict in favor of Dow Corning. The jury found neither misrepresentation nor concealment of any significant facts that might have affected Dow Corning's ability to obtain insurance.

According to a Dow Corning spokesperson, the forthcoming insurance proceeds, estimated at between $700 million and $1 billion, would make more money available to compensate women pursuing liability claims against the company. A Dow Corning attorney pointed out that the verdict bolsters Dow Corning's contention that the implants are safe and that there is no scientific proof of their causing disease. Regarding the latter assertion, lawyers for women with outstanding lawsuits against Dow Corning have expressed concern that the verdict could hurt their cases should they come to trial since the jury found that the company did not withhold information on product risks, a key allegation in most of the lawsuits. This concern has not lessened despite an earlier ruling, by a Nevada court in October 1995, that the Dow Chemical Company was solely liable for health problems caused by Dow Corning's breast implants. In that case, the jury awarded a Nevada woman $14 million in compensatory and punitive damages. The Nevada verdict had raised hopes that other claimants would soon receive damage payments from Dow Corning or its larger joint owner, Dow Chemical, but these hopes proved to be premature. They were further undercut when attorneys for the insurance companies announced that they would appeal the Michigan verdict that made them responsible for paying claimants.

Just weeks before the Michigan verdict, Dow Corning announced its fourth-quarter profits for 1995 had risen 21.5 percent, to $39.6 million, because of strong overseas sales. However, the company also announced that it had lost over $30 million for the year as a result of a $221 million after-tax charge in the second quarter, reflecting an accounting change related to the breast-implant litigation settlement fund. It was the second straight year of losses for the firm; in 1994 it had posted a $6.8 million dollar loss when it took a $152 million charge for implant litigation.

Dow Corning used to pride itself on being a leader in business ethics, but manufacturing and marketing silicone gel implants with possible health risks tarnished its excellent reputation.

Questions

1. What are the ethical issues related to a product that can alter the human body? Breast implants alter the body and could affect the results of a mammogram or have an impact on lactating women. Is it up to women to decide whether the risk outweighs vanity, or is it the manufacturer's duty to be socially responsible toward its clients and therefore sell a safe product, or not sell the product at all?

2. Consumers make the final decision to have surgery for problems that are not life-threatening. Given the risks involved when a foreign substance is put into the body, who bears the responsibility of potential hazards: The consumer, for making the final decision? The surgeon, for not discouraging the procedure? Or the manufacturer, for making the option available? (Assume that all know the risks involved.)

3. Dow Corning was praised for its ethics program prior to the silicone gel implant controversy. How valid are the reports of the whistle blowers and internal memos today if they were deemed unimportant in 1976?

4. Given the Michigan jury's finding that Dow Corning did not misrepresent product risks to liability insurers, should the company now be free of further legal responsibility and charges of ethical wrongdoing? What is the parent company's — Dow Chemical's — responsibility in the case, as evidenced by the Nevada court finding?

These facts are from Geoffrey Cowler, "Silicone: Juries vs. Science," *Newsweek,* November 13, 1995, p. 75; "Dow Corning Insurers Must Pay Up, Jury Says," *Los Angeles Times,* February 15, 1996, p. D1; Barnaby J. Feder, "Dow Corning in Bankruptcy over Lawsuits," *New York Times,* May 16, 1995, p. A1; "Financial Digest," *Washington Post,* February 3, 1996,

p. H1; Barry Meier, "Implant Jury Finds Dow Chemical Liable," *New York Times,* October 29, 1995, sec. 1, p. 33; Joseph Nocera, "Fatal Litigation," *Fortune,* October 16, 1995, p. 60; John Byrne, "The Best Laid Ethics Programs Couldn't Stop a Nightmare at Dow Corning. What Happened?" *Business Week,* March 9, 1992, pp. 67–69; Alison Frankel, "From Pioneers to Profits: The Splendid Past and Muddled Present of Breast Implant Litigation," *American Lawyer* (June 1992): 82–91; Philip J. Hilts, "FDA Tells Company to Release Implant Data," *New York Times,* January 21, 1992, p. C7; Philip J. Hilts, "Strange History of Silicone Held Many Warnings," *New York Times,* January 18, 1992, pp. 1, 8; Tim Smart, "Breast Implants: What Did the Industry Know, and When?" *Business Week,* June 10, 1992, pp. 94–98; and Tim Smart, "This Man Sounded the Silicone Alarm — in 1976," *Business Week,* January 27, 1992, p. 34.

SPAM versus Muppets

im Henson Productions, Inc., had created a new Muppet character, Spa'am, to debut in its movie *Muppet Treasure Island.* Spa'am, an exotic wild boar, was meant to be a humorous link with the tame domestic luncheon meat SPAM. But Hormel Foods Corporation, the producer of SPAM, wasn't laughing. It claimed that the association would have a negative effect, causing a drop in the consumption of SPAM. Consequently, Hormel filed a civil lawsuit to determine the legality of Henson Productions' use of the Spa'am character. This is an instance of seeking from the legal system a solution to what is really an ethical dispute over the ownership and use of a brand name.

HORMEL AND SPAM

Hormel has made and marketed its popular SPAM luncheon meat since 1937. Made of pork and pork byproducts, SPAM is a distinctive, well-known brand and trademark. Along with the luncheon meat itself, Hormel produces, markets, and licenses other products bearing the SPAM trademark: clothing items, such as T-shirts, and sports items, such as golf balls. In the mid-1990s the SPAM name became more popular and, to some extent, a fashionable brand name.

The ancillary items, a secondary source of income for Hormel, are also meant to promote the sale of SPAM luncheon meat. It is assumed that those who purchase SPAM T-shirts and golf balls are consumers of the luncheon

---

This case was prepared by Phylis Mansfield for classroom discussion rather than to illustrate either effective or ineffective handling of an administrative, ethical or legal decision by management.

meat and that they associate these items with the meat product. Hormel also promotes the luncheon meat through its character SPAM-man, a person dressed as a giant can of SPAM. In addition, SPAM is featured in cooking contests seeking the most original use for the luncheon meat, as well as in contests focusing on how many different uses one can find for the product. SPAM has even been featured in a new book by Joey Green on secondary uses of household products, *Polish Your Furniture with Panty Hose,* in which Green assures the reader that one can use sliced SPAM (and a polishing rag) to polish wood furniture.

At the same time, SPAM is often the target of jokes and disparaging remarks. In SPAMarama, an annual SPAM cooking contest, one of the entries was "SPAMpers," which involved a mother and her baby girl, a diaper pail, and a SPAM pâté. According to SPAMarama's founder, a lot of the judges became ill. SPAM has almost become an icon in itself; a recent surfing expedition on the Internet uncovered a "Church of SPAM," a "SPAM-page," a "SPAM joke-a-day," and numerous anti-SPAM spoofs.

JIM HENSON PRODUCTIONS AND THE MUPPETS

In the 1950s Jim Henson created a group of puppets, known as the Muppets. Over the years many new puppets have been added to the original cast, and they have been featured in television programs as well as movies. The Muppets characters are well known as parodies of brand names, fictional characters, or celebrities. Even television programs and trademarks have been lampooned. The Muppets characters are primarily intended as children's entertainment, and are part of two very popular television programs, *Sesame Street* and *Fraggle Rock.*

In addition, the Muppets are promoted through various articles of clothing, toys, and other products. Some of the Muppet alliances include Henson's joint venture with Hasbro and the makers of Calgon to produce a bath line of licensed products for children. Henson's company has also teamed up with Hasbro toys and General Mills to develop a cross-promotion with the Muppets on 10 million boxes of Cheerios. Another cross-licensing program includes Henson's contract with the National Hockey League, in which its "Muppets Take the Ice" promotes Minute Maid, the league's "official juice sponsor," and the NHL.

THE MUPPET MOVIE: *MUPPET TREASURE ISLAND*

Jim Henson Productions scheduled a movie, *Muppet Treasure Island,* for release in February 1996. Familiar characters such as Kermit the Frog, Miss Piggy, and Rizzo Rat star alongside some newly created puppets. The story line has Kermit, Miss Piggy, and Rizzo Rat landing on Treasure Island, which is inhabited by a tribe of wild boars. They encounter the leader, Spa'am, High Priest of the Boars, a newly created puppet character. At their initial meeting, Spa'am and his tribe capture Kermit and Rizzo, accusing them of "violating" the island, and Spa'am orders the trio to be tied to stakes. However, by the end of the picture, Spa'am has joined forces with Kermit, Miss Piggy, and Rizzo Rat, and the group barely escapes the clutches of the truly evil Long John Silver.

Henson entered into several promotional agreements in connection with the movie, including contracts with General Mills, McDonald's, Hershey Chocolate, Baskin Robbins, and Dole. General Mills used characters from the movie on its boxes of Cheerios, and McDonald's used movie scenes on its Happy Meals boxes. Hershey added candies shaped like the characters from the movie to its Hershey's Amazin' Fruit line. Besides the food product promotions, Henson had licensing agreements that would put the Muppet characters in a CD-ROM video game, in books, and on clothing, including T-shirts. In all merchandise, the character's likeness, as well as its name, would appear on the product, and the name of the movie, *Muppet Treasure Island*, would be prominently displayed. Pending the outcome of the lawsuit, the Spa'am character was dropped from the licensing guide, but before that, the guidelines described Spa'am as "the noble . . . leader of the tribe of wild boars that live on Treasure Island . . . proud, yet grotesque . . . what they lack in personal hygiene, they make up for in bravery, and loud, spirited grunting." All pages of the licensing guide state in small print that "character names and likenesses are trademarks of Jim Henson Productions, Inc." A "TM" symbol accompanies the characters' names. Henson Productions asserted that consumers would purchase the movie-related merchandise, including Spa'am merchandise, because they liked the movie and/or the Muppets.

CONFLICT RESOLUTION

Hormel made several accusations against Jim Henson Productions in regard to the Muppet character Spa'am. According to Hormel, the character, seen as wild, untidy, and unattractive, will tarnish consumers' attitudes about its product SPAM. Hormel suggested that its related products, such as T-shirts and golf balls, will be confused with those sold with Spa'am, reducing Hormel's sales. Furthermore, Hormel charged that Henson's use of the Spa'am character in the movie, as well as on ancillary merchandise, constituted both an infringement on its trademark, SPAM, and false advertising, in violation of the Lanham Act. The firm also raised state claims of unfair competition, deceptive practices, and trademark dilution.

Hormel focused on the damaging effect that the character Spa'am might have because of his unattractive physical appearance and hostile behavior. According to Hormel, consumers are likely to perceive Spa'am as unhygienic and generally unpleasant. To support its charges, Hormel brought in an expert witness, Dr. Laura Peracchio, who has expertise in consumer behavior. In her statement to the court, she noted that the character Spa'am is "unappealing and will lead to negative associations on the part of consumers because he has small eyes, protruding teeth, warts, a skull on his headdress, is generally untidy, and speaks in a deep voice with poor grammar and diction." She added that Spa'am is threatening in his initial contact with Kermit and the others and that his later camaraderie with the trio is inconsistent behavior and will not dispel the negative impression stemming from the earlier negative conduct.

THE LANHAM ACT AND TRADEMARK INFRINGEMENT

The Lanham Act addresses trademark infringement in part:

> Any person who shall, without the consent of the registrant . . . use in commerce any reproduction, counterfeit, copy or colorable imitation of a registered mark in connection with the sale, offering for sale, distribution or advertising of any goods or services on or in connection with which such use is likely to cause confusion, or to cause mistake, or to deceive . . . shall be liable in a civil action by the registrant for the remedies hereinafter provided.

A critical issue in trademark infringement is whether a considerable number of consumers are likely to be misled or confused about the original source of the goods in question. Some of the factors that might cause this confusion are the strength of the registrant's trademark, similarity of uses of the two products, their proximity, the defendant's good or bad faith in using the mark, the quality of the second product, and the sophistication of the consumer. The primary factor in court decisions is the extent to which consumers might confuse the sources of the two products.

However, the Lanham Act also gives some protection to artistic expression. With regard to parodies, which are a form of artistic expression protected by the First Amendment, a decision on trademark protection would be made by weighing the public interest in free expression against the public interest in avoiding consumer confusion. Therefore, if a parody was very likely to confuse a consumer about the source of a product or service, the First Amendment would not protect it. The definition of a parody is that it must convey two messages simultaneously: that it is both imitating and mocking the original. If something presented as a parody does not sufficiently convey the latter message, it is vulnerable under trademark law. Usually, the more distinctive a trademark, the more likely it is that consumer confusion will occur if imitative products are traded. However, in the case of parody — that is, the successful blending of imitation and mockery — the more well known the original trademark, the easier it is to convey a message that the second item is a spoof. A parody relies upon a difference from the original mark, presumably a humorous difference, in order to produce its desired effect.

THE DEBATE IN COURT

SPAM and Spa'am are similar, a requirement for parody; yet they are also easily distinguishable in written form, as well as when spoken. The word *Spa'am* is pronounced in two distinct syllables in the Muppet movie; additionally, it is always used in context with a Muppet character, whether in the movie or in related merchandise. Because the Muppets are well known for parodying brand names and celebrities, consumers are unlikely to confuse the character Spa'am with the luncheon meat SPAM. They would be more likely to conclude that the spoof came from Jim Henson Productions than to believe that Hormel sponsored the joke. While Henson representatives acknowledged that they did mean to conjure up a joke regarding Hormel's trademark, they denied any intent to confuse consumers about the two entities.

Hormel contended that the character Spa'am was competing directly with its SPAM-man, as well as with its own line of clothing. Yet Hormel's own witnesses testified that purchasers of the SPAM clothing line were generally consumers of the luncheon meat. Since the Spa'am character looked like a Muppet-style puppet and was being marketed in association with the movie *Muppet Treasure Island,* it was highly likely that the customers of its ancillary products would associate it with the Muppets. Therefore, the products of luncheon meat and puppet entertainment were sufficiently far apart to prevent consumer confusion. Hormel's argument was further weakened by evidence submitted by Jim Henson Productions: cartoons, news articles, and television clips suggesting that SPAM should consider itself fortunate to be linked to a Muppet parody of its product rather than some other, more negative version.

THE COURT'S DECISION

Although no one enjoys being the butt of a joke, the requirement for a violation under trademark law is that confusion of the source, sponsorship, or affiliation had occurred or is likely to occur. That is not the same as a trademark having the "right not to be made fun of." Possibly, the humorous depiction of the Spa'am character actually reinforces the distinctiveness of the SPAM trademark by its reliance on SPAM's mark to successfully pull off the joke.

The court decided that Jim Henson Productions and its representatives acted in good faith, without "predatory intent" to capitalize on consumer confusion between the two products or to appropriate for itself any goodwill associated with SPAM. Hormel's claims against Jim Henson Productions were judged not sufficient to warrant a decision in its favor, and all claims against the Spa'am characterization, including trademark infringement, unfair competition, and false advertising, were denied. Kimba M. Wood, U.S. district judge, ruled that the Spa'am likeness and name "may be used on merchandise that clearly identifies Spa'am as a character from a Muppet motion picture, because such uses would be unlikely to cause consumer confusion or dilute Hormel's trademark."

Questions

1. Are there ethical implications when a company profits at the expense of another company's product or name, even if a parody is involved? Is the Lanham Act (as described in this case) sufficient for dealing with this type of situation?

2. Should a portion of the income gained from parodies of other trademarks or celebrities be shared with the targets of the spoofs?

3. Because the court ruled that there were no legal violations or damages in this case, does it mean that there were no ethical issues? Justify your answer.

4. What should an organization do in order to not violate the Lanham Act and to avoid costly court disputes over damages in matters such as trademarks and copyrights?

These facts are from Pam Weisz, "Muppetbath Takes Kids Away," *Brandweek*, April 18, 1994, p. 12; Terry Lefton, "Hasbro Bets Muppets Will Be Cereal Killers," *Brandweek*, February 14, 1994, pp. 1, 6; Terry Lefton, "NHL Strikes Minute Maid Promo Pact," *Brandweek*, December 5, 1994, p. 4; segment on *The Today Show*, NBC, December 4, 1995; *Austin American Statesman*, March 30, 1995, p. 16; and U.S. District Court, Southern District of New York, *Hormel Foods Corporation, Plaintiff* v. *Jim Henson Productions, Inc., Defendant.* 95 Civ. 5473 (KMW) Opinion & Order, September 22, 1995.

FIVE

Lincoln Savings and Loan: Symbol of the U.S. Savings and Loan Crisis

During the 1980s and early 1990s, a number of savings and loan (S&L) associations failed. The resulting crisis has been called everything from the "greatest financial scandal in U.S. history" to "the greatest bank robbery ever." The rash of S&L failures continues to haunt the financial world. Many government agencies, the media, and individuals have investigated the crisis and have blamed everything from deregulation of the banking industry in the early 1980s to unscrupulous lawyers, from poor management decisions to outright fraud. Few charges, however, have been as serious as those leveled against Charles Keating and his California-based Lincoln Savings and Loan, the failure of which will probably cost American taxpayers $2.6 billion. Keating and Lincoln Savings have in many ways come to represent the entire S&L crisis. So how did the Lincoln Savings scandal come about and why did it continue for so long?

KEATING'S ACQUISITION OF LINCOLN SAVINGS

Charles H. Keating, Jr., crusader against pornography and abortion and a champion swimmer, earned his law degree from the University of Cincinnati in 1948 and subsequently founded the law firm Keating, Meuthing, and Klekamp. One of his firm's largest accounts was American Financial Corp., a large insurance and banking firm. Carl H. Linder, American Financial's chairman, soon invited Keating to join the firm, where he became vice presi-

This case was prepared by John Fraedrich and Tanuja Srivastava for classroom discussion rather than to illustrate either effective or ineffective handling of an administrative, ethical or legal decision by management. Research assistance was provided by Gwyneth M. Vaughn.

dent and a director. Keating helped American Financial, which at the time was experiencing a decline in profits, to raise money from the public without the help of Wall Street underwriters.

Trouble began in 1979, when the Securities and Exchange Commission (SEC) charged that Keating and Linder had received insider loans from Provident Bank, a subsidiary of American Financial Corp. Keating and Linder did not admit to any violations, but they agreed to leave American Financial and not to violate securities laws in the future. Soon after, with Linder's assistance, Keating started American Continental Corporation, a Phoenix home construction company.

In 1984 American Continental acquired California's Lincoln Savings and Loan Association for $51 million. In its application for change of ownership, American Continental indicated that its intentions for Lincoln were slow growth, that its principal business would remain mortgage lending, and that it would retain existing management. At the time of the acquisition, 48 percent of Lincoln's $1.1 billion in assets were in residential mortgages. The institution held no brokered deposits on record, and only 24 percent of its assets were classified as risk assets. Keating had big plans for Lincoln.

However, Keating soon began breaking the promises made in the application. In February 1985 Alan Greenspan, then a financial consultant, wrote to the Federal Home Loan Bank Board on Keating's behalf to request permission for Lincoln Savings to exceed the board's new 10 percent limit on direct investments. The board denied Greenspan's request, but Keating was not deterred. By December he had dismissed Lincoln's old management and set about changing the way Lincoln did business. His new business tactics certainly propelled Lincoln's growth: Its assets increased to more than $2.8 billion, but 54 percent of those assets were considered risk assets. At the same time its residential loans fell to 15 percent, while brokered deposits increased to 37 percent of all deposits — despite the terms set out in the change-of-ownership application in 1984.

BUILDING AN EMPIRE OF STRAW

In 1987 Keating raised $200 million by selling subordinated debentures (unsecured bonds) of American Continental through twenty-nine branches of Lincoln Savings. Then, in 1988, he attempted to raise another $300 million through American Continental's own branches. Keating lured investors with high interest rates, which, at 9.5 to 12 percent, looked better than the 7.8 to 8.3 percent that insured bank certificates of deposits yielded. However, American Continental's bonds had higher levels of risk. The 1987 and 1988 bond offerings were subordinate to the parent company's $113 million in debt and, because there was no secondary market for them, they could not be sold easily. No brokerage firm underwrote the bonds, which meant that there was no name behind the offerings. However, bondholders were told that the bonds were federally insured.

Most of the people who bought American Continental's bonds were small investors looking for a secured long-term investment. Thus their investment gave American Continental and Lincoln Savings access to long-term stable money. Instead of putting the money into stable home mortgage lending, however, Keating used it for high-risk speculative investments, such as a $280 million luxury resort hotel in Scottsdale, Arizona, the purchase of Detroit's Pontchatrain hotel, and junk bonds.

If these speculative transactions had paid off, things might have turned out differently for Keating and Lincoln Savings. However, most of the investments were losing money. These losses, combined with the $34 million in salaries, bonuses, and stocks that Keating paid himself and his family between 1986 and 1988, further depleted Lincoln's coffers.

Before he bought Lincoln Savings, Keating had used interest capitalization, a scheme that allows interest payments to be reported as assets rather than expenses, to report inflated earnings at American Continental. He used the same tactics at Lincoln Savings. Additionally, he transferred about $95 million from Lincoln to its parent company through a tax-sharing plan allowed by the Internal Revenue Service (IRS). Through this plan, subsidiaries can advance cash to their parent company to cover their tax liabilities. However, during the period that the money was advanced, there were no taxes payable by American Continental to the IRS.

Other practices that Keating used included creating "straw borrowers." The loans Lincoln made to these borrowers were never intended to be repaid in full. In fact, the government would later contend that Lincoln loaned money to these borrowers so that they could pay interest on the previous loans.

These and other practices allowed Lincoln to report inflated earnings and profits when in fact it was losing money. It seems apparent that — despite mounting losses, faulty accounting practices, and loopholes — liberal California investment rules and Keating's powerful friends in Washington permitted Lincoln to continue its operations long after it should have been shut down.

EXPOSING THE PROBLEMS OF LINCOLN SAVINGS

San Francisco regulators sensed that something was amiss as early as 1985. On December 5, 1985, Lincoln was notified by the San Francisco office of the Federal Home Loan Bank Board that it had violated banking regulations and that there was concern over its high-risk activities. An examination of Lincoln's activities and books commenced in March 1986. From the start, bank board examiners had trouble obtaining necessary documents from Lincoln officials. Even after a meeting with Lincoln officials — including Keating and his lawyer — bank examiners' requests for information and documents were often denied. At one point, the institution publicly charged that the examiners were "harassing the thrift and that Bank Board Chairman Edwin J. Gray had a personal 'vendetta' against Lincoln." In August 1986 the San Francisco Federal Home Loan Bank notified its headquarters in Washington, D.C., of its many concerns about Lincoln. Among other things, it had uncovered $135 million of unreported losses, primarily the result of overappraised property values and bad equity investments. However, no action was taken until November, when the examination of Lincoln was completed and one of the board's vacancies was filled.

By 1987 the regulators recommended that Lincoln be placed in receivership — taken over by the federal government. However, Keating's political and financial clout was great, and Danny Wall, then chairman of the Federal Home Loan Bank Board, overruled the regulators' recommendations. In fact, Wall decided in September 1987 to transfer regulatory supervision of Lincoln Savings from the San Francisco Federal Home Loan Bank Board to Washington, the first time a thrift had been transferred from the regulatory authority of a district bank. This decision was partly the result of the lobbying efforts of several senators who had received large campaign contributions from Keating.

THE "KEATING FIVE"

In February 1987 Lincoln asked its private outside auditor Jack D. Atchison, of the accounting firm Arthur Young, to meet with U.S. Senator Donald W. Riegle, Jr. Atchison presented a seven-page letter summarizing the "unduly harsh" examination report and other alleged abuses against Lincoln. Later, the letter was sent to Senators Dennis DeConcini and John McCain. Soon afterward, Riegle met with the board chairman to discuss the possible mishandling of Lincoln's audit. Riegle suggested that Bank Board Chairman Edwin Gray meet with the other senators who were concerned about the issue. In March, Lincoln filed a formal petition with the Federal Home Loan Bank Board, asking to have Gray removed from the case because of his alleged "animosity" toward Lincoln Savings. The petition was never acted on because Gray's term as chairman ended a few months later, in June.

However, Gray did meet with Senators DeConcini, McCain, Alan Cranston, and John Glenn for about an hour on April 2, 1987. Details of that meeting are disputed, but it is known that a two-page memorandum, dated March 19, 1987, on "what American Continental wants from Gray for concessions," was presented. The senators denied that they discussed any deal with Gray. However, a week later the five senators — whom the media would later label "the Keating Five" — met, after hours, with examiners from both the San Francisco and Washington offices of the Federal Home

Loan Bank Board in DeConcini's office to discuss Lincoln and what they would do to get some slack from the regulators. When the examiners disclosed the fact that Lincoln's case was being referred to the U.S. Department of Justice for possible criminal charges, the meeting ended.

The Keating Five senators quickly tried to distance themselves from Charles Keating and Lincoln Savings. However, when the media learned of their role in the affair, it publicized a list of contributions Keating gave the five senators: Cranston received over $1.2 million; DeConcini, over $80,000; Glenn, approximately $235,000; McCain, approximately $112,000; and Riegle, approximately $78,000. When the case became public, Riegle, McCain, and DeConcini returned their contributions to Keating. The Senate Ethics Committee later found DeConcini, Riegle, Glenn, and McCain guilty of poor judgment but took no further action against them. Senator Cranston, however, was found to have "engaged in an impermissible pattern of conduct in which fund-raising and official activities were substantially linked," and the Ethics Committee called for a further investigation.

THE FALLOUT

Lincoln continued to lose money, a fact that could not remain hidden for long. Thus it was only a matter of time before the Resolution Trust Corporation (RTC) filed a $1.1 billion lawsuit against Keating and other American Continental directors and officers in 1989 for fraud and racketeering in the sale of American Continental bonds. The nearly insolvent Lincoln Savings was shut down and taken over by the RTC, and the FBI was brought in to further investigate wrongdoing at Lincoln. Keating was indicted in 1992.

Keating was convicted in California courts and sentenced to ten years in prison. He was also convicted in federal court and sentenced to another twelve and a half years. In addition, he was ordered to pay restitution of $122.4 million and to forfeit another $265 million. Keating appealed the decision on the grounds that his accusers "distorted, interfered with, and, for all practical purposes, nullified any chance of justice, fairness or due process" by drowning him in litigation. He also argued that he was the primary scapegoat of the savings and loan crisis. He claimed, too, that he was a "pauper" who could not even afford legal counsel. As of 1996 Keating's appeal in the Ninth U.S. Circuit Court of Appeals was rejected and he continues to reside in a federal prison in Tucson, Arizona.

Others linked with Lincoln Savings have either settled their cases or are being pursued by regulators. The accounting firm of Arthur Andersen agreed to pay $30 million to settle investor claims and another $25 million to settle federal charges. Another accounting firm, Deloitte and Touche, is being sued by Lincoln bondholders, despite the fact that it came on board only six months before the seizure of Lincoln by regulatory authorities and had not conducted a single audit of the firm.

The prestigious New York law firm of Kaye, Scholer, Fierman, Hays, and Handler was sued for $275 million in damages and had to settle for $41 million for its role in the Lincoln Savings failure. The Office of Thrift Supervision charged that the firm had assisted Lincoln in carrying out its fraud. Another law firm, Jones, Day, Reavis, and Pogue, is being sued for $50 million for its failure to report questionable transactions to the thrift's board. It has already settled for $23 million in a separate suit filed by bondholders.

As a result of Lincoln's collapse, taxpayers have paid over $2.6 billion to depositors and over $190 million to small investors, including a large portion of legal expenses.

Questions

1. What are the ethical issues in this case?

2. Discuss the financial accountability of Charles H. Keating, Jr., toward the bondholders.

3. What lessons can be learned from the S&L failures in general and from the Lincoln Savings failure in particular?

These facts are from John R. Cranford, "History of the Keating Case," *Inside Congress,* November 10, 1990, pp. 3791–3793; John R. Cranford, "Keating and the Five Senators: Putting the Puzzle Together," *Inside Congress,* January 26, 1991, pp. 221–227; John R. Cranford, Janet Hook, and Phil Kuntz, "Decision in Keating Five Case Settles Little for Senate," *Inside Congress,* March 2, 1991, pp. 517–523; Paula Dwyer, "The Worst Is Probably Over for the Keating Five," *Business Week,* February 4, 1991, p. 63; Paula Dwyer, Catherine Yang, and Ronald Grover, "The Seduction of Senator Alan Cranston," *Business Week,* December 4, 1989, pp. 82–84; Louise Kertesz, "Keating Seeks Defense Cover in S&L Lawsuits," *Business Insurance,* June 11, 1990, p. 4; Kathleen Kerwin, "For Charlie Keating, the Best Defense Is a Lawsuit," *Business Week,* May 1, 1989, p. 32; Kathleen Kerwin, "Mr. S&L Faces the Music," *Business Week,* November 25, 1991, p. 36; "Lincoln Savings: An Amazing Tale," *The Economist,* August 26, 1989, p. 66; Robert E. Norton, "Seeking the Roots of the S&L Mess," *Fortune,* November 19, 1990, pp. 207ff; Paul Craig Roberts, "Mike Milken, Scapegoat for the Feds," *Business Week,* September 30, 1991, p. 12; Howard Rudnitsky, "Good Timing Charlie," *Forbes,* November 27, 1989, pp. 140–142, 144; Eric Schine, "Charlie Keating Gets a Taste of L.A. Law," *Business Week,* October 8, 1990, p. 46; Tim Smart, "Jones Day: Did It Do Its Duty in the Keating Affair?" *Business Week,* May 4, 1992, pp. 120–121; Tim Smart, Gail DeGeorge, and Michele Galen, "Somebody Has to Pay — and That Means S&L Lawyers Too," *Business Week,* March 16, 1992, p. 38; and "Who's Left Holding the Bag? As Things Stand Now, the Taxpayers (Of Course)," *Barrons,* August 27, 1989, p. 13; James R. Adams, *The Big Fix: Inside the S&L Scandal: How an Unholy Alliance of Politics and Money Destroyed America's Banking System* (New York: Wiley, 1990); Michael Binstein and Charles Bowden, *Trust Me: Charles Keating and the Missing Billions* (New York: Random House, 1993); Kathleen Day, *S&L Hell: The People and the Politics Behind the $1 Trillion Savings and Loan Scandal* (New York: Norton, 1993); Martin Mayer, *The Greatest-Ever Bank Robbery: The Collapse of the Savings and Loan Industry* (New York: Scribner's, 1990); Stephen Pizzo, Mary Fricker, and Paul Muolo, *Inside Job: The Looting of America's Savings and Loans* (New York: McGraw-Hill, 1989); and Senate Select Committee on Ethics, *Preliminary Inquiry into Allegations Regarding Senators Cranston, DeConcini, Glenn, McCain, and Riegle and Lincoln Savings and Loan: Hearings Before the Senate Select Committee on Ethics,* 101st Congress, 2nd sess., 1991.

Sexual Harassment in the Workplace

*I*n the fall of 1991 workplaces across the United States were abuzz over allegations of sexual harassment that lawyer Anita Hill had made against Supreme Court nominee (now Justice) Clarence Thomas, who had been her supervisor ten years before. Thomas eventually gained the seat on the nation's highest court despite the charges, but their conflict sparked a national debate on the issue of sexual harassment in the workplace.

Sexual harassment charges are being made with greater frequency, and many more examples have been publicized in recent years. Soon after Hill's testimony against Thomas, a *New York Times*/CBS news poll found that 38 percent of those surveyed said they had been subjected to sexual harassment by their male supervisors in the form of "propositions or unwanted sexual discussions," and that only 4 percent had reported the incidents. One of the most highly publicized examples was the Tailhook scandal, in which at least twenty-six women say they were sexually assaulted or harassed by a group of naval officers at the 1991 convention of the Tailhook Association. Attempts by members of the navy to cover up the scandal made matters worse and damaged the military's reputation with regard to its treatment of women. A recent study by the Center for Women in Government found that 1,546 employees were awarded $25.2 million for back pay, remedial relief, damages, promotions, and reinstatements.

This case was prepared by Tanuja Srivastava for classroom discussion rather than to illustrate either effective or ineffective handling of an administrative, ethical or legal decision by management.

WHAT IS SEXUAL HARASSMENT?

What exactly constitutes sexual harassment? Is it harassment when a man displays photos of nude women or tells off-color jokes in the presence of women colleagues? What about the situation where a woman repeatedly refuses a coworker's request for a date, but he won't give up? What about instances when a man feels harassed by a woman?

The issue is complicated by the fact that men and women have different attitudes about what constitutes sexual harassment. According to one study, 67 percent of the men surveyed would be flattered to be propositioned at work, but 63 percent of the women would be offended by such behavior from men. Another survey, by the *Harvard Business Review,* reported that 23 percent of the men surveyed would be flattered if a woman looked at them suggestively, whereas only 8 percent of the women felt likewise about such a look from a man.

The Michigan Task Force on Sexual Harassment in the Workplace has noted that sexual harassment includes "continual or repeated verbal abuse of a sexual nature including but not limited to graphic commentaries on the victim's body, sexually suggestive objects or pictures in the workplace, sexually degrading words used to describe the victim, or propositions of a sexual nature." This seemingly straightforward explanation, however, does not capture the wide spectrum of situations that may or may not be construed as sexual harassment, an issue that has serious consequences for companies.

The issue is no longer taken lightly. The New England Patriots and three of its football players were fined nearly $50,000 for making lewd gestures and remarks to a female reporter in their locker room. The majority leader of Florida's House of Representatives lost his position because he allowed an atmosphere of sexual innuendo to be created by his staff. Two Long Beach, California, female police officers won $3.1 million in a lawsuit after enduring three years of ridicule, vulgar language, and obscene behavior from their male colleagues. Indeed, employers are just beginning to realize the pervasiveness of the problem. A poll by the National Association for Female Executives revealed that 53 percent of the 1,300 members surveyed had been or knew someone who had been sexually harassed. Another poll found that half of the men surveyed admitted having done something that a woman might view as harassment.

Sexual harassment laws can be abused as well. AT&T has estimated that 5 percent of the allegations filed against it were false. Desire for revenge against the boss, disappointing job-performance appraisals, and even the desire for a transfer to another department have been found to be catalysts for sexual harassment complaints.

THE HISTORY OF THE ISSUE

Sexual harassment was not recognized as a legal issue until after the 1970s. Sexual discrimination was made illegal by the 1964 Civil Rights Act, but the act contained no specific provisions to deal with sexual harassment. In the mid-1970s, a Washington, D.C., woman complained of retaliation after she declined to have an after-hours affair with her boss. A federal judge ruled that the 1964 Civil Rights Act did not apply to her case.

As women joined the work force in increasing numbers, many in professions previously dominated by men, they became targets of harassment more often. However, it took the Equal Employment Opportunity Commission (EEOC) more than a decade after the Civil Rights Act of 1964 to develop specific definitions of and guidelines on sexual harassment. Recognition by the law came when the EEOC incorporated sexual harassment into the Civil Rights Act of 1964, making it possible for victims to seek compensatory damages.

In general, sexual harassment is not limited to any one profession or to any level of employment. Victims range from secretaries to renowned neurosurgeons. One of the nation's leading brain surgeons at the prestigious Stanford University Medical School finally resigned after being subjected to sexual harassment by a male colleague. A machinist at American National Can Corp. saw that her excellent performance did not compensate for her being a woman. When she filed suit, her boss told her that she had provoked the incidents and had not done enough to stop the treatment. In fact, winning a sexual harassment claim is anything but easy, especially if the woman has allowed the behavior to continue or is viewed as having sent "mixed signals."

THE LAW

The guidelines passed by the EEOC in 1980 view sexual harassment as a form of sexual discrimination. As such, sexual harassment is illegal under Title VII of the Civil Rights Act of 1964. These guidelines identify two forms of sexual harassment:

- *Quid pro quo harassment,* in which the person being sexually harassed is promised career or job advancement in return for sexual favors or is threatened with unwelcome consequences in the absence of compliance with the advances
- *Environmental harassment,* in which unwelcome sexual conduct "unreasonably interferes" with the person's working environment or creates an "intimidating, hostile, or offensive working environment"

In 1985 a harassment case, *Meritor Savings Bank* v. *Vinson*, went to the Supreme Court, which ruled that sexual harassment does violate Title VII of the Civil Rights Act if it is unwelcome, sufficiently severe, and creates such an abusive environment that the victim's performance is harmed. The Court further ruled that although employers are not automatically liable for acts of sexual harassment committed by their employees, lack of knowledge on the employers' part does not absolve them of liability. Employers could limit their liability for harassment claims by implementing antiharassment policies and procedures in the workplace. Finally, the Court ruled that the victim's consent does not absolve the employer of liability if the victim's conduct indicated that the behavior was unwelcome.

A recent ruling by the Supreme Court has shed more light on the sexual harassment issue. In *Harris* v. *Forklift Systems Inc.,* Teresa Harris argued that she was working in a "hostile" environment because she was made to serve coffee at meetings of the other managers although her superior never asked the male managers to do so. Her boss also made comments such as "You're a woman, what do you know" and referred to her as "a dumb ass woman." In addition, he would ask her to retrieve coins from his front pockets and then comment on or make sexual innuendoes about her attire. On one occasion Hardy suggested in front of other employees that they go to a motel to negotiate her raise. Harris endured these comments for two years. She began to have a drinking problem and told her boss that she found his behavior offensive, but to no avail. When the case went to court, the judge did not believe that Harris was "subjectively so offended that she suffered injury, despite her testimony."

The Supreme Court agreed to hear the case to resolve the issue of whether a plaintiff is required to prove psychological harm in a hostile work environment. Justice Sandra Day O'Connor argued that while proof of psychological harm may be relevant to a determination of whether the conduct meets the standard, as laid out in Title VII, it is not necessarily required. Rather, all of the circumstances must be reviewed, including the "frequency of the discriminatory conduct; its severity; whether it is physically threatening or humiliating, or a mere offensive utterance; and whether it reasonably interferes with an employee's work performance." All these factors are relevant, but none is a "required" element. Justice Ruth Bader Ginsburg also pointed out that proof of a tangible decline in productivity is not required to establish unreasonable interference with work performance.

Ellison v. *Brady,* a San Francisco case heard before the Ninth U.S. Court of Appeals, introduced the notion of a "reasonable woman." The court ruled that analyzing both the victim's and perpetrator's perspectives is necessary to assess the intent, but the victim can establish that a hostile environment existed by showing that a "reasonable woman" would consider the conduct under question severe enough to be labeled sexual harassment. This notion has been controversial, however, and some have called for a more gender-neutral standard.

BUSINESSES BEGIN TO RESPOND

In response to these rulings, companies are beginning to incorporate sexual harassment policies into personnel handbooks and manuals and to take charges of sexual harassment more seriously. Although the number of quid pro quo cases has declined steadily, the number of environmental-harassment cases has been increasing. Between 1989 and 1993 sexual harassment cases reported to the EEOC grew from a total of 5,623 to 11,908. Most of these cases were filed by women, although a few were filed by men against women or men against other men. However, because the EEOC allows only compensatory damages to victims (who have to file a private action in order to recover punitive damages), cases filed with the EEOC do not reflect the actual magnitude of the problem.

The controversy surrounding sexual harassment has reaffirmed changes already made at companies such as E. I. du Pont de Nemours, Corning, and Digital Equipment; these companies have made combating sexual harassment a top priority to avoid lawsuits and to recruit and retain high-quality female employees. Du Pont has a twenty-four-hour hotline to provide guidance for sexual harassment victims, and it has started a four-hour workshop, "A Matter of Respect," for its employees. AT&T has a policy of responding to sexual harassment inquiries within three to twenty days. Other companies are seeking the advice of consultants on how to set up grievance procedures or expand training sessions.

AVOIDING SEXUAL HARASSMENT COMPLAINTS

Experts advise that companies should focus on prevention. They recommend that employers develop and distribute policies that precisely define unacceptable conduct and the punishment for violating the policy. They also advise holding training seminars that sensitize workers to the issue through videos, lectures, and role-playing exercises. Finally, companies should set up dispute-resolution procedures that permit confidential complaints of harassment and do not require one to report the harassment to immediate supervisors, who often are the harassers.

Companies should measure the consequences of sexual harassment in more than monetary terms. The costs of lawsuits in the form of compensatory and punitive damages are obvious. Less obvious and longer lasting are the costs associated with increased stress, strained personal relationships for the victims, decreased work effectiveness, absenteeism, higher turnover, lower morale among peers, and an overall loss of image for the company.

Sexual harassment will plague the business world for many years because of its complexity and the difficulty in proving and enforcing measures against it. However, some chief executives suggest that the recent controversy has heightened their awareness of the problem and will improve the ways companies follow up sexual harassment charges.

Questions

1. What is your evaluation of the "reasonable woman" clause in sexual harassment cases? Would it be preferable to use a gender-neutral standard? If so, why?

2. A male colleague repeatedly asks a female colleague for a date. She does not go out with him, but she never really declines the invitations openly. He has no decision-making authority over her. After receiving a bouquet of flowers from this man, she files a sexual harassment suit. In your opinion, does his behavior constitute sexual harassment?

3. Some argue that sexual harassment is not as severe as it has been made out to be. They suggest that because women have decided to join the work force, they should learn to tough it out. Some also argue that women are overly sensitive and take even a "harmless joke" too personally. Discuss.

These facts are from Alan Deutschman, "Dealing with Sexual Harassment," *Fortune,* November 4, 1991, pp. 145, 148; Michele Galen, Zachary Schiller, and Joan O'C. Hamilton, "Ending Sexual Harassment: Business Is Getting the Message," *Business Week,* March 18, 1991, pp. 98–100; Michele Galen, Joseph Weber, and Alice Z. Cuneo, "Out of the Shadows: The Thomas Hearings Force Businesses to Confront an Ugly Reality," *Business Week,* October 28, 1991, pp. 30–31; Susan B. Garland and Troy Segal, "Thomas vs. Hill: The Lessons for Corporate America," *Business Week,* October 21, 1991, p. 32; Ted Gest, Amy Saltzman, Betsy Carpenter, and Dorian Friedman, "Harassment: Men on Trial," *U.S. News and World Report,* October 21, 1991, pp. 38–40; John Leo, "Getting Reasonable About Feelings," *U.S. News and World Report,* November 18, 1991, p. 30; Sarah J. McCarthy, "Cultural Fascism," *Forbes,* December 9, 1991, p. 116; Gretchen Morgenson, "May I Have the Pleasure . . . ," *National Review,* November 18, 1991, pp. 36–41; Gretchen Morgenson, "Watch that Leer, Stifle that Joke," *Forbes,* May 15, 1989, pp. 69–72; Daniel Niven, "HBR Case Study: The Case of the Hidden Harassment," *Harvard Business Review* 70 (March–April 1992): 12–14; Eloise Salholz and Douglas Waller, "Tailhook: Scandal Time," *Newsweek,* July 6, 1992, pp. 40–41; Daniel Seligman, "The Milestone Menace," *Fortune,* January 15, 1990, p. 153; Geoffrey Smith, "Consciousness Raising Among Plain Old White Boys," *Business Week,* October 28, 1991, p. 32; and Charlene Marmer Solomon, "Sexual Harassment After the Thomas Hearings," *Personnel Journal* 70 (December 1991): 32.

Love Canal Revisited

Hooker Chemical Company, the tenth-largest chemical company in the United States, manufactures chemicals used in a wide variety of products, from defense-industry compounds to diapers. Between 1942 and 1953, Hooker disposed of its chemical wastes in the Love Canal area near Niagara Falls, New York. The canal, which had been dug in the 1890s as part of an abandoned hydropower project, was considered an ideal site for the disposal of wastes because the area was sparsely populated and its impervious clay soil created a natural "vault" for storing chemical residues and other industrial wastes. The chemical wastes were stored in drums in isolated sections of the canal area, either in the canal bed itself or in new excavations, and covered with several feet of clay material.

By 1952 the board of education of the city of Niagara Falls wanted the Love Canal site for a school. Knowing that the land might be seized through eminent domain, Hooker in 1953 deeded the land to the city for $1. However, the deed contained an admonition, advising the city that the land had "been filled, in whole or in part, to the present grade level thereof with waste products resulting from the manufacturing of chemicals by the grantor [Hooker] at its plant in the City of Niagara Falls, New York, and the grantee [the city] assumes all risk and liability incident to the use thereof." The deed also stipulated that, as a condition of the deal, the city, or its successors, could make no claim, suit, action, or demand of any nature against Hooker as a result of death or loss of or damage to property caused by the presence of the industrial wastes.

After acquiring the land, the school board subdivided it and built a school near the central part. The northern part of the land was deeded to the

Contributed by George S. Vozikis, The Citadel, and Timothy S. Mescon, Kennesaw State College. Reprinted by permission of the authors.

city, and the southern portion was eventually sold to a private developer. In time, despite Hooker's warning, houses and shopping centers were built in the area (no homes, however, were built directly on the Love Canal property). The basements of many of these houses expanded into the impervious clay. When construction crews removed the topsoil covering the surface of Love Canal, rain and snow gradually began seeping into the canal, forcing a chemical mixture to leach out of the sealed containers of chemical wastes.

THE NIGHTMARE BEGINS

As early as 1958 some children playing above the Love Canal dump site had to be treated for chemical burns; these incidents, however, were only a harbinger of the problems to come. Heavy rains throughout the 1970s accelerated the erosion of the more than 199,900 tons of contaminated waste, representing 150 chemical compounds. As the waste seeped to the surface, some ominous statistics began to emerge. An unusually high incidence of miscarriages, serious birth defects, liver abnormalities, chromosome breakdown, and cancer was detected among residents in the area. Moreover, a strong smell emitted by the chemicals prompted one local resident to claim that "the whole area stinks."

In 1978, 239 Love Canal families were forced to abandon their homes after toxic fumes were detected in area basements and nearby drainage ditches were found to contain traces of trichlorophenal (which breaks down into dioxin and can cause cancer, nervous system disorders, depression, liver and kidney damage, and irritations of the skin and mucous membranes). In addition a study by the Environmental Protection Agency (EPA) found signs of chromosome breakdown in some area residents. As a result, the federal government and the state of New York agreed in 1980 to relocate another 710 Love Canal area families to other housing.

In December 1979 the EPA filed a complaint against Hooker Chemical, the city of Niagara Falls, and the Niagara Falls Board of Education. Among other charges, the EPA stated that Hooker had failed to warn residents and developers that contact with the chemical wastes could be harmful and that it had failed to take action to prevent further deaths and injuries due to exposure to the wastes. Few school board members who had accepted the deed to the land in 1953 could be found, but one of them, Irma Runals, insisted that Hooker warned no one of any dangers.

However, minutes from board of education meetings held in 1957, before the subdivision of the land, indicate that representatives from Hooker urged the board not to approve construction on the site. According to the minutes of a November 7, 1957, meeting, Arthur Chambers, a representative of Hooker's legal department, reminded the board that "the land was not suitable for construction where underground facilities are necessary. It was their [Hooker's] intent that the property be used for a school and for parking."

Three weeks later, Chambers again warned the board that "there are danger-ous chemicals buried there in drums, in loose form, in solids and liquids. It was understood the land would be used for a park or some surface activity if it was developed."

Hooker, which had been acquired by Occidental Chemical Corporation, had not owned the land for nearly forty years and did not consider that it had any responsibility in the matter. The company did, however, volunteer to share the cost of an engineering study and to contribute one-third of the original estimate for the cost of recapping the southern portion of the canal. The school board and the city were to assume the other two-thirds of the cost. However, the school board was unable to raise the necessary funds, and re-medial efforts were delayed. Consequently, a state of emergency was de-clared in 1980, and the federal and state governments assumed the costs of the remedial program. According to sources at Hooker, the company was still willing to share the cost, as long as the school board and the local govern-ment also participated. In 1988, the state and federal governments declared that most of the area was again suitable for residential use. Many of the aban-doned homes were again sold.

TEN YEARS LATER

There have been physiological and psychological changes for the people who once lived in the Love Canal area. More than 150 chemicals were found in soil and sediment samples from Love Canal, including dioxin, the most toxic manmade chemical known; benzene, known to be linked to leukemia; and many other substances associated with nervous-system disorders, kidney problems, respiratory distress, deafness, and birth defects. Some Love Canal children were born with two rows of teeth, three ears, or one kidney. How-ever, it has been difficult to prove a connection between this chemical smor-gasbord and the health problems experienced by the Love Canal residents.

In addition to physiological problems, the Love Canal refugees experi-enced psychological harm, ranging from feelings of anxiety and depression to higher rates of divorce. The worst part is their fear of the unknown, a sense that tomorrow may bring new tragedies to them and their loved ones. This fear has transformed trusting, innocent people into enemies of business and crusaders against their government. One mother of two children was ar-rested after screaming at state and local officials and throwing a microphone at the mayor. She says now, "My kids were getting sick, and I wanted to kill."

A LEGAL MORASS

In 1988 Hooker Chemical and Plastics Corporation, and its parent company, Occidental Chemical Corporation, were held liable for cleanup costs at the polluted Love Canal landfill. The company appealed the decision and pursued lawsuits against dozens of its liability insurers for coverage of its pollution-related losses. U.S. District Judge John T. Curtin ruled that Occidental must reimburse the U.S. government and the state of New York for the costs of remedial action at Love Canal under the Comprehensive Environmental Response, Compensation, and Liability Act. In its lawsuit against the insurance companies, Occidental claims that it has incurred $80.1 million in damages because of the insurance companies' failure to pay defense costs and contribute to settlements and cleanup costs.

According to the Love Canal litigation, active polluters and their insurance companies, as well as the insurance firms that insure the county in which the polluter is located, are liable if citizens sue, even if the insurance policies were expressly devoid of any liability provision. Standard comprehensive general liability (CGL) insurance policies protect policyholders whenever someone imposes, or seeks to impose, legal liability on them. This protection includes all legal liability from pollution or environmental damage unless the policy explicitly excludes such liability. Since 1973, however, standard CGL policies have done just that in the case of clearly intentional pollution acts by a company. They have excluded coverage for personal injury or property damage from discharge of pollutants into the environment, unless the discharge is "sudden and accidental."

This pollution exclusion has caused considerable controversy and litigation. Most courts have interpreted it in a manner favorable to the insured. Courts have ruled that policyholders are covered for legal liability as a result of pollution unless the pollution occurred over an extended period of time as part of the regular course of the policyholder's business, the policyholder knew of the pollution, and the injury resulting from the pollution was foreseeable. Except in such fairly extreme circumstances, pollution has been interpreted as "sudden and accidental," so that the pollution exclusion did not apply.

After the 1988 verdict, Occidental charged that nearly all of its insurers breached their policies by refusing to contribute to settlements unconditionally or to agree to cover Occidental for future judgments and settlements. In a statement, the company also said, "Although we believe we are protected by insurance, we intend further to protect our rights by appealing this extraordinary decision."

Under the settlement, the Love Canal residents received $20 million, in addition to the $30,000 or $40,000 that they got for each of their homes. Individual settlements ranged from $2,000 to $40,000, with nearly one thousand cases still pending as of 1996. In 1994 Occidental agreed to pay $98 million to settle a lawsuit with the state of New York. The city also was seeking $4 million for unreimbursed costs and lost interest. In 1996 Occidental finally agreed to pay $129 million to cover the federal government's cleanup costs at Love Canal.

THE FUTURE

The full consequences of the Love Canal episode are still not clear. A comprehensive study on the health of the area residents has yet to be done. Besides the health effects of pollution, the contamination obviously resulted in severe declines in property values. Nevertheless, "acceptable" soil samples taken in 1990 have led officials to allow resettlement of some parts of the Love Canal area.

Robert G. Smerko, president of the Chlorine Institute, predicts that the chemical industry will eventually be regulated in the same restrictive fashion as the nuclear industry. Environmental issues have been increasingly politicized, as illustrated by the Love Canal case. The chemical industry's public image has been tarnished by problems of product safety and damage to the environment. Love Canal, the Union Carbide Corp. disaster in Bhopal, India, and the *Exxon Valdez* oil spill were major turning points in the public demand for a safer and cleaner environment.

The main problems in pollution control are ethics, politics, liability determination, technology, and, most important, lack of communication with the public. There is no simple solution, for overly restrictive regulatory policies could harm society by stifling technical and economic progress and development. What, then, should be done?

Some analysts claim that the right approach is to expand local control over industry and strengthen the liability approach by focusing federal resources on technical forensic assistance in tracing pollutants as they are emitted. Others emphasize steps to be taken by companies. In 1985 the Chemical Manufacturers Association implemented a Community Awareness and Emergency Response program to encourage chemical plant managers to reassess emergency response procedures. Some have argued that a company's chief executive officer should ensure the integration of social accountability issues into the company's culture and structure. Businesspeople, according to this view, should realize that social responsibility initiatives are in the firm's best interest and that socially responsible companies can still be profitable.

In the meantime, there is no escape for the former residents of Love Canal. A woman whose son Jon died at the age of seven, two months after the state declared a health emergency in Love Canal, still laments, "I keep thinking Jon could still be here. You can't ever get over a child's death. I still can't get over the questions: What if he didn't play in the backyard? What if the chemicals weren't there?"

Questions

1. Given that Hooker's activities were legal at the time and that it warned the board of education not to use the property for anything other than

a school, should Hooker (and, subsequently, Occidental) be held responsible?

2. Discuss the insurance companies' refusal to pay claims stemming from Hooker's activities. Are "pollution exclusion" policies ethical?

3. What are the board of education's responsibility and liability in this case?

This case is based on information from *Environmental Laboratory Report,* January 8, 1996, LRP Publications; Ann Caslan, "Insurer's Duty to Defend in Hazardous Waste Litigation," *CPCU Journal* 40 (September 1987): 174–181; Leo J. Eikmeyer, "Pollution: An Effect on Value," *Canadian Appraiser* 29 (Spring 1985): 21–23; "EPA Hits Hooker with Suits Asking $118M for Clean Up of Hazardous Waste Dumps," *Chemical Marketing Reporter,* December 24, 1979, p. 47; Gregg LaBar, "Chemical Industry: Regulatory Crunch Coming?" *Occupational Hazards* 50 (November 1988): 36–39; "Letter from Love Canal," *U.S. News & World Report,* May 28, 1990, p. 18; "Love Canal Lessons," *Wall Street Journal,* May 22, 1980, p. 24; Steven D. Lydenberg, Alice T. Marlin, and Sean O. Strub, "Rating America's Corporate Conscience," *Business and Society Review* 60 (Winter 1987): 27–31; Conrad B. MacKerron, "Superfund Cleanup: The Lessons of Love Canal and Springfellow," *Chemical Week,* September 2, 1987, pp. 36–40; Douglas McLeod, "Pollution: Oxy Told to Pay Love Canal Cleanup," *Business Insurance,* February 29, 1988, pp. 1, 29; Timothy S. Mescon and George S. Vozikis, "Hooker Chemical and the Love Canal," in *Business Ethics: Readings and Cases in Corporate Morality,* ed. W. Michael Hoffman and Jennifer Mills Moore (New York: McGraw-Hill, 1984), pp. 421–426; Irwin Molosky, "A Love Canal Warning No One Can Recall," *New York Times,* April 14, 1979, p. 22L; Avraham C. Moskowitz, "CGL Pollution Exclusion: Courts Take a Narrow View," *Business Insurance,* October 29, 1984, pp. 25–27; David Shribman, "Even After 10 Years, Victims of Love Canal Can't Quite Escape It," *Wall Street Journal,* March 9, 1989, pp. A1, A7; Richard L. Stroup, "Environmental Policy," *Regulation,* 12, no. 3 (1988): 43–49; and "What Hooker Told Whom, When About Love Canal," *Wall Street Journal,* June 19, 1980, p. 18.

The Old Joe Camel Controversy: A Case of Commercial Free Speech

When the R.J. Reynolds Tobacco Co. (RJR) introduced its Cool Joe promotion campaign for Camel filter cigarettes, the company saw Camel's market share rise from 2.6 percent to 3.1 percent in just three years. RJR revived the campaign in 1987, featuring the "smooth character" of a cartoon camel named Old Joe or Cool Joe, but the promotion may be influencing what many say is an unacceptable market for cigarettes. According to *The Journal of the American Medical Association (JAMA)*, Old Joe increased RJR's share of the children's cigarette market from 0.5 percent before the campaign to 32.8 percent in 1990. Although RJR has repeatedly asserted that it is not targeting children or encouraging kids to smoke, the company has been unable to put out the controversy.

HISTORY OF CIGARETTE ADVERTISING

As a result of growing public pressure and concern, the health hazards of cigarette smoking were investigated in the early 1950s. In 1953 the Sloan-Kettering report linked smoking to cancer in rats. The first attempt to regulate the cigarette industry came in 1955, when the Federal Trade Commission (FTC) prohibited claims of the presence or absence of any positive physical effects of smoking in cigarette advertising or labeling. On January 11, 1964, the then surgeon general, Luther Terry, declared cigarettes to be a cause of cancer. The following year the Trade Regulation Rules were formulated, mandating a

This case was prepared by Tanuja Srivastava for classroom discussion rather than to illustrate either effective or ineffective handling of an administrative, ethical or legal decision by management.

health warning on all cigarette packaging and prohibiting cigarette advertising to people under 25 years of age. However, these regulations did not result in any noticeable decline in cigarette consumption; in fact, consumption increased.

A decline in smoking did not come about until soon after the "fairness doctrine" was implemented in 1967. Although it was developed for political advertising, the fairness doctrine was applied to require radio and television broadcasters to give equal time to antismoking advertisements. In 1971 the Cigarette Advertising and Labeling Act banned cigarette advertisements from television and radio altogether. A 1984 amendment requires cigarette manufacturers or importers to display on cigarette packaging and advertising one of four different health warnings, which are rotated every quarter.

The tobacco industry has vehemently opposed all legislation restricting cigarette advertising. In contrast, the medical profession and various consumer groups want even more stringent regulation of the industry; many advocate a complete ban on cigarette advertising. Recent findings published in *JAMA*, which suggest that RJR's Old Joe promotion is being used to target children and teenagers, have fueled the controversy further.

COMMERCIAL FREE SPEECH

Viewed in isolation, a ban on cigarette advertising could be challenged under the First Amendment of the U.S. Constitution, which prohibits Congress from making any law that would restrict the freedom of speech. Historically, the notion of freedom of speech applied to expressions of political and social ideas. However, over the years and through various court cases, it was expanded to cover some aspects of commercial expression. Should the Old Joe promotion wind up in court, RJR would probably invoke the free speech clause. However, unlike noncommercial speech, commercial speech is regulated to prohibit false and deceptive advertising.

THE EVIDENCE AGAINST OLD JOE

The cartoon Old Joe Camel has apparently served as a "cool" role model for younger smokers. Health advocates claim that the cartoon dromedary seems more appealing to kids than, for example, rival Marlboro's macho cowboy. These claims have been given substance by three surveys published in *JAMA*'s December 1991 issue, which concluded that RJR's Old Joe Camel character is extremely effective in reaching children and teenagers. When teenagers were shown the advertisements featuring Old Joe Camel, 98 percent accurately associated him with the Camel brand of cigarettes. A relatively low percentage of adults (67 percent) identified the brand. The study also found that 6-year-olds "were nearly as familiar with Joe Camel as they were with the Disney Channel's Mickey Mouse Logo." As a result, anti-smoking forces petitioned the Federal Trade Commission to "take immediate action against RJR's cartoon animal."

Despite RJR's claims to the contrary, its share of filter cigarettes has grown. The *JAMA* study found that since RJR began the Old Joe campaign, Camel sales have increased to $476 million. Consumer groups argue that this increase came from sales to the under-18 market, which has grown from 0.5 percent to 33 percent. Another study found that 98 percent of a total of 1,055 students between ages 12 and 19 recalled seeing Old Joe. About the same number recognized the association between the character and the product, with 58 percent saying they thought Old Joe looked "cool." Another 35 percent reported liking Joe as a friend, while 33 percent listed the brand as their favorite. With overall unit sales in the industry declining by about 3 percent annually, this study highlights the impact these advertisements have had on recruiting new, younger smokers.

RJR'S RESPONSE

RJR denies the charges, claiming that its advertisements are meant only to encourage smokers in the age group of 21 to 35 to switch brands. It faults the *JAMA* study for having an inadequate sample size, inaccurate definition of underage smokers, and lack of countercomments; it also claims that the study draws conclusions not supported by statistical evidence. In January 1992, as health groups were clamoring for a halt to the Old Joe campaign, RJR responded with a letter to the Federal Trade Commission requesting a chance to present its own research on young smokers.

RJR is also sponsoring antismoking advertisements targeting young children. One of the advertisements features two boys smoking in a men's room, with a cartoon character in the style of Old Joe Camel asking, "And you think this looks cool?" However, that advertisement has itself proven controversial. While RJR touts it as an antismoking appeal to younger children, antismoking activists claim that the advertisement does characterize the rebellious boys as cool. Critics also charge that these advertisements portray smoking as an adult activity, further encouraging kids to smoke because they want to be more adult.

Whatever the motives behind Old Joe Camel, RJR is unlikely to discontinue one of the most successful promotion campaigns in its history. On the other hand, some marketing experts suggest that RJR's strong attempts to defend its campaign may backfire. They cite the example of Philip Morris's 1989 campaign celebrating the bicentennial of the Bill of Rights, which was viewed by antismoking groups as an attempt to duck the 1971 ban on radio and television advertising of cigarettes. The expensive campaign was the subject of a congressional inquiry, perhaps resulting in damage to Philip Morris's reputation.

HIGH STAKES

Despite evidence of declining demand in recent years, cigarettes continue to be big business. With approximately 600 billion cigarettes smoked annually at a cost of $28 billion, the economic stakes are enormous. Twenty-two states grow tobacco, making it the sixth-largest cash crop in the United States. The vast and complex tobacco-supply network extends the chain of economic dependence on tobacco to include manufacturers of farm equipment, advertising agencies, advertising media, and other businesses. Advertising and related industries alone collect a billion dollars annually from cigarette advertising. Arguably, banning cigarette advertising could have serious repercussions for the economy.

Moreover, even many nonsmokers believe cigarette advertising is commercial speech protected under the First Amendment. A total ban on advertising by RJR or any other company would be tantamount to suppression of commercial information and speech, something clearly forbidden by the First Amendment. There are also those who fear that a ban on cigarette advertising would set a dangerous precedent for more government interference in commercial activities.

TRUTH IN ADVERTISING

Opponents of the commercial free-speech argument counter that if commercial speech is to be free, it should not be deceptive and misleading, which, they say, RJR's Old Joe campaign is. RJR has been accused of misleading advertising before. In 1985 it ran an advertisement in the *New York Times* and other newspapers around the country entitled "Of Cigarettes and Science." The Federal Trade Commission filed a formal complaint against the company, saying that the advertisement was a distortion of an important study demonstrating the relationship between a number of risk factors and heart disease. RJR countered by arguing that "Of Cigarettes and Science" was an expression of opinion on an issue of social and political importance and was therefore protected by the First Amendment. A commercial law judge dismissed the complaint, concluding that "Of Cigarettes and Science" was not commercial speech and therefore not subject to Federal Trade Commission regulation. The court did not consider whether the advertisement was deceptive, false, or misleading.

Can RJR hide behind the First Amendment if Old Joe winds up in court? The answer to that question depends on whether the advertisements can be shown to be deceptive, false, or misleading and whether they are found to represent a "clear and present danger" that indeed encourages children to smoke. The success or failure of a freedom-of-speech defense will depend on the attitude of the public, who may be outraged by subtle attempts to target children.

In addition, recent documents, as well as an affidavit given by Jeffrey Wigand, former research executive of Brown & Williamson Tobacco Corp., to several state prosecutors, show strong evidence that for decades the tobacco industry has known of the dangers of its product. In response to the Wigand deposition, Brown & Williamson developed a five-hundred-page dossier attacking Wigand. After careful review of this dossier, the *Wall Street Journal* in 1996 asserted that much of it was poorly substantiated, thus giving rise to the argument that a smear campaign was being created. National news shows such as *60 Minutes* opened the debate as to whether tobacco companies should be legally liable for damages caused by smoking. When these cases finally come to court, the issue of free speech may be superseded by the judgment of intentional wrongdoing by executives within the tobacco industry and governmental representatives.

Questions

1. Which ethical issues are becoming legal issues?
2. If selling cigarettes to minors is illegal, where is the ethical issue?
3. What are the arguments for and against the issue of free speech?
4. Should cigarette advertising be banned altogether?
5. Is selling a potentially harmful or addictive product that is legal a problem for businesspeople?
6. If cigarettes become cost prohibitive to sell in the United States, what, if any, are the ethical ramifications of selling cigarettes in other countries?

These facts are from *American Voices: Prize Winning Essays on Freedom of Speech, Censorship, and Advertising Bans* (New York: Philip Morris USA, 1987); Daniel Seligman, "Camel Rights," *Fortune*, May 18, 1992, p. 120; Kathleen Deveny, "Joe Camel Is Also Pied Piper, Research Finds," *Wall Street Journal*, December 11, 1992, pp. B1, B4; Walecia Konrad, "I'd Toddle a Mile for Camel," *Business Week*, December 23, 1991, p. 34; Gary Levin, "Poll: Camel Ads Effective with Kids: Brand Recognition Highest Among Preteens," *Advertising Age*, April 27, 1992; Joanne Lipman, "Why Activists Fume at Anti-Smoking Ads," *Wall Street Journal*, February 20, 1992, p. B3; Barbara Lippert, "Camel's Old Joe Poses the Question: What Is Sexy?" *AdWeek's Marketing Week*, October 3, 1988, p. 55; "RJ Reynolds Takes on the AMA, Defending Joe Camel Cartoon Ad," *Wall Street Journal*, February 5, 1992, p. B8; Camille P. Schuster and Christine Pacelli Powell, "Comparison of Cigarette and Alcohol Advertising Controversies," *Journal of Advertising*, 16, no. 2 (1987): 26–33; Fara Warner, "Novello Throws Down the Gauntlet: The Surgeon General's Crusade to Kill Off Joe Cool," *AdWeek's Marketing Week*, March 16, 1992, pp. 4–5; Larry C. White, *Merchants of Death* (New York: Beech Tree Books, Inc., 1988); Alan Blum, *New England Journal of Medicine* 324 (March 28, 1991): 913–916; Kevin Goldman "Philip Morris Dresses Up Virginia Slims," *Wall Street Journal*, February 26, 1993; US DHHS, National Center for Chronic Disease Prevention and Health Promotion Study, cited in *Wall Street Journal*, April 2, 1993, p. A1; US DHHS, National Institute on Drug Abuse, press release, 1989 National High School Senior Drug Abuse Survey, "Monitoring the Future Survey," February 13, 1990; STAT, "Cigarette Advertising Increases Smoking," *Tobacco Free Youth Reporter* (Fall 1992); A. O. Goldstein, P. M. Fischer, J.W. Richards, and D. Creten, "The Influence of Cigarette Advertising on

Adolescent Smoking," 1987; Joe B. Tye, "Lusting After Children: The Tobacco Industry's Investment in a Profitable Future," *Social Science Record, Journal of the New York State Council for the Social Studies* (Fall 1988); World Health Organization (WHO), press release, "World No-Tobacco Day: Health Versus Smoking," May 27, 1993; William Ecenbarger, "America's New Merchants of Death," *Reader's Digest* (April 1993); "Africa: Ashtray of the World," *Sunday Times (London),* May 13, 1990; L. Bird, "Joe Smooth for President," *Adweek's Marketing Week,* May 20, 1991; Paul M. Fischer, Meyer P. Schwartz, John W. Richards, Jr., Adam O. Goldstein, and Tina H. Rojas, "Brand Logo Recognition by Children Aged Three to Six Years," *Journal of the American Medical Association (JAMA),* December 11, 1991; Joseph R. DiFranza, John W. Richards, Paul M. Paulman, Nancy Wolf-Gillespie, Christopher Fletcher, Robert D. Jaffe, and David Murray, "RJR Nabisco's Cartoon Camel Promotes Camel Cigarettes to Children," *JAMA,* December 11, 1991; Karen Lewis, "Addicting the Young: Tobacco Pushers and Kids," *Multinational Monitor* (January–February 1992); and Stop Teenage Addiction to Tobacco (STAT), "RJR Nabisco: Targeting Teens for Addiction," *Tobacco Free Youth Reporter* (Fall 1992).

The Fall of Michael Milken

$\mathbb{D}$rexel Burnham Lambert, Inc., was an investment banking firm that rose to prominence during the 1980s, only to be toppled by one of the biggest scandals ever to hit Wall Street. Michael Milken, senior vice president and head of Drexel's high-yield and convertible bond department, based in Beverly Hills, California, also succumbed to the scandal. Milken's and Drexel's rapid rise to the top came about as a result of their virtual creation and subsequent domination of the billion-dollar "junk bond" market that helped finance the 1980s takeover boom and change the face of corporate America. Their downfall was the result of a Securities and Exchange Commission (SEC) investigation, which eventually led to Milken's incarceration and Drexel's bankruptcy.

THE "JUNK BOND KING"

Before Milken's ascent to the top of financial circles, junk bonds were a relatively obscure financial investment shunned by most investors. Junk bonds are debt securities that offer high rates of return at high risk. Often they are securities that previously had been graded as "investment quality" but later were downgraded to low-grade, high-risk, high-yield status because of doubts about the issuer's financial strength. Drexel preferred to call these securities "high-yield bonds."

Milken was the driving force behind Drexel's domination of the high-yield bond market. People familiar with the firm say Milken's office was

This case was prepared by O. C. Ferrell and Gwyneth M. Vaughn for classroom discussion rather than to illustrate either effective or ineffective handling of an administrative, ethical or legal decision by management.

responsible for 80 to 90 percent of Drexel's profits. In addition to bringing in huge profits for the company, Milken also amassed a huge fortune for himself. In the four-year period ending in 1987, he is believed to have made over $1.1 billion. In 1987 alone he earned $550 million in salary and bonuses — more than the firm he worked for — making him easily the highest-paid employee in history.

During the early 1980s Milken recognized a tremendous opportunity in borrowing needs of relatively small companies. At that time only about eight hundred companies issued bonds labeled investment grade, but there were thousands of firms with annual revenues of $25 million or more. Drexel's success was built on meeting those financing needs. The company's ability to raise capital through the high-yield bond market allowed many firms to borrow much-needed funds although they had not previously been considered creditworthy. In this sense, Drexel's activities supported growth. Nevertheless, Milken and Drexel have been sharply criticized, particularly in recent years, because their financial activities helped fuel the bitter takeover battles of the 1980s. Investment analysts generally view junk bonds and the companies that issue them as risky and unsafe. Milken continues to defend the use of high-yield bonds; he argues that at the time, "We were matching capital to entrepreneurs who could use it effectively. We were creating investments that money managers needed in volatile markets."

THE CASE AGAINST MILKEN

In addition to some criticism on Wall Street, Drexel and Milken also attracted the attention of the Securities and Exchange Commission, which between 1980 and 1985 launched four separate investigations of Drexel's activities. None of the investigations turned up enough evidence of wrongdoing to justify action. Only in 1986, when Ivan Boesky agreed to cooperate with prosecutors, was the government able to put together a case strong enough to warrant bringing charges against Drexel. During government investigations into a Wall Street insider-trader ring, Dennis Levine, a former Drexel investment banker, blew the whistle on Boesky. As part of his deal with prosecutors, Boesky agreed to name people who had participated in insider trading and other illegal activities. Boesky's testimony led prosecutors to Drexel and to Milken, their number-one target.

In September 1988, after an investigation spanning two and a half years, the SEC filed a 194-page civil lawsuit against Drexel Burnham Lambert, Inc. The SEC also named Michael Milken, his brother Lowell, and other Milken aides in the suit. In its most sweeping enforcement action since the securities laws were written, the SEC charged Drexel with insider trading, stock manipulation, "parking" of securities to conceal their true ownership, false disclosures in SEC filings, maintaining false books and records, aiding and abetting capital rules violations, fraud in securities-offerings materials, and various other charges. (Parking involves hiding ownership of securities by selling them to another with the understanding that they will be sold back to the original owner, usually at a prearranged time and price.)

The SEC suit also raised questions about Drexel's supervision of Milken's Beverly Hills operations. Milken reported to Edwin Kantor, head of trading in New York. The two allegedly spoke several times a day over the phone, but otherwise Milken ran the office with little intervention. In an interview held after the investigation and ensuing criminal case had been completed, Drexel's chief executive officer, Fred Joseph, stated that he was "appalled and surprised by the organized nature of the crime wave." In retrospect, he admitted to "surprising naiveté." With leadership so loose, it is not clear who, if anyone, was overseeing Milken's activities.

While the SEC was putting together its case, the U.S. Department of Justice was building a criminal case against Drexel and its employees. This effort was led by Rudolph Giuliani, the U.S. attorney for the Manhattan district. At the same time that the SEC filed its civil suit against Drexel, Giuliani's office notified Michael Milken, his brother Lowell (who managed many of Michael's accounts), and two other key traders that they would probably soon be indicted on securities laws violations. Drexel was notified of its impending indictment a few weeks later. Notification of an impending indictment usually means that the prosecution has completed its investigation and is prepared to go to court.

The SEC and the U.S. attorney's office had worked together, sharing resources, information, and investigators, and both had good cases. Their adversary was also well prepared. Drexel had 115 lawyers to the SEC's 15, and the firm made it clear that it could outspend the SEC. In fact, Drexel's legal defense budget was bigger than the entire SEC budget. Drexel had $2.3 billion in capital, and for two years it had been setting aside huge reserves to cover any litigation. Despite the bad publicity Drexel experienced, it continued to gain market share and became more profitable throughout the investigation. Even competitors were impressed by the loyalty of Drexel's clients, many of whom at the time of the SEC announcement had vowed to stand by Drexel and especially Milken, who had helped many of them make millions of dollars.

Drexel faced charges from the U.S. attorney's office on securities, wire, and mail fraud as well as charges of racketeering under the Racketeering Influenced and Corrupt Organizations Act (RICO). RICO was enacted in 1970 to give the government a powerful weapon to go after organized crime; under the act, a person or business that commits two or more felonies as part of a pattern can be charged with racketeering. RICO allows prosecutors to charge entire organizations with crimes and to seize assets before trial to ensure payment of any subsequent penalties. In addition, RICO requires firms to forfeit any profits made or any property used during the period of wrongdoing. RICO laws carry heavy fines and long prison sentences, and they award triple damages to successful plaintiffs in civil suits.

RICO was first used against a securities firm in August 1988, when Giuliani's office indicted the five general partners of Princeton/Newport Partners, a small New Jersey–based investment firm, on racketeering charges. A former Drexel trader was involved in the transactions for which the partners were indicted. The firm folded within five months of the indictment. Princeton/Newport officials blamed the firm's demise on the fact that clients were scared off from doing business with a racketeer. At the time of the charges against Drexel, some observers expressed surprise that Drexel itself was named rather than the senior executives as individual persons, as in the Princeton/Newport Partners case.

Giuliani's office set out to prove that Drexel used Boesky as a front for secretly trading some stocks. By so doing, Drexel could increase the price of takeover stocks so that it could get higher fees and trigger unwanted takeovers. The profits were then funneled back into the firm using dubious payments, with false paperwork covering the trail. In many cases Drexel's goal appeared to be power as much as profit — the ability to control the outcome of the deals it financed. Giuliani's case against the firm centered on a $5.3 million payment Boesky made in March 1987 to Drexel for "consulting services." The prosecution alleged that this amount was actually part of the profits on stock that Drexel had parked with Boesky's firm. There were also allegations that Drexel and Boesky deliberately destroyed documents to cover up their activities. Of the six charges initially brought against Drexel, all involved transactions allegedly initiated by Michael Milken, and five of the six transactions allegedly involved Boesky. Drexel set out to discredit Boesky as Giuliani's office supported his claims against Drexel with written documentation and other informants — Charles Thurnher, James Dahl, Cary Maultesch, and Terrence Peizer — all of whom had worked for Michael Milken.

As the possibility of a court trial increased, defense lawyers began negotiations with prosecutors to drop the racketeering charges. They argued that RICO was intended to be used against the Mafia and that such charges would be unfair to business, disruptive to the equity and debt markets, and harmful to the economy. Giuliani initially wanted Drexel and its employees to waive their attorney-client privileges so that he could get access to Drexel's records on its own internal investigation of employees in the matter. After several rounds of negotiations, it was clear that Giuliani wanted a settlement. It was also clear that he would not hesitate to invoke the full force of the RICO statutes if he did not get one.

In December 1988, after spending more than $100 million on its legal defense and denying any misconduct or wrongdoing for more than two years, Drexel pleaded guilty to a six-count felony indictment on charges of securities, wire, and mail fraud and agreed to pay a record $650 million in fines and restitution. Drexel also gave in to the government demand that it had vehemently opposed: it agreed to cooperate in all continuing investigations, including investigations of some of its own clients and employees — including

Michael Milken. In return, the prosecutor dropped the racketeering charges against the company. CEO Fred Joseph said that Drexel's decision was the only alternative that gave the company a chance to survive.

The settlement with the Justice Department was contingent on Drexel's settling with the SEC, which it did in the spring of 1989. Under that agreement, Drexel submitted to unprecedented federal supervision, agreed to a three-year probation, and had to appoint board members approved by the SEC. In addition, Drexel was required to move its Beverly Hills operation back to New York and to sever ties with Michael Milken. In the agreement, Drexel neither admitted nor denied guilt. By agreeing to plead guilty to the felony charges in which Michael Milken was also implicated and by cooperating with the prosecution in all continuing investigations, Drexel in effect withdrew all support from its most productive employee. The firm was also asked to withhold Milken's 1988 salary and bonus. Some saw the guilty plea as a bargaining chip that Drexel used to gain other concessions from the prosecutor and said Drexel was passing sentence on Milken before he got a trial. Milken's attorney later protested that this denied his client due process.

MILKEN IS INDICTED

Michael Milken was handed his own ninety-eight count felony indictment, including charges of racketeering, in March 1989. In June he resigned from Drexel to form his own company — just before the federal court approved the terms of the SEC settlement that would have forced his termination anyway. This, along with the fact that Milken continued to proclaim his innocence, widened a rift that had existed in the firm since 1978, when Milken had set up the junk bond operations on the West Coast. Milken's office had become a company within a company, employing about 600 of the elite among Drexel's 9,100 people. Those in "Drexel East," as they came to be called by those in the Beverly Hills office, were often jealous of the high commissions and big bonuses paid to the employees in the junk-bond department. Those in the West saw the men on the board as nonproducers who got rich off Milken and then sold him out to preserve their positions and capital.

Drexel's CEO, Joseph, had been a principal negotiator in working out the settlement. He was caught between trying to wring as many concessions from Giuliani as he could and trying to keep an increasingly bitter work force of traders, analysts, and brokers from quitting. However, Joseph made matters worse for himself when, at the board meeting held to accept or reject the settlement, he and five of the other twenty-two members of the board voted against the agreement he had just negotiated. This token support for Milken fooled no one and, in the view of some, made him appear hypocritical. Joseph later admitted privately that what he had done had been a mistake. In talking with a client who happened to be a Milken supporter, Joseph mentioned that he viewed Giuliani as a worthy adversary and that the prosecutor could have come down harder on the firm if he had chosen to do so. The client saw the prosecutor as having "taken Joseph, turned him, and made him his own." Many Milken loyalists within the firm regarded Joseph as a "traitorous wimp."

Some observers say that RICO is a tool that allows prosecutors to scare defendants into submission before getting close to court. Certainly, Joseph initially had no intention of settling, for he believed that firms that had recently settled with the government in other types of cases had not fared well. Other observers, however, are less sympathetic. The $650 million fine, they point out, is not due all at once and is partially (20 percent) tax deductible. Moreover, $650 million may not be a very significant penalty for a firm that made as much as $200 million on a single deal. In fact, for a while the most popular joke on Wall Street was that the "latest buyout" referred to the way Drexel handled the U.S. attorney's office.

Drexel did manage to avoid a lengthy court trial and its accompanying expense and publicity. It avoided the severe penalties of RICO, including jail sentences for top management and the stigma of a racketeering-conviction label. In addition, Drexel was not prohibited from doing business in the junk-bond market. It was, however, a convicted felon and without the services of Michael Milken and other key employees. And, although many clients remained loyal to the firm, others followed Milken or broke ties altogether. Drexel lost its dominance in the junk-bond market.

THINGS GET WORSE

To maintain some degree of profitability, Drexel sold its retail brokerage and mutual fund businesses and trimmed about 40 percent of its work force from the payroll. Despite the company's efforts to remain a player in financial markets, it suffered the final blow with the collapse of the junk-bond market in late 1989. Unable to maintain the liquidity needed to buy and sell huge quantities of securities, Drexel declared bankruptcy in February 1990.

In a plea-bargain arrangement, Michael Milken pleaded guilty on April 24, 1990, to six felony charges, ranging from mail and wire fraud to conspiracy and net-capital violations. He was sentenced to ten years in prison and three years of community service on his release. He must pay $200 million in fines and penalties as well as $400 million in restitution to victims of his crimes. Additionally, he was barred forever from the securities industry. In return, prosecutors dropped all charges against Lowell Milken (although he, too, was forever barred from the securities industry) and the remaining charges filed against Michael Milken in 1989.

Michael Milken was released to a halfway house in Los Angeles on January 3, 1993. After he had served twenty-two months in federal prison, his original ten-year sentence was reduced to two years. He spent two months in the halfway house work-release program, but he is still barred by the Securities and Exchange Commission from the investment brokerage industry. His halfway house employment was through his lawyer's firm, Victor and Sandler, researching civil legal cases. In early 1993, it was estimated that Milken had paid $1.1 billion in fines and settlements connected with his work in the securities business at Drexel.

On leaving prison at the age of 46, Milken indicated that he had inoperable prostate cancer. Milken said he was the victim of a Wall Street witch-hunt that had him as a prize trophy. Milken pointed out thousands of emerging businesses he had helped to grow, including MCI, Turner Broadcasting, and the largest black-owned business, TLC Beatrice. In June 1993, he was worth $500 million after paying $1.1 billion in fines and settlements. He continues to work on eighteen hundred hours of court-ordered community service with a drug prevention program in inner-city Los Angeles. In a June 5, 1993, interview with Barbara Walters, on the television program *20/20,* he presented himself as a humanitarian, philanthropist, and builder of business. He told Walters in the interview that "I was involved with over 3 million transactions in my career. Did we have an oversight in bookkeeping in one or two transactions? Yes. No one thought it was criminal. I am not perfect, and I've never met a person who was."

As of 1996 Milken is still active in charities such as Prostrate Cancer Research, writing books on how to pick stocks, and giving speeches at such educational institutions as the Wharton School of Business.

Questions

1. What are the ethical issues in this case?

2. In Michael Milken's decision-making process, which of the elements of the ethical decision-making process appeared to have the most significant influence: his personal moral values or Drexel's corporate culture?

3. Discuss the costs and benefits of Drexel's actions, considering the outcomes presented in the case.

4. What should Drexel have done?

These facts are from Stephen J. Adler and Laurie P. Cohen, "Using Tough Tactics, Drexel's Lawyers May Advance While Appearing to Lose," *Wall Street Journal,* October 12, 1988, p. 138; Laurie P. Cohen, "Drexel Lawyers, Justice Agency to Meet, Discuss RICO Status in Possible Charges," *Wall Street Journal,* October 20, 1988, p. A3; Laurie P. Cohen, "Drexel Learns U.S. May Soon Ask an Indictment from Grand Jurors," *Wall Street Journal,* October 19, 1988, p. A3; Laurie P. Cohen, "Drexel Pact Contains Concessions by U.S.," *Wall Street Journal,* December 27, 1988, p. A3; Laurie P. Cohen, "Milken's Stiff 10-Year Sentence Is Filled with Incentives to Cooperate with the U.S.," *Wall Street Journal,* November 23, 1990, p. A3; Laurie P. Cohen, "SEC, Drexel Expected to Request Approval of Proposed Settlement," *Wall Street Journal,* June 15, 1989, p. B4; Laurie P. Cohen and Stephen J. Adler, "Indicting Milken, U.S. Demands $1.2 Billion of Financier's Assets," *Wall Street Journal,* March 30, 1989, p. A1; John R. Emshwiller, "Milken's Pursuit of Business Opportunity Built a Personal Fortune, Brought Drexel to the Fore," *Wall Street Journal,* September 8, 1988, p. 7A; Michael Galen, with Dean Foust and Eric Schine, "'Guilty, Your Honor'; Now, Will Milken Help the Feds

Nab Other Wall Street Criminals?" *Business Week,* May 7, 1990, pp. 33–34; Colin Lernster and Alicia Hills Moore, "I Woke Up with My Stomach Churning," *Fortune,* July 3, 1989, p. 120; Michael Milken, interviewed by Barbara Walters, *20/20,* June 5, 1993; Michael Milken, as told to James W. Michaels and Phyllis Berman, "My Story — Michael Milken," *Forbes,* March 16, 1992, pp. 78–100; "Milken Move," *USA Today,* December 28, 1992, p. B1; "Mixed Feelings About Drexel's Decision; Some Call It Wise; Others, a Lack of Will," *Wall Street Journal,* December 23, 1988, p. B1; Thomas E. Ricks, "SEC's Failed Probes of Milken in Past Show Difficulty of Its Mission," *Wall Street Journal,* January 30, 1989, p. A1; Michael Siconolfi, William Power, Laurie P. Cohen, and Robert Guenther, "Rise and Fall: Wall Street Era Ends as Drexel Burnham Decides to Liquidate; Junk Bonds' Creator Becomes Their Victim as Securities It Holds Plunge in Value," *Wall Street Journal,* February 14, 1990, pp. A1, A12; Randall Smith, "How Drexel Wields Its Power in Market for High Yield Bonds," *Wall Street Journal,* May 26, 1988, pp. 1, 12; James B. Stewart, Steven J. Adler, and Laurie P. Cohen, "Out on a Limb, Drexel's Milken Finds Himself More Isolated as Indictment Nears," *Wall Street Journal,* December 23, 1988, p. A1; James B. Stewart and Daniel Hartzberg, "SEC Accuses Drexel of a Sweeping Array of Securities Violations," *Wall Street Journal,* September 8, 1988, pp. 1B, 7B; James B. Stewart and Daniel Hartzberg, "U.S. Reportedly to Seek Charges Tied to Transactions of Princeton/Newport," *Wall Street Journal,* August 4, 1988, pp. 2, 4; James B. Stewart, Daniel Hartzberg, and Laurie P. Cohen, "Biting the Bullet, Drexel Agrees to Plead Guilty and Pay Out a Record $650 Million," *Wall Street Journal,* December 22, 1988, p. A1; "Still Drawing a Crowd," *USA Today,* January 6, 1993, p. B3; Steve Swartz, "Why Mike Milken Stands to Qualify for Guinness Book," *Wall Street Journal,* March 31, 1989, p. A1; Steve Swartz and Bryan Burrough, "Tough Choice, Drexel Faces Difficulty Whether It Settles Case or Gambles on a Trial," *Wall Street Journal,* September 9, 1988, pp. 1, 7; Blair S. Walker, "Milken Rewrites his Life Story," *USA Today,* June 7, 1993, p. 3B; Monci Jo Williams, "Can Fred Joseph Save Drexel?" *Fortune,* May 8, 1989, p. 89; and Monci Jo Williams, "Drexel's Profit and Potential Loss," *Fortune,* February 27, 1989, p. 8.

Ben & Jerry's Homemade Balances Social Responsibility and Growth

en Greenfield and Jerry Cohen opened their first ice cream shop in 1978 in a converted gas station in Burlington, Vermont, investing $12,000 in some secondhand equipment. Their business credentials consisted of lots of enthusiasm and a $5 Penn State University correspondence course in ice cream making. Driven by Greenfield and Cohen's 1960s ideals, Ben & Jerry's Homemade, Inc., has become very successful. By 1995 the company's sales had grown to nearly $150 million. With 500 employees, Ben & Jerry's had brand-name recognition of a company much greater than its size.

From the beginning, Cohen and Greenfield have incorporated into their business a strong sense of social responsibility — to their employees, the community, and the world at large. The company lives by its mission statement: "We're not part of the economic machine that makes profits and oppresses people. We think there should be a spiritual aspect to business. As we help others, we cannot help but help ourselves." Although Ben & Jerry's has experienced some trying times of late, it remains firmly based on its original socially responsible corporate vision.

THE BEN & JERRY'S STORY

Cohen and Greenfield's converted gas station served up rich, all-natural ice cream, full of sweet crunchy bits of cookies and candies, which quickly became popular with local residents. When winter came, however, the customers

---

This case was prepared by O. C. Ferrell and Terry Gable for classroom discussion rather than to illustrate either effective or ineffective handling of an administrative, ethical or legal decision by management.

turned to warmer treats, so Cohen and Greenfield had to come up with new ideas to survive their first year. Soon they were packaging their ice cream and hauling it around to local restaurants. Gradually, they began to include grocery stores among their customers, soon gaining shelf space in 150 stores across the state. Since then the company has grown to include franchises in eighteen states and four countries, including Russia. Cohen and Greenfield continue to hold active positions with the company they started. Cohen is chairman and chief taste tester; Greenfield holds the titles of director of company promotions, cochairman, and "Big Cheese."

In keeping with the founders' 1960s ideals, Ben & Jerry's has always been a bit unorthodox in its business practices, from its executive titles to its products. A popular Ben & Jerry's ice cream flavor is Cherry Garcia, named after (now deceased) guitarist Jerry Garcia, of the rock band the Grateful Dead. Another flavor, Wavy Gravy, is named after the master of ceremonies at Woodstock and, naturally, is packaged in a tie-dyed container.

When the company went public in 1984 as Ben & Jerry's Homemade, Inc., Cohen initially limited the sale of the company's stock to Vermont residents; his idea was that if local residents were part owners of the firm, the community would share in the success of the business. A national stock offering did follow two years later, but the company has continued its philosophy of supporting the local community. In Cohen's words: "What a strange thing we're discovering: As our business supports the community, the community supports us back."

"CARING CAPITALISM"

When Cohen and Greenfield first went into business together, they wrote their own rules, including a corporate mission statement requiring the firm to initiate "innovative ways to improve the quality of life of a broad community — local, national, and international." But by the early 1980s they felt they were losing control of their wildly successful company — its growth, creativity, organization, and values. Greenfield even dropped out of the business for a time. When Cohen considered selling the company at one point, a friend pointed out to him that he could make the company into whatever he wanted. Cohen then developed the concept of "caring capitalism," which he applies by donating part of the company's profits to worthy causes, as well as by finding creative ways to improve the quality of life of the firm's employees and of the local community. Greenfield rejoined the company soon after.

In 1985 Cohen set up the Ben & Jerry's Foundation, which is dedicated to encouraging social change through the donation of 7.5 percent of Ben & Jerry's yearly pretax profits. However, Ben & Jerry's social concern can be seen most clearly in some of its products. One of the firm's ventures is the Peace Pop, an ice cream bar on a stick, from which 1 percent of the profits are used to build awareness and raise funds for peace. The company purchases rain forest nuts for its Rainforest Crunch ice cream, thus providing a market for goods that do not require destruction of the rain forests. Additionally, sales of Rainforest Crunch are funneled back into rain-forest preservation efforts. Ben & Jerry's also buys brownies made by homeless people for its Chocolate Fudge Brownie ice cream and Brownie Bars.

Cohen and Greenfield extend their social awareness to their own employees. A seven-to-one salary ratio at the firm limits the salaries of top executives to seven times the salary earned by the lowest-paid workers. This helps give all employees a sense of working together as a team. And, when it seemed that the company was expanding too quickly (the company went from 150 people to 300 almost overnight), company executives made a conscious decision to slow growth to ensure that the company's family atmosphere and core values would not be lost. Employees also get three pints of ice cream a week, free health-club memberships, and a partially subsidized company child-care center.

Rather than buy television, radio, or newspaper advertising, Ben & Jerry's promotes things and events of value to the community. The company sponsors peace, music, and art festivals around the country and tries to draw attention to the many social causes it undertakes. One such cause is opposition to bovine growth hormone (a substance injected into cows to increase milk production) because Greenfield and Cohen fear that its use will drive small dairy farmers out of business. A local venture is the Giraffe Project, which recognizes people willing to stick their own necks out and stand tall for what they believe; local customers of Ben & Jerry's scoop shops nominate the recipients of Giraffe Commendations. The company also plans to open a new scoop shop in Karelia, Russia, the profits from which will be used to fund cultural exchanges between Americans and Russians.

ARE THE TIMES A-CHANGIN' FOR BEN & JERRY'S?

Based on his thirty-five years of international development and citizen-action experience, David Korten, a former Harvard Business School professor, contends that long-term-oriented, socially responsible companies often face hard times in today's fast-paced, often shortsighted, and profit-minded economic system. According to this perspective, the economic system, in its focus on the current value of company stock, rewards cost efficiency and punishes those that it sees as inefficient. Firms that are able to externalize or shift their costs to other parties are rewarded whereas the socially responsible organization is considered inefficient and wasteful. Consequently, the firm's stock price suffers and the company is labeled as "in trouble." According to Korten,

> With financial markets demanding maximum short-term gains and corporate raiders standing by to trash any company that isn't externalizing every possible

cost, efforts to fix the problem by raising the social consciousness of managers misdefine the problem. There are plenty of socially conscious managers. The problem is a predatory system that makes it difficult for them to survive. . . . They must either compromise their vision or run a great risk of being expelled by the system. . . . Corporate managers live and work in a system that is virtually feeding on the socially responsible.*

Ben & Jerry's appears to be one socially responsible firm faced with such issues. While some analysts say that the company is merely going through a sort of "midlife crisis," from which it will soon recover, others harshly criticize its motives and direction. Examples of such criticisms include the following:

- That it is questionable how much good the social work championed and engaged in by Ben & Jerry's really does. For example, the company bought pie crust and "goo" ingredients from a New Jersey bakery staffed by recovering alcoholics and drug addicts. But critics allege that when Ben & Jerry's Apple Pie Frozen Yogurt flopped in the marketplace, the company caused the bakery, which had no other customers, to lay off twenty employees and fall deeply into debt.

- That a much publicized campaign to find a new CEO for Ben & Jerry's "turned into a ruse." Critics allege that the campaign, in which prospective CEO candidates were asked to send in essays stating their qualifications and their vision for the firm, was nothing more than a publicity stunt and that the eventual "winner" was in fact recruited by a New York–based headhunter and wrote his essay after being hired.

- That some of Ben & Jerry's products contain a legal but potentially harmful growth hormone.

- That Ben & Jerry's "save the world" marketing focus is little more than "a series of feel-good stunts to sell high-priced ice cream."

- That the firm's recent flattened sales and financial losses are clear signs of a company on the brink of collapse. (Ben & Jerry's lost $1.9 million on sales of $148 million in 1994.)

One commentator stated that while some internal miscues have negatively affected the company's financial performance, the best explanation for flat sales is that increasingly health-conscious consumers are demanding less fat- and calorie-laden products from Ben & Jerry's. Ben and Jerry's has received criticism and admits it has made some mistakes. The company believes that perceived mistakes are always made when a position is taken on social issues.

---

*David C. Korten, *When Corporations Rule the World* (West Hartford, Conn.: Kumarian Press, 1995), pp. 212–214.

THE BEAT GOES ON . . .

Despite their detractors, Cohen and Greenfield remain committed to the socially responsible vision that Ben & Jerry's was founded on.

According to Cohen, "It's very possible for business to make a profit and integrate a concern for the community into its day-to-day activity. If most businesses operated in that fashion, we wouldn't have all these social and environmental problems that we have." He adds, "I'm certainly aware that there are a lot of business and economic theorists that believe that spiritual values, a concern for the people, a concern for the general public welfare have no place in business. . . . I disagree very strongly."

Each year Ben & Jerry's asks someone to conduct a social audit to measure whether the company is fulfilling its self-stated obligations. While the company will probably continue to struggle in its efforts to balance growth and profits with social responsibility, its customers — mostly 25 to 45 years old — will probably continue to buy its ice cream not only for the good taste but also to feel that they are doing something good for society.

Questions

1. Ben & Jerry's has sought innovative ways to improve the quality of life of the community, both locally and on a global basis. How can other firms initiate "caring capitalism" that incorporates ethics and social responsibility?

2. Ben & Jerry's donates 7.5 percent of its yearly pretax profits to encourage social change. Is this the appropriate role for a profit-making corporation?

3. Discuss how the corporate culture at Ben & Jerry's, as described in this case, influences the daily implementation of ethical decision making.

4. Do you feel that the criticism directed at Ben & Jerry's is warranted? What, do you think, are the grounds for this criticism?

5. Why are there so few companies as proactively and visibly socially responsible as Ben & Jerry's?

These facts are from Mark Albright, "At Ben & Jerry's, Social Agenda Churns with Ice Cream," *St. Petersburg Times,* November 11, 1995, p. 1E; Peter Newcomb, "Is Ben & Jerry's BST-free?" *Forbes,* September 25, 1995, p. 98; Hanna Rosin, "The Evil Empire: The Scoop on Ben & Jerry's Crunchy Capitalism," *The New Republic,* September 11, 1995, p. 22; Andrew E. Serwer, "Ben & Jerry's Corporate Ogre," *Fortune,* July 10, 1995, p. 30; David C. Korten, *When Corporations Rule the World* (West Hartford, Conn.: Kumarian Press, 1995), pp. 212–214; Erik Larson, "Forever Young," *Inc.* (July 1988): 50–62; Maxine Lipner, "Ben & Jerry's: Sweet Ethics Evince Social Awareness," *Compass Readings* (July 1991): 22–30; Blair S. Walker, "Good-Humored Activist Back to the Fray," *USA Today,* December 8, 1992, pp. 1B, 2B; and Eric J. Wieffering, "Trouble in Camelot," *Business Ethics* 5 (January–February 1991): 16–19.

The Wreck of
the Exxon Valdez

*I*n 1989 Exxon Corporation and Alyeska Pipeline Service Company — an eight-company consortium that operates the Trans-Alaska pipeline and the shipping terminal in Valdez, Alaska — were severely criticized for their handling of a major oil spill from an Exxon tanker. The *Exxon Valdez* ran aground near Valdez, Alaska, on March 24, 1989, and spilled 240,000 barrels — eleven million gallons — of crude oil that eventually covered 2,600 square miles of Prince William Sound and the Gulf of Alaska. Although the Exxon spill was not the largest ever, it was one of the worst in terms of environmental damage and disruption of industry, and it has jeopardized the future of oil production in environmentally sensitive areas of Alaska. As of early 1996, the extent of the damage done, as well as the level of Exxon's responsibility, was still being debated in the U.S. judicial system and the media.

THE WRECK

At 12:04 A.M. on March 24, 1989, the *Exxon Valdez* was under the command of Third Mate Gregory Cousins, who reportedly was not licensed to pilot the vessel through the treacherous waters of Prince William Sound. The ship's captain, Joseph Hazelwood, apparently was asleep below deck. In an effort to dodge floating ice in the sound, Cousins performed what officials later described as an unusual series of right turns. The ship ran aground on Bligh Reef, spilling much of its cargo through the ruptured hull. The spill spread

This case was prepared by O. C. Ferrell, Gwyneth M. Vaughn, and Terry Gable for classroom discussion rather than to illustrate either effective or ineffective handling of an administrative, ethical or legal decision by management.

rapidly over the next few days, killing thousands of sea birds, sea otters, and other wildlife; covering the coastline with oil; and closing the fishing season in the sound for several years.

The Prince William Sound area was home to abundant wildlife. More than two hundred species of birds have been reported there, including one-fifth of the world's trumpeter swans. The fishing industry derived annual sales of $100 million from the sound's herring, salmon, Pacific cod, Alaska pollock, rockfish, halibut, flounder, and sharks, as well as crab and shrimp. The world's largest concentration of killer whales and about one-fourth of the total U.S. sea otter population inhabited the sound at the time of the wreck.

THE RESPONSE TO THE DISASTER

The events following the March 24 spill reveal what some observers say is a pattern of unpreparedness, mismanagement, and negligence. According to the transcripts of radio conversations between Captain Hazelwood on the *Exxon Valdez* and the Coast Guard immediately after the accident, the captain tried for an hour to rock the tanker free from the reef, an action that Coast Guard officials claim might have sunk the ship and spilled more oil. They say that Hazelwood ignored their warnings that rocking the ship might make the oil spill almost five times as bad.

When Coast Guard officers boarded the tanker at 3:30 A.M., they reported that 138,000 barrels of crude oil had already been spilled. According to a contingency plan filed when the Valdez terminal first began operations, Alyeska crews should already have arrived at the ship with containment equipment. They had not. A frantic Coast Guard officer radioed, "We've got a serious problem. . . . She's leaking and groaning. There's nobody here. . . . Where's Alyeska?"

After being notified of the accident, Alyeska Pipeline Service, in the first line of defense against oil spills, sent an observation tug to the scene and began to assemble its oil-spill containment equipment, much of which was in disarray. It loaded containment boom and lightering equipment (emergency pumps to suction oil from the *Exxon Valdez* onto other vessels) onto a damage barge. The Coast Guard then decided, however, that the barge was too slow and the need for the lightering equipment more urgent, so Alyeska crews had to reload the lightering equipment onto a tug, losing still more time.

Coast Guard officers tested Captain Hazelwood for alcohol nine hours after the wreck; they apparently did not realize that the ship was equipped with a testing kit. The test showed that Hazelwood had a blood-alcohol content of 0.061; it is a violation of Coast Guard regulations for a person operating a ship to have a blood-alcohol level in excess of 0.04. Four other crewmen, including the third mate, tested negative for alcohol. Exxon officials later admitted that they knew the captain had gone through an alcohol detoxification program, yet they still gave him command of the *Exxon Valdez,* Exxon's largest tanker.

The first Alyeska containment equipment did not arrive at the scene until 2:30 in the afternoon; the rest of the equipment came the next morning. Neither Alyeska nor Exxon had enough containment booms and chemical dispersants to fight the spill. They were not ready to test the effectiveness of the dispersants until eighteen hours after the spill, and then they conducted the test by tossing buckets of chemicals out the door of a helicopter. The helicopter's rotor dispersed the chemicals, and they missed their target altogether. Moreover, the skimmer boats used to scoop oil out of the sea were so old that they kept breaking down and clogging. The skimmers filled up rapidly and had to be emptied into nearby barges, taking them out of action for long periods. Some of the makeshift work crews were assigned to boats with no apparent mission. Cleanup efforts were further hampered by communication breakdowns between coordinators on shore and crews at the scene because of technical problems and limited range. Messages had to be relayed through local fishermen. And, although a fleet of private fishing boats was standing by ready to assist with the containment and cleanup, Exxon and Alyeska failed to mobilize their help. Exxon has admitted that the early efforts were chaotic, but says that they were no more so than the response to any major disaster.

The tanker was not fully encircled by containment booms until Saturday afternoon, thirty-six hours after the accident. By then, the oil spill covered an area of twelve square miles. Exxon conducted more tests with chemical dispersants Saturday night, but the tests were inconclusive because conditions were too calm. (The chemical dispersants require wave action to be effective.) On Sunday afternoon the Coast Guard gave Exxon permission to use the dispersants on the spill. But that night a storm with winds as high as seventy-three miles an hour drove the oil slick thirty-seven miles into the southwestern section of the sound. All cleanup efforts were halted until the next afternoon because of the weather. Exxon eventually applied 5,500 gallons of chemical dispersants, but by then, because of the delay caused by the storm, the oil had become too emulsified for dispersants to work properly. By the end of the week, the oil slick had spread to cover 2,600 miles of coastline and sea.

ALYESKA'S CONTAINMENT PLAN

Since the early 1970s, Alaskan officials and fishermen have expressed concern that a major oil spill was inevitable. In response, Alyeska Pipeline Service, its eight oil company owners, and federal officials promised in 1972 that the tanker fleet operating out of Valdez would incorporate safety features such as double hulls and protective ballast tanks to minimize the possibility of spills. By 1977, however, Alyeska had convinced the Coast Guard that the safety features were not necessary, and only a few ships in the Valdez fleet incorporated them. The *Exxon Valdez* did not.

Alyeska Pipeline Service had filed a comprehensive contingency plan detailing how it would handle spills from the pipeline or the Valdez terminal. In the event of an oil spill from a tanker, emergency crews were to encircle the spill with containment booms within five hours — yet, it took them a day and a half to encircle the *Exxon Valdez.* Alyeska's contingency plan further specified that an emergency crew of at least fifteen would be on hand at all times. By 1981, however, much of the team had been disbanded to cut costs. In 1989 Alyeska maintained a crew of eleven to monitor terminal operations, but because the *Valdez* spill occurred at the beginning of the Easter holiday weekend, the company had trouble rounding up the team. Furthermore, Exxon's staff of oil spill experts had been cut back since 1985. At least nine oil spill managers, including Exxon's chief environmental officer, had left or retired. An Exxon spokesman said that he was not aware that the cutbacks affected Alyeska's initial readiness to combat a spill.

A state audit of Alyeska's equipment demonstrated that the company was unprepared for the spill. It was supposed to have three tugboats and thirteen oil skimmers available but in fact had only two and seven, respectively. The company also had only fourteen thousand feet of boom for containing spills; the contingency plan specified twenty-one thousand feet. The barge that carried the booms and stored skimmed oil was also out of service because it had been damaged in a storm. In any case, the required equipment would not have been enough, because a tanker like the *Exxon Valdez* is almost one thousand feet long and holds 1.2 million barrels of oil. The booms available could barely encircle the giant ship, much less a sizable slick.

Alyeska violated its own contingency plans when it failed to notify state officials that the barge was out of service. A key piece of equipment in the contingency plan, the barge should have been loaded with seven thousand feet of boom, but the boom had been removed during the repair. A replacement barge had been ordered and was on its way from Texas. On March 24, it was in Seattle.

Although Alyeska conducted regular "spill drills," state monitors said that drills in the previous few years had been bungled and were considered unsuccessful. Among other things, the drills showed that crew members often did not know how to operate their assigned equipment and that Alyeska's equipment and responses were inadequate. Reporters Ken Wells and Charles McCoy wrote in the *Wall Street Journal,* "The oil companies' lack of preparedness makes a mockery of a 250-page containment plan, approved by the state, for fighting spills in Prince William Sound." Arlon R. Tussing, a Seattle oil consultant, commented, "The system that was set up early on has disintegrated."

CLEANING UP OIL AND MANAGING A PUBLIC RELATIONS DISASTER

Exxon's chairman, Lawrence Rawl, apologized to the public for the spill in full-page advertisements in many newspapers and in a letter to Exxon stockholders. The company accepted liability for the spill and responsibility for its cleanup. By summer Exxon had ten thousand people, one thousand vessels, thirty-eight oil skimmers (including one sent by the former Soviet Union to help out for a short time), and seventy-two aircraft working to clean up beaches and wildlife. Exxon hoped to complete its cleanup before September 15, 1989, because winter weather would make further efforts difficult.

Exxon claims that it saved $22 million by not building the *Exxon Valdez* with a second hull. But, as of March 22, 1990, the company had spent $2 billion on cleaning up the spill, of which insurance companies would pay only $400 million. (Exxon was, however, able to take an after-tax charge of $1.7 billion to cover legal bills and cleanup costs in 1989.) In addition, thirty-one lawsuits and thirteen hundred claims had been filed against Exxon within a month of the spill. On August 15, 1989, the state of Alaska also filed suit against Exxon and the largest of the other firms involved in Alyeska Pipeline Services for mismanaging the response to the oil spill. The suit demanded both compensatory and punitive damages that could exceed $1 billion. Captain Hazelwood, who was fired by Exxon soon after the accident, was found guilty in March 1990 of negligent discharge of oil, a misdemeanor. He was acquitted on three other more serious charges, including drunk driving.

Exxon also faced heated criticism from the public and from state and federal officials who believed cleanup efforts were inadequate. A Coast Guard spokesman in Valdez said, "We're running into a problem with the definition of the word 'clean.' The concept of being clean makes you think no oil is there. The oil is still there, but it may be three feet or two feet beneath the surface." Lee Raymond, Exxon's president, said, "Assuming that we can have people working till mid-September, we have a good shot at having all the beaches treated. But not clean like Mr. Clean who shows up in your kitchen. Our objective is to make sure the ecosystems are back in shape." Many Alaskans and environmentalists did not believe Exxon's idea of "clean" was clean enough. In addition, there were disputes as to how much oil had actually been cleaned up. By July 25, 1989, six hundred miles of shoreline had been "treated," but another two hundred miles still required treatment. Moreover, incoming tides often brought new oil slicks to cover just-treated beaches, slowing cleanup efforts considerably.

In addition, Exxon came under fire for the way it had managed the crisis. Chairman Lawrence Rawl did not comment on the spill for nearly six days, and then he did so from New York. Although Rawl personally apologized for the spill, crisis management experts say that it is important for the chief executive to be present at the site of an emergency. Harry Nicolay, a Boston crisis management consultant, said, "When the most senior person in the company comes forward, it's telling the whole world that we take this as a most serious concern." The crisis management experts believe that Rawl's delayed response and failure to appear on the scene angered the public despite Exxon's efforts to clean up the spill.

Some of Exxon's statements to the public have also been criticized as bad public relations moves. For example, one Exxon executive told reporters that consumers would pay for the costs of the cleanup in the form of higher gas prices. Although that statement may have been truthful, it did nothing to placate already angry consumers. The public also reacted skeptically to Exxon officials' attempts to blame cleanup delays on the Coast Guard and Alaskan officials. And Gerald C. Meyers, a specialist in corporate crisis management, said that Exxon's newspaper apology was "absolutely insincere. They were ill-advised to say they sent 'several hundred people' to the scene. This is a company with more than 100,000 employees." Furthermore, Exxon insisted that it would stop all cleanup operations on September 15, 1989, regardless of how much shoreline remained to be cleaned. In a memo released in July, that September deadline was said to be "not negotiable." After much public and government protest, however, the company's president promised that Exxon would return in the spring of 1990 if the Coast Guard determined that further cleanup was warranted. "It's our best guess that there will be a lot less oil than people think," he said. "But if the conclusion is reached by the Coast Guard that something needs to be made right and it can be made right, we'll be there. We're not trying to run off." (Exxon did return in the spring for further cleanup efforts.)

Exxon's response to the crisis certainly hurt its reputation and credibility with the public. National consumer groups have urged the public to boycott all Exxon products, and nearly twenty thousand Exxon credit card holders cut up their cards and returned them to the company to express their dissatisfaction with its cleanup efforts.

THE EFFECTS OF THE *VALDEZ* DISASTER

Many changes have been made since the *Valdez* incident. Because Captain Hazelwood was found to have a high blood-alcohol content after the spill, three of Alyeska's largest owners (including Exxon) have begun mandatory random drug and alcohol searches of all ships using the Valdez port. In April 1989, Alaska Governor Steve Cowper ordered Alyeska Pipeline to restock the Valdez terminal with all the booms, skimmers, and other equipment that were required by the original contingency plan. Alyeska was also ordered to form an emergency crew to respond immediately to spills. Governor Cowper demanded that Alyeska stock enough additional equipment to allow it to respond within two hours to a ten-million-gallon spill in Prince William Sound. Alyeska is now required to encircle all tankers with containment booms as they are loading and unloading, and it also had to change certain other procedures. In addition, on May 8, 1989, the state eliminated many of the tax exemptions granted to oil companies producing in many Alaskan oil fields. The elimination of the tax breaks was expected to cost the affected oil companies about $2 billion over the next twenty years. Exxon will probably have to pay an extra $35 million in taxes annually. Other legislation that would increase the oil companies' liability in spills is also under consideration by state lawmakers.

In contrast to strong public sentiment that the cleanup efforts were too little too late, many experts believed the spill's effects would not be permanent and that nature would clean the area. John Robinson, head of the National Oceanic and Atmospheric Administration's hazardous materials response unit, said that wind and wave action would make the spill all but invisible by the summer of 1990. Nature would purge the toxic effects from the oil in two years, he believed. Robinson also pointed out that North Slope crude is fairly heavy; lighter crudes, such as the Arabian crude spilled by the *Amoco Cadiz* off the coast of France in 1979, are more toxic. The spill from the *Amoco Cadiz* has been almost completely cleaned up by the action of wind and wave, although the process took nearly ten years. Exxon's chairman, Rawl, agreed that the spill's effects would not be permanent. When asked what people will find on returning to Valdez in ten years, Rawl replied, "Nothing. I would think they can return to Valdez a lot sooner than ten years from now. I don't think they will find much in terms of environmental damage."

Nevertheless, the spill has jeopardized further oil exploration and production in other parts of Alaska. Before the spill, a U.S. Senate committee and a House panel passed separate bills to allow drilling in Alaska's environmentally sensitive Arctic National Wildlife Refuge, but neither came up for a final vote. Alaska State Senator Frank Murkowski, who supported further drilling, believed it was "premature" to introduce additional legislation until the oil industry develops stronger contingency plans to deal with spills and accidents.

THE MATTER REMAINS UNRESOLVED

The extent of the damage done by the massive *Exxon Valdez* oil spill, as well as Exxon's responsibility in the matter, is still being debated in both the media and the U.S. court system. With regard to Exxon's level of responsibility, court proceedings have passed through three distinct stages and are now in the fourth.

In the first stage, as noted earlier, the captain of the *Exxon Valdez*, Joseph Hazelwood, was found to be negligent and reckless for his role in the spill. The second phase focused on compensatory damages; fishermen and fisheries were awarded $286 million for losses incurred as a result of not being able to fish in the spill area. The third phase of court proceedings dealt with punitive damages. In this stage, concluded on September 16, 1994, Exxon was ordered to pay $5.3 billion — $15 billion had been sought — to a group of four-teen thousand fishermen and citizens in the Prince William Sound region. Of the total amount — roughly equal to what Exxon was then earning in profits each year — $4 billion was allocated to cover environmental costs, with the remaining $1 billion awarded as retribution for Exxon's insensitivity in the matter. The fourth stage, still in process in 1996, has involved Exxon's appeal of both the compensatory and punitive damage awards. As a result of the appeals process, Exxon is able, at least temporarily, to avoid paying both the damages themselves and interest on them. With regard to the money thus saved on the $5.3 billion award, one reporter estimated that the amount would accrue $648,000 in interest per day, or $300 million per year, if Exxon should fail to have the judgment set aside by the court. Exxon has yet to pay any amount of either the $286 million or $5.3 billion judgments against it as individual portions of the complex lawsuits are debated further in court. According to Steve Schroer, an attorney for the Alaskan fishermen and citizens, "Exxon has made it clear that it is going to appeal this to the end of the earth."

But the court debate does not end there. Exxon is also involved in a hotly contested lawsuit with its numerous insurance providers over their refusal to pay Exxon for its spill cleanup efforts. The insurance companies, led by Lloyd's of London, refused to pay Exxon because (1) the cleanup efforts engaged in were not required by law; (2) these efforts were conducted in substandard fashion; (3) Exxon's level of liability coverage was well below the expenses sought; and (4) the spill itself was a result of "intentional misconduct," thus disqualifying insurance coverage of the accident. In short, the insurance companies contend that Exxon's cleanup activities were little more than "an expensive public relations exercise" designed to make the public think of Exxon as an ethical and socially responsible corporation. Claiming that it had incurred between $3.5 billion and $4 billion in expenses for the cleanup, Exxon in turn filed suit against the 250 insurance companies, originally seeking around $3 billion in compensation, even though it was covered for only $850 million. Most of the original amount sought from the insurers, $2.15 billion, was for "bad faith" conduct related to initial refusal to pay, interest charges, and attorneys' fees. The original figure of $3 billion was later reduced to about $1 billion, and insurers agreed to pay Exxon $300 million as a partial settlement of claims related to cleanup activities.

Seven years after the *Exxon Valdez* spill the extent of the damage it caused is still unclear and Exxon's responsibilities to those harmed by its negligence remain unresolved. Although Exxon's court battles now draw little media attention, an oil spill (not an Exxon spill) in early 1996 off the Rhode Island coast prompted commentary on the changes since 1989. A *Boston Globe* reporter noted that "the oil industry handles oil more carefully since the *Exxon Valdez* disaster. . . . The mess shocked Congress into passing the Oil Pollution Act of 1990, the world's toughest oil spill law. . . . Six years later, the volume of oil spilled in U.S. waters has dropped, but it began increasing again in

1993. . . . From 1993 to 1994, the number of significant U.S. spills — more than 10,000 gallons — doubled, to a total discharge of 967,000 gallons."* According to another analyst, "We're still seeing the same number of spills. What has improved is the response to those spills."

As these assessments suggest, the one positive consequence of the *Exxon Valdez* oil spill has been better industry response to the spilling of oil into our waters. However, this hardly compensates for the harm inflicted by Exxon's negligent spillage of 11 million gallons of crude oil into the Prince William Sound area. Years later the area is still trying to recover fully.

Questions

1. In relation to this incident and the circumstances that led up to it, discuss the role of individual moral development, organizational factors, and significant others in decisions.

2. If Exxon had an ethics program as described in Chapter 9, would this have prevented the wreck of the *Exxon Valdez?*

3. Should Exxon and Alyeska be held responsible for cleaning up the spill, or should taxpayers and consumers pay for it (in the form of higher gasoline prices and taxes)? In future oil production efforts, which should take precedence: the environment or consumers' desires for low-priced gasoline and heating oil?

---

*Scott Allen, "Oil Spills a Fossil–Fuel Fact of Life," *Boston Globe,* January 27, 1996, p. 13.

These facts are from Reed Abelson, "Tax Reformers, Take Your Mark," *New York Times,* February 11, 1996, sec. 3, p. 1; Scott Allen, "Oil Spills a Fossil-Fuel Fact of Life," *Boston Globe,* January 27, 1996, p. 13; "Exxon Will Pay $3.5 Million to Settle Claims in Phase Four of Valdez Case," *BNA State Environment Daily,* January 19, 1996; Aliza Fan, "Exxon May Still Get More Than $3 Billion in Dispute with Lloyd's," *Oil Daily,* January 22, 1996, p. 3; Tony Freemantle, "Billion-Dollar Battle Looms over Spill Costs: Exxon Corp. Trying to Collect from Its Insurance Companies," *Anchorage Daily News,* September 5, 1995, p. 1A; *Institute for Crisis Management Newsletter,* 4, (March 1995): 3; Dave Lenckus, "Exxon Seeks More Spill Cover: Oil Giant Reaches Partial Agreement with Insurers," *Business Insurance,* January 22, 1996, p. 1; Natalie Phillips, $3.5 Million Settles Exxon Spill Suit," *Anchorage Daily News,* January 18, 1996, p. 1B; Wayne Beissert, "In Valdez's Wake, Uncertainty," *USA Today,* July 28, 1989, p. 3A; Amanda Bennett, Jolie Solomon, and Allanna Sullivan, "Firms Debate Hard Line on Alcoholics," *Wall Street Journal,* April 13, 1989, p. B1; Cable Network News, March 22, 1990; Carrie Dolan, "Exxon to Bolster Oil-Cleanup Effort After Criticism," *Wall Street Journal,* May 11, 1989, p. A10; Carrie Dolan and Charles McCoy, "Military Transports Begin Delivering Equipment to Battle Alaskan Oil Spill," *Wall Street Journal,* April 10, 1989, p. A8; Stuart Elliot, "Public Angry at Slow Action on Oil Spill," *USA Today,* April 21, 1989, pp. B1, B2; William Glasgall and Vicky Cahan, "Questions That Keep Surfacing After the Spill," *Business Week,* April 17, 1989, p. 18; Kathy Barks Hoffman, "Oil Spill's Cleanup Costs Exceed $1.3B," *USA Today,* July 25, 1989, p. B1; "In Ten Years You'll See 'Nothing'" (interview with Exxon chairman, Lawrence Rawl), *Fortune,* May 8, 1989, pp. 50–54; Charles McCoy, "Alaska Drops Criminal Probe of Oil Disaster," *Wall Street Journal,* July 28, 1989, p. A3; Charles McCoy, "Alaskans End Big Tax Breaks for Oil Firms," *Wall Street Journal,* May 10, 1989, p. A6; Charles McCoy, "Heartbreaking Fight Unfolds in Hospital for Valdez Otters," *Wall Street Journal,* April 20, 1989, pp. A1, A4; Charles McCoy and Ken Wells, "Alaska, U.S.

Knew of Flaws in Oil-Spill Response Plans," *Wall Street Journal,* April 7, 1989, p. A3; Peter Nulty, "The Future of Big Oil," *Fortune,* May 8, 1989, pp. 46–49; Wayne Owens, "Turn the Valdez Cleanup Over to Mother Nature," editorial, *Wall Street Journal,* July 27, 1989, p. A8; Lawrence G. Rawl, letter to Exxon shareholders, April 14, 1989; "Recordings Reveal Exxon Captain Rocked Tanker to Free It from Reef," [Texas A&M University] *Battalion,* April 26, 1989, p. 1; Michael Satchell, with Steve Lindbeck, "Tug of War over Oil Drilling," *U.S. News & World Report,* April 10, 1989, pp. 47–48; Richard B. Schmitt, "Exxon, Alyeska May Be Exposed on Damages," *Wall Street Journal,* April 10, 1989, p. A8; Stratford P. Sherman, "Smart Ways to Handle the Press," *Fortune,* June 19, 1989, pp. 69–75; Caleb Solomon and Allanna Sullivan, "For the Petroleum Industry, Pouring Oil Is in Fact the Cause of Troubled Waters," *Wall Street Journal,* March 31, 1989, p. A4; Allanna Sullivan, "Agencies Clear Exxon Oil-Cleanup Plan Despite Coast Guard Doubts on Deadline," *Wall Street Journal,* April 19, 1989, p. A2; Allanna Sullivan, "Alaska Sues Exxon Corp., 6 Other Firms," *Wall Street Journal,* August 16, 1989, pp. A3, A4; Allanna Sullivan and Amanda Bennett, "Critics Fault Chief Executive of Exxon on Handling of Recent Alaskan Oil Spill," *Wall Street Journal,* March 31, 1989, p. B1; Ken Wells, "Alaska Begins Criminal Inquiry of Valdez Spill," *Wall Street Journal,* March 30, 1989, p. A4; Ken Wells, "Blood-Alcohol Level of Captain of Exxon Tanker Exceeded Limits," *Wall Street Journal,* March 31, 1989, p. A4; Ken Wells, "For Exxon, Cleanup Costs May Be Just the Beginning," *Wall Street Journal,* April 14, 1989, pp. B1, B2; Ken Wells and Marilyn Chase, "Paradise Lost: Heartbreaking Scenes of Beauty Disfigured Follow Alaska Oil Spill," *Wall Street Journal,* March 31, 1989, pp. A1, A4; Ken Wells and Charles McCoy, "How Unpreparedness Turned the Alaska Spill into Ecological Debacle," *Wall Street Journal,* April 3, 1989, pp. A1, A4; and Ken Wells and Allanna Sullivan, "Stuck in Alaska: Exxon's Army Scrubs the Beaches, but They Don't Stay Cleaned," *Wall Street Journal,* July 27, 1989, pp. A1, A5.

Ethics Training at WMX Technologies, Inc.

When Dean L. Buntrock and H. Wayne Huizenga began their small garbage collection service, they could not have foreseen that it would grow into the world's largest solid waste and disposal company. Before they were partners, Buntrock started with Ace Scavenger Service of Illinois, which had 12 collection trucks, and Huizenga was running 2 waste collection routes in Broward County, Florida. In 1971 they came together to form Waste Management, Inc. Concern over air quality in the 1960s and the subsequent ban of on-site waste-burning during that period caused the waste-disposal industry to boom. In its first year of operations, Waste Management had revenues of close to $17 million and customers in Florida, Illinois, Indiana, Minnesota, Ohio, and Wisconsin.

With Waste Management's success under his belt, Wayne Huizenga left the company for other business pursuits. Dean Buntrock remained as CEO. In 1993, the company became known as WMX Technologies, Inc. Currently, WMX employs more than 63,000 people and operates in 20 countries, including Argentina, Venezuela, Australia, New Zealand, Germany, Italy, France, Finland, and the Netherlands. WMX has expanded into the only full-line, global company offering services ranging from environmental consulting, design, and engineering to construction, management, and disposal, and has controlling interest in four other public companies. WMX services twelve million residential and one million commercial and industrial customers.

WMX'S CONCERN FOR ETHICS

Because WMX was fined $2 million for violation of antitrust laws and $12.5 million for pollution ordinance infringements, the company has become increasingly concerned with the environment and ethical business practices. As evidence of WMX's success in implementing ethical and environmental practices, the Occupational Safety and Health Administration (OSHA) currently uses a facility of one of its subsidiaries, Chemical Waste Management, as a model for addressing recent safety laws thorough good faith efforts in complying. WMX also has garnered the support of several zoning boards through their proactive environmental activities. Because of these efforts, the company recently received a permit to develop an area for which many other applicants from the disposal industry were turned down.

A NEED FOR ETHICS TRAINING

The business community as a whole is being forced to consider ethics due to society's recent upsurge in concern over the ethical wrongdoing of companies. Highly publicized cases, such as the suspension of General Dynamics from doing business with the federal government after overcharging the Pentagon and Ivan Boesky's insider trading, have helped to create a public perception that standards in business need to be raised.

In the past companies operated under the assumption that if employees with strong ethical values were hired, the company also would be ethical. Research has indicated, however, that an individual's personal belief system and moral philosophy are only part of what is considered when making ethical decisions. The environment and culture of the company and the influence of fellow workers are also key determinants in ethical decision making. Ethics training and its support by top officials in the organization have been shown to greatly affect an organization's ethical climate.

Ethics training has increased dramatically over the past five years due to a number of developments. First, more companies understand that ethics, like most other activities in an organization, are influenced by the organizational culture. Values, attitudes, beliefs, language, and behavioral patterns on a day-to-day basis define an organization's operating culture and subsequently the ethical behavior of its employees. Marketers who fail to institute ethical leadership and systems that facilitate ethical choice share the responsibility of ethical behavior within the company. Companies such as Sears provide evidence that a lack of ethical leadership can be costly. The company lost an estimated $60 million from its failure to clarify the difference between unnecessary service and legitimate preventive automobile maintenance. The company had developed an incentive program requiring service consultants to sell a certain quota of services from brake jobs to front-end alignments on an hourly basis. Sears did not set out to defraud the public, but a number of organizational factors contributed to unethical sales practices.

Another influential factor in the development of ethics training programs is the 1991 Federal Sentencing Guidelines. The Federal Sentencing Guidelines reward companies that develop programs to emphasize the prevention of unlawful conduct, primarily through compliance standards and procedures. Under the guidelines, firms committing unlawful acts have been fined from 5 to 200 percent of the loss suffered by customers, depending on whether an effective program to prevent or detect unethical and unlawful conduct has been established. In other words, an approach to ethics training is to channel behavior in ethical directions and act as a deterrent to irresponsible behavior. It is hoped that companies will avoid the old cliché, "if it's legal, it's ethical."

WMX CODE OF ETHICS

Ethics training at WMX is designed to help employees recognize ethical issues and make ethical choices well above the standards set for legal compliance. WMX's code of ethics and training program get employees involved in making decisions. Through ethical leadership and group problem resolution, employees practice recognizing ethical issues and improving decisions. The following include some specific components of the WMX ethics training program.

In WMX's code of ethics booklet, "Ethics in Our Workplace: Guidelines for Our People," the following words appear under a picture of CEO Dean Buntrock:

> Our ethics and our business practices. These are the "bonding agents." Qualities like fairness, honesty, integrity and trust shape our behavior—as a Company and as individuals.
> It's our reputation we are talking about. Companies with shaky ethics and shabby standards simply will not be able to cut it when they're stacked against the competition. We want to be winners! Leaders! The best of the best!
> That means calling up the best in each of us. Practicing sound ethical values in each and every undertaking. Making "ethical excellence" a way of life. Having a good, solid name.

WMX's success in improving the organization's ethical decisions is partly due to its code of ethics. The four-page booklet outlines what WMX expects from its employees when they are faced with ethical situations. It begins by defining what "ethics" means to WMX. It specifically identifies what is ethical and what is unethical. "Treating values such as fairness, honesty, integrity, and trust as ground rules, not options, in making decisions" is ethical, and "misrepresenting the facts" to a customer, "bad-mouthing the competition," "doing shoddy work," "promising more than we can deliver," and "conspiring to 'cover-up' illegal or unethical customer activities" are unethical practices, for example.

The code also provides information concerning how to recognize an ethical problem in day-to-day activities in the workplace. It supplies a set of rules to follow and establishes principles to consider when a situation is not specifically addressed. The activities covered range from those with customers, suppliers, and government regulators to dealings with fellow employees and competitors. WMX makes the information easy to follow and understand through the use of cartoons, pictures, and short moral quotes sprinkled throughout the pamphlet. A final important component is the outline of what to do and whom to contact when faced with a moral dilemma at work. The employee, who may remain anonymous, is provided a toll-free telephone Helpline number and guaranteed to be "treated with respect and dignity." Anyone in a position of authority over the employee is subject to disciplinary action or dismissal if an attempt is made to harass or stop the employee from using the Helpline. Concerns also may be submitted by fax, letter, or computer E-mail.

WMX VIDEO TRAINING PROGRAM

In addition to the WMX code of ethics, a video is used in ethics training. Produced by WMX's Audio-visual Department, the videotape presents ethical situations commonly faced by WMX employees. Dealings with outside vendors, fellow workers, and supervisors are played out in settings employees are familiar with.

One such vignette shows a project manager faced with pressure from her general manager to falsify reports to a government agency about the project. Tests had been run to determine how well the lining of a new dump site would contain chemical waste. Though enough successful tests had been run, weather had possibly caused weaknesses in areas of the lining which had already been tested. Reworking the areas would cause the project to be finished late and over budget. Under pressure to come in on time and under budget, the general manager tells the project manager to finish the project and turn in the successful reports. As the scene fades, the project manager turns to the camera and asks, "What would you do?" Faced with the possibility of being fired for disobeying her supervisor, what should she do?

Providing ethically questionable cases to WMX employees creates discussion about what the most ethical action might be. The code of ethics booklet offers the project manager guidelines in the environmental principles section under compliance as to the correct action, and indicates the steps the company expects of her. Each scenario in the video offers an opportunity to answer similar ethical questions the employees may face. Without company-supported guidelines and principles, employees may see an opportunity or feel pressured to make unethical decisions.

RESULTS OF THE ETHICS PROGRAM

Ethics training is only a part of an overall ethics program. It must be supported by top management and tools such as the code of ethics and video used at WMX. Tools alone, however, are not sufficient. If a program is to be effective, it must be enforced.

WMX's success in being considered environmentally conscious and ethical by society is a result of the ethics training program and the supportive philosophy adopted by its management. WMX now has reputation for being socially responsible and has realized a better relationship with government agencies due to its ethics program. Ethics programs such as WMX's benefit society by creating a cleaner environment and a greater degree of protection from unethical business practices.

Questions

1. Evaluate the need for an ethics training program, such as the WMX ethics training approach.

2. What are some of the characteristics of WMX's code of ethics that have made it successful?

3. Discuss the strategy WMX used when addressing social responsibility issues. How was WMX rewarded?

4. Do you feel WMX's financial success is related to its social responsibility and ethics? Why?

Sources: "Ethics in Our Work Place; Guidelines for Our People," WMX Code of Ethics, 1993; *Ethics Combo* (video), WMX Technology and Services, Audi Services Department, Feb. 14, 1994; O. C. Ferrell and John Fraedrich, *Business Ethics* (Boston: Houghton Mifflin Co., 1994); Subrata Chakravarty, "Dean Buntrock's Green Machine," *Forbes,* Aug. 2, 1993, pp. 96–100; Kevin Kearney, "Process Safety Management," *Professional Safety,* Aug. 1993, pp. 16–22; Christel Cothran, "Pro-active Environmental Activity Eases Permitting Process," *Journal of Environmental Permitting,* Summer 1993, pp. 293–300; Gary Hoover, Alta Campbell, and Patrick Spain, eds. *Hoover's Handbook of American Business* (Austin, TX: The Reference Press, 1994), pp. 1130–1131; and Lynn Sharp Paine, "Managing for Organizational Integrity," *Harvard Business Review,* March–April 1994, pp. 106–111.

Crazy Eddie, Ethics, and the Law

The Crazy Eddie, Inc., chain of electronic stores began in the 1970s as a family-owned business, with Eddie Antar as the key figure. Eddie Antar, and his brother Mitchell, seemed to trade being the company's president and chairman of the board until December 1986, when Eddie permanently resigned as presi dent. Mitchell continued as president until he resigned on June 5, 1987.

The chain was built on low prices and quality merchandise. This strategy was very successful through the 1970s and 1980s. Before the chain went public (selling stock to public investors on a stock exchange), it had stores in four states, with reported annual sales of over $300 million.

On September 13, 1984, Crazy Eddie made the first public offering of its stock. The asking price was $8 per share. By 1986 the stock was selling at $75 per share, and so those who had invested in the chain seemed to have found a gold mine. However, in August 1987 the Securities and Exchange Commission (SEC) began an investigation into allegations of fraud. After two years of searching, the SEC filed a civil action alleging that Eddie Antar and several others had falsified financial statements.

The indictment alleges that Eddie directed employees to inflate year-end inventory figures and falsify company books to improve its position to the SEC. As a result of these favorable statements, second and third public offerings of Crazy Eddie stock were made. The government also alleges that Eddie and other defendants engaged in cash skimming. Cash skimming involves keeping certain cash receipts off the books so that the money can be put to tax-free, personal use.

This case was prepared by John Fraedrich for classroom discussion rather than to illustrate either effective or ineffective handling of an administrative, ethical or legal decision by management.

The Crazy Eddie chain looked so good as an investment that in April and May 1987 Elias Zinn of Entertainment Marketing Inc. attempted a takeover by buying a controlling interest through the purchase of Eddie stock. In May the Antars countered by buying their company's stock from the public domain. Although Zinn withdrew his initial offer to purchase the company, he aligned himself with the Oppenheimer-Palmieri Fund, which began a proxy fight to take control of Crazy Eddie's board of directors. By November 6, 1987, the Antars had lost control, with Zinn and the Fund taking over. The first item of business was to take a physical count of the company's inventory. When the numbers were tallied, Crazy Eddie was short about $45 million.

In 1989 the court notified the Antars of pending suits. On January 24, 1990, a U.S. District Court for the District of New Jersey ordered Eddie Antar to:

> . . . transfer all assets, funds or other property representing or derived from the $43,898,640.38 transferred to Bank Leumi Israel on or about February 17, 1987, or from the funds in the aggregate amount of $8,367,325.25 presently held in foreign locations in the name of Eddie Antar, for his benefit, under his control or over which he exercises actual investment or other authority, to be held and invested in accordance with such instructions as the Court may issue upon notice to the parties.

Antar failed to comply with the court order, asserting his Fifth Amendment privilege against self-incrimination. On February 9, 1990, when Eddie Antar did not comply with the court's order to transfer the funds, he was found in contempt of court and ordered to be jailed until he complied.

This must have gotten Antar's attention because he and his lawyer went to another court and judge to argue against the contempt charges. At the hearing, Antar agreed to appear later that month to have his lawyer address the charges. But he never appeared in court; instead, he left for Israel. On June 29, 1990, in response to a motion by the SEC, the court determined that Eddie Antar had made illegal profits of $52,519,548 from the sale of the stock of Crazy Eddie and had to pay that amount, as well as $20,976,884 in prejudgment interest. In July the court entered a final judgment against Antar for $52,519,548. Almost two years later, on June 11, 1992, a federal grand jury returned a multicount indictment against Eddie Antar, Mitchell Antar, Allen Antar, and Eddie Gindi, one count of which had to do with the RICO act. In all there were nineteen counts against them.

Between 1992 and 1993 Eddie Antar decided to return to the United States to stand trial. All defendants initially pleaded not guilty, but Gindi's case was severed and he became a government witness at trial. On February 2, the court heard the following arguments concerning Eddie Antar and his bail.

> THE COURT: What about somewhat between $50 and $100 million that lay out there some place? What if Mr. Antar were to be put in a situation, escape, go run and through some way get his hands on $50 or $100 million that might be available to him in other places? . . .

MR. ARSENEAULT (Antar's lawyer): Your Honor, I have two responses. . . . [T]he reality, your Honor, is the assets of Mr. Antar abroad are frozen. They have been frozen since at least June of this year. . . . So there is no realistic possibility that those assets are available for anybody.

THE COURT: Is he willing to sign the papers necessary to have those funds brought under the control of this Court or with the trustee/receiver to abide whatever events may occur in either this criminal case or the civil case?

MR. ARSENEAULT: It may be, your Honor, under certain circumstances. But independent of that issue, your Honor, I don't believe that issue is tied to the bail application. That money is unattainable. It is where it is. It can't be touched. It can't be moved. The government has stood up time and time again before your Honor in this courtroom and said those assets have nothing to do with bail. They have no impact on bail. They can't be posted as bail.

THE COURT: Simpson from the SEC says "they belong to me." He takes the position they belong to him as the judgment creditor. Whether they do or not, Mr. Arseneault, is not an issue I'm addressing. At least titularly they're in the names of Mr. Antar or one of his pseudonames [sic]. What I'm saying is what I think is one of the things that is lacking in your bail application is the agreement by Mr. Antar to unequivocally throw before this Court all of those assets and say: Judge, they will abide the events, whether they be criminal or civil, and let those moneys go. If I'm right — and I have no reason, from the outset, to indicate in a criminal context that he's guilty or not guilty. I express no opinion at all. But abide the events. And — it seems to me he should say, Judge, if I'm right, I'll get them all back. These are fake charges. Everything is wrong. I'm an innocent man. I'm as innocent as the chorus of confidence people say I am. Why doesn't he throw it all out, give it to the good old judge here and say: Judge, you hold it pending the final outcome of the matter and that that [sic] is security for the fact that I'm not going to flee. And, by the way, Judge, I will also get on the stand and under oath disclose to you each and every asset that I have, and I will swear under oath to you, Judge, that I don't have another pittance any place else, either directly or indirectly controlled by me? Wouldn't that be a nice, pure way to come before me? Then, you know, it might start triggering the mind a little bit here.

MR. ARSENEAULT: Without being redundant . . . I ask your Honor to remember, we're more than willing to post whatever surety if the issue is an issue of flight. I've been told before it is not a flight issue. . . .

THE COURT: The surety part doesn't make sense. There is $60 million laying [sic] out there. I'm not going to divorce myself from my knowledge. . . . Your client has refused to sign over to the trustee. So we're not talking about surety. Come on. Does he want to sign the $60 million over?

Bail for Eddie and Mitchell Antar was never given and both waited in jail for their trial, which began on June 15, 1993, and lasted nineteen days. The jury deliberated for another five days. It convicted Eddie Antar on all nineteen counts and Mitchell on six; Allen Antar was acquitted. At the sentencing hearing, the following discussion occurred:

> MR. CHERTOFF (class action attorney): Finally, your Honor, in connection with the court's observation about the fact that the public is to be the beneficiary of this, . . . which I think would be those who on a net — those investors, other than co-conspirators of the offense or the defendants, themselves, who on a net basis lost money trading in the securities of Crazy Eddie before June 2nd, 1988. And to the extent there is money left over, that any third parties who had to make compensation to those victims be themselves compensated.

> THE COURT: Because that is a more complex issue, I'd like to get the input from the SEC and experts. I will defer to another day the disposition of the moneys so far as the public is concerned. My Trustee-Receiver will hold it. Then I would anticipate the U.S. Attorney's office, in connection with the SEC, will make appropriate applications on notice to the defendant and the defendant's counsel so that we can get everyone's total input. My object in this case from day one has always been to get back to the public that which was taken from it as a result of the fraudulent activities of this defendant and others. We will work the best possible formula we can to be as fair as possible to the public. If we can get the $120 million back, we would have accomplished a great deal in this case.

On April 29, 1994, the District Court sentenced Eddie Antar to 151 months in prison and ordered him to pay $121 million in restitution. The court sentenced Mitchell Antar to 51 months in prison and ordered him to pay $3 million in restitution. Eddie and Mitchell both filed appeals.

On appeal, the verdicts of Eddie and Mitchell were set aside and a new trial ordered. Mitchell Antar was released on $50,000 bail, which means that he put up at least 10 percent ($5,000) in cash and a bail bondsman put up the rest. Eddie Antar was not released because he had fled once before; hence the court felt that he was too much of a flight risk.

Questions

1. Why were Eddie and Mitchell Antar's appeals granted?
2. What ethical issues are present in this case?
3. What are the reasons that Eddie might have had for the nineteen counts charged against him?

These facts are from Wade Lambert, "Crazy Eddie Founder's Conviction in Stock Fraud Case Is Reversed," *Wall Street Journal,* April 13, 1995, p. B4; and U.S. Court of Appeals for the Third Court, Opinion of the Court, pp. 2–5.

The Fall of Kidder, Peabody

*T*o understand the demise of Kidder, Peabody, an investment firm, several people and companies need to be brought into the case. The first is John Welch, Jr., the chief executive officer of General Electric (GE). Under his leadership, GE had 51 uninterrupted quarters of earning gains, and in 1994 GE made over $4 billion in net earnings on more than $60 billion of revenue. People called Welch (Jack) a "no-nonsense, get-it-done" type of person. As a result, the GE corporate culture was results-oriented. "Jack can be tough and intimidating and that's the reason they [GE] do so well." Welch has also created, as one professor puts it, "a culture of individual fiefdoms, and that decentralized responsibility leaves a firm like GE vulnerable." As will be presented later, GE owned Kidder, Peabody when it fell.

GE's 1994 annual report gives a glimpse of GE's corporate culture and of John Welch:

> Boundaryless behavior has become the "right" behavior at GE, and aligned with this behavior is a rewards system that recognizes the adapter or implementer of an idea as much as its originator. Today's global environment, with its virtually real-time information exchanges, demands that an institution embrace speed. Faster, in almost every case, is better. Across every business, the focus on shorter cycles — on simply getting faster — has been the driver of our improved asset turnover rate and strong cash flow. A stretch atmosphere replaces a grim, heads-down determination to be as good as you have to be, and asks, instead, how good can you be?

This case was prepared by John Fraedrich for classroom discussion rather than to illustrate either effective or ineffective handling of an administrative, ethical or legal decision by management.

John Welch supposedly first met Michael Carpenter when the latter worked at Boston Consulting Group. One of Carpenter's colleagues at the time described him as a wonderful analyst who had the ability to develop insights into complex problems. In 1983 Carpenter became vice chairman of GE's strategic planning, whereafter he convinced executives to purchase RCA. In 1986, when GE paid $602 million for Kidder, Peabody, Carpenter was reassigned to it.

Along with Carpenter, Melvin R. Mullin was hired by GE to work at Kidder, Peabody. Associates described Mullin as a "make-money-at-all costs" kind of boss. He was also a "hands off" supervisor who allowed employees latitude in performing their jobs. His philosophy was to allow employees significant creativity to pursue what they saw to be avenues for making money.

Another individual hired by Kidder, Peabody was Joseph Jett. In 1983 Jett began his career as an engineer at GE. Superiors evaluated Jett as a bright, outgoing, and charming person, but one who fell short of expectations. Jett seemed to be a hard-working and aggressive employee who sometimes had difficulty with the details of his job. In 1987 Jett, after getting his MBA, was hired by Morgan Stanley Inc. (an investment firm). There he began his financial career by becoming a bond trader. From Morgan Stanley Inc., he went to CS First Boston, taking a position in which he created packages of mortgage-backed securities. Colleagues recall that Jett spent tremendous amounts of time computer programming and seemed less attentive to the nitty-gritty task of calculating cash flows. From CS First Boston Jett then went to Landover Associates, a firm specializing in finding computer experts to develop programs for investment firms.

As a result of his experience at Landover Associates and his other workplaces, Jett was hired by Kidder, Peabody. Although his background pointed toward a job in the mortgage area, Jett was offered a job trading government securities, something he had never done. Later Jett was promoted because of his high energy level and his drive to succeed.

No one could say that Jett didn't work hard at Kidder, Peabody. On the government trading desk, he was the first one in and the last one out, arriving at 7:30 A.M. and leaving at about 7:00 P.M. But after a while colleagues began to question his abilities.

In April 1992, Jett started looking around for job opportunities, in part because of allegations that he had been "mismarking," or inflating, the prices of the securities he held. It was also alleged that he informed a potential employer of a "yield curve" trading strategy that consisted of betting millions on small interest-rate changes he predicted through a computer program he had created. Jett explained that all trading bets were "hedged," which made his trading strategy risk-free.

How this computer program functioned in relation to hedging was later discovered by Kidder, Peabody. Kidder, Peabody found that Jett was using a glitch in its accounting system that allowed him to book gains up front before his trades were actually completed. For example, Jett was supposed to be exchanging government bonds for other bonds and vice versa. Usually, these exchanges are completed within one day; however, Jett was setting up the trades so that they were settled as far off as ninety days. At a certain point, instead of selling them, he would roll them over, circumventing the accounting system, which would have eliminated any false profit or loss at the time of settlement. To make this work, it is purported that Jett made it seem like he was doing business with the Federal Reserve Bank.

At the end of 1992 Jett had nearly doubled the revenues in his area to $30 million. In 1993 Jett was promoted and was given a mandate to grow quickly. By mid-1993 Jett's career was on a roll, with alleged profits up sharply. On the strength of these profits, Jett was paid $9 million and promoted to managing director, one of only 135 at Kidder, Peabody. In January 1994 Jett was given Kidder's coveted Chairman's Award. By this time Jett's trading revenues had soared to more than $100 million.

Because his success was so phenomenal, people started trying to understand how he was achieving it. By early April Cerullo, Jett's superior, had been asked a series of hard questions to which he had few concrete answers. When Cerullo asked Jett how he was profiting from these small market inefficiencies, Jett told him that the back office couldn't handle the volume of trade he was generating and that he (Jett) had set up two custodial accounts for the Federal Reserve to enable operations personnel to keep track of his transactions. At the time these questions were being asked, Jett suffered trading losses of about $90 million. On the morning of April 15, Jett was to have another meeting with Cerullo and others to explain his losses as well as $95 million in false profits that had been discovered. He never kept his appointment.

On April 16 a messenger gave Jett a two-sentence termination letter. Four days later Kidder, Peabody filed an arbitration claim with the New York Stock Exchange seeking part of Jett's $9 million 1993 compensation. On June 23 Kidder, Peabody's chairman and chief executive officer was fired. One month later Cerullo quit as head of the fixed-income division and denied any knowledge of Jett's improprieties. Three days later Jett accused Cerullo of knowing about his activities and of helping him with the trades.

On October 16, 1994, Paine Webber bought Kidder, Peabody for $670 million and laid off half its five thousand workforce. One and a half months later, the New York Stock Exchange (NYSE) barred Jett from the securities industry for refusing to testify at an NYSE inquiry. In New York on January 9, 1995, the SEC filed civil fraud charges against Jett and charges against his supervisors for failure to supervise.

In his 1994 end-of-year speech to investors and employees, Welch said the following:

> The unfortunate part of 1994 was that many achievements and terrific performances of GE people were often overshadowed by the well-chronicled prob-

lems with Kidder, Peabody. The Kidder story, and its $1.2 billion loss, is not a pleasant one; and it is tempting to simply relegate it to the past — but we can't. Whether or not it was a good idea to buy Kidder in 1986 is academic — in the end, it simply didn't work out. In 1994, weak trading markets lowered Wall Street earnings by billions of dollars from the levels of 1993, and Kidder was not immune to the weaknesses in these markets. But Kidder had another problem: a phantom trading scheme by a single employee, directed not against customers but against the firm itself, which cost it $210 million in net income. The combination of the two circumstances — a downturn in earnings and an employee's wrongdoing — made it clear to us that it was time to get out; thus the sale of the brokerage assets of Kidder to Paine Webber, in return for 25 percent equity in that firm, and the liquidation of the trading operation. None of this is to say it couldn't have done better, but the bottom line is that the type of business Kidder had become — a cyclical trading business — was simply not the place for GE to be. The tragedy of businesses that are not market leaders, that don't have a broadly based competitive edge — be they brokerage houses or manufacturing plants — is exactly the same; and it goes beyond "one-time charges" — dollars and cents. It's the people — the factory or office workers — who can't just "go down the street" — like traders and managers can — for another job. This human toll reminds us, once again, that nothing we do is more important than staying competitive — keeping that winning edge. Nothing.

The Jett case continued to be confusing in mid-1996. The Securities and Exchange Commission indicated that there were wide discrepancies in Kidder, Peabody records being used to prove its fraud case against now ex-trader Joseph Jett. A prosecution witness said under oath that she could not tell from the records whether Jett had misrepresented profits. The records supplied by Kidder, Peabody are central in the Securities and Exchange Commission allegations that Jett misrepresented $350 million in profits on government bond trades to hide $80 million in losses. In May 1996 Jett went public and was quoted in the mass media as saying he planned to work hard to prove his innocence.

Questions

1. What are the legal issues of the key people in the case?
2. What are the ethical issues of the key people in the case?
3. Is John Welch correct when he says that managers and traders are different from factory workers in that they can easily find jobs?
4. Discuss the GE–Kidder corporate culture as it relates to Kidder's demise.
5. Do you believe that Jett acted alone? Why or why not?

These facts are from Michael Siconolfi, "Jett Fires Back, Says Kidder Refuses Data," *Wall Street Journal*, September 7, 1994, pp. C1, C25; William M. Carley, Michael Siconolfi, and Amal Kumar Naj, "Major Challenge: How Will Welch Deal with Kidder Scandal? Problems

Keep Coming," *Wall Street Journal*, May 3, 1994, pp. A1, A6; Michael Siconolfi, "Jettisoned: With Scandal Report Due Today, Kidder Ousts Another Official," *Wall Street Journal*, August 4, 1994, pp. A1, A4; Michael Siconolfi, "Report Faults Kidder for Laxness in Jett Case," *Wall Street Journal*, August 5, 1994, pp. C1, C10; William Carley, "A Corporate Gadfly Takes Boss Seriously — A Serious Mistake," *Wall Street Journal*, April 14, 1995, p. A1; Michael Siconolfi, "An Employee Fired by Kidder Peabody Casts a Pall of Fear," *Wall Street Journal*, April 29, 1994; William M. Carley and Amal Kuman Naj, "Multifaceted Case: Price-Fixing Charges Put GE and DeBeers Under Tough Scrutiny," *Wall Street Journal*, February 22, 1994, pp. A1, A8; Alix M. Freedman and Laurie P. Cohen, "Jett's Passage: How a Kidder Trader Stumbled Upward Before Scandal Struck," *Wall Street Journal*, June 3, 1994, p. A4; and David Carrig, "Jett Case," *USA Today*, May 22, 1996, p. 1B.

Archer Daniels Midland Company

The humble origins of Archer Daniels Midland Company (ADM), based in Decatur, Illinois, can be traced to 1902, when John Daniels formed the Daniels Linseed Company in Minneapolis, Minnesota. Daniels had been crushing flaxseed to produce linseed oil since 1878. George Archer, also an experienced flaxseed crusher, joined the Daniels firm in 1903. With the purchase of Midland Linseed Products in 1923, the company became known as Archer Daniels Midland.

After ADM's rapid domestic and international expansion not only in the production of linseed oil, but also in flour milling and soybean processing in the 1930s, 1940s, and 1950s, its leadership passed to the current chairman and chief executive officer, Dwayne O. Andreas, in 1966. Under Andreas, ADM has further expanded its operations into corn processing, soybean-based vegetable protein, sugar, peanuts, citric acid, and a variety of vitamin products and additives for both human and animal consumption. Company sales and net income have increased significantly over the course of the last decade. In 1986 ADM posted sales and profits of $5.3 billion and $236 million, respectively. Those figures climbed to $12.7 billion and $796 million for 1995. Today as the largest U.S. processor of agricultural commodities, ADM employs nearly 15,000 persons and operates 200 plants processing 150,000 tons of grain, seed, and vegetable products each day. The firm's extensive reach into the products eaten and drunk by consumers around the globe is reflected in its promotional efforts: it proudly calls itself the "supermarket to the world."

This case was prepared by Terry Gable for classroom discussion rather than to illustrate either effective or ineffective handling of an administrative, ethical or legal decision by management.

While 1995 was a banner year for ADM in terms of record sales and profits, it was also a time of turmoil for the food-processing giant. There was ongoing discussion in the media and among competitive firms that ADM had gained special access to the political process, resulting in laws, regulations, and loopholes favoring its individual interests. This access was seen as a consequence of Andreas's close personal relationships with both President Bill Clinton and Senator Bob Dole, as well as other major political figures, and of the company's history of large political contributions to legislators. Allegations circulated that ADM and several of its larger competitors in the flour-milling industry had grown too large and powerful, thus potentially limiting consumer choice. There were also charges that ADM's board of directors had grown too large, was too well paid, and was excessively dominated by nonobjective company insiders. Although these issues raised potentially damaging ethical, legal, and performance problems at ADM, the firm's turmoil had another source. It stemmed from widespread allegations that it worked with competitors to set, or "fix," artificially high prices for a biochemical product, lysine. These allegations grew out of a lengthy Federal Bureau of Investigation (FBI) probe, conducted with the cooperation of ADM bioproducts executive and projected future company president, Mark Whitacre.

MARK WHITACRE: RISING STAR AT ADM

After earning bachelor's and master's degrees in animal science from Ohio State University and a Ph.D. in nutritional biochemistry from Cornell University, Mark Whitacre went to work briefly for Ralston Purina in St. Louis and then for Degussa, a German chemical company. While at Degussa, Whitacre negotiated with ADM in hopes of striking a joint venture between the two firms involving lysine production. The alliance was never forged, but Whitacre was hired by ADM in 1989 to run its newly formed biochemical products division. Chairman Andreas's son, Michael, himself vice chairman of the firm, was particularly instrumental in Whitacre's hiring. The younger Andreas told Whitacre that success in the new division he was to head was a high priority for the company.

Whitacre's first objective was to move ADM into the production and marketing of lysine, an amino acid derived from corn and used in swine and poultry feed to promote the growth of lean muscle. He was so successful at this task and others that toward the end of 1992 he was promoted to corporate vice president and given responsibility for all of ADM's Asian market development projects. In early 1993 Whitacre was informed by ADM's president, Jim Randall, that he was "the top candidate to be the next president of this company." However, Whitacre's then secret involvement in the FBI investigation of alleged lysine price fixing eventually halted his rapid ascension up ADM's corporate ladder of command.

ADM ENTERS THE LYSINE MARKET

When Whitacre was hired to propel ADM into the promising lysine market, there were no American firms in the industry, which was dominated by two Japanese companies, Kyowa Hakko and Ajinomoto. To establish itself in the market, ADM made an initial investment of $150 million in lysine production, sales, and marketing. According to Whitacre, ADM's first strategy as the new market entrant "was to get customers," as evidenced in market share. Consistent with ADM philosophy and practice, profitability would then follow.

After plant construction was completed, ADM formally entered the lysine market in early 1991. ADM gained market share quickly and a fierce price war followed, with the per-pound price of lysine dropping from about $1.30 to around 60 cents. In early 1992 Michael Andreas and Jim Randall informed Whitacre that he would be working more closely with the corn-processing division president, Terry Wilson. Whitacre states that during his first year with ADM he had been told "to beware" of Wilson because of his alleged involvement in price-fixing activities in several of the firm's other divisions. According to Whitacre, Andreas and Randall told him that he would be working with Wilson so that Wilson could "teach me some things about how ADM does business."

Whitacre claims that when he and Wilson met in February 1992, the content of their initial discussion was far different from what he had expected. Rather than asking Whitacre about his sales force or the location of ADM lysine offices and other typical strategic issues, Wilson asked Whitacre if he "knew our competitors." He told him that he wanted to meet with these Japanese firms because ADM was losing several million dollars a month on its lysine operations, despite gaining a 30 percent share of the global lysine market. According to Whitacre, Wilson then stated that "We're not blaming that on you. Obviously we needed to get market share first, and that's what we did. That was stage one. But now we need to take the business to a different tier."*

WILSON AND WHITACRE MEET THE COMPETITION

After representatives of Kyowa Hakko and Ajinomoto declined an invitation to come to ADM's Decatur headquarters, Wilson and Whitacre flew to Tokyo in April 1992. There the ADM executives were met with coldness, understandable given the fact that their aggressive price-cutting, market-entry strategy had pushed their Japanese competitors from a comfortable position of profitability to one of large losses on their lysine operations.

---

*Mark Whitacre and Ronald Herkoff, "My Life as a Corporate Mole for the FBI," *Fortune,* September 4, 1995, pp. 52–62.

Whitacre claims that Wilson's initial tactic to overcome the coldness of the Japanese was to suggest that the three firms form a cooperative amino acids association to jointly promote and expand lysine sales. Kyowa Hakko and Ajinomoto representatives were receptive to this idea. Following a meeting at Kyowa's headquarters, additional meetings in Hawaii and Mexico City were planned. According to Whitacre, Wilson summed up ADM's proposal at the Mexico City meeting as follows:

> "Well, gentlemen," he said, "here is our problem. We have about 20% to 25% more production capacity than what usage levels are." He took demand and multiplied it by 60 cents. Then he said, "Well, Mark, what was the price before we built our plant?" And I said, "Well, about $1.30 a pound." So he took that same usage level and multiplied it by $1.30 a pound. And the difference was about $200 million. Then he said, "Well, gentlemen, there's $200 million that we're giving to our customers. In other words, the customer is benefiting, not the people who spent hundreds of millions of dollars building these plants." Then he said something that was a common phrase around ADM. . . ." The competitor is our friend, and the customer is our enemy."*

When Whitacre and Wilson returned to Decatur, Whitacre claims that several people from Wilson's corn-processing division said to him, "Oh, you and Terry have been at one of your price-fixing meetings."

In retrospect, Whitacre told *Fortune* magazine that ADM's original thinking was that their aggressive market entry strategy would force one of the weaker competitors to drop out of the lysine market. Whitacre reasoned that since this had not happened, "now we were going to do business by the Terry method."†

JAPANESE COMPETITORS SUSPECTED OF SABOTAGE

ADM continued to lose money on its lysine operations. Production costs continued to run at roughly twice the market price due to contamination problems long since mastered by the Japanese producers, both of whom had sent representative engineers to inspect ADM facilities later in the summer of 1992. During one of his phone conversations with technical personnel at Ajinomoto, Whitacre, frustrated by the lingering contamination problem, jokingly stated: "Hey, you guys don't have a guy out here sabotaging our plant, do you?" The lack of a response made Whitacre wonder if there was in fact competitive sabotage taking place. He contacted Michael Andreas about the issue, and Andreas suggested that the Ajinomoto technician be offered a finder's fee for information regarding the problem. When Whitacre made the

*Ibid.
†Ibid.

offer — a perfectly legal practice — he again received a vague, neutral response, further confirming his suspicion that the Japanese competitor had indeed planted someone inside ADM's lysine production facility.

In further conversations with Michael Andreas, Whitacre claims he was told that maybe it would be more productive to worry less about finding the mole planted by the Japanese and to see instead if the informant would be willing to divulge inside technological information. Such information might not only help end the contamination problem, but also improve ADM's competitive position in other ways. Although Whitacre says that he was aware that ADM had gained technological information in this manner in the past, he also admits that the practice can be very risky: "They're stealing in-house technology, and you can end up with quite a lawsuit on your hands." Conversations with the technician took place with no deal being struck.

CHAIRMAN ANDREAS CALLS IN THE FBI

On hearing about the potential sabotage problem, Chairman Andreas called a personal friend at the FBI, who expressed great interest in the matter. According to Whitacre, Michael Andreas was not pleased with his father's decision, saying that "his father hadn't thought about all the ramifications." Whitacre claims that he was then coached by Michael Andreas about what to say and what not to say to the FBI:

> . . . he said I should tell them about the contamination, but . . . he didn't want the FBI to know that we had approached this guy about the technology; he said he wanted the FBI to think that the Japanese had approached us. The other thing he wanted to know was which phone I had been talking on to the Japanese about lysine pricing. I told him that I had mainly used my home phone and Mick (Michael Andreas) asked me if I had any other phones in my house. Did I have an OPX line, which is a company phone? And I said yeah. And he said I should tell them that's the line that I used to talk to the Ajinomoto guy. . . . That way, he said, if they decided to tap the phone, maybe they would tap the wrong phone. So at that point, he told me to lie to the FBI about those two points: trying to buy the technology and the phone line.*

Whitacre, accompanied by ADM's head of security, Mark Cheviron, met with FBI officials at FBI offices located in Decatur. As instructed, Whitacre lied to the FBI about the attempted technology purchase and the phone line.

Whitacre did not feel comfortable lying to the FBI. When FBI agent Brian Shepard arrived at Whitacre's home the evening of their initial meeting to install phone taps, Whitacre told him the truth. According to Whitacre:

---

*Ibid.

> I explained everything to him. I told him that what was happening on the one phone line was talk about price fixing. I said it wasn't going on yet, but I was concerned about it. I said there were discussions with competitors on pricing and buying, something we weren't doing yet on lysine, but something that ADM does on other products, and I told him it was pretty well known and that it was in the process of getting there on lysine.*

Whitacre contends that he would have told Shepard the truth in their first meeting if it had not been for the presence of Cheviron, who, Whitacre feels, was sent along with him to make sure that he had lied as instructed.

MARK WHITACRE: FBI MOLE

As Whitacre talked to his contacts at Kyowa and Ajinomoto about the proposed lysine association, the FBI listened. Highly interested in what it heard, the FBI asked for and received permission from Whitacre to supply him with a small, wired recorder that was concealed, which was used to tape ADM lysine and other product-type meetings.

Near Christmas 1992, the FBI informed Whitacre, based on what it had learned from the secretly taped ADM meetings, that he had to choose between three alternatives. He could: (1) stay with the company and engage in price-fixing; (2) leave the company having committed no wrongdoing; or (3) work with the FBI to prevent price-fixing from occurring. Whitacre chose the last alternative.

Whitacre met with FBI agents on the case "on average a couple of nights a week for three years." They discussed meetings recorded both by Whitacre using a tape recorder concealed inside a panel in his briefcase and by the FBI itself, which would wire hotel rooms where meetings were to take place after receiving advance notice from Whitacre as to the location of the meeting. According to Whitacre:

> It's amazing, some of the stuff that came up on the tapes. There were recordings where agreements on world volume were reached, as well as prices. And it was important to get tapes showing that I wasn't leading this activity. So we have tapes with Terry Wilson saying "Before we go to this meeting I'm going to go to Mick (Michael Andreas) and get our marching orders." . . . Sometimes there were real surprises. Once we were at Meigs Field, an airport in Chicago. We got out of the plane, and Terry Wilson and I were on our way to meet with one of the competitors. The general counsel and the assistant counsel were getting into a different taxi. I had already turned the briefcase on so we would get Terry's marching orders in the car, and the general counsel says: "Hey, guys, good luck with your price-fixing meeting." . . . We also have a tape of me going to an

---

*Ibid.

ADM staff attorney and telling him these kinds of things were going on. And of him telling me he doesn't want to hear about it. So there really wasn't any way to fix this problem internally. It was too far up. Too far up.*

As a result of what it had heard, the FBI conducted a raid on ADM corporate headquarters in search of further evidence regarding alleged price-fixing practices.

ADM'S RESPONSE TO PRICE-FIXING ALLEGATIONS

ADM responded to Whitacre's and the FBI's allegations by stating that it had not engaged in price-fixing. Chairman Andreas pointed out that fixing the price of a commodity item such as lysine would be nearly impossible because artificially inflated prices would cause customers to switch to alternative feed-additive products, such as soy meal. Furthermore, Andreas stated that Whitacre, once a rising star in the firm, was telling "fairy tales" to cover up his alleged theft of $9 million from the firm. Whitacre, in hiding due to alleged threats on his family's well-being, furiously denied the embezzlement charges.

An unnamed friend of Whitacre told *Fortune* reporters that a large sum of money — $2.5 million — was transferred from ADM to Whitacre after his firing and that the money was not stolen but rather was an "agreed-upon part" of Whitacre's compensation. This friend further informed *Fortune* that ADM disguised the money as disbursements to outside suppliers, then funneled it into foreign bank accounts, an executive compensation practice referred to by the individual as common. The legal director of an advocacy group based in Washington, D.C., commented about ADM charges against Whitacre that "Organizations under threat do everything they can to neutralize that threat. If there is one common denominator among whistle-blowers, it is that they face harassment, retaliation, and professional apocalypse."†

ADM's response, however, was not limited to denial and countercharges against Whitacre. Angry shareholders and other critics contended that the root of the problem was in the firm's complacent and insider-dominated seventeen-member board of directors. Critics claimed that the alleged price-fixing, along with other antitrust and compensation-related activities that were also being investigated, were clear signs of director oversight. They argued that these doings should have been detected and dealt with long before they were published and broadcast in major national news media. Specific reasons cited for the neglect were the board's unusually large size, extraordinarily high levels of member compensation, and the fact that ten of the sev-

---

*Ibid.
†Ibid.

enteen directors were either retired ADM executives or relatives of senior management.

These issues were addressed at a spirited annual meeting of ADM shareholders in October 1995. At one point in the meeting, Chairman Andreas shouted down shareholders and ordered audience microphones silenced. To one company pension official who questioned ADM's top-management style, Andreas shouted "This meeting, sir, runs according to my rules." However, it was decided that change in the composition and nature of the board was required. Two board members not related to the Andreas family, O. Glenn Webb and Ray A. Goldberg, were entrusted with overseeing this transformation. However, the fact that both had long-time close personal and business ties with the Andreases and ADM caused some to question whether meaningful change would indeed take place.

Despite being shaken by the consequences of his actions, Whitacre continues to stand firmly behind his allegations that ADM conspired with its major competitors to fix lysine and other product prices. He believes that he did the right thing in exposing these practices. Shortly after the FBI raid, he described the sequence of events as follows:

> The night they came in, they interviewed me and took stuff out of my office just like everybody else. They had warned me that I would need an attorney and told me not to get one tied to ADM, but they didn't stress it, and I didn't think about it enough. I spent from six to ten that night talking to John Dowd, the attorney from Akin Gump Strauss Hauer & Feld hired by ADM. Dowd promised me he wouldn't tell anybody about my real role. But by 11 A.M. the next day, someone at ADM called me and said, "Hey, Dwayne told me your attorney just told him that you're the mole. You're the one who caused all this. . . . And it's been pure hell ever since. . . . " It amazes me how just a few weeks ago I was potentially the next president of the company, and now it's pure character assassination. . . . We've been threatened a lot. How serious they are, I don't know. But we've had to move. The bottom line is that I know my story will eventually be confirmed by the FBI. . . . And the nice thing is that I can have every single thing that happened at ADM confirmed by tape. It's all on tape. Everything that happened.*

The ADM case is a tough one for the Justice Department. As of mid-1996, there have been no indictments. Although the government is pressing on with charges, prosecutors have found that the company has a high degree of internal organizational cohesiveness. The prosecutors have encountered tough resistance from employees, and at this time, not a single Archer Daniels Midland employee has come forward to help the government, although dozens have been questioned by prosecutors. Wilson and Michael

---

*Laurie P. Cohen, "Tough Battle Looms as ADM Lawyers Plot Price–Fixing Defenses," *Wall Street Journal,* March 27, 1996, p. A1.

Andreas refused to plea bargain and continue to maintain their innocence. In addition, the government has not been helped by some of ADM's largest customers — the reported victims in any price-fixing allegations. ADM did settle a $45 million class action civil suit with customers without admitting to the alleged misconduct in order to avoid the enormous uncontrollable costs of protracted litigation.

Questions

1. Was ADM's response to the allegations of price-fixing adequate? Do you think that the firm was simply "blaming the messenger" for reporting what he perceived as a widespread aspect of ADM corporate culture, or did the firm adequately exonerate itself from alleged misconduct?

2. Do you see changes in ADM's board of directors as sufficient to deter future ethical and legal problems, such as those arising from the price-fixing allegations?

3. How could ADM have dealt better with the potentially serious ethical and legal dilemmas it now faces regarding alleged price-fixing practices? Suggest an ethical compliance program that could have prevented the problem.

4. Comment on Mark Whitacre's expressed opinion that he was doing the right thing by cooperating with the FBI and that he felt that he would eventually stay with and prosper at ADM. Was he "doing the right thing"? Was he naive in thinking that he could stay with the firm? Why or why not?

These facts are from John Bovard, "Corporate Welfare Fueled by Political Contributions: Archer Daniels Midland's Ethanol Program," *Business and Society Review,* June 22, 1995, p. 22; Greg Burns and Richard A. Melcher, "A Grain of Activism at Archer Daniels Midland," *Business Week,* November 6, 1995, p. 44; Dan Carney, "Dwayne's World: Archer Daniels Midland CEO Dwayne Orville Andreas," *Mother Jones,* July 1995, p. 44; Major Garrett, "The Supermarket to the World Pols: Clinton, Dole Helped Campaign Contributor ADM, Now Probed for Price Fixing," *Washington Times,* September 5, 1995, p. A1; Ronald Henkoff, "So Who Is This Mark Whitacre, and Why Is He Saying These Things About ADM?," *Fortune,* September 4, 1995, pp. 64–68; David C. Korten, *When Corporations Rule the World* (West Hartford, Conn.: Kumarian Press, 1995) pp. 75, 224; Joann S. Lublin, "Is ADM's Board Too Big, Cozy, and Well-Paid?" *Wall Street Journal,* October 17, 1995, p. B1; "10 Little Piggies: Corporations That Receive Government Benefits," *Mother Jones,* July 1995, p. 48; Mark Whitacre and Ronald Henkoff, "My Life as a Corporate Mole for the FBI," *Fortune,* September 4, 1995, pp. 52–62; and Laurie P. Cohen, "Tough Battle Looms as ADM Lawyers Plot Price-Fixing Defenses," *Wall Street Journal,* March 27, 1996, p. A1.

APPENDIX A

Association and Industry Codes of Ethics

AMERICAN ASSOCIATION OF UNIVERSITY PROFESSORS: *Statement on Professional Ethics**

The statement that follows, a revision of a statement originally adopted in 1966, was approved by Committee B on Professional Ethics, adopted by the Council as Association policy, and endorsed by the Seventy-third Annual Meeting in June 1987.

Introduction

From its inception, the American Association of University Professors has recognized that membership in the academic profession carries with it special responsibilities. The Association has consistently affirmed these responsibilities in major policy statements, providing guidance to professors in such matters as their utterances as citizens, the exercise of their responsibilities to students and colleagues, and their conduct when resigning from an institution or when undertaking sponsored research. The *Statement on Professional Ethics* that follows sets forth those general standards that serve as a reminder of the variety of responsibilities assumed by all members of the profession.

In the enforcement of ethical standards, the academic profession differs from those of law and medicine, whose associations act to assure the integrity of members engaged in private practice. In the academic profession the individual institution of higher learning provides this assurance and so should normally handle questions concerning propriety of conduct within its own framework by reference to a faculty group. The Association supports such local action and stands ready, through the general secretary and Committee B, to counsel with members of the academic community concerning questions of professional ethics and to inquire into complaints when local consideration is impossible or inappropriate. If the alleged offense is deemed sufficiently serious to raise the possibility of adverse action, the procedures should be in accordance with the 1940 *Statement of Principles on Academic Freedom and Tenure*, the 1958 *Statement on Procedural Standards in Faculty Dismissal Proceedings*, or the applicable provisions of the Association's *Recommended Institutional Regulations on Academic Freedom and Tenure*.

The Statement

I. Professors, guided by a deep conviction of the worth and dignity of the advancement of knowledge, recognize the special responsibilities placed upon them. Their primary responsibility to their subject is to seek and state the truth as they see it. To this end professors devote their energies to developing and improving their scholarly competence. They accept the obligation to exercise critical self-discipline and judgment in using, extending, and transmitting knowledge. They practice intellectual honesty. Although professors may follow subsidiary interests, these interests must never seriously hamper or compromise their freedom of inquiry.

II. As teachers, professors encourage the free pursuit of learning in their students. They hold before them the best scholarly and ethical standards of their discipline. Professors demonstrate respect for students as individuals and adhere to their proper roles as intellectual guides and counselors. Professors make every reasonable effort to foster honest academic conduct and to assure that their evaluations of students reflect each student's true merit. They respect the confidential nature of the relationship between professor and student. They avoid any exploitation, harassment, or discriminatory treatment of students. They acknowledge significant academic or scholarly assistance from them. They protect their academic freedom.

III. As colleagues, professors have obligations that derive from common membership in the community of scholars. Professors do not discriminate against or harass colleagues. They respect and defend the free inquiry of associates. In the exchange of criticism and ideas professors show due respect for the opinions of others. Professors acknowledge academic debt and strive to be objective in their professional judgment of colleagues. Professors accept their share of faculty responsibilities for the governance of their institution.

IV. As members of an academic institution, professors seek above all to be effective teachers and scholars. Although professors observe the stated regulations of the institution, provided the regulations do not contravene academic freedom, they maintain their right to criticize and seek revision. Professors give due regard to their paramount responsibilities within their institution in determining the amount and character of work done outside it. When considering the interruption or termination of their service, professors recognize the effect of their decision upon the program of the institution and give due notice of their intentions.

V. As members of their community, professors have the rights and obligations of other citizens. Professors measure the urgency of these obligations in the light of their responsibilities to their subject, to their students, to their profession, and to their institution. When they speak or act as private persons they avoid creating the impression of speaking or acting for their college or university. As citizens engaged in a profession that depends upon freedom for its health and integrity, professors have a particular obligation to promote conditions of free inquiry and to further public understanding of academic freedom.

CASE WESTERN RESERVE UNIVERSITY: *Information Services Ethics Policy**

The general standards of conduct expected of members of the Case Western Reserve University community also apply to the use of the University computers, network facilities, information services and resources. These facilities and resources include:

- wiring or infrastructure used for communications;

- electronics, digital switches and communication equipment used for processing or communications;

- programs, programming languages, instructions, or routines which are used to perform work on a computer;

- digital information such as records, images, sounds, video or textual material stored on or accessible through a computer;

- computers used for automation or the administration of information services;

- information such as CWRUnet IDs, authorization codes, account numbers, usage and billing records, or textual material stored on or accessible through the network or other communication lines.

Property Rights

University computers, network facilities, information services and resources are made available to individuals to assist in the pursuit of educational goals. In order to promote the most effective use of these, it is expected that users will cooperate with each other and respect the privacy of information even though it may be in electronic form rather than printed form. Individuals and organizations will be held no less accountable for their actions in situations involving University computers, network facilities, information services and resources than they would be in dealing with other media.

Though some of them are intangible, these University computers, network facilities, information services and resources are the property of the University. Rules prohibiting theft or vandalism apply to authorization codes, long distance telephone services, television signals and service information as well as to physical equipment.

Conduct which violates the University's property rights with respect to University computers, network facilities, information services and resources is subject to University disciplinary action. This conduct includes:

- using University computers, network facilities, information services and resources for purposes other than those intended by the University body granting access to those resources (especially using them for personal financial gain or allowing access to them by unauthorized persons even if they are members of the University community);

- using any portion of University computers, network facilities, information services and resources for the purpose of:
  - copying University-owned or licensed information to another computer system for personal or external use without prior written approval;
  - attempting to modify University-owned or licensed information (including software and data) without prior approval;
  - attempting to damage or disrupt the operation of computer equipment, communications equipment, or communication lines;

- knowingly accepting or using University owned or licensed information (including software and data) which has been obtained by illegal means;

- from a single CWRUnet faceplate, receiving more than one set of television signals or distributing these signals to multiple receivers;

- knowingly accepting or using television signals which have been obtained by illegal means.

Confidentiality

The University seeks to protect the civil, personal, and property rights of those actually using its computers, network facilities, information services and resources and seeks to protect the confidentiality of University records stored on its computer systems. The University also seeks similarly to protect those computers, network facilities, information services and resources of other institutions to whom University personnel have access via the University computers, network facilities, information services and resources. Conduct which involves the use of University computers, network facilities, information services and resources to violate another's rights is subject to University disciplinary action. This conduct includes:

- invading the privacy of an individual by using electronic means to ascertain confidential information, even if an individual or department inadvertently allows access to information;

- copying another user's information without the permission of the owner, even if it is readily accessible by electronic means;

- knowingly accepting or using information which has been obtained by illegal means;

- abusing or harassing another user using the University computers, network facilities, information services and resources.

Accessibility/Use

Some of the University computers, network facilities, information services and resources require that each user have a unique identity (i.e. CWRUnet ID, telephone long distance authorization code). The identity is used to represent a user in various University computers, network facilities, information services and resources activities; to provide access to certain University computers, network facilities, information services and resources based on his/her credibility and purpose for requiring such access; and to associate his/her own service use and information with his/her identity. As such, this identity is another instrument of identification and its misuse constitutes forgery or misrepresentation.

Conduct which involves inappropriate access or misuse of University computers, network facilities, information services or resources and service identities is subject to University disciplinary action. This conduct includes:

- allowing another individual to use one's unique identity;

- using another individual's identity, even if the individual has neglected to safeguard it;

- using the University computers, network facilities, information services or resources in the commission of a crime;

- gaining access to non-public computers, network facilities, information services and resources.

Case Western Reserve University's computers, network facilities, information services and resources are networked on the CWRU campus and to other locations. Information on the University's networks and communication lines is considered to be private. Tapping the University's network or communication lines for the purpose of examining or using information other than that destined for the intended user is considered unacceptable conduct and is subject to disciplinary action.

State and National Laws

Conduct in violation of the principles set forth above, with respect to the use of University information services and facilities may be subject to criminal or civil legal action in addition to University disciplinary action.

U.S. DEPT. OF COMMERCE: *Model Business Principles*

The following statement of Model Business Principles and subsequent procedures were released by the U.S. Dept. of Commerce and should be viewed as voluntary guidelines for U.S. businesses.

Recognizing the positive role of U.S. business in upholding and promoting adherence to universal standards of human rights, the Administration encourages all businesses to adopt and implement voluntary codes of conduct for doing business around the world that cover at least the following areas:

1. Provision of a safe and healthy workplace.

2. Fair employment practices, including avoidance of child and forced labor and avoidance of discrimination based on race, gender, national origin or religious beliefs; and respect for the right of association and the right to organize and bargain collectively.

3. Responsible environmental protection and environmental practices.

4. Compliance with U.S. and local laws promoting good business practices, including laws prohibiting illicit payments and ensuring fair competition.

5. Maintenance, through leadership at all levels, of a corporate culture that respects free expression consistent with legitimate business concerns, and does not condone political coercion in the workplace; that encourages good corporate citizenship and makes a positive contribution to the communities in which the company operates; and where ethical conduct is recognized, valued and exemplified by all employees.

In adopting voluntary codes of conduct that reflect these principles, U.S. companies should serve as models, encouraging similar behavior by their partners, suppliers, and subcontractors.

Adoption of codes of conduct reflecting these principles is voluntary. Companies are encouraged to develop their own codes of conduct appropriate to their particular circumstances. Many companies already apply statements or codes that incorporate these principles. Companies should find appropriate means to inform their shareholders and the public of actions undertaken in connection with these principles. Nothing in the principles is intended to require a company to act in violation of host country or U.S. law. This statement of principles is not intended for legislation.

Model Business Principles: Procedures

When President Clinton announced his decision to renew China's MFN status, he also announced a commitment to work with the business community to develop a voluntary statement of business principles relating to corporate conduct abroad. The President made clear that U.S. business can and does play a positive and important role promoting the openness of societies, respect for individual rights, the promotion of free markets and prosperity, environmental protection, and the setting of high standards for business practices generally.

The Administration today is offering an update on our efforts to follow through on the President's commitment to promote the Model Business Principles and best practices among U.S. companies. The Principles already have gained the support of some U.S. companies. A process is ongoing to elicit additional support for these Principles and to continue to examine issues related to them.

The elements of this process are as follows:

Voluntary Statement of Business Principles

The Administration, in extensive consultations with business and labor leaders and members of the Non-Governmental Organization (NGO) community, developed these model principles, which were reported widely in the press earlier this spring. A copy is attached. This model statement is to be used by companies as a reference point in framing their own codes of conduct. It is based on a wide variety of similar sets of principles U.S. companies and business organizations already have put into global practice. The Administration encourages all businesses everywhere to support the model principles. (Copies of the model statement are available by calling the U.S. Department of Commerce Trade Information Center, 1-800-USA-TRADE.)

Efforts by U.S. Business

As part of the ongoing effort, U.S. businesses will engage in the following activities:

Conferences on Best Practices Issues

In conjunction with Business for Social Responsibility, a non-profit business organization dedicated to promoting laudable corporate practices, and/or other appropriate organizations, the Administration will work to encourage conferences concerning issues relating to the practices contained in the Model Business Principles. Such conferences can provide a forum for information-sharing on new approaches for the evolving global context in which best practices are implemented. (For further information on Business for Social Responsibility, contact Bob Dunn, President, (415) 865-2500.)

Best Practices Information Clearinghouse and Support Services

One or more non-profits will work with the U.S. business community to develop a clearinghouse of information regarding business practices globally. The clearinghouse will establish a library of codes of conduct adopted by U.S. and international companies and organizations, to be catalogued and made available to companies seeking to develop their own codes. The clearinghouse would be available to provide advice to companies seeking to develop or improve their codes, advice based on the accumulated experience of other companies. Business for Social Responsibility (described above) is highly respected and is one resource that businesses and NGOs alike can turn to for information on best business practices.

Efforts by the U.S. Government

The U.S. Government also will undertake a number of activities to generate support for the Model Business Principles:

Promote Multilateral Adoption of Best Practices

The Administration has begun and will continue its effort to seek multilateral support for the Model Business Principles. Senior U.S. Government officials already have met with U.S. company officials and U.S. organizations operating abroad as well as with foreign corporate officials to seek support for the Principles. For example, the American Chambers of Commerce in the Asia Pacific recently adopted a resolution by which their members agreed to work with their local counterparts in the countries in which they operate to seek development of similar best practices among their members. The United States also will present the Model Business Principles at the Organization for Economic Cooperation and Development (OECD) and the International Labor Organization (ILO) as part of these organizations' ongoing behavior. Therefore, on an annual basis, the Administration will offer a series of awards to companies for specific activities that reflect best practices in the areas covered by the Model Business Principles. The awards will be granted pursuant to applications by interested companies. NGOs and private citizens will be encouraged to call attention to activities they believe are worthy of consideration. (For further information on the Best Practices Awards Program, contact Melinda Yee, U.S. Department of Commerce, (202) 482-1051.)

Presidential-Business Discussions   The President's Export Council (PEC), a high-level advisory group of Chief Executive Officers, provides a forum for the President to meet regularly with U.S. business leaders to discuss issues relating to U.S. industries' exports and operations abroad. The Administration will put the Model Business Principles on Appropriate PEC meeting agendas.

For further general information about the Model Business Principles, please contact U.S. Commerce Department, (202) 482-5151, or U.S. Department of State, (202) 647-1625.

AMERICAN ADVERTISING FEDERATION: *The Advertising Principles of American Business**

Truth Advertising shall tell the truth, and shall reveal significant facts, the omission of which would mislead the public.

Substantiation Advertising claims shall be substantiated by evidence in possession of the advertiser and advertising agency, prior to making such claims.

Comparisons Advertising shall refrain from making false, misleading, or unsubstantiated statements or claims about a competitor or his products or services.

Bait Advertising Advertising shall not offer products or services for sale unless such offer constitutes a bona fide effort to sell the advertised products or services and is not a device to switch consumers to other goods or services, usually higher priced.

Guarantees and Warranties Advertising of guarantees and warranties shall be explicit, with sufficient infor-

mation to apprise consumers of their principal terms and limitations or, when space or time restrictions preclude such disclosures, the advertisement should clearly reveal where the full text of the guarantee or warranty can be examined before purchase.

Price Claims Advertising shall avoid price claims which are false or misleading, or savings claims which do not offer provable savings.

Testimonials Advertising containing testimonials shall be limited to those of competent witnesses who are reflecting a real and honest opinion or experience.

Taste and Decency Advertising shall be free of statements, illustrations or implications which are offensive to good taste or public decency.

INTERNATIONAL FRANCHISE ASSOCIATION: *Code of Ethics†*

Section I: Preamble

Franchising is a business relationship utilized in more than 65 different industries. A wide variety of franchise relationships exist between thousands of franchisors and hundreds of thousands of franchisees.

Business format franchising offers the best opportunity for individuals who are seeking to enter into business for themselves by providing a framework for a mutually beneficial business relationship.

In recognition of the increasing role of franchising in the marketplace, and the very beneficial and positive contributions of franchising to the American economy, the members of the International Franchise Association believe that franchising must reflect the highest standards of ethical business practices. This can best be achieved by means of a strong and effective *Code of Ethics.*

To protect and to promote the interests of consumers, franchisees, and franchisors, and to ensure that this unique form of entrepreneurship continues to flourish with a high degree of success and security, we, the members of the International Franchise Asso-

*Courtesy of the American Advertising Federation.
†Reprinted by permission. International Franchise Association.

ciation (IFA), do hereby set forth the following principles and standards of conduct.

Section II: Principles

Franchisors shall conduct their business professionally, with truth, accuracy, fairness, and responsibility.

Franchisors shall use ethical business practices in dealings with franchisees, consumers, and government agencies.

Franchisors shall comply with all applicable laws and regulations in all business operations.

Franchisors shall offer equal opportunities in franchising for minorities, women, and the disabled.

Section III: Compliance and Enforcement

1. Applicability. The Code of Ethics shall be applicable to all IFA members in their United States operations.

2. Compliance. The policies and practices of members shall be consistent with the Code of Ethics.

3. Enforcement. IFA shall investigate complaints concerning possible violations of the Code of Ethics and, if appropriate, shall suspend, terminate, or take other appropriate action with respect to a member which is found to be in violation of the Code of Ethics.

Section IV: Standards of Conduct

1. Franchise Sales and Disclosure. In the advertisement and grants of franchises, a franchisor shall comply with all applicable laws and regulations. Offering circulars shall be complete, accurate, and not misleading.

All matters material to the granting of a franchise shall be contained in or referred to in one or more written documents, which shall clearly set forth the terms of the relationship and the respective rights and obligations of the parties. Such documents shall be provided to a prospective franchisee on a timely basis as required by law.

A franchisor shall encourage prospective franchisees to seek legal or other professional advice prior to the signing of a franchise agreement.

A franchisor shall encourage prospective franchisees to contact existing franchisees to gain a better understanding of the requirements and benefits of the business.

2. Good Faith Dealings. Franchisors and franchisees shall deal with each other fairly and in good faith, which means dealing honestly, ethically, and with mutual respect, in accordance with the terms of their franchise agreements. "Good faith dealing" is not intended to modify the terms of franchise agreements.

3. Franchisee Advisory Councils and Franchisee Associations. A franchisor shall foster open dialogue with franchisees through franchisee advisory councils and other communication mechanisms.

A franchisor shall not prohibit a franchisee from forming, joining, or participating in any franchisee association.

4. Termination of Franchise Agreements. A franchisor shall apply the following standards in connection with the termination of franchise agreements:

(a) A franchise agreement may only be terminated for good cause, which includes the failure of a franchisee to comply with any lawful requirement of the franchise agreement.

(b) A franchisee shall be given notice and a reasonable opportunity to cure breaches of the franchise agreement, which need not be more than 30 days.

(c) A franchise agreement may be terminated immediately, without prior notice or opportunity to cure, in the event of a franchisee's insolvency, abandonment of the franchised business, criminal misconduct or endangerment of public health or safety.

(d) The franchise agreement may be terminated pursuant to an express provision in the franchise agreement providing for a reciprocal right to terminate the agreement without cause.

5. Expiration of Franchise Agreements. A franchisor shall apply the following standards in connection with the expiration of franchise agreements:

(a) A franchisee shall be given notice at least 180 days prior to expiration of a franchisor's intention not to grant a new franchise agreement to the franchisee.

(b) The franchisor may determine not to grant a new franchise agreement:

(1) for good cause, which includes the failure of the franchisee to comply with any lawful requirement of the franchise agreement; or

(2) if the franchisor permits the franchisee to:

(i) during the 180 days prior to the expiration of the franchise, sell the business to a purchaser meeting the then-current qualifications and requirements specified by the franchisor; or

(ii) continue to operate the business under a different trade identity at the same location or within the same trade area.

(c) The franchisor may determine not to grant a new franchise agreement to a franchisee, without prior notice, in the event of the franchisee's insolvency, abandonment of the franchise business, criminal misconduct or endangerment of public health or safety.

(d) The franchisor may exercise any existing right to purchase the franchisee's business as provided in the franchise agreement.

(e) The franchisor may determine not to grant a new franchise agreement to a franchisee if the franchisor is withdrawing from the market.

6. Transfer of Franchise.

A franchisor shall not withhold approval of a proposed transfer of a franchise when the following criteria are met:

(a) The transferring franchisee is in compliance with the terms of the franchise agreement;

(b) The proposed transferee meets the then-current qualifications of the franchisor;

(c) The terms of the transfer meet the then-current requirements of the franchisor and the transfer provisions of the franchise agreement;

(d) The franchisor determines not to exercise a right of first refusal in accordance with the franchise agreement.

7. Encroachment.

In determining whether to open, or to authorize the opening of, an outlet in proximity to an existing franchised outlet, that will offer products or services similar to those of the existing outlet, a franchisor shall take into account the following:

(a) Territorial rights of the existing franchisee contained in the franchise agreement.

(b) The similarity of the new outlet and the existing outlet in terms of products and services to be offered.

(c) Whether the new outlet and the existing outlet will sell products or services to the same customers for the same occasion.

(d) The competitive activities in the market.

(e) The characteristics of the market.

(f) The ability of the existing outlet to adequately supply anticipated demand.

(g) The positive or negative effect of the new outlet on the existing outlet.

(h) The quality of operations and physical condition of the existing outlet.

(i) Compliance by the franchisee of the existing outlet with the franchise agreement.

(j) The experience of the franchisor in similar circumstances.

(k) The benefit or detriment to the franchise system as a whole in opening the new outlet.

(l) Relevant information submitted by existing franchisees and the prospective franchisee.

8. Alternative Supply Sources.

A franchisor may offer a turnkey business. A franchisor may require that franchisees purchase products and services which utilize or embody the franchisor's trade secrets or proprietary processes or ingredients, or for which it is not practical to issue specifications or standards, from the franchisor or a supplier selected exclusively by the franchisor. A franchisor will permit franchisees to obtain other equipment, fixtures, supplies, and services from sources chosen by the franchisee, provided that the chosen suppliers demonstrate to the franchisor's reasonable satisfaction:

(a) that the supplier meets the franchisor's specifications, standards and requirements regarding quality, variety, service, safety and health for the equipment, products and services supplied and the facilities used in the production and distribution of such equipment, products and services;

(b) that the supplier has the capacity to supply franchisee requirements;

(c) that the supplier has a sound financial condition and business reputation; and

(d) that the supplier will supply equipment, products or services to a sufficient number of franchisees of the franchisor to enable the franchisor to economically monitor compliance by the supplier with the franchisor's specifications, standards and requirements.

9. Disputes. Whenever practical, a franchisor shall make a diligent effort to resolve disputes with a franchisee by negotiation, mediation, or internal appeal procedures. A franchisor will consider the use of additional alternative dispute resolution procedures in appropriate situations to resolve disputes that are not resolved by negotiation, mediation, or internal appeal.

10. Discrimination. A franchisor shall not discriminate in the operations of its franchise system on the basis of race, color, religion, national origin, age, disability or sex. A franchisor may grant franchises to some franchisees on more favorable terms than are granted to other franchisees as part of a program to make franchises available to persons lacking capital, training, business experience or other qualifications ordinarily required of franchisees. A franchisor may implement other affirmative action programs.

AMERICAN MARKETING ASSOCIATION: *Code of Ethics**

Members of the American Marketing Association (AMA) are committed to ethical professional conduct. They have joined together in subscribing to this Code of Ethics embracing the following topics:

Responsibilities of the Marketer

Marketers must accept responsibility for the consequences of their activities and make every effort to en-

sure that their decisions, recommendations, and actions function to identify, serve, and satisfy all relevant publics: consumers, organizations and society. Marketers' professional conduct must be guided by:

1. The basic rule of professional ethics: not knowingly to do harm;

2. The adherence to all applicable laws and regulations;

3. The accurate representation of their education, training and experience; and

4. The active support, practice and promotion of this Code of Ethics.

Honesty and Fairness

Marketers shall uphold and advance the integrity, honor, and dignity of the marketing profession by:
1.   Being honest in serving consumers, clients, employees, suppliers, distributors and the public;
2.   Not knowingly participating in conflict of interest without prior notice to all parties involved; and
3.   Establishing equitable fee schedules including the payment or receipt of usual, customary and/or legal compensation for marketing exchanges.

Rights and Duties of Parties

Participants in the marketing exchange process should be able to expect that:

1. Products and services offered are safe and fit for their intended uses;

2. Communications about offered products and services are not deceptive;

3. All parties intend to discharge their obligations, financial and otherwise, in good faith; and

4. Appropriate internal methods exist for equitable adjustment and/or redress of grievances concerning purchases.

It is understood that the above would include, *but is not limited to,* the following responsibilities of the marketer:

---

*Reprinted by permission of the American Marketing Association.

In the Area of Product Development Management:

- Disclosure of all substantial risks associated with product or service usage
- Identification of any product component substitution that might materially change the product or impact on the buyer's purchase decision
- Identification of extra-cost features

In the Area of Promotions:

- Avoidance of false and misleading advertising
- Rejection of high pressure manipulations, or misleading sales tactics
- Avoidance of sales promotions that use deception or manipulation

In the Area of Distribution:

- Not manipulating the availability of a product for purpose of exploitation
- Not using coercion in the marketing channel
- Not exerting undue influence over the resellers' choice to handle a product

In the Area of Pricing:

- Not engaging in price fixing
- Not practicing predatory pricing
- Disclosing the full price associated with any purchase

In the Area of Marketing Research:

- Prohibiting selling or fund raising under the guise of conducting research
- Maintaining research integrity by avoiding misrepresentation and omission of pertinent research data
- Treating outside clients and suppliers fairly

Organizational Relationships

Marketers should be aware of how their behavior may influence or impact on the behavior of others in organizational relationships. They should not encourage or apply coercion to obtain unethical behavior in their relationships with others, such as employees, suppliers or customers.

1. Apply confidentiality and anonymity in professional relationships with regard to privileged information.

2. Meet their obligations and responsibilities in contracts and mutual agreements in a timely manner.

3. Avoid taking the work of others, in whole, or in part, and representing this work as their own or directly benefit from it without compensation or consent of the originator or owner.

4. Avoid manipulation to take advantage of situations to maximize personal welfare in a way that unfairly deprives or damages the organization or others. Any AMA members found to be in violation of any provision of this Code of Ethics may have his or her Association membership suspended or revoked.

STANDARDS OF ETHICAL CONDUCT FOR MANAGEMENT ACCOUNTANTS*

Management accountants have an obligation to the organizations they serve, their profession, the public, and themselves to maintain the highest standards of ethical conduct. In recognition of this obligation, the Institute of Management Accountants, formerly the National Association of Accountants, has adopted the following standards of ethical conduct for management accountants. Adherence to these standards is integral to achieving the *Objectives of Management Accounting.* Management accountants shall not commit acts contrary to these standards nor shall they condone the commission of such acts by others within their organizations.

Competence

Management accountants have a responsibility to:

- Maintain an appropriate level of professional competence by ongoing development of their knowledge and skills.

---

*Statement of Management Accounting IC, Institute of Management Accountants (formerly National Association of Accountants), Montvale, NJ 07645. Reprinted by permission.

- Perform their professional duties in accordance with relevant laws, regulations, and technical standards.
- Prepare complete and clear reports and recommendations after appropriate analyses of relevant and reliable information.

Confidentiality

Management accountants have a responsibility to:

- Refrain from disclosing confidential information acquired in the course of their work except when authorized, unless legally obligated to do so.
- Inform subordinates as appropriate regarding the confidentiality of information acquired in the course of their work and monitor their activities to assure the maintenance of that confidentiality.
- Refrain from using or appearing to use confidential information acquired in the course of their work for unethical or illegal advantage either personally or through third parties.

Integrity

Management accountants have a responsibility to:

- Avoid actual or apparent conflicts of interest and advise all appropriate parties of any potential conflict.
- Refrain from engaging in any activity that would prejudice their ability to carry out their duties ethically.
- Refuse any gift, favor, or hospitality that would influence or would appear to influence their actions.
- Refrain from either actively or passively subverting the attainment of the organization's legitimate and ethical objectives.
- Recognize and communicate professional limitations or other constraints that would preclude responsible judgment or successful performance of an activity.
- Communicate unfavorable as well as favorable information and professional judgments or opinions.
- Refrain from engaging in or supporting any activity that would discredit the profession.

Objectivity

Management accountants have a responsibility to:
Communicate information fairly and objectively. Disclose fully all relevant information that could reasonably be expected to influence an intended user's understanding of the reports, comments, and recommendations presented.

Resolution of Ethical Conflict

In applying the standards of ethical conduct, management accountants may encounter problems in identifying unethical behavior or in resolving an ethical conflict. When faced with significant ethical issues, management accountants should follow the established policies of the organization bearing on the resolution of such conflict. If these policies do not resolve the ethical conflict, management accountants should consider the following course of action:

- Discuss such problems with the immediate superior except when it appears that the superior is involved, in which case the problem should be presented initially to the next higher managerial level. If satisfactory resolution cannot be achieved when the problem is initially presented, submit the issues to the next higher managerial level.

   If the immediate superior is the chief executive officer, or equivalent, the acceptable reviewing authority may be a group such as the audit committee, executive committee, board of directors, board of trustees, or owners. Contact with levels above the immediate superior should be initiated only with the superior's knowledge, assuming the superior is not involved.

- Clarify relevant concepts by confidential discussions with an objective advisor to obtain an understanding of possible courses of action.

- If the ethical conflict still exists after exhausting all levels of internal review, the management accountant may have no other recourse on significant matters than to resign from the organization and to submit an informative memorandum to an appropriate representative of the organization.

Except where legally prescribed, communication of such problems to authorities or individuals not employed or engaged by the organization is not considered appropriate.

WATER QUALITY IMPROVEMENT INDUSTRY: *Code of Ethics** promulgated by the Water Quality Association

Preamble

The Water Quality Association is dedicated to promoting the highest principles of honesty, integrity, fair dealing, and professionalism in the water quality improvement industry. It is equally dedicated to preserving the consuming public's right to quality water. The primary purpose of this Code of Ethics is to educate industry members concerning standards of conduct in their dealings with their customers, among themselves, with members of related industries, and the public at large.

Article I
General Obligations

Industry members shall conduct themselves as informed, law abiding citizens. They shall be informed of and adhere to those federal, state, and local laws, statutes, ordinances, codes, and regulations applicable to the industry and to their businesses such as those dealing with restraint of trade, consumer protection, truth in advertising, truth in lending, selling, sanitation, registration, and effluent disposal.

Article II
Obligations to the Public

Industry members shall dedicate themselves to sound and competitive business practices. Specifically, they shall strive to:

A. Compete lawfully and honestly.

B. Build their businesses on the merits of their own products, services, and abilities; and not falsely disparage the products, services, or abilities of competitors, water purveyors, or others.

C. Accurately represent the characteristics or effects of the source water supply.

D. Accurately represent the characteristics or effects of the water improvement process or its product.

E. Accurately represent the benefits of the products or services that are to be provided and the changes to be made therefore.

F. Accurately represent their credentials, training, experience, and abilities and those of their employees and agents.

G. Base product performance, benefit or other promotion claims, either written or verbal, on factual data obtained from tests conducted by personnel technically competent to conduct such tests following scientifically valid test procedures, which data is in existence and available at the time such claims are made.

H. Avoid the omission of material facts in promoting their products or services if the effect would be to mislead or misrepresent.

I. Be familiar with and adhere to the Water Quality Improvement Industry Promotion Guidelines.

Article III
Promotion Guidelines

1. The word "product" as used in these Guidelines and Procedures includes publicly and privately supplied water, bottled water, and water quality improvement products and services or systems.

2. Product performance, benefit, or other promotion claims, either verbal or written, shall be based on factual data obtained from tests conducted by personnel technically competent to conduct such tests following scientifically valid test procedures, which data is in existence and available at the time such claims are made.

3. When the attributes or benefits claimed are not readily apparent to or verifiable by consumers, these claimed attributes or benefits shall be described and qualified with proven facts and in complete, comprehensive, and detailed terms.

---

*Water Quality Improvement Industry Code of Ethics, 1993.

4. Those who develop or disseminate, either in writing or verbally, product promotion claims or materials, including packaging, labeling, and installation, operation or maintenance materials, shall be responsible for making available reputable, verifiable, factual substantiation for those product promotion claims or materials.

5. Statements, either verbal or written, which are false, misleading, deceptive, fraudulent, or which falsely or deceptively disparage publicly or privately supplied water, bottled water, water quality improvement products or systems, or other competitors or competitive products, shall not be used.

6. Pictures, exhibits, graphs, charts, or other portrayals used in product promotion shall not be used in a false or misleading manner.

7. Sweeping, absolute statements, either verbal or written, shall not be made if they are false or not applicable in all situations which they purport to cover.

8. It shall not be stated or implied that the water to which the word "pure" is applied is "pure," unless the word "pure" is clearly defined by the user or by regulation. These words have been both used and defined in a variety of ways. Their capacity to mislead consumers is considerable. Therefore, the substantial definition problems with the words "pure," "purification," "purifier," or other derivatives of the word "pure" dictate that such words be used only with extreme caution.

9. Advertisements or promotional materials and practices, either verbal or written, shall be true and accurate in their entirety. Not only shall each sentence or statement, standing alone and separately considered, be literally true, but the combined overall effect of the materials shall also be accurate and not misleading.

10. Material facts shall not be omitted from product advertising or promotional material or practices if the effect would be to mislead or to misrepresent.

11. Devices or techniques, used to demonstrate hardness, the presence of chlorine, color, or other water characteristics of the individual consumer's water, shall not be used in sales presentations without, at the same time, accurately informing the consumer of their scope.

12. The words "warranty," "guarantee," or equivalent terms (hereinafter "warranty") shall not be used verbally or in writing in connection with industry products unless such use meets the requirements of the Federal Trade Commission's Guides for the Advertising of Warranties and Guarantees, 16 CFR 239.1 et seq., effective May 1, 1985, and corrected May 21, 1985, as they may be amended from time to time.

13. The composition of advertisements or other forms of product promotion materials shall be such as to minimize the possibility of misleading the reader. Product performance or benefit claims shall not be so placed in advertisements or promotional material or used in sales presentations so as to give the impression that they apply to additional or different merchandise when such is not the fact.

14. An asterisk may be used to direct attention to additional information about a word or term which is not in itself inherently deceptive. The asterisk or other reference symbols shall not be used as a means of contradicting or substantially changing the meaning of statements or graphic portrayals.

15. Prior to an advertiser's publishing or otherwise using an endorsement or testimonial (hereinafter both referred to as "endorsement"), the person whose endorsement is being used ("endorser") shall have previously made or shall have approved the contents and given permission for the advertiser's use of the endorsement.

B. The published or printed portion of an endorsement shall fairly reflect the spirit and content of the complete endorsement.

C. A proper endorsement may be advertised although given for compensation. The receipt of compensation need not be disclosed unless the context or contents of the endorsement implies that there was no compensation given.

Article IV
Obligations to the Customer

Industry members shall serve their customers competently, honestly, and promptly. Specifically, they shall strive to:

A. Be open and honest in their communications and dealing with customers and potential customers.

B. Factually represent their products and services to their customers.

C. Ensure that their products or services are properly applied or installed when they are responsible for such application or installation.

D. Respond promptly to customer complaints.

E. Provide for the availability of timely and competent service for their products.

F. Inform their customers of the maintenance and service requirements and related costs.

G. Honor contracts and warranties without undue delay.

Article V
Obligations to Professionalism

Industry members shall maintain and advance their knowledge and skills in the technologies utilized in the water quality improvement industry. Specifically, they shall strive to:

A. Ensure that their employees and agents, through continuing education, have a practical working knowledge of the technologies used in, and the capabilities of the products and services they provide.

B. Improve their own professional expertise by staying abreast of industry technological and scientific developments.

C. Adhere to and promote the business ethics embodied in this Code.

Company Codes of Ethics

E. I. DU PONT DE NEMOURS & COMPANY*

The policy was first adopted by the company in October 1975 and was last amended by the Board of Directors on October 26, 1988. It consolidates in one document all policies with respect to Business Ethics and Conflict of Interest for E. I. du Pont de Nemours and Company and its subsidiaries in which it has a majority interest or for which it has operating responsibility.

Business Ethics Policy

It always has been and continues to be the intent of the company that its employees maintain the highest ethical standards in their conduct of company affairs. The following sets forth in summary form for the benefit of all company employees, wherever located, the company's long-standing policy with respect to (1) gifts, favors, entertainment and payments given or received by employees, (2) potential conflicts of interest, and (3) certain other matters.

The essence of this policy is that each employee will conduct the company's business with integrity, in compliance with applicable laws, and in a manner that excludes considerations of personal advantage.

A. Payments by the Company

1. Gifts, favors and entertainment may be given others at company expense only if they meet *all* of the following criteria:

a. they are consistent with customary business practices,

b. they are not excessive in value and cannot be construed as a bribe or pay-off,

c. they are not in contravention of applicable law or ethical standards, and

d. public disclosure of the facts will embarrass neither the company nor the employee.

2. In connection with sales by the company, commissions, rebates, discounts, credits and allowances should be paid or granted only by the company on whose books the related sale is recorded, and such payments should:

a. bear a reasonable relationship to the value of goods delivered or services rendered,

b. be by check or bank transfer to the specific business entity with whom the agreement is made or to whom the original related sales invoice was issued — not to individual officers, employees or agents of such entity or to a related business entity.

c. be made only in the country of the entity's place of business, and

d. be supported by documentation that is complete

---

and that clearly defines the nature and purpose of the transaction.

Agreements for the company to pay commissions, rebates, credits, discounts or allowances should be in writing. When this is not feasible, the payment arrangement should be supported by an explanatory memorandum for file prepared by the approving department and reviewed by Legal Department.

3. In connection with the company's purchases of goods and services, including commissions related thereto, payments should be made only in the country of the seller's or provider's place of business or in the country in which the product was delivered or service rendered. All such payments shall be consistent with corporate and trade practice.

B. Gifts Received

1. Employees shall neither seek nor accept for themselves or others any gifts, favors or entertainment without a legitimate business purpose, nor seek or accept loans (other than conventional loans at market rates from lending institutions) from any person or business organization that does or seeks to do business with, or is a competitor of, the company. In the application of this policy:

    a. Employees may accept for themselves and members of their families common courtesies usually associated with customary business practices.

    b. An especially strict standard is expected with respect to gifts, services, discounts, entertainment or considerations of any kind from suppliers.

    c. It is never permissible to accept a gift in cash or cash equivalents (e.g., stocks or other forms of marketable securities) of any amount.

C. Conflicts of Interest

1. Employees should avoid any situation which involves or may involve a conflict between their personal interests and the interests of the company. As in all other facets of their duties, employees dealing with customers, suppliers, contractors, competitors or any person doing or seeking to do business with the company are to act in the best interests of the company to the exclusion of considerations of personal preference or advantage. Each employee shall make prompt and full disclosure in writing to his Department Management of a prospective situation which may involve a conflict of interest. This includes:

    a. Ownership by an employee or, to the employee's knowledge, by a member of the employee's family of a significant financial interest* in any outside enterprise which does or seeks to do business with or is a competitor of the company.

    b. Serving as a director, officer, partner, consultant, or in a managerial position with, or employment in a technical capacity by, any outside enterprise which does or is seeking to do business with or is a competitor of the company.

    c. Acting as a broker, finder, go-between or otherwise for the benefit of a third party in transactions involving or potentially involving the company or its interests.

    d. Any other arrangement or circumstance, including family or other personal relationships, which might dissuade the employee from acting in the best interest of the company.

All information disclosed to management as required by this policy shall be treated confidentially, except to the extent necessary to protect the company's interests.

---

*As a minimum standard, a "significant" financial interest is a direct or indirect aggregate interest of an employee and family members of more than:
(a) 1% of any class of the outstanding securities of a firm or corporation,
(b) 10% interest in a partnership or association, or
(c) 5% of the total assets or gross income of such employee.

D. Inside Information

1. Employees shall not:

    a. Give or release, without proper authority, to anyone not employed by the company, or to another employee who has no need for information, data or information of a confidential nature obtained while in company employment.

    b. Use nonpublic information obtained while in company employment (including information about customers, suppliers or competitors) for the personal profit of the employee or anyone else. This includes, but is not limited to, taking advantage of such information by (1) trading or providing information for others to trade in securities, (2) acquiring a real estate interest of any kind, including but not limited to plant or office sites or adjacent properties, or (3) acquiring (or acquiring options to obtain) interests in oil and gas leases, royalties, minerals or real property for the purpose of obtaining mineral or royalty interest, or any interest in oil or gas production or profits from the same.

E. Political Contributions

1. Employees shall not make any contribution of company funds, property or services to any political party or committee, domestic or foreign, or to any candidate for or holder of any office of any government — national, state, local or foreign. This policy does not preclude (a) the operation of a political action committee under applicable laws, (b) company contributions, where lawful, to support or oppose public referenda or similar ballot issues, or (c) political contributions, where lawful and reviewed in advance by the Executive Committee or by a committee appointed by the Executive Committee for this purpose.

F. Accounting Standards and Documentation

1. All accounts and records shall be documented in a manner that:

    a. clearly describes and identifies the true nature of business transactions, assets, liabilities or equity, and

    b. properly and timely classifies and records entries on the books of account in conformity with generally accepted accounting principles.

    No record, entry or document shall be false, distorted, misleading, misdirected, deliberately incomplete or suppressed.

    Strict adherence to this policy will protect the company and its employees from criticism, litigation or embarrassment that might result from alleged or real conflicts of interest or unethical practices. Employees should report apparent violations of this policy through their line organization or, if they prefer, directly to the company's General Auditor or a member of internal auditing management. The Auditing Division can be contacted by writing the General Auditor in Wilmington, Delaware, or by calling (302) 774-1300. Every effort will be made to protect the identity of the employee, or an employee may elect to report anonymously.

GEORGIA POWER COMPANY: *Code of Ethics**

We are wholeheartedly dedicated to providing our service in an ethical manner so that all who interact with us — our customers, our employees, our shareholders, our regulators, our suppliers and our competitors, as well as the public at large — can trust the company to deal with them in an honest and open manner in all transactions.

The commitment to honesty and integrity at Georgia Power goes back to our earliest history as a company. It is reflected in the speeches of Preston Arkwright, the company's first president. In a speech in 1922 he said, "Men in business should not forget that their character and self-respect are invested in the enterprise as well as their money and their work. Their reputation for moral character, in addition to the

---

*Georgia Power Company. Reprinted by permission.

personal happiness it brings, has for them a distinct commercial value. We have an even greater need than men generally for a strict adherence to moral principles." On another occasion Arkwright noted, "This Company will not wrong anyone intentionally. If by chance it commits a wrong, it will right it voluntarily."

Following this long-standing management philosophy, we must have the confidence and courage to recognize our duty to our customers, our employees and the communities we serve.

This summary of the character of the company is for the guidance of those just joining the company, to remind ourselves of the importance of our most important resource — our integrity — and so that the reasons for many of our policies based on this code of ethics will be understood.

Fairness

Above all else, it is our intention to treat everyone in a fair and equitable manner. No action of the company will be undertaken that does not meet this test. No person representing Georgia Power shall take unfair advantage of any customer, employee or representative of any concern with which we do business. Furthermore, we will display dignity and courtesy in business dealings with those inside and outside the company.

An organization this size must have numerous policies and procedures to ensure as nearly as possible consistent business behavior. In no case, however, should a policy or procedure of the company be used as an excuse for treating an employee, customer, or shareholder in an unfair manner. Common sense and our sense of ethics should prevail.

Resources

The resources of the company, including its money, its property and the time and talent of its employees, are to be used for conducting our business and meeting the needs of those we serve. These resources are to be handled prudently by those to whom they are entrusted. They most certainly are not to be diverted to the personal use of any of us.

Information

We have a great deal of information available to us about the company, its customers, its employees, its shareholders and its business transactions. All who have dealings with Georgia Power should know that we will not use this information for any purpose except that for which it was developed or given.

Truth

The internal and external reporting and exchange of information is a critical part of the conduct of our business. We will be complete, candid and accurate in our internal and external communication and take all practical steps to ensure that reliable information is provided by this company.

Business Relationships

All decisions made on behalf of Georgia Power are to be made in the best interest of the company, its customers, its shareholders and the public at large. Thus the acceptance in a business context of gifts, loans, entertainment, personal favors or anything that would influence a business decision, or appear to influence a business decision, must be avoided. Since our families have enormous influence over us, it is necessary that family members also avoid such compromising situations.

We will not make illegal payments, whether as money, services or other considerations, to persons to influence their actions regarding the company.

Laws and Regulation

The company and its officials, employees and representatives will obey all laws and regulations.

Politics

Employees should feel free to personally support political activities as citizens of a free nation. However, it is in some cases illegal for the company to support political candidates. No company asset can be used to support any political candidate. Furthermore, no official of the Company shall coerce any employee, supplier or customer to take any political action that is inconsistent with his personal beliefs.

Conflict of Interest

Every employee should avoid any activity in which his or her personal interests are at odds with the company's interests. As employees, we must exhibit at all times loyalty to our company. Engaging in any activity that dilutes employees' attention or loyalty to their careers and the company, even if only in appearance, constitutes a conflict of interest and cannot be allowed to continue.

Safe and Responsible Behavior

Competent and safe performance on the job is part of every employee's daily duty. In the interest of the safety and well being of ourselves, our fellow workers and our customers, we will be careful and responsible. Included in this is employees' responsibility to keep themselves totally free from the influence of alcoholic beverages while at work and at all times totally free from the influence of illegal drugs.

WM. WRIGLEY JR. COMPANY: *Principal Corporate Standards of Conduct**

The following policies apply to the Wm. Wrigley Jr. Company and all of its domestic and international associated companies and operations.

1. All presidents, managing directors, or managers of operations or departments shall be responsible for the enforcement of, and compliance with, the policies as set forth herein and have the responsibility for necessary distribution of this policy statement to insure full employee knowledge and compliance.

2. Any officer, director, or employee having information or knowledge of any unrecorded corporate fund or asset shall immediately report such matter to the Chairman of the Audit Committee, the internal auditors, or directly to the Chief Financial Officer of the Wrigley Company in Chicago, who, in turn, is required to report to the Audit Committee of the Board of Directors. Any officer, director, or employee of the Company possessing knowledge of any violation of corporate policy, the Compliance Guide or any prohibited corporate act, shall immediately report such violation to the Chief Financial Officer, the internal auditors, the Compliance Officer, or the Assistant

Secretary-Legal, who in turn, is required to report to the Audit Committee of the Board of Directors.

3. The use of corporate or associated company funds or other assets for any unlawful or improper purpose, including purposes that may be legal under non-U.S. laws but which are illegal under the laws of the United States is strictly prohibited.

4. No undisclosed or unrecorded funds or other assets shall be established for any purpose by the corporation or any of its associated companies or operations.

5. No false or artificial entries shall be recorded, or any omissions made, in the books or records of the corporation, or any of its associated companies or operations for any reason whatsoever, and no employee shall engage in or agree to any arrangement that results in such prohibited acts.

6. No payment on behalf of the corporation or any of its associated companies or operations shall be approved or made with the intention or understanding that any part of such payment is to be used for any purpose other than those described by the documents supporting all payments.

7. No payments or deposits, relating to any commitments made to an individual, a corporation or a partnership, shall be made to any individual, or to bank accounts in the names of individuals, or to corporate or partnership bank accounts in countries other than the countries in which the goods or services were received or their country of origin, or to a third party in behalf of such individual, corporation or partnership regardless of where such party is located.

8. No gifts in cash or in kind shall be accepted by any employee or his or her immediate family from any person, firm, or corporation that is either a competitor of the Wrigley Company or who supplies or seeks to supply merchandise, materials, property, or services to the Company.

The foregoing excludes *occasional* gratuitous items or services with a value of less than $150 or nominal promotional items. Also excluded is partici-

---

*Reprinted courtesy of the Wm. Wrigley Jr. Company.

pation in reasonable and infrequent entertainment sponsored by a current or prospective supplier of goods or services, provided there is a positive business intent and conforms to the ethics of the Wrigley Company.

Gifts or entertainment of this nature can easily be misinterpreted, and when proffered, must be thoroughly considered. Should you have any doubts whatsoever, concur with your immediate supervisor. If unusual circumstances require the acceptance of a gift in excess of $150 or entertainment that may not be considered reasonable, promptly report this to the Company's Chief Financial Officer.

There may be an occasion where a personal or family friend, who fits the criteria set forth at the beginning of this section, will give you or a member of your family a gift exceeding $150 in value for a special event, such as a wedding or birthday, etc. When such a gift is clearly personal and has no connection with your business relationship, it may be accepted, but must be promptly reported, in writing, to the Company's Chief Financial Officer with the situation fully explained.

9. No employees or their family members are to have non-business travel, living expenses, or entertainment advanced or absorbed by any person, firm, or corporation that is either a competitor of the Wrigley Company or supplying, or seeking to supply merchandise, materials, property, or services to the Company.

10. No gifts in cash or in kind shall be offered or given by any employee to any person or his or her immediate family who is an employee or is otherwise related to a person, firm or corporation that is either a competitor of the Wrigley Company or purchasing or who may seek to purchase merchandise, materials, property, or services from the Company. This excludes infrequent nominal business entertainment and gifts of nominal value which are necessitated by long-standing custom, gifts that are awarded to contestants of company-sponsored contests and items normally distributed for promotional purposes.

There may be an occasion where you wish to give a gift exceeding $150 in value for a special event, such as a wedding or birthday, etc., to a personal or family friend who fits the criteria set forth at the beginning of

this section. When such a gift is clearly personal and has no connection with your business relationship, it may be given, but must be promptly reported in writing, to the Company's Chief Financial Officer with the situation fully explained.

11. No employee shall offer or provide at corporate expense non-business travel, living expenses, or entertainment to any person or his or her immediate family, who is an employee or otherwise related to a person, firm, or corporation that is either a competitor of the Wrigley Company or purchasing or who may seek to purchase merchandise, materials, property, or services from the Company.

12. All procurement agents are charged with the responsibility of obtaining the best possible value under ethical guidelines for the Company in their procurement activities.

Employees directly involved in the procurement of merchandise, materials, property, or services are prohibited from investing in the companies that supply or who may seek to supply merchandise, materials, properties, or services to the Wrigley Company if the amount of business which the Wrigley Company conducts, or might conduct, with that supplier, represents, or might represent, a material portion of the supplier's annual gross revenues, or if the cost of such investment to the employee is less than that paid by other investors or is otherwise reduced because the Wrigley Company is conducting, or might conduct, business with that supplier.

Employees or their immediate families are prohibited from personal financial dealings with any individual or business organization supplying or seeking or who may seek to supply merchandise, materials, property, or services to the Company. This includes commissions, royalties, property, profit sharing, loans (excluding bank loans or accounts), or anything of value except as outlined above.

13. As with all other business conduct, employees shall take great care to ensure that when making political contributions the reputation of the Wrigley Company and its employees is not compromised. Contributions to political candidates in the U.S. or other countries is an individual citizen's decision, and contributions must not be made, or even appear to be made, with the Company's funds, or be reimbursed from the Company's funds. Likewise, no employee shall be required to specify that a portion of his or her salary or bonus be used for a political contribution, and no solicitations for political contributions shall be conducted in Company facilities. Any consideration of Company facilities, properties, or personnel to assist in a political campaign must first be submitted to the Compliance Officer for review.

14. Employees are expected to interact with U.S. and foreign government officials in accordance with the Wrigley Company's policy of conducting all business with the utmost integrity. Accordingly, Company or personal funds may not be used to offer payments (including money, gifts of substantial value, lavish entertainment and loans) directly or indirectly to a government official. This includes payments to obtain favorable legislation, regulations or rulings which would benefit the Company's business.

15. All employees must take care to conduct their business in accordance with the highest ethical standards. No individual who represents or is employed by the Wrigley Company shall engage in fraudulent behavior or make misrepresentations designed to obtain money or property. Wrigley Company employees are expected to treat their fellow associates, customers, suppliers, and others in an honest and straightforward manner.

16. All employees on international assignment represent and are identified with the Company in every country where they reside or visit. Their conduct cannot help but reflect directly upon the Company. To maintain and foster the reputation of the Wrigley Company at the highest possible level, these employees are expected to adhere to acceptable and proper standards of business and personal conduct and abide by host country laws and regulations. This includes the satisfaction of personal income tax liabilities, if applicable.

17. Appropriate officers, managers, or employees will be required at periodic intervals to certify compliance with these policies.

The policies mentioned above will be specifically included in the normal audit procedures, including internal audits, and may be further expanded and defined from time to time in the future.

Gray Matters*

This ethics training exercise provides an opportunity to practice ethical decision making.

Instructions:

1. You and the rest of the class are managers at Lockheed Martin Corporation, Orlando, Florida. You are getting ready to do the group exercise in an ethics training session. The training instructor announces you will be playing *Gray Matters: The Ethics Game*. You find out that *Gray Matters*, which was prepared for Lockheed Martin employees, is also played at 41 universities, including Harvard University, and at 65 other companies. There are 55 scenarios in *Gray Matters*, but you will have time during this session to complete only the nine scenarios that your group draws from the stack of cards.

2. The training instructor asks you to form into groups of four to six managers and to appoint a group leader who will read the case to the group, conduct a discussion of the case, obtain a consensus answer to the case, and then be the one to report the group's answers to the training instructor. You will have five minutes to reach each decision, after which time all groups will discuss their answers, and the instructor will give the point values and rationale for each choice. Then you will have five minutes for the next case, etc., until all nine cases have been completed. Keep track of your group's score for each case; the winning team will be the group scoring the most points.

3. Since this game is designed to reflect life, you may believe that some cases lack clarity or that some of your choices are not as precise as you would have liked. Also, some cases have only one solution, while others have more. In still others there is no good answer, and you must choose the answer that is the best of those presented. Each choice is assessed points to reflect which answer is the most correct. **Your group's task is to select only one option in each case.**

Your group draws cards 4, 5, 7, 12, 20, 31, 36, 40, and 51.

4

MINI-CASE

For several months now, one of your colleagues has been slacking off, and you are getting stuck doing the work. You think it is unfair. What do you do?

POTENTIAL ANSWERS

A. Recognize this as an opportunity for you to demonstrate how capable you are.
B. Go to your supervisor and complain about this unfair workload.
C. Discuss the problem with your colleague in an attempt to solve the problem without involving others.
D. Discuss the problem with the human resources department.

---

*Source: Permission granted by the author of *Gray Matters*, George Sammet, Jr., Vice President, Office of Corporate Ethics, Lockheed Martin Corporation, Orlando, Florida, to use these portions of *Gray Matters: The Ethics Game*© 1992. If you would like more information about the complete game, call 1-800-3ETHICS.

5
MINI-CASE

A defense program has not yet been formally approved nor have the funds been allocated. Nevertheless, because it all looks good and you need to get started in order to meet schedule, you start negotiating with a supplier. What do you tell the supplier?

POTENTIAL ANSWERS

A. "This is a 'hot' program for both of us. Approval is imminent. Let's get all the preliminary work under way."
B. "The program is a 'go.' I want you under contract as soon as possible."
C. "Start work and we will cover your costs when we get the contract."
D. "If you want to be part of the team on this important, great program, you, like us, will have to shoulder some of the start-up costs."

12
MINI-CASE

Your price is good on a program contract you are bidding, but you think it will take you several months longer than your competitor to develop the system. Your client, the U.S. Army, wants to know the schedule. What do you say?

POTENTIAL ANSWERS

A. Tell the Army your schedule is essentially the same as what you believe your competitor's will be.
B. Show the Army a schedule the same as what you believe your competitor's is (but believing you can do better than what your engineers have told you).
C. Explain to the Army the distinct advantage of your system irrelevant of schedule.
D. Lay out your schedule even though you suspect it may cause you to lose points on the evaluation

7
MINI-CASE

You are aware that a fellow employee uses drugs on the job. Another friend encourages you to confront the person instead of informing the supervisor. What do you do?

POTENTIAL ANSWERS

A. You speak to the alleged user and encourage him to get help.
B. You elect to tell your supervisor that you suspect an employee is using drugs on the job.
C. You confront the alleged user and tell him either to quit using drugs or you will "turn him in."
D. Report the matter to employee assistance.

20
MINI-CASE

You work in finance. Another employee is blamed for your error involving significant dollars. The employee will be able to clear himself, but it will be impossible to trace the error back to you. What do you do?

POTENTIAL ANSWERS

A. Do nothing. The blamed employee will be able to clear himself eventually.
B. Assist the blamed employee in resolving the issue but don't mention your involvement.
C. Own up to the error immediately, thus saving many hours of work.
D. Wait and see if the matter is investigated and at that time disclose your knowledge of the case.

31

MINI-CASE

A close relative of yours plans to apply for a vacancy in the department that you head. Hearing of this, what would you say to that person?

POTENTIAL ANSWERS

A. "Glad to have you. Our organization always needs good people."
B. "I would be concerned about the appearance of favoritism."
C. "It would be best if you did not work for me."
D. "If you get the job, expect no special consideration from me."

40

MINI-CASE

Your coworker is copying company-purchased software and taking it home. You know a certain program costs $400, and you have been saving for a while to buy it. What do you do?

POTENTIAL ANSWERS

A. You figure you can copy it too since nothing has ever happened to your coworker.
B. You tell your coworker he can't legally do this.
C. You report the matter to the ethics office.
D. You mention this to your supervisor.

36

MINI-CASE

You work for a company that has implemented a policy of a smoke-free environment. You discover employees smoking in the restrooms of the building. You also smoke and don't like having to go outside to do it. What do you do?

POTENTIAL ANSWERS

A. You ignore the situation.
B. You confront the employees and ask them to stop.
C. You join them, but only occasionally.
D. You contact your ethics or human resources representative and ask him or her to handle the situation.

51

MINI-CASE

A current supplier contacts you with an opportunity to use your expertise as a paid consultant to the supplier in matters not pertaining to your company's business. You would work only on weekends. You could:

POTENTIAL ANSWERS

A. Accept the job if the legal department poses no objection.
B. Accept the job.
C. Report pertinent details to your supervisor.
D. Decline the position.

Chapter 1

1. Paul W. Taylor, *Principles of Ethics: An Introduction to Ethics,* 2nd ed. (Encino, Calif.: Dickenson, 1975), p. 1.
2. Copyright © 1992 by Houghton Mifflin Company. Adapted and reprinted by permission from *The American Heritage Dictionary of the English Language,* Third Edition.
3. Wroe Alderson, *Dynamic Marketing Behavior* (Homewood, Ill.: Irwin, 1965), p. 320.
4. Archie B. Carroll, *Business and Society: Ethics and Stakeholder Management* (Cincinnati, Ohio: South-Western, 1989), pp. 30–33.
5. Del Jones, "Denny's Faces Another Claim of Racial Bias," *USA Today,* September 28, 1995, p. B1.
6. Linda Himelstein, "Law and Order in Cyberspace?" *Business Week,* December 4, 1995, p. 44.
7. Peter Eisler, "Alert Center Keeps Prodigy Users in Line," *USA Today,* September 5, 1995, p. 1A.
8. Material in this section was adapted from Richard T. DeGeorge, "The Status of Business Ethics: Past and Future," *Journal of Business Ethics,* 6 (April 1987): 201–211.
9. Carroll, *Business and Society,* pp. 225–227.
10. Alan R. Yuspeh, "Development of Corporate Compliance Programs: Lessons Learned from the DII Experience," in *Corporate Crime in America: Strengthening the "Good Citizenship" Corporation* (Washington, D.C.: U.S. Sentencing Commission, 1995), pp. 71–79.
11. Eleanor Hill, "Coordinating Enforcement Under the Department of Defense Voluntary Disclosure Program," in *Corporate Crime in America: Strengthening the "Good Citizenship" Corporation* (Washington, D.C.: U.S. Sentencing Commission, 1995), pp. 287–294.
12. "Huffing and Puffing in Washington: Can Clinton's Plan Curb Teen Smoking?" *Consumer Reports,* 60 (October 1995): 637.

13. Richard P. Conaboy, "Corporate Crime in America: Strengthening the Good Citizen Corporation," in *Corporate Crime in America: Strengthening the "Good Citizenship" Corporation* (Washington, D.C.: U.S. Sentencing Commission, 1995), pp. 1–2.

14. *United States Code Service* (Lawyers Edition), 18 U.S.C.S. Appendix Sentencing Guidelines for the United States Courts (Rochester, NY: Lawyers Cooperative Publishing, 1995), § 8A.1.

15. Conaboy, "Corporate Crime," p. 1.

16. Cyndee Miller, "Sexy Sizzle Backfires," *Marketing News,* September 25, 1995, pp. 1, 2.

17. Ken Wells, "Blood-Alcohol Level of Captain of Exxon Tanker Exceeded Limits," *Wall Street Journal,* March 31, 1989, p. A4.

18. Peter Eisler, "Complaints Now Sit for at Least a Year," *USA Today,* August 15, 1995, p. 1A.

19. Ibid.

20. "Officials Call for Crackdown on Garment Work Conditions," *Washington Post,* September 10, 1995, pp. A1, A12.

21. Madeline Jaynes, "When to Rat on the Boss," *Fortune,* October 2, 1995, p. 183.

Chapter 2

1. Ethics in American Business: Policies, Programs and Perceptions (Washington, D.C.: Ethics Resource Center, 1944), p. .

2. Ibid., p. 54.

3. Jathon Sapsford, Michael Sesit, and Timothy O'Brien, "How Daiwa Bond Man in New York Cost Bank $1.1 Billion in Losses," *Wall Street Journal,* September 27, 1995, pp. A1, A9.

4. Gene R. Laczniak, Marvin W. Berkowitz, Russell G. Brooker, and James P. Hale, "The Ethics of Business: Improving or Deteriorating?" *Business Horizons,* 38 (January–February 1995) 39–47.

5. Andy Pasztor, "Lockheed Willing to Plead Guilty, Pay Fine in Egyptian Plane Sales," *Wall Street Journal,* January 20, 1995, p. B6.

6. Bryan Burrough, "Slick Operators: Long Acceptance of Thefts Tied to Kickbacks Today; You Got to Buy Business," *Wall Street Journal,* January 15, 1985, p. 1.

7. Steve Stecklow, "Cheat Sheets: Colleges Inflate SAT's and Graduation Rates in Popular Guidebooks," *Wall Street Journal,* April 5, 1995, pp. A1, A4.

8. Vernon R. Loucks, Jr., "A CEO Looks at Ethics," *Business Horizons,* 30 (March–April 1987): 4.

9. "Law on Treating Poor Patients Faces Key Test," *Wall Street Journal,* May 2, 1991, pp. B1, B8.

10. Eric H. Beversluis, "Is There 'No Such Thing as Business Ethics'?" *Journal of Business Ethics,* 6 (February 1987): 81–88. Reprinted by permission of Kluwer Academic Publishers, Dordrecht, Holland.

11. Ibid., p. 82.

12. G. Bruce Knecht, "When Visa and American Express Go to War, Truth May Be the Big Loser," *Wall Street Journal,* October 14, 1994, pp. B1, B5.

13. Teri Agins, "Go Figure: Same Shopper Wears Size 6, 8, 10, 12," *Wall Street Journal,* November 11, 1994, p. B1.

14. Alix M. Freedman and Suein L. Hwang, "Why Don't Low-Tar Cigarettes Have Lower Nicotine?" *Wall Street Journal,* July 14, 1995, p. A1.

15. Archie B. Carroll, *Business and Society: Ethics and Stakeholder Management* (Cincinnati: South-Western, 1989), pp. 228–230.

16. "Lawyers' Billing Practices Are Scrutinized," *Wall Street Journal*, April 6, 1992, p. B7.

17. "Collusion, Price Fixing Have Long Been Rife in Treasury Market," *Wall Street Journal*, August 19, 1991, pp. A1, A5.

18. Matt Murray, "Former Phar-Mor President Guilty in Fraud Case," *Wall Street Journal*, May 26, 1995, p. B1.

19. Timothy L. O'Brien, "Law Firm's Downfall Exposes New Methods of Money Laundering," *Wall Street Journal*, May 26, 1995, pp. A1, A6.

20. Suein L. Hwang, "The Executive Who Told Tobacco's Secrets," *Wall Street Journal*, November 28, 1995, pp. B1, B6.

21. Milo Geyelin, "Du Pont Faces Criminal Probe Tied to Benlate DF Test Results," *Wall Street Journal*, October 18, 1995, p. B3.

22. Steve Stecklow, "False Profit: How New Era's Boss Led Rich and Gullible into a Web of Deceit," *Wall Street Journal*, May 19, 1995, pp. A1, A4.

23. Barbara Carton, "Unlikely Hero: A Persistent Accountant Brought New Era's Problems to Light," *Wall Street Journal*, May 19, 1995, pp. B1, B6.

24. William M. Carley, "Rigging Computers for Fraud or Malice Is Often an Inside Job," *Wall Street Journal*, August 27, 1992, pp. A1, A4.

25. Ibid., pp. A1, A4.

26. Margaret A. Jacobs, "Riding Crop and Slurs: How Wall Street Dealt with a Sex-Bias Case," *Wall Street Journal*, June 9, 1994, pp. A1, A8.

27. "Internal Suspicions: GE's Drive to Purge Fraud Is Hampered by Workers' Mistrust," *Wall Street Journal*, July 22, 1992, pp. A1, A4.

28. Andy Pasztor, "Probe of Rockwell Unit Expands; Hazardous Waste Disposal at Issue," *Wall Street Journal*, December 21, 1995, p. B7.

29. Milo Geyelin, "Why Many Businesses Can't Keep Their Secrets," *Wall Street Journal*, November 20, 1995, pp. B1, B3.

30. Edward Felsenthal, "Honesty Often a State Policy in Real Estate," *Wall Street Journal*, June 13, 1994, pp. B1, B3.

31. "Data Tap: Patients' Records Are Treasure Trove for Budding Industry," *Wall Street Journal*, February 27, 1992, pp. A1, A4.

32. "Cut Down: Timber Town Is Bitter over Efforts to Save the Rare Spotted Owl," *Wall Street Journal*, January 6, 1992, pp. A1, A8.

33. Charles McCoy, "A Giant Logger and a Tiny Bird Test Limits of Conservation Law," *Wall Street Journal*, October 20, 1994, pp. B1, B4.

34. Thomas M. Buton, "Dow's Role in Implants Is Given New Light," *Wall Street Journal*, December 21, 1994, p. B4.

35. "Doctor Assails J&J Price Tag on Cancer Drug," *Wall Street Journal*, May 20, 1992, pp. B1, B8.

36. Amal Kumar Naj, "Medical Group Questions Benefits of MRI," *Wall Street Journal*, May 16, 1994, p. B6.

37. Heidi Evans, "Doctors Who Perform Fetal Sonograms Often Lack Sufficient Training and Skill," *Wall Street Journal*, June 20, 1995, pp. B1, B2.

38. "CPA's Nightmare: How Audit of a Bank Cost Price Waterhouse $388 Million," *Wall Street Journal*, August 14, 1992, pp. A1, A4.

39. Patrick M. Reilly, "Woolworth Is Shaken by Accounting Probe at a Very Bad Moment," *Wall Street Journal*, April 8, 1994, pp. A1, A6.

40. Lee Berton, "Code May Force CPAs to Inform on Employees," *Wall Street Journal,* August 4, 1995, pp. B4, B12.

Chapter 3

1. James R. Rest, *Moral Development Advances in Research and Theory* (New York: Praeger, 1986), p. 1.
2. Tricia Welsh, "Best and Worst Corporate Reputations," *Fortune,* February 7, 1994, pp. 58–95.
3. "American Express Public Responsibility; A Report of Recent Activities," Office of Public Responsibility, American Express Company, 1987, p. 8; and Patricia A. Galagan, "Joining Forces: Business and Education Take on Competitiveness," *Training and Development Journal* (July 1988): 28.
4. Welsh, "Best and Worst Corporate Reputations," pp. 58–95.
5. John R. Emshwiller, "Having Lost Thousands to Con Artists, Elderly Widow Tells Cautionary Tale," *Wall Street Journal,* September 20, 1995, pp. B1, B5.
6. Suzanne Alexander Ryan and John R. Wilke, "Banking on Publicity, Mr. Marks Got Fleet to Lend Billions," *Wall Street Journal,* February 11, 1994, pp. A1, A5.
7. Richard Brandt, *Ethical Theory* (Englewood Cliffs, N.J.: Prentice-Hall, 1959), pp. 253–254.
8. J.J.C. Smart and B. Williams, *Utilitarianism: For and Against* (Cambridge, England: Cambridge University Press, 1973), p. 4.
9. C. E. Harris, Jr., *Applying Moral Theories* (Belmont, Calif.: Wadsworth, 1986), pp. 127–128.
10. Immanuel Kant, "Fundamental Principles of the Metaphysics of Morals," in *Problems of Moral Philosophy: An Introduction,* 2nd ed., ed. Paul W. Taylor (Encino, Calif.: Dickenson, 1972), p. 229.
11. Example adapted from C. E. Harris, Jr., *Applying Moral Theories* (Belmont, Calif.: Wadsworth, 1986), pp. 128–129.
12. Gerald F. Cavanaugh, Dennis J. Moberg, and Manuel Velasquez, "The Ethics of Organizational Politics," *Academy of Management Review* 6 (July 1981): 363–374.
13. John R. Wilke, "A Publicly Held Firm Turns X-Rated Videos into a Hot Business," *Wall Street Journal,* July 11, 1994, pp. A1, A2.
14. Kant, "Fundamental Principles," p. 229.

Chapter 4

1. Archie B. Carroll, "The Pyramid of Corporate Social Responsibility: Toward the Moral Management of Organizational Stakeholders," *Business Horizons* (July–August 1991): 42.
2. Ibid.
3. Linda Ferrell, "Corporate Social Responsibility and Financial Return to Investors: Future Directions for Research," *Southern Management Association Proceedings,* (1992): 343.
4. Christina Duff, "Big Stores' Outlandish Demands Alienate Small Suppliers," *Wall Street Journal,* October 27, 1995, p. B1.
5. Udayan Gupta, "'Teleconomic' Expert Helps Towns Develop," *Wall Street Journal,* October 19, 1995, pp. B1, B2.
6. Joseph B. White, "Factory Towns Start to Fight Back Angrily When Firms Pull Out," *Wall Street Journal,* March 8, 1988, p. 1.

7. Gregory T. Gundlach, "Price Predation: Legal Limits and Antitrust Considerations," *Journal of Public Policy & Marketing*, 14 (Fall 1995): 278.

8. Ibid.

9. William M. Carley, "Secrets War: GE Presses Campaign to Halt Rivals' Misuse of Turbine-Parts Data," *Wall Street Journal*, August 16, 1988, pp. 1, 10.

10. Alix M. Freedman and Suein L. Hwang, "Reynolds Marketing Plan Urged Focus to Get Young Adults to Smoke Camels," *Wall Street Journal*, November 2, 1995, p. B4.

11. Paul Raeburn, "Magazine Spread Tobacco Views to Kids, Study Says," *Commercial Appeal*, November 1, 1995, p. B6.

12. Scott McCartney, "Compaq Suit Claims Packard Bell Sells New Computers Containing Used Parts," *Wall Street Journal*, April 11, 1995, p. A2.

13. Official Court Notice, U.S. District Court Southern District of Georgia, as published in *USA Today*, September 22, 1995, p. 4B.

14. Fred W. Morgan, Drue K. Schuler, and Jeffrey J. Stoltman, "A Framework for Examining the Legal Status of Vulnerable Consumers," *Journal of Public Policy & Marketing*, 14 (Fall 1995): 267.

15. Bob Davis, "FCC Starts Inquiry on the Regulation of Children's TV," *Wall Street Journal*, October 21, 1992, p. 58.

16. Alan Freeman, "Quebec Law Protecting Kids from Ads Rankles Companies," *Wall Street Journal*, December 19, 1985, p. 23.

17. Allanna Sullivan and Bradley A. Stertz, "Alternative Fuels Strutting Their Stuff," *Wall Street Journal*, August 17, 1989, p. B1.

18. CNN News, "Not in My Backyard," CNN Special Report, December 19, 1988.

19. Russell Mitchell, "A Word of Advice, Benjamin: Stay Out of Plastics," *Business Week*, April 17, 1989, p. 23.

20. Brad Edmondson, "Work Slowdown," *American Demographics* (March 1996): 4.

21. Ibid., p. 6.

22. Win Swenson, "The Organizational Guidelines' 'Carrot and Stick' Philosophy, and Their Focus on 'Effective' Compliance," in *Corporate Crime in America: Strengthening the "Good Citizenship" Corporation*, (Washington, D.C.: U.S. Sentencing Commission, 1995), pp. 17–26.

23. *United States Code Service* (Lawyers Edition), 18 U.S.C.S. Appendix, Sentencing Guidelines for the United States Courts (Rochester, NY: Lawyers Cooperative Publishing, 1995) § 8A.1.

24. Lynn Sharp Paine, "Managing for Organizational Integrity," *Harvard Business Review* (March-April 1994): 111.

25. Carroll, "Pyramid of Corporate Social Responsibility," p. 41.

26. G. A. Steiner and J. F. Steiner, *Business, Government, and Society* (New York: Random House, 1988).

27. Milton Friedman, "Social Responsibility of Business Is to Increase Its Profits," *New York Times Magazine*, September 13, 1970, pp. 122–126.

28. Excerpted from R. Edward Freeman and Daniel R. Gilbert, Jr., *Corporate Strategy and the Search for Ethics* (Englewood Cliffs, N.J.: Prentice-Hall, 1988), p. 90. Reprinted by permission.

29. Ibid., p. 105. Reprinted by permission.

30. Ibid., p. 7. Reprinted by permission.

31. Ibid. Reprinted by permission.

32. M. Cash Matthews, *Strategic Intervention in Organizations: Resolving Ethical Dilemmas* (Newbury Park, Calif.: Sage Publications, 1988), pp. 78–79.

33. Emily T. Smith and Vicki Cahan, with Naomi Freundlich, James E. Ellis, and Joseph Weber, "The Greening of Corporate America," *Business Week,* April 23, 1990, pp. 96–103.

34. Adapted from O. C. Ferrell and Geoffrey Hirt, *Business: A Changing World,* (Homewood, Ill.: Richard D. Irwin, Inc., in a joint venture with Austen Press, 1993), pp. 45–46. Reprinted by permission.

35. Stan Crock, "When Charity Doesn't Begin at Home," *Business Week,* November 27, 1995, p. 34.

36. Nelson Schwartz and Tim Smart, "Giving — And Getting Something Back," *Business Week,* August 28, 1995, p. 81.

37. Ibid.

38. Ibid.

39. Julia Lawlor, "Homeless Can Reserve Room, Job at Days Inns," *USA Today,* July 20, 1990, p. 2B.

Chapter 5

1. Thomas M. Jones, "Ethical Decision Making by Individuals in Organizations: An Issue-Contingent Model," *Academy of Management Review,* 16 (February 1991): 366–395; O. C. Ferrell and Larry G. Gresham, "A Contingency Framework for Understanding Ethical Decision Making in Marketing," *Journal of Marketing,* 49 (Summer 1985): 87–96; O. C. Ferrell, Larry G. Gresham, and John Fraedrich, "A Synthesis of Ethical Decision Models for Marketing," *Journal of Macromarketing,* 9 (Fall 1989): 55–64; Shelby D. Hunt and Scott Vitell, "A General Theory of Marketing Ethics," *Journal of Macromarketing,* 6 (Spring 1986): 5–16; William A. Kahn, "Toward an Agenda for Business Ethics Research," *Academy of Management Review,* 15 (April 1990): 311–328; and Linda K. Trevino, "Ethical Decision Making in Organizations: A Person-Situation Interactionist Model," *Academy of Management Review,* 11 (March 1986): 601–617.

2. Jones, "Ethical Decision Making," pp. 367, 372.

3. Donald P. Robin, R. Eric Reidenbach, and P. J. Forrest, "The Perceived Importance of an Ethical Issue as an Influence on the Ethical Decision-Making of Ad Managers," *Journal of Business Research,* 35 (January 1996): 17.

4. Ibid.

5. Ibid.

6. Jay Koblenz, "Avoiding Dealer Discrimination," *Black Enterprise* (November 1995): 177.

7. Del Jones, "Denny's Faces Another Claim of Racial Bias," *USA Today,* September 28, 1995, p. B1.

8. Robin, Reidenbach, and Forrest, "The Perceived Importance of an Ethical Issue," p. 17.

9. Lawrence Kohlberg, "Stage and Sequence: The Cognitive Developmental Approach to Socialization," in *Handbook of Socialization Theory and Research,* ed. D. A. Goslin (Chicago: Rand McNally, 1969), pp. 347–480.

10. Ibid.

11. Charles Peters and Taylor Branch, *Blowing the Whistle: Dissent in the Public Interest* (New York: Praeger, 1972), pp. 182–185.

12. Rebecca Goodell, *Ethics in American Business: Policies, Programs and Perceptions,* (Washington D.C.: Ethics Resource Center, 1994), p. 15.

13. Ibid.

14. John Fraedrich and O. C. Ferrell, "Cognitive Consistency of Marketing Managers in Ethical Situations," *Journal of the Academy of Marketing Science*, 20 (Summer 1992), 245–252.

15. John Fraedrich, Debbie M. Thorne, and O. C. Ferrell, "Assessing the Application of Cognitive Moral Development Theory to Business Ethics," *Journal of Business Ethics*, 13 (1994): 829–838.

16. Ibid.

17. Jeffrey A. Trachtenberg and Mark Robichaux, "Crooks Crack Digital Codes of Satellite TV," *Wall Street Journal*, January 12, 1996, p. B1.

18. Richard T. De George, *Business Ethics*, 3rd ed. (New York: Macmillan Publishing Company, 1990), pp. 14, 26–27, 40, 63, 79–80, 83–85, 105–108, 160–178.

19. Margaret H. Cunningham and O. C. Ferrell, "Ethical Decision-Making Behavior in Marketing Research Organizations," working paper, School of Business, Queen's University, Kingston, Ontario, 1993.

20. Ferrell and Gresham, "A Contingency Framework," pp. 87–96.

21. Rhonda L. Rundle, "Sunrise, Restating Net Lower, Claims Faked Data," *Wall Street Journal*, January 5, 1996, p. A2.

22. Ibid.

23. "SEC Charges Three in Kidder 1994 Bond Trading Scandal," *St. Petersburg Times*, January 10, 1996, p. 6E.

24. Margaret H. Cunningham and O. C. Ferrell, "Ethical Decision-Making Behavior in Marketing Research Organizations," working paper, School of Business, Queen's University, Kingston, Ontario, 1993.

25. Christina Duff, "Big Stores' Outlandish Demands Alienate Small Suppliers," *Wall Street Journal*, October 27, 1995, p. B1.

26. Ibid.

Chapter 6

1. Wendy L. Wall, "Commodity Firm's Selling Tactics Spotlighted in Legal Proceedings," *Wall Street Journal*, August 14, 1986, p. 19.

2. Ken Wells and Charles McCoy, "How Unpreparedness Turned the Alaska Spill into Ecological Debacle," *Wall Street Journal*, April 3, 1989, p. A1.

3. Andrea Gerlin, "Spread of Illegal Home Sewing Is Fueled by Immigrants," *Wall Street Journal*, March 15, 1994, pp. B1, B8.

4. O. C. Ferrell and Steven J. Skinner, "Ethical Behavior and Bureaucratic Structure in Marketing Research Organizations," *Journal of Marketing Research*, 25 (February 1988): 103–109.

5. Peter D. Bennett, ed., *Dictionary of Marketing Terms* (Chicago: American Marketing Association, 1988), p. 45. Reprinted by permission.

6. Richard L. Daft, *Organizational Theory and Design* (St. Paul, Minn.: West Publishing, 1983), p. 482.

7. Stanley M. Davis, quoted in Alyse Lynn Booth, "Who Are We?" *Public Relations Journal* (July 1985): 13–18.

8. T. E. Deal and A. A. Kennedy, *Corporate Culture: Rites and Rituals of Corporate Life* (Reading, Mass.: Addison Wesley, 1982), p. 4.

9. G. Hofstede, "Culture's Consequences: International Differences," in *Work-Related Values* (Beverly Hills, Calif.: Sage Publications, 1980), p. 25.

10. N. M. Tichy, "Managing Change Strategically: The Technical, Political and Cultural Keys," *Organizational Dynamics* (Autumn 1982): 59–80.

11. J. W. Lorsch, "Managing Culture: The Invisible Barrier to Strategic Change," *California Management Review,* 28 (Winter 1986): 95–109.

12. R. Eric Reidenbach and Donald P. Robin, *Ethics and Profits* (Englewood Cliffs, N.J.: Prentice-Hall, 1989), p. 91.

13. W. B. Tunstall, "Cultural Transition at AT&T," *Sloan Management Review* (Fall 1983): 15–26.

14. Teri Agins, "Gitano Jeans' Fall Is Saga of Corruption and Mismanagement," *Wall Street Journal,* February 18, 1994, pp. A1, A4.

15. Meg Cox and Johnnie L. Roberts, "How the Despotic Boss of Simon & Schuster Found Himself Jobless," *Wall Street Journal,* July 6, 1994, pp. A1, A12.

16. Francis C. Brown III, "American Airlines Boss Blossoms as Champion of the Poor Passenger," *Wall Street Journal,* March 4, 1988, pp. 1, 10.

17. Reidenbach and Robin, *Ethics and Profits,* p. 92.

18. Ibid.

19. N. K. Sethia and M. A. Von Glinow, "Arriving at Four Cultures by Managing the Reward System," in *Gaining Control of the Corporate Culture* (San Francisco: Jossey-Bass, 1985), p. 409.

20. Alex Markels and Joann S. Lublin, "Longevity-Reward Programs Get Short Shrift," *Wall Street Journal,* April 27, 1995, pp. B1, B3.

21. Joann S. Lublin, "Less-Than-Watchful Eyes Didn't Oversee Expenses of a Utility's Chairman," *Wall Street Journal,* June 15, 1994, pp. B1, B4.

22. Robert Frank, "As UPS Tries Harder to Deliver More to Its Customers, Labor Problems Grow," *Wall Street Journal,* May 23, 1994, pp. A1, A5.

23. Elyse Tanouye, "J&J to Admit to Shredding Retin-A Papers," *Wall Street Journal,* January 11, 1995, pp. B1, B4.

24. Patrick E. Murphy, "Implementing Business Ethics," *Journal of Business Ethics,* 7 (December 1988): 909.

25. Ibid.

26. Bruce Hager, "What's Behind Business' Sudden Fervor for Ethics," *Business Week,* September 23, 1991, p. 65.

27. Ricky Griffin, *Management,* 3rd ed. (Boston: Houghton Mifflin Co., 1990), pp. 522–524.

28. Ibid.

29. Margaret Cunningham, "Walking the Thin White Line: A Role Conflict Model of Ethical Decision Making Behavior in the Marketing Research Process," Ph.D. dissertation, Texas A&M University, 1991.

30. Ibid.

31. O. C. Ferrell, Larry Gresham, and John Fraedrich, "A Synthesis of Ethical Decision Making Models for Marketing," *Journal of MacroMarketing* (Fall 1989): 58–59.

32. Micheline Maynard, "GM: Pickups 'Do Not Have Safety Defect,'" *USA Today,* April 30, 1993, p. B1.

33. Michael Clements and Micheline Maynard, "Groups Claim Design at Fault in Fiery Deaths," *USA Today,* December 9, 1992, p. B1.

34. Rinier Buck, "Super Mario Fiasco," *Ad Week's Marketing Week,* September 20, 1991, p. 8.

Chapter 7

1. John Fraedrich and O. C. Ferrell, "Cognitive Consistency of Marketing Managers in Ethical Situations," *Journal of the Academy of Marketing Science,* 20 (Summer 1992): 243–252.

2. Rebecca Goodell, "National Business Ethics Survey Findings," *Ethics Journal* (Fall/Winter 1994): 1–3.

3. Karl Perez, "Today's Lesson: Do Your Homework," *Crain's International* (Fall, 1995): 1–11.

4. John R. Emshwiller, "How Low-Key Style Let a Con Man Steal Millions from Bosses," *Wall Street Journal,* December 4, 1995, p. A1.

5. Margaret Cunningham, "Walking the Thin White Line: A Role Conflict Model of Ethical Decision Making Behavior in the Marketing Research Process," Ph.D. dissertation, Texas A&M University, 1991, p. 323.

6. Mary Zey-Ferrell and O. C. Ferrell, "Role-Set Configuration and Opportunity as Predictors of Unethical Behavior in Organizations," *Human Relations,* 35, no. 7 (1982): 587–604.

7. O. C. Ferrell and K. Mark Weaver, "Ethical Beliefs of Marketing Managers," *Journal of Marketing* (July 1978): 69–73.

8. *Wall Street Journal,* June 25, 1992.

9. Vikki Kratz, "Don't Be Shy," *Business Ethics* (January–February 1996): 15.

10. E. Sutherland and D. R. Cressey, *Principles of Criminology,* 8th ed. (Chicago: Lippincott, 1970), p. 114.

11. O. C. Ferrell and Larry G. Gresham, "A Contingency Framework for Understanding Ethical Decision Making in Marketing," *Journal of Marketing,* 49 (Summer 1985): 90–91.

12. Mary Zey-Ferrell, K. Mark Weaver, and O. C. Ferrell, "Predicting Unethical Behavior Among Marketing Practitioners," *Human Relations,* 32 (1979): 557–569.

13. James S. Bowman, "Managerial Ethics in Business and Government," *Business Horizons,* 19 (October 1976): 48–54; William C. Frederick and James Weber, "The Value of Corporate Managers and Their Critics: An Empirical Description and Normative Implications," in *Research in Corporate Social Performance and Social Responsibility,* ed. William C. Frederick and Lee E. Preston (Greenwich, Conn.: JAI Press, 1987), pp. 149–150; and Linda K. Trevino and Stuart Youngblood, "Bad Apples in Bad Barrels: A Causal Analysis of Ethical Decision Making Behavior," *Journal of Applied Psychology,* 75 (August 1990): 38.

14. Keith H. Hammonds, "A Whistle-Blower Gets His Reward," *Business Week,* August 28, 1995, p. 38.

15. Ross Kerber, "Suit Says Dartmouth Fudged Data Used in Business-School Rankings," *Wall Street Journal,* January 11, 1996, p. B2.

16. Madeline Jaynes, "When to Rat on the Boss," *Fortune,* October 2, 1995, p. 183.

17. Ibid.

18. Maynard M. and Carolyn C. Dolecheck, "Ethics: Take It from the Top," *Business* (January–March 1989): 12–18.

19. John Bussey, "Lee Iacocca Calls Odometer Policy 'Dumb,'" *Wall Street Journal,* July 2, 1987, p. 2.

20. Janet Guyon, "GE Chairman Welch, Though Much Praised, Starts to Draw Critics," *Wall Street Journal,* August 4, 1988, pp. 1, 7.

21. Ibid.

22. Lyman W. Porter, "Job Attitudes in Management: II. Perceived Importance of Needs as a Foundation of Job Level," *Journal of Applied Psychology,* 47 (April 1963): 141–148.

23. Clayton Alderfer, *Existence, Relatedness, and Growth* (New York: Free Press, 1972), pp. 42–44.

24. John R. P. French and Bertram Ravin, "The Bases of Social Power," in *Group Dynamics: Research and Theory,* ed. Dorwin Cartwright (Evanston, Ill.: Row, Peterson, 1962), pp. 607–623.

25. Laurie P. Cohen and Elyse Tanouye, "Drug Makers Set to Pay $600 Million to Settle Suit by Small Retailers," *Wall Street Journal,* January 18, 1996, p. A1.

26. Pamela Sebastian, "ITT Pleads Guilty in Conspiracy Case over Defense Data," *Wall Street Journal,* October 25, 1988, p. A24.

27. Frederick and Weber, "The Value of Corporate Managers," pp. 149–150.

28. Gene R. Laczniak and Patrick E. Murphy, *Ethical Marketing Decisions: The Higher Road* (Boston: Allyn & Bacon, 1993), p. 14.

Chapter 8

1. O. C. Ferrell and Larry G. Gresham, "A Contingency Framework for Understanding Ethical Decision Making in Marketing," *Journal of Marketing,* 49 (Summer 1985): 92.

2. John R. Emshwiller, "How Low-Key Style Let a Con Man Steel Millions from Bosses," *Wall Street Journal,* December 4, 1995, pp. A1, A7.

3. Michael Schroeder, "Heart Trouble at Pfizer," *Business Week,* February 26, 1990, pp. 47–48.

4. Don Clark, "Some Scientists Are Angry over Flaw in Pentium Chip, and Intel's Response," *Wall Street Journal,* November 25, 1994, p. B6.

5. Andrea Gerlin, "A Sandoz Drug Generates a Wave of Lawsuits," *Wall Street Journal,* August 16, 1994, pp. B1, B6.

6. Dean M. Krugman and O. C. Ferrell, "The Organizational Ethics of Advertising: Corporate and Agency Views," *Journal of Advertising,* 10, no. 1 (1981): 21–30.

7. "CEO Pay Foes Will Give Peace a Chance," *Business Ethics* (November–December 1992): 10.

8. Leslie Scism, "Some Agents 'Churn' Life-Insurance Policies, Hurt Their Customers," *Wall Street Journal,* January 3, 1995, pp. A1, A4.

9. Eric Schine, "At Teledyne, a Chorus of Whistle Blowers," *Business Week,* December 14, 1992, p. 40.

10. Gregory Strucharchuk, "Bounty Hunter: Ex-Foreman May Win Millions for His Tale About Cheating at GE," *Wall Street Journal,* June 23, 1988, pp. 1, 12.

11. Ben Brown, "POLL: Most Say Rose Bet on Baseball," *USA Today,* August 25, 1989, p. 1A; and Mike Lopresti, "For Baseball Legend, 'A Very Sad Day'" (commentary), *USA Today,* August 25, 1989, pp. 1A, 2A.

12. "Convenience Stores Lose Stamp Approval," *Commercial Appeal,* December 10, 1992, p. B3.

13. Joseph Pereia and Barbara Carton, "Toys 'R' Us to Banish Some 'Realistic' Toy Guns," *Wall Street Journal,* October 18, 1994, pp. B1, B7.

14. Alix M. Freedman and Michael J. McCarthy, "New Smoke from RJR Under Fire," *Wall Street Journal,* February 20, 1990, pp. B1, B6; and Alix M. Freedman and Suein

L. Hwang, "Reynolds Marketing Plan Urged Focus to Get Young Adults to Smoke Camels," *Wall Street Journal*, November 2, 1995, p. B4.

15. Paul Raeburn, "Magazine Spread Tobacco Views to Kids, Study Says," *Commercial Appeal*, November 1, 1995, p. B6.

16. Morton Mintz, *The Progressive*, 55 (May 1991): 24–25.

17. Charles McCoy, "Businesses Are Battling Environmentalism with Its Own Laws," *Wall Street Journal*, April 28, 1994, pp. A1, A4.

18. "If the Shoe Fits," *Business Ethics* (November–December 1992): 10.

19. Michael Satchell, "Trashing the Reservations?" *U.S. News and World Report*, January 11, 1993, pp. 24, 27.

Chapter 9

1. Rebecca Goodell, "National Business Ethics Survey Findings," *Ethics Journal* (Fall–Winter 1994): 1–3.

2. Ibid.

3. U.S. Sentencing Commission, *Federal Sentencing Guidelines Manual* (St. Paul, Minn.: West Publishing, 1994).

4. John R. Emshwiller, "Hot Special at Small Stores: Food Stamp Fraud," *Wall Street Journal*, June 1, 1995, pp. B1, B6.

5. The facts and excerpts used in discussing the Texas Instruments ethics code come from "Cornerstone," TI Ethics Office, Texas Instruments Incorporated, 1988; and "Ethics in the Business of TI," Texas Instruments Incorporated, 1987. Reprinted by courtesy of Texas Instruments, Inc.

6. Curt S. Jordan, "Lessons in Organizational Compliance: A Survey of Government-Imposed Compliance Programs," *Preventive Law Reporter* (Winter 1994): 4.

7. Susan Gaines, "Handing Out Halos," *Business Ethics*, 8 (March–April 1994): 21.

8. Alan L. Otten, "Ethics on the Job: Companies Alert Employees to Potential Dilemmas," *Wall Street Journal*, July 14, 1986, p. 17.

9. Jordan, "Lessons in Organizational Compliance," p. 7.

10. Robert Howard, "Values Make the Company: An Interview with Robert Haas," *Harvard Business Review*, 68 (September–October 1990): 134.

11. William C. Frederick and James Weber, "The Value of Corporate Managers and Their Critics: An Empirical Description and Normative Implications," in *Research in Corporate Social Performance and Social Responsibility*, ed. William C. Frederick and Lee E. Preston (Greenwich, Conn.: JAI, 1987), pp. 149–150.

12. Linda K. Trevino and Stuart Youngblood, "Bad Apples in Bad Barrels: Causal Analysis of Ethical Decision Making Behavior," *Journal of Applied Psychology*, 75 (August 1990): 390.

13. Ibid., p. 400.

Chapter 10

1. Adi Ignatius, "Money to Be Made," *Wall Street Journal*, March 1, 1994, pp. A1, A7.

2. Robert W. Armstrong and Jill Sweeny, "Industry Type, Culture, Mode of Entry and Perceptions of International Marketing Ethics Problems: A Cross-Cultural Comparison," *Journal of Business Ethics*, 13 (October 1994): 775–785; and Mee-Kau Nyaw and Ignace Ng, "A Comparative Analysis of Ethical Beliefs: A Four-Country Study," *Journal of Business Ethics*, 13 (October 1994): 543–555.

3. David A. Ricks, *Big Business Blunders: Mistakes in Multinational Marketing* (Homewood, Ill.: Dow-Jones Irwin, 1983), pp. 83–84.

4. Ibid.

5. Ibid., pp. 16–18.

6. Ibid., p. 8.

7. Joann S. Lublin, "Companies Use Cross-Cultural Training to Help Their Employees Adjust Abroad," *Wall Street Journal,* August 4, 1992, pp. B1, B6.

8. Dana Milbank and Marcus W. Brauchli, "Greasing Wheels," *Wall Street Journal,* September 29, 1995, pp. A1, A14.

9. Jennifer Cody, "To Forge Ahead, Career Women Are Venturing Out of Japan," *Wall Street Journal,* August 29, 1994, pp. B1, B5, C4.

10. Subhash C. Jain and Lewis R. Tucker, *International Marketing Management Perspectives,* 2nd ed. (Boston: Kent, 1986), pp. 1–23.

11. Louis Turner, "There's No Love Lost Between Multinational Companies and the Third World," *Business and Society Review* (Autumn 1974), reprinted in Michael W. Hoffman and Jennifer Mills Moore, *Business Ethics* (New York: MacGraw-Hill, 1990), p. 531.

12. Peter Gumbel and E. S. Browning, "The Agnellis of Italy Learn How Not to Do a Takeover in Paris," *Wall Street Journal,* March 4, 1992, pp. A1, A10; and Yumiko Ono, "Borden's Breakup with Meiji Milk Shows How a Japanese Partnership Can Curdle," *Wall Street Journal,* February 21, 1991, pp. B1, B4.

13. Jonathan Friedland, "Did IBM Unit Bribe Officials in Argentina to Land a Contract?" *Wall Street Journal,* December 11, 1995, pp. A1, A5.

14. William C. Frederick, "The Moral Authority of Transnational Corporate Codes," *Journal of Business Ethics,* 10 (1991): 564–575.

15. Craig Torres, "The Banking Disaster in Mexico Whipsaws an Ailing Economy," *Wall Street Journal,* January 25, 1996, pp. A1, A10.

16. Michael Williams, "Many Japanese Banks Ran Amok While Led by Former Regulators," *Wall Street Journal,* January 19, 1996, pp. A1, A9.

17. Faye Rice, "Should You Work for a Foreigner?" *Fortune,* August 1, 1988, pp. 123–124.

18. Yumiko Ono, "Women's Movement in Corporate Japan Isn't Moving Very Fast," *Wall Street Journal,* June 6, 1991, pp. A1, A14.

19. Frederick Rose, "How a U.S. Company used Anti-Japan Mood to Help Reverse a Loss," *Wall Street Journal,* April 22, 1992, pp. A1, A4.

20. John B. Matthews, Kenneth E. Goodpaster, and Laura L. Nash, *Policies and Persons* (New York: McGraw-Hill, 1985), pp. 415–429.

21. "The Federal Spotlight on Mitsui," *Business Week,* April 13, 1981, p. 44.

22. Eileen White Read and Joseph P. Manguno, "Seoul Brother: Northrop Signed on Secret Lobbyist to Try to Sell F-20 to Korea," *Wall Street Journal,* June 8, 1988, pp. 1, 10.

23. Fred T. Allen and Stephen J. Korbin, "Morality, Political Power, and Illegal Payments by Multinational Corporations," *Columbia Journal of World Business* (Winter 1976): 105.

24. Friedland, "Did IBM Unit Bribe Officials in Argentina," pp. A1, A5.

25. David Weir and Mark Schapiro, *Circle of Poison* (San Francisco: Institute for Food and Development Policy, 1981), p. 22.

26. Clemens P. Work, with Eva Pomice and Jim Impoco, "Where There's Smoke," *U.S. News & World Report,* March 5, 1990, p. 58.

27. Alix M. Freedman, "Cigarette Defector Says CEO Lied to Congress About View of Nicotine," *Wall Street Journal,* January 26, 1996, pp. A1, A4.

28. Craig S. Smith, "China Becomes Industrial Nations' Most Favored Dump," *Wall Street Journal,* October 9, 1995, p. B1.

29. "Nestlé Infant Formula: The Consequences of Spurning the Public Image," in *Marketing Mistakes,* 3rd ed., ed. Robert F. Hartley, (Columbus, Ohio: Grid Publishing, 1986), pp. 47–61; and "Nestlé and the Role of Infant Formula in Developing Countries: The Resolution of a Conflict," a series of reports, articles, and press releases provided by Nestlé Coordination Center for Nutrition, Inc., 1984.

30. Junda Woo and Jared Sundberg, "Copyright Law Is Easy to Break on the Internet, Hard to Enforce," *Wall Street Journal,* October 10, 1994, p. B4.

31. Teri Agins, "Fashion Knockoffs Hit Stores Before Originals as Designers Seethe," *Wall Street Journal,* August 8, 1994, pp. A1, A3.

Index